FORGOTTEN HEROES

of Ireland's Great Hunger

In remembrance of our dear friend and colleague,
Ray Gillespie (1955–2024).
He inspired us, and generations of students and scholars of Irish history.

FORGOTTEN HEROES

of Ireland's Great Hunger

Edited by
CHRISTINE KINEALY
and **GERARD MORAN**

QUINNIPIAC UNIVERSITY PRESS
CORK UNIVERSITY PRESS

Published by:
Quinnipiac University Press
275 Mount Carmel Ave
Hamden, CT 06518–1908
www.quinnipiac.edu
for

Ireland's Great Hunger Institute:
www.qu.edu/institutes-and-centers/irelands-great-hunger-institute/
Cork University Press:
www.corkuniversitypress.com

ISBN: 978–1–7361712–3–3

Cover design by the Office of Integrated Marketing Communications

Interior design and typesetting by Marsha Swan
Printed in Villatuerta, Spain, by GRAPHYCEMS

Contents

INTRODUCTION

Christine Kinealy and Gerard Moran

This is the third publication in a series that looks at heroes of Ireland's Great Hunger. When the first volume appeared in 2021, inspired by the Covid–19 pandemic, it was not intended for more volumes to follow, but its publication triggered a realization that there were multiple famine heroes who, for too long, had been ignored in the historiography. Even as this volume appears, it is apparent that it will take more than three collections of essays to do justice to the variety of men and women whose actions were motivated by a desire to assist the Irish poor and to highlight their suffering. The work of recovery continues, some of which is made possible by the discovery of new archival resources.

This series has acknowledged and highlighted the role and exertions of organizations and individuals in Ireland and internationally, who came to the aid of those facing starvation and death. While some provided substantial financial aid, others, such as the Indigenous Nations in Canada and the United States, not only contributed more than they could afford, but also showed empathy with people who lived thousands of miles away. Moreover, in many cases they had never met an Irish person, but the plight of people who were starving and who had little was a position with which they could relate, given their own experiences. Their involvement indicated the international dimension of famine relief during the Great Hunger, which was to be replicated once again during the 'Forgotten Famine' of 1879 to 1881 when international intervention played a pivotal role in ensuring that the scenes of the late 1840s were not repeated. James Hack Tuke and James Redpath were amongst those who drew lessons from the earlier famines.

What is the moral responsibility of governments to save the lives of the poorest members of society? Are governments responsible for the welfare and safety of their citizens during periods of emergency? Clearly, this does not always happen either because resources are scarce, they are overwhelmed by the scale of the disaster, they are bound by ideological or financial constraints, or they are following a deliberate policy of withholding medicines and food. Whatever the reason, it is often left to private bodies to fill this void. Consequently, during a time of crisis, especially wars, natural disasters and famines, the role of international relief agencies and individuals play an important role in intervening and helping to counteract death and starvation. Often, they can only play a limited, but important, role in the efforts to keep people alive and fed. They often do so at a personal risk to their own well-being or even their lives. Unfortunately, the role of charitable bodies and others do not generally get the recognition they deserve and their work goes unacknowledged. Moreover, the majority of those who provide practical assistance in emergency situations do not look for accolades or acknowledgement, but continue their exertions based on charitable and philanthropic motives.

It is difficult to provide a definitive definition as to who is a 'hero' and many covered in this series of Famine Heroes would never have regarded themselves as such. There were many instances where they refused to be acknowledged publicly, wanting their endeavours to be kept secret and unrecorded. In contrast to the international interventions of Indigenous Peoples, others confined their charitable activities to the localities in which they resided, where they witnessed death and starvation, and concluded that intervention—however partial and piecemeal—was needed to save their communities and neighbours. These are often the unsung 'Forgotten Heroes' of the Great Hunger and only when in-depth local studies are undertaken will their activities be revealed and honoured. While they came from different economic, social, and religious backgrounds, what bound them together was their desire and commitment to assist those in their communities who needed help and protection from a calamity that was generally unprecedented in its severity and extent.

At the same time, the role of many outsiders during these crises has yet to be fully acknowledged. During the Great Hunger it was frequently people who were not connected with Ireland who highlighted the catastrophe that was unfolding, especially in the more remote parts of the country such as Connemara, County Mayo, and west Cork. These 'heroes' included Asenath Nicholson, the American evangelical, and Polish explorer, Paul Strzelecki, both of whom featured in earlier volumes, and a number of Quakers such as William Forster, William Bennett, and James Hack Tuke, who are highlighted in Rob Goodbody's essay. They observed and provided eye-witness testimony of the misery, desolation, and death that they observed on their travels which otherwise would not have been recorded. By placing themselves in the frontline of relief activity, they were doing so at a risk to their own health and, unsurprisingly, many of them did contract 'famine fever'. The observations from those who came from outside Ireland were also important in counteracting the arguments of the authorities in London and sections of the British media who maintained that the Irish exaggerated what was happening in the country. Individuals like Bennett, Nicholson and Tuke were objective observers who reported the scenes of starvation and death in an unbiased way. While the authorities maintained that the Irish poor always survived on a knife edge and the failure of the potato was nothing new, the Society of Friends and others were able to record that the crisis of the late 1840s was exceptional and that the extent of the calamity was not exaggerated.

The contributions of heroes can be varied and are rarely confined to one particular approach. While some have been acknowledged in this series through their financial and material contributions, an unknown number paid the ultimate price, dying because of their exertions, as was with Rev. Francis Kincaid and the better-known Rev. Robert Traill, both Church of Ireland clergymen. Others had life-lasting illnesses because of contracting disease. Several attempted to change the government's relief policies, as with Lord George Bentinck, a British politician who was praised in Ireland for exposing the inadequacies of official relief. John Robert Godley pushed for a major colonization scheme to Canada, to be financed by the British government, which would provide both immediate relief and longer-term benefits. Bentinck and Godley may not have achieved their ultimate objectives, but they were influencers who attempted to provide solutions during a crisis on a scale that had not been previously witnessed in Europe.

While the exploits of many of the heroes in this series concentrated on providing immediate aid and relief to the starving and destitute, others adopted a more long-term approach. Often, the problem for communities who face famine and natural disasters were systemic—while their immediate needs and requirements were met, the fundamental underlying structural problems were not dealt with. During the Great Hunger, some of the heroes adopted a more holistic approach, concluding that poverty in Ireland was perennial and structures needed to be put in place that would combat the periodic famines and food shortages. The Society of Friends were to the forefront of this approach as noted in Rob Goodbody's study. As Goodbody shows, the Quaker intervention involved members from Britain, the United States, as well as Ireland, indicating the international aspect of their involvement. In addition to opening private soup kitchens, they established several model farms in County Galway and sponsored an investigation into the feasibility of developing fishing along the west coast, which would have long-term benefits for coastal communities.

These heroes came from many walks of life: clergymen of all denominations, landlords and landladies, politicians and government officials, philanthropists, students, and people who simply sympathized with people who were suffering. This volume concludes by examining the interventions from individuals who themselves had been colonized and who were familiar with poverty and hunger.

The chapters that follow are written by contributors from both sides of the Atlantic, who are drawn from a range of disciplines and backgrounds. They all, however, have expertise in the topics they have chosen to write about. The inclusion of authors from America and Canada indicates how important the Great Hunger topic is not only in Ireland, but internationally. This is in part due to the 2.1 million who were forced to leave Ireland and seek refuge in foreign lands between 1845 and 1855 as a result of hunger and evictions. It also indicates how the Famine had an impact on countries as far away as Australia, Canada, and the United States, and as near as Britain. The duality of emigration, as both escape and exile, is captured in the beautiful cover image by Jack B. Yeats, aptly entitled 'A Young Man's Troubles', which depicts 'a shop interior in a Connaught town; a sad-faced young man stands brooding at one side of a broad board or counter; behind him pasted on the wall are a row of emigration notices'.[1] Emigration, both during and after the Great Hunger, may have provided an economic safely valve but, as Gerard Moran's chapter shows, it was an option disliked by many nationalists.

Some groups of heroes may be familiar, such as the Society of Friends or Quakers. The important role played by the Friends, or Quakers, was recognized, even as famine raged in Ireland. According to Asenath Nicholson, known for her forthright commentary:

> These men, moved by high and lofty feelings, spent no time in idle commenting on the Protestant and the Papist faith—the Radical, Whig, or Tory politics, but looked at things as they were, and faithfully recorded what they saw. Not only did they record, but they relieved.[2]

Goodbody's chapter provides insights into a number of these individuals by recounting in detail how they contributed to Famine relief.

Acts of heroism are not confined to any age group. An earlier volume examined the role of Captain Kennedy in Kilrush, and his remarkable 7-year-old daughter, Elizabeth, famously depicted in the *Illustrated London News* handing out clothes to the local poor. Nor were they confined to any religious group, with Jews, Muslims and Hindus proving to be generous benefactors to Ireland.[3] The responses of the principal churches in Ireland to the Great Hunger remains under-researched.[4] This is especially true regarding the involvement of the main Protestant churches, whose activities went far beyond that of using the famine as an opportunity to proselytize. Brendan Hoban looks at the role of several Church of Ireland clergymen in Ballina, County Mayo, but in particular at Rev. Frances Kincaid. Kincaid worked with clerics from all religious denominations in the town to provide relief. This collaboration was replicated in many other parts of the country.

Many heroes had no direct connection with Ireland but were motivated by a humanity that transcended national borders or class. One of the most flamboyant—and ridiculed—friend of the Irish poor was Alexis Soyer, a French chef with an international reputation. His infamous soup provoked a lively public debate that deflected attention from government policies that were increasingly desperate to throw the whole financial burden for famine relief on Ireland. Soyer's unique, and controversial, contribution is assessed by Christine Kinealy.

While many of the individuals in this volume were directly involved in providing and distributing relief, others attempted to influence government policy and provide greater and more specific levels of assistance. Among those were Lord George Bentinck, an MP who tried to influence government policy-making by issuing a number of powerful appeals to his colleagues in parliament. Bentinck's contribution is explored by Peter Murphy. A similar approach was adopted by John Robert Godley who petitioned the government to fund a major colonization scheme to Canada by which two million people would relocate to North America. His endeavours were supported by many Irish landowners and politicians including the influential Lord Monteagle. Godley is examined by Gerard Moran

In March 1847, the nationalist *Pilot* published an article entitled 'Landlords who do their duty'. After listing several instances of benevolence, they concluded, 'How happy we feel in recording such instances of landlord appreciation in the duties of property. Alas, that they should be so rare'.[5] Clearly, landlords were not a homogenous group and, as the Famine progressed, a number were under increasing financial pressure with falling income from rents and rising poor law taxation. Regardless of this double pressure, a number did assist their tenants in a variety of ways. Previous volumes have outlined the contributions of Lady Sligo and her son, and of Lord

George Hill, Sir Robert Gore Booth, and Daniel O'Connell, as examples of positive responses by landlords. This volume examines the role of George Henry Moore of Moore Hall in County Mayo, the subject of Fiona White's contribution. Amongst other things, Moore devoted part of his winnings from a horse-race in England to feed his tenants. He also combined with other landowners in County Mayo to purchase grain, which was then distributed locally. A female landowner who took a personal interest in her starving tenants in County Antrim was Frances Anne, the wealthy Third Countess of Londonderry. Her contributions, which are assessed by Anthony Russell, included the construction of a harbour at Carnlough and rent reductions for the less well-off tenants on her estate.

Eamonn McKee looks at the life of Frederick Hamilton-Temple-Blackwood, Lord Dufferin, a student at Oxford University who travelled to Skibbereen in early 1847 with his fellow student, the Honourable George Boyle. What Dufferin witnessed both appalled and galvanized him. Dufferin subsequently became a major diplomat for the British Empire, serving as Governor General in India and Canada. He proposed improvements for Ireland in the decades following the Great Hunger, tailored by what he had witnessed in west Cork when a young student. While influencers like Dufferin, Godley and Bentinck may not have achieved their objectives, they set out to change government policies towards the famine Irish and to highlight to the authorities alternatives ways of responding.

The long-term impact of the Great Hunger on those who witnessed it first-hand is hard to gauge. Clearly, there were those who were deeply moved by this experience as the chapters on James Hack Tuke, Lord Dufferin and others have shown. While the American journalist, James Redpath, may not have been present in Ireland to personally view the horrors of the Great Hunger, when he came to Ireland in 1879 to report on another food crisis and the land agitation, he was aware of the devastation that it had caused in those communities which were once again being ravaged by famine. As Catherine Shannon points out in her essay, Redpath, in his articles to publications in the United States and his speeches at land meetings, resurrected the memories and horrors that these people had experienced in the late 1840s. More practically, he raised large amounts of money that helped to assuage the impact of the successive harvest failures in the west of Ireland. Shannon's chapter provides a reminder that famines continued to occur in Ireland after 1852.

The involvement of the Society of Friends has been widely applauded, but generally they are referred to collectively rather than as individuals who shared a common objective. Goodbody's chapter helps to rectify this by outlining the actions of several key participants. Christine Kinealy's expands on some of his work by focussing on the multiple contributions of women in relief work, including Quaker women. Women were at the heart of multiple philanthropic activities, yet, too often they remain hidden in history.

The concluding three chapters again highlight the involvement of disinterested strangers, whose donations were prompted by the concept of giving to those in need, and by a belief in the common humanity of all people. These acts of kindness are outlined in the chapters by Anelise Shrout, Mark McGowan, and Jason King. While the donation by the Choctaw Nation in 1847 has, quite rightly, been widely celebrated, the participation of other Indigenous Peoples have been forgotten or overshadowed. Shrout assesses the contribution of the Cherokee Nation: people who, like the Irish, had suffered from colonization and displacement. The chapters by McGowan and King make use of recently discovered archives relating to Indigenous Peoples in Canada. In the former, McGowan shows that, despite being repeatedly betrayed by their colonial rulers, the Anishinaabe, Haudenosaunee, and Wendat Peoples adhered to their treaties and abided by a set of principles that were grounded in empathy and compassion. Similarly, King describes how the Mississaugas of the Credit First Nation, who were themselves facing hunger and about to be removed from their ancestral home, donated to Irish relief. Like the Choctaw and Cherokee Nations, the First Nations in Canada also deserve to be remembered and honoured.

This collection looks at the role of individuals and organizations who came to the aid of the starving Irish. Not all of them can be considered heroes in the traditional sense, nor were all of their interventions effective, or even totally altruistic. Yet, to a downtrodden and starving people, their interest and actions not only could give the Irish poor a chance of survival, they also could give dignity to the voiceless and suffering in Ireland. While this series on unsung heroes has highlighted the endeavours and contributions of over 40 individuals and organizations, both Irish and international, it only skims the surface, in acknowledging that there are many other men, women, groups and organisations, whose story has yet to be uncovered and told, and hopefully in time they will get the recognition and credit they deserve.

NOTES

1. This painting is part of the Great Hunger Collection owned by Quinnipiac University. http://collections.ighm.org/mDetail.aspx?rID=2011.26&db=objects&dir=ART&osearch=yeats&list=res&rname=&rimage=&page=1
2. Mrs A. Nicholson, *Annals of the famine in Ireland in 1846, 1847 and 1848* (New York: E. French, 1851), p. 54.
3. For more on the diversity of donations see Christine Kinealy, *Charity and the Great Hunger. The kindness of strangers* (London: Bloomsbury, 2011).
4. Donal Kerr, *A Nation of Beggars? Priests, People, and Politics in Famine Ireland, 1846–1852* (Oxford: Clarendon Press, 1994), still remains one of the most thorough accounts of the Catholic Church during this crisis.
5. 'Landlords who do their duty', *Pilot*, 22 March 1847.

Individual Benefactors

CHAPTER ONE

FRANCIS KINCAID (1812–1847)

Curate of the Established Church, Ballina

Brendan Hoban

In the horrendous world of the Great Famine (1845–1852), a dispirited Catholic population sometimes found unlikely heroes in the clergy of the Established Church. Unlikely, because of the twin challenges with which Catholics then grappled—sheer survival amid a pervasive elemental hunger coupled with an assault on their religion by the forces of evangelical Protestantism. Protestant clergy—especially in the Established Church—driven by a combined sense of their civic responsibility to support their distressed fellow-citizens and by their biblical conviction to love their neighbours, often became unlikely heroes for their Catholic neighbours. This chapter explores the contribution of a number of those unlikely heroes in the diocese of Killala, situated in north Mayo and west Sligo, and one of the noted theatres of desolation and death during the nightmare years of the Famine. In particular, it examines the contribution of Rev. Francis Kincaid, a curate of the Established Church in the parish of Kilmoremoy (Ballina) in County Mayo, who was a particular and exceptional example of a Protestant hero for his Catholic neighbours.[1] While this is not the full story, it proved to be a common experience in an exceptional number of instances for the Catholics of Killala diocese.

The town of Ballina in the years before the Great Famine had an approximate population of 5,000 with an estimated 5,000 more in the wider parish, and of the total population, 1,400 (or 14 per cent) were Protestants, with Catholics overwhelmingly comprising the remainder.[2] At the time, the town and parish could be viewed as a microcosm of the religious world of the west of Ireland with Baptists, Methodists, Presbyterians, Catholics and members of the Established Church mingling happily and unhappily.[3] Adding to the mix of personalities and theologies were various clergy archetypes. In the Established Church all shades were evident from the old-fashioned, well-connected, easy-going rector of Kilmoremoy, Joseph Verschoyle, to his curates, the evangelical but respectful Francis Kincaid, and the confrontational evangelical George Read. The Catholic Church typology mirrored the same broad spectrum from the tolerant and respectful Hugh Conway, administrator of the Catholic cathedral in Ballina, to his curate, the belligerent Catholic evangelical, Patrick Malone.

At either end of Ballina town, the lanes of Ardnaree and the shacks of Bohernasop were full of families living on their wits and the charity of their neighbours, and when their staple diet, the potato, disappeared with the coming of the blight in 1845, the loss of life and its fall-out among the poorest of Ballina's poor was particularly harrowing. Ballina workhouse—under-funded and often overwhelmed with too many seeking admittance—struggled to keep going.[4] At one point during 'Black '47', an estimated 90 people were dying each week in the parish.[5]

In the convulsion of the Famine years in Ballina, when starvation and religious rivalry conspired to undermine a joint effective approach to relieving the distress, few clergy had the breadth of vision or the Christian conviction to overcome narrow denominational interests. However, one such exception was Rev. Francis Kincaid, who expended himself selflessly in acquiring and distributing relief for the poor of Ballina. Kincaid represented 'the best type of Established Church clergyman of the age—one who combined the fresh spirit of evangelical zeal with the traditional sense of social responsibility held by the resident gentleman school of parsons'.[6] Exemplary to a fault in living out his Christian convictions, Kincaid stood head and shoulders over clergy of every denomination in the diocese of Killala in his uncompromising commitment to feeding the starving poor of Ballina and the surrounding area, regardless of religious or other denomination. In the course of undertaking what to him was a sacred duty, he would eventually pay the highest of all prices when 'the fever' took him on 27 January 1847. He was just 35-years-old.[7]

Francis Kincaid was born in Dublin and at 18 years of age entered Trinity College where he graduated with a BA degree in 1834.[8] The following year, John Lewis, a Fellow of Trinity, recommended him for 'the sacred order of deacon'. Kincaid, he wrote, 'soberly, honourably and diligently' had applied himself to his studies and never held or taught anything 'contrary to the doctrine or the discipline of the united

Church of England and Ireland'.[9] Shortly afterwards, Michael Moore who had, Lewis said, 'every opportunity of judging Kincaid's habits and dispositions' assessed him as 'a fine scholar and a person of correct moral character'. He concluded, 'I consider him qualified to undertake the office of a minister of the Gospel'.[10] At the time, Kincaid's bishop, the Honorable Power le Poer Trench,[11] was taking the waters in Bath[12] and he delegated the responsibility of examining Kincaid to the Archdeacon of Kildare.[13] In December 1835, Kincaid writing to his friend, Edward Maturin,[14] a contemporary in Trinity, was happily looking forward to his ordination in the new year, 'I have devoted my existence to him who gave it in the sure and certain hope of the resurrection from the dead and life in the world to come'.[15]

Kincaid was ordained in Glasnevin Parish Church by Richard Whately, Archbishop of Dublin, on 4 October 1835.[16] In February 1836, the Archdeacon of Kildare, writing to his counterpart in Ardagh where Kincaid had been ministering in a temporary capacity, concluded:

> I hope my selection of him (Kincaid) for the clerical office and his unremitting and arduous labours in the ministry have met with your approbation so fully, as well as mine, as to induce you to comply with my request to present him to his Grace for the order of priest.[17]

After his ordination, Kincaid was appointed curate in Aughaval parish (Tuam), and later the same year in Athenry (also in Tuam),[18] before his appointment as curate in Ballina in 1837.[19] His rector was the patrician Joseph Verschoyle who, by 1837, had already served 20 years in Ballina and would serve another 30.[20] Thomas Armstrong,[21] the Presbyterian minister in Ballina, described Verschoyle as 'not marked by high talent, but kindly and courteous' and as 'an aristocrat, who only visited among the gentry class, and then not as a pastor but as a friend'.[22]

Ballina (or Kilmoremoy) was a busy Church of Ireland parish of over 1,000 members and with, usually, a rector and two curates. It was a comfortable, even it might be said, a lucrative position in that Verschoyle left a fortune of £35,000 when he died, though the indications are that he barely exerted himself—he had a stock of 12 sermons from which limited source he repeatedly drew his inspiration.[23] The evidence too is that he presided rather than worked or ruled, delegating the pastoral care of his parishioners to his youthful, energetic curates. Kincaid settled into Ballina, soon demonstrating his evangelical zeal and his concern for the needy, the two great impulses of his life and work. An indication of the latter was founding with others the Ballina Charitable Loan Fund Society in 1838, of which he became manager and secretary. The focus was on giving 'the poor man' access to a grant of money sufficiently large to place within his reach the materials of industry in order to enable him to navigate 'the limit where poverty ends and pauperism begins'.[24] While the Society was unashamedly Protestant in its provenance, trustees and membership, it was clear from the relatively small number of Protestants in Ballina (14 per cent of the overall population) that the recipients of the loans were not confined to membership of the Protestant churches.[25] The great and good of Ballina and the surrounding area acted as trustees and committee members,[26] and an indication of its success was the figure contained in its sixth annual report indicating that, in the 11 months since the previous report, 1,940 loans had been issued with a total pay-out of £6,514, and the only loss incurred was one loan.[27]

Kincaid was very happy in Ballina though his relative serenity was disturbed in 1839 when he was offered a lucrative promotion by the Rev. Philip Brabazon Ellis.[28] Ellis wrote to him offering him the position of superintendent of the proposed Connemara Mission and Asylum Centre for Persecuted Protestants.[29] The most arduous duties would include a yearly trip to England to raise funds for the asylum and Brabazon Ellis assured him that 'at least £500 a year' would come his way if he accepted it.[30] For a young curate on £75 a year and with plans to marry, the offer must have been tempting, but Kincaid decided to remain in Ballina.[31] His decision was final even though Ellis pressed him to accept and even indicated that he was happy to go to Ballina to talk 'more painstakingly' about whether Kincaid might be disposed 'to take the spiritual charge of the proposed settlement'.[32] Kincaid refused the overture and indicated very clearly that he wished to remain in Ballina. His decision may not have been unconnected with his marriage the following year to Elizabeth, the eldest daughter of Henry Crofton of Longford House, Dromard.[33] It may well too have been that his pastoral work in Ballina, including his reluctance to become involved in sectarian rivalry, had mellowed his previous evangelical fervour, or, more particularly, made him more sceptical of, and uncomfortable with, ultra-evangelical clergy colleagues like Brabazon Ellis in Connemara and Edward Nangle in Achill.

Kincaid was an impressive presence in Ballina, respected and liked in equal measure by both Protestants and Catholics. The evangelical *Christian Examiner* described him as a 'combination of firmness and suavity'.[34] The *Tyrawly Herald* called him 'an enlightened scholar, a pious clergyman and a public benefactor', while Thomas Armstrong, the Presbyterian minister in Ballina and assistant editor of the *Tyrawly Herald,* described him as an 'eloquent preacher and diligent minister of the gospel'.[35] For the *Mayo Constitution* he was an 'estimable gentleman and indefatigable Christian minister'.[36] The American evangelical missionary, Asenath Nicholson, a shrewd observer, praised him for 'being free from sectarianism'.[37] Kincaid was

Nicholson's hero.[38] It was this disinterest in sectarian divisions that allowed Kincaid to comfortably accept other denominations and be accepted by them, which placed him in a strong position to confront issues of poverty and neglect across the palpable religious divide in Ballina. His rector, Joseph Verschoyle, delegated responsibility for social concern to Kincaid and, while it suited both, Verschoyle was a quiet and supportive presence. This was evident in Verschoyle's backing of the Sick and Indigent Room Keepers' Benevolent Society and the Ballina Charitable Loan Fund Society and Kincaid's advocacy of a fever hospital and a dispensary for Ballina. That such societies were founded by a clergyman of the Established Church in Ballina was unsurprising—what was different was that Kincaid drew no distinction between Protestant and Catholic.

When the Famine struck Ballina and its hinterland, Kincaid was well placed to respond, and his reputation as a respectful presence, as well as his even-handedness, gave him a status that allowed the Ballina Relief Committee to form around him. Kincaid was friendly with Hugh Conway, the Catholic administrator of the cathedral, and when the effect of famine began to bite, Conway asked Kincaid whether he could suggest anything that might give direct relief to the people. Kincaid's response was to suggest the establishment of a relief committee and this was soon formed with representatives from across the religious divide in Ballina, with the Protestant rector of Ballina, Joseph Verschoyle in the chair, Kincaid as secretary, and Conway and Thomas Armstrong as active members. Whereas the patrician and detached Verschoyle adopted a supervisory hands-off approach, Kincaid and Conway immersed themselves in directly aiding the starving. In general, Kincaid supervised the local soup kitchen and Conway moved through the cabins of the poor, surveying the abject needs of the impoverished 'paupers' as they struggled to survive hunger, fever and the elements. But on occasion the roles alternated, with Kincaid visiting those at risk of death by starvation and Conway helping with the organisation of relief.

Kincaid and Conway worked hand in glove in an unusual partnership—one man, Protestant, urban and Trinity-educated, the other, Catholic, rural, Maynooth-educated—that flowered into a strong friendship with a growing conviction that they had an absolute obligation to do whatever they could to preserve the lives of the destitute poor of Ballina. Astutely, Conway saw his role as supportive, he recognising that the key players in relieving distress were the clergy of the Established Church (as well as the landlords) because without them, Kincaid and himself would have been unable to feed, for example, the 3,000 people who received relief in Ballina from October to Christmas 1846. He acknowledged that, without their intervention, hundreds, if not thousands, would have died. The key was not just a growing friendship based on respect, mutual conviction and close co-operation, but an effective blend of roles: Kincaid's contacts in sourcing financial and other support and organising the actual distribution of relief, and Conway's access to situations of greatest need.

Resources poured into the Ballina Relief Committee, sourced mainly from the Society of Friends and from around the world with regular acknowledgements in the local papers from Francis Kincaid and later Hugh Conway. It is indicative of the high regard in which Kincaid was held that when the Catholic bishop of Killala, Thomas Feeny—though exercised on occasion by the proselytising allegations directed against some Protestant clergy—received donations from the British Relief Association, from Archbishop Daniel Murray of Dublin, and from Catholic contacts around the world, he forwarded them to the committee. But while the soup kitchen continued to feed over 1,000 people a day, deaths continued. However, as Conway was always happy to accept, Kincaid was the key person on what was soon called the Ardnaree and Ballina Relief Committee. Kincaid had contacts in Dublin and in England and the energy and commitment to write a constant stream of letters drawing attention to the distressing situation in Ballina, as the blight ravaged the potato crop. A letter to the London *Times* was typical of his pragmatic approach, his directness, and his unvarnished service to the poorest of the poor:

> Ballina, County Mayo, Ireland.
> November 6, 1846
>
> Sir,
>
> The pressure of extreme distress with which this town has been visited in the Providence of God is the claim made upon your attention to the following facts. Ballina, a large town in the west of Ireland, contains 10,000, of them at least 4,000 depended on the potato crop for their maintenance throughout the year. That crop has totally failed in this the most destitute part of impoverished Ireland. Our Poorhouse, capable of containing at the utmost 1,200 paupers, has nearly 100 above that amount. Hundreds more seek admission, but there is no room for them. A committee, selected for the purpose, containing the ministers of all denominations, the local medical gentlemen and the principal traders and shopkeepers of the town, have [sic] visited this week the abodes of the poor and returned upwards of 1,300 human beings as withering to death from intense privations, subsisting many of them on one meal a day and that composed of a scant supply of cabbage or mill-dust mixed with a portion of meal, a last resource to retain life a little longer.
>
> They reported 'no tongue can describe the state in which we found the poor'. Our trade—the exportation of corn—is at an end. The price of meal, the only substitute here for the potato, is about double the ordinary cost and we have had demands on us for the last four months, far exceeding our ability to meet. We are making another effort to stay the Famine moving through our streets, but it will be in vain if the affluent and the benevolent of other places do not come to our assistance.

> I am directed by the Committee, the first hurried proceedings of which I send you a report of, to solicit your aid to save some of the lives of your fellow-creatures.
> I remain,
> Your obedient servant,
> Francis Kincaid,
> Secretary to Ardnaree and Ballina Relief Committee.[39]

Kincaid, as secretary of the Relief Committee, enlisting 'the sympathy of the rich and noble in England and in Ireland', sought help from every source available, and as funds poured in, over 3,000 people were kept alive from October to Christmas 1846. Kincaid's wife, Elizabeth, was the secretary of the Ballina Ladies' Institution for the Encouragement of Industry and her contribution to the relief of distress was lauded by Asenath Nicholson.[40] Together with some women friends, who had set up the Ballina Benevolent Society to extend relief to the poor of Ballina and Ardnaree,[41] they decided early in 1847 that instead of giving relief directly, they would employ poor women in spinning wool and flax.[42]

By the turn of the year, Kinkaid was immersed in battling the ravages of famine, at times almost singlehanded as others fled the contagion that the poor brought with them everywhere they went. Kincaid must have realised how susceptible he was to fever as the mortality rate among the higher classes was much higher than among the poorer people. Many of the latter had a low form of infection that was endemic among them and to which they had built up a certain immunity. But while only one in four or five among the poor died of fever, among the gentry, about seven in ten who were infected died.[43] The particular distress in Ballina was exacerbated by a number of factors: a huge percentage of the population lived in chronic poverty and overwhelmingly in inadequate 'fourth-class housing'; a populous under-class, particularly in areas like Bohernasop and Ardnaree, already struggled to survive in a warren of filthy streets and alley-ways full of squalid hovels; an estimated 300 vagrants and beggars lived on the streets of Ballina with no local authority to improve or even maintain minimal conditions of cleanliness and hygiene; outbreaks of cholera and other fevers were widespread; the Ballina Workhouse, beyond its maximum complement of 1,200 residents, was surviving on a knife-edge as it struggled to meet its responsibilities in law with 'landed proprietors' (or landlords) failing or unable to provide financial support;[44] and a constant influx of people from surrounding parishes seeking relief, thus compounded the mix of problems.[45]

Examples of extreme distress were widespread: starving people selling their last possessions to buy food; the constabulary protecting food depots; in Bohernasop, a survey of 47 families comprising 183 individuals, revealed that only 18 were able to leave their houses to seek relief due to a general lack of adequate clothing. The *Herald* reported:

> On Tuesday last, as Dr Atkinson was passing though Bohernasop, a densely populated street on the outskirts of this town [Ballina], he happened to go into a house, where he found the remains of Ellen and John Clarke, brother and sister. They were dead for two or three days, and yet, strange to say, none of the neighbours were aware of the circumstance. The mother and another of her children were in the house but were in a dying state induced by excessive want.[46]

On 2 January 1847, Kincaid wrote to his friend, Dr Edmund Sharkey:

> People are dying in multitudes around us. We have had a soup kitchen in operation for the last six weeks, distributing upwards of 1,100 meals daily to as many totally destitute inhabitants of this town and we have 500 more on the list. I have not been in bed before 2 o'clock each morning for the past month but it has pleased God to continue my health with little diminishment. If you can do anything for us. I have no time to write of other matters.[47]

However, the effort to source funds, to convert the money into food, and to organise relief for thousands of people, took its toll. Almost inevitably, Kincaid, in his almost constant contact 'with the crowds of lice-ridden skeletons' that surrounded him daily in his relief work, in his exhausted state, making him more vulnerable to infection, succumbed to the fever.[48]

All seemed to be well with Kincaid when an issue of the *Tyrawly Herald*, dated 14 January 1847, reported an acknowledgement from him of a donation of £10 that he had received from St Jude's Committee of Liverpool.[49] A week later, however, the same paper reported:

> We deeply regret to state that this Rev. Gentleman, the talented and efficient secretary of the relief committee of this town (Ballina), is at present seriously ill of fever, brought on, there is little doubt, by his incessant labours in the cause of the suffering people of the neighbourhood since the commencement of the fearful visitation with which they are afflicted. Mild, courteous and charitable he has, since his first entrance on this mission, endeared himself to the poorer classes of society, who must now deplore that illness, which, it is to be hoped, will only for a short time deprive them of his great and valuable services.[50]

Kincaid's work as secretary of the relief committee was curtailed by his illness and acknowledgements of contributions, the committee reported, would have to await his recovery. But it was not to be. Kincaid never recovered. He died from the fever on 27 January 1847, contracted after working at a soup kitchen and visiting the starving poor in their homes.[51] Asenath Nicholson wrote: 'Mr Kincaid, who was but 35, left a widow and son and daughter. The widow is worthy to bear his name. She too, like him, is found among the poor, promoting spiritual good in every possible way'.[52]

Under the heading 'Public Calamity—Death of the Rev. Francis Kincaid', the *Tyrawly Herald* attempted 'to give a brief notice of this melancholy event':

> The Rev. Francis Kincaid, curate of Kilmoremoy, the mild, the gentle, the humane, the charitable, beyond all power of expression, is no more. On yesterday morning, fever put a period to his existence and 'the spirit from him passed'. Ever since the commencement of the present awful visitation, which has fallen on this country, his labours to mitigate the misfortunes to sooth the sorrows of the distressed have been unremitting and unceasing. By night and by day, he exercised all the energies of his body and his mind for them, and to his powerful appeals on their behalf, is mainly to be ascribed the establishment and success of the (Ardnaree and Ballina) Relief Committee. An enlightened scholar, a pious clergyman and a public benefactor has passed away from us, but he has left behind him an example whereby we should walk, and though meteor-like, his light shone but for a brief period on us here on earth, we may surely trust that it is only transferred to a brighter and more glorious world.[53]

Hugh Conway was devastated by Kincaid's death. In later years, reflecting on the experience, he wrote that at the time he was 'so overcome by grief that I never since on any occasion experienced as much sorrow and grief for anyone's death, as I did for him'. He continued:

> He was decidedly the most charitable, the most benevolent and the most philanthropic man that ever I met. His heart and soul were occupied in the work of relief and visiting poor cabins to look after the sufferers from the famine, and while engaged in this merciful mission he took the fever himself and died. He was the guiding star of the committee, the man who formed it and drew up the rules, and I thought when he was carried away that I would not be able to do the work after him.[54]

This proved to be the case. Conway, in the wake of Kincaid's death, through 'overexertion and mental anxiety, took to bed with but little hope of recovering'. However, despite his worries and reservations about carrying the added burden of responsibility, Conway recognised that the work had to continue.[55] There was no alternative. A week before Kincaid died, the managers of the soup kitchen informed a meeting of the Relief Committee that each day they were distributing 1,387 quarts of soup to 563 families. On the day after Kincaid died, the *Telegraph* reported that the Committee was distributing 3,427 gallons of soup every day to 1,309 people in Ballina and Ardnaree.[56] The grim statistics were a measure of the vital contribution Kincaid was making in sourcing funds and in organising a constant mammoth operation of dispensing food to the starving families. It is no exaggeration to state that without Kincaid's ministrations thousands more people would have been added to the statistics of death from starvation in Ballina during the Great Famine.

Feeding the starving without Kincaid was an exceptionally daunting task, made even more difficult because the Ballina Union was forever in difficulty and struggling to survive a bank debt with closure an ongoing possibility.[57] The loss of Kincaid, it was feared, could convert into hundreds, even thousands of deaths:

> At present (in Ballina) six hours in each day are occupied in procuring and dispensing the food, to which 1,400 people look as nearly their sole means of existence. Something should be done, and that immediately, or hundreds, thousands, may perish by a fearful death.[58]

The statement was indicative of the reliance on the contribution of Kincaid as the central driving force of relief in Ballina. The *Tyrawly Herald* in a lengthy obituary underlined the enormous contribution Kincaid had made:

> His sole object was the comfort and happiness of the poor and to the accomplishment of that object his time and his talents were unweariedly devoted for the last ten years, and when the present terrible visitation made its appearance, when famine and disease entered into the habitations of the poor and demanded and carried off their victims, his exertions on behalf of the sufferers were not merely redoubled, they became almost superhuman and his life was sacrificed to his love. What more glorious example of undeviating devotion to the welfare of a people does history afford?[59]

In the same issue, James Collins, the Protestant Dean of Killala, described himself as 'crest-fallen' when he heard the news of Kincaid's death:

> Surely the Lord's hand is upon us. The Rev. Francis Kinkead [sic] has fallen. The mild, the pious, the faithful, the zealous, the efficient minister of the Gospel, and indefatigable servant of the starving poor, has been called away by typhus fever, caught in his benevolent labours! Well, he has gone from his cross to his crown. He sleeps in Jesus. Who next? Thou, O Lord, knowest.[60]

Soon after Kincaid's death Conway was appointed secretary of the Relief Committee in succession to Kinkaid and, predictably, Conway was involved in and contributed towards a plaque in Kincaid's memory that would be erected in St Michael's Church, Ardnaree, and would attract cross-community support. It was one of many tributes paid to him:

To the memory of Rev. Francis Kincead (sic)
This tablet was erected by his sorrowing friends and the parishioners of Kilmoremoy, where for almost 10 years he laboured with faithfulness, patience and untiring zeal.
Exemplary as a minister, he was in his early walk
a consistent servant of his heavenly master.
Gifted with high intellectual endowments,
he consecrated them all to his redeemer's service,
for the excellency of the knowledge of whom
he coveted all things but loss.
His work of faith and labour were terminated by
typhus fever contracted in his unwearying efforts
to relieve the wants of the poor
during the season of grievous famine.
Obiit [61] 27 January 1847, *Aeta*[62] 35.

Asenath Nicholson wrote:

> His simple tablet hangs in the church where he preached, but he needed no marble monument, for his name will be held in everlasting remembrance. He was eyes to the blind, and the cause he knew not he sought out. Free from sectarianism, he relieved all in his power, and he spoke kindly to the bowed down; he wiped the tear from the eye of the widow and fatherless and brought joy and gladness into the abode of those who were forgotten by their neighbours.[63]

Nicholson's biographer, Maureen Murphy, wrote that the American evangelical admired Kincaid for two things: his concern for the poor and his efforts to provide employment. A third reason for Nicholson's admiration was that Kincaid was, in her own words, 'free from sectarianism', a considerable accolade in the circumstances of the time.[64]

While Francis Kincaid stood head and shoulders above Protestant clergy during the Great Hunger in relieving the distress of the starving poor regardless of religious denomination, others shared the same moral perspective. Among them were James Burrowes, rector of Castleconnor and Kilglass, and George Trulock, rector of Skreen, both in the deanery of Tireragh in west Sligo. James Annesley Burrowes, a native of Longford, came to Killala diocese as private tutor to Bishop Joseph Stock's children. He was appointed rector of Castleconnor and Kilglass in 1804 and married Catherine Stock, Bishop Joseph Stock's daughter, in 1809.[65] By 1847, Burrowes and his family were the sole providers of relief in Castleconnor and, often aided by Kincaid, sourced Indian meal for 80 families.[66] Later, at one point, he was issuing nearly two tons of meal a week from his rectory in Killanley.[67] After years of struggling mightily side by side with his wife, Catherine and their daughters, as much of the actual relief work fell to him and his family, Burrowes would die of exhaustion and famine fever in 1849. A daughter, Helen, was also taken by the fever, two years before her father. She was 28-years-old.

Burrowes, as part of the Established Church, saw himself as responsible not just for his own parishioners but for all citizens. He eschewed proselytising tendencies but was still distrusted by the parish priest, Patrick Duffy, who seemed in awe of the more academically qualified and theologically literate Burrowes.[68] When Burrowes collapsed in June 1847 from overwork and famine fever, his friend Robert Noble, the vicar of Athboy in Meath, rushed to help him. In a letter to the *Tyrawly Herald*, Noble outlined Burrowes predicament:

> I came here 100 miles to assist the aged vicar of this parish in his onerous duties of feeding the hungry, attending the dying and burying the dead.[69] Four hundred families received food weekly at this glebe house for five months, given out by the vicar and his wife and daughters, and there was none to assist him ... the crowds brought infection with them, coming out of fever houses. One daughter, aged 28, has died of malignant typhus fever. The mother of this large family ... is ill of the same fever.[70]

A response in the *Standard* summed up what it called 'the picture of misery' represented by the predicament of the Burrowes family:

> Pestilence invades the once happy home ... his beloved child is snatched from him in the summer of her years; her mother, the partner of the afflicted parent's life, the sharer of his early happiness and hopes, is laid upon a sick bed, stricken by a disease that has already sent a daughter to the grave.[71]

On 24 May, Noble wrote to the *Achill Missionary Herald* describing 'the temporal want and destitution' he found in Castleconnor:

> A dead body of a female, in a state of putrefaction, was thrown into the churchyard (at Killanley) without coffin or clothes last week. She had evidently died of starvation. Crowds amounting to hundreds, surrounded the Glebe-House (at Killanley) every day, famine-stricken, woe-begone creatures, walking skeletons, in many of them the swelling in their lower limbs betokening death. If it had not been for the active and untiring manner in which the Vicar's family have given up their whole time to distribute food ... the whole population of this parish would have died of starvation.[72]

There is no doubting the extent of the selfless contribution of Burrowes and his family in feeding the hungry of Castleconnor and Kilglass, most of whom were Catholics. Such, indeed, was the sacrifice of James Burrowes that, in the summer of

1847, he collapsed from overwork and famine fever and, though he struggled on, his health was impaired. He died in 1849 from exhaustion and fever. In recording his death, the *Ballina Chronicle* commented: 'Seldom have we had to record the departure of one whose removal will be (more) regretted than that of the vicar of Killanley'.[73]

Other clergy of the Established Church who extended relief to their Catholic neighbours included: George Trulock, rector of Skreen, who co-operated with John Hopkins, PP, Skreen;[74] James Collins,[75] rector of Killala, worked with Anthony Corcoran, PP, Killala; Richard St. George, rector of Crossmolina co-operated with Bartholomew Costello, PP, Crossmolina in running soup kitchens;[76] and Francis Little, rector of Doonfeeney (Ballycastle), and Martin Hart(e), the parish priest of Ballycastle, enjoyed a mutual respect born out of extended periods of simultaneous service—Little serving for 32 years and Hart(e) for 31 years—during which time their solidarity was enhanced by the robust presence of Presbyterian evangelical missionary, Rev. Michael Brannigan, who targeted their flocks.[77] Peter Dowdican, parish priest of Dromard, under the pressure of his dying parishioners, made his peace with Rev. Lewis Potter, rector of Dromard, and agreed to cooperate with him in jointly establishing soup kitchens; George Bermingham, rector of Lacken, worked with Peter Neary, PP, Lacken; Samuel Stock, rector of Kilcommon, co-operated with Michael Kelly, PP, Belmullet;[78] and, not least, Henry Knox, who served for a time in Moygownagh as curate to his father-in-law, Richard St George, rector of Crossmolina. Henry, with his wife, Fanny, ran an effective soup kitchen in Fahy, Kilfian parish, where they were at one point spending £200 a week from their own resources to feed 200 families as well as an estimated 300 beggars who arrived every day at the family home.[79] Unfortunately, in this instance, the co-operation of the Catholic priest was not forthcoming as John Jordan, the PP of Kilfian, while he was an active member of the local relief committee, was critical of what he regarded as Knox's 'souperist' mentality. There were others who sang from the same Catholic hymn-sheet as Jordan. It was not, in the words of famine historian, Donal A. Kerr, 'an ecumenical age'.[80]

Research into the parishes of Killala diocese has uncovered a significant and unexpected degree of co-operation between Christian denominations, particularly between the Catholic Church and the Established Church.[81] The work and contributions of Church of Ireland clergymen during the Great Hunger has been largely ignored or forgotten as can be seen in the case of Francis Kincaid. While much has been written on the proselytising campaign carried out by evangelical Protestants during this period, there were many clergymen who worked on their own or with their Catholic counterparts to save the destitute and starving within their parishes and communities and, in many cases, as with Kincaid, they paid the ultimate sacrifice with their lives. By joining forces with Hugh Conway and others in Ballina, Kincaid ensured total community engagement in the relief efforts. Kincaid, like many others, was prepared to devote considerable amounts of time on the relief committees and in the process endangered their health and their lives. The town of Ballina and its hinterland were among the places that suffered most during the Great Hunger as can be noted from the local workhouse being unable to cope with the numbers who sought shelter there, but were refused relief.[82] Clerics like Kincaid played a vital role in filling this void. They were also prepared to highlight the extent of the problem within their localities to the outside world and the authorities. The Great Hunger brought death, starvation and diseases to Ireland and while philanthropy was largely the prerogative of privileged classes who possessed the resources and time to assist the dying and starving, a number paid the ultimate prices with their lives. The heroics of individuals like Kincaid and others should not be confined to a footnote in the historiography of the Great Hunger, but they should be given the recognition they deserve for their actions during Ireland's darkest period.

NOTES

1. 'Kincaid' was sometimes written 'Kincead' or 'Kinkead'.
2. Samuel Lewis, *Topographical Dictionary of Mayo*, vol. 1 (London, 1837) p. 104.
3. Desmond Bowen, *Souperism, Myth or Reality, A Study of Catholics and Protestants during the Great Famine* (Cork: Mercier Press, 1970), p. 217.
4. The workhouse had been built to accommodate 1,200 but sometimes contained in excess of that number.
5. *Tyrawly Herald*, 1 January 1847.
6. Bowen, *Souperism,* p. 219.
7. *Castlebar Telegraph*, 26 May 1847.
8. J.B Leslie/D.W.T. Crooks, *Clergy of the Diocese of Tuam, Killala and Achonry, Biographical Succession Lists* (Tuam, 2008), p. 424.
9. Trinity College Archives, File 3207/12, 15 July 1835.
10. Ibid., File 3207/14.
11. When Bishop Joseph Verschoyle of Killala died in 1834, Killala and Achonry were united with Tuam under Archbishop Power le Poer Trench.
12. The natural thermal springs in Bath with over 42 different minerals were regarded as medicinal, especially for curing skin disease.
13. Trinity Archives, File 3207/15, 30 September 1835.
14. Maturin was later a Professor of Greek at Charleston, South Carolina and widely regarded as a talented Irish American scholar and writer.
15. Trinity Archives, File 3207/17, 5 December 1835.

16. Ibid., File 3207/59, 4 October 1835. A scroll of his ordination is in his archives in Trinity College, Dublin.
17. Ibid., File 3207/19, 5 February 1836.
18. Ibid., File 3207/22, 11 July 1836.
19. Leslie/Crooks, *Clergy*, p. 424.
20. Ibid., pp 653–4. After serving 50 years in Ballina, Verschoyle died on 24 January 1867.
21. Monaghan-born Armstrong arrived in Ballina in November 1845. Rooted in a more refined and nuanced Presbyterian evangelical tradition than his Protestant colleagues, Armstrong's instinct as famine intensified was to co-operate with his fellow Christians in providing relief for the distressed and he befriended Francis Kincaid and Hugh Conway. In the *Tyrawly Herald*, where Armstrong worked in a part-time editorial capacity, he famously opposed the notorious 'moral' campaign of Father Patrick Malone, then Catholic curate in Ballina, against the activities of prostitutes. Malone's favoured policy of dissuading them was to physically attack them in the streets of Ballina and on occasion forcibly to cut off their hair. In his own defence, Malone sought to justify his behaviour by comparing himself to Jesus Christ clearing out the money changers from the Temple in Jerusalem. Hugh Conway—a relative of Malone—disagreed with Malone's approach and retained all his life a close friendship with Armstrong. Clearly, Malone had the support of Bishop Thomas Feeny for his campaign as otherwise Feeny, a robust disciplinarian, would have intervened to stop him. Malone's notoriety earned him the unhappy designation, 'The Clipper'. Brendan Hoban, *Trouble & Strife, Fifty Killala Priests, 1600–2000* (Dublin: Banley House, 2012), pp 519–528.
22. Thomas Armstrong, *My Life in Connaught, with sketches of mission work in the west* (London: Elliot Stock. 1906), p. 4. Armstrong's critical remarks reflect the tension between the Established Church and the Presbyterian Church which resulted from stiff competition for adherents.
23. It was a huge sum, the equivalent in 2024 of over €4 million, part of which he may have inherited from his father, Bishop James Verschoyle, and from the Earl of Charleville, whose niece he had married.
24. *Tyrawly Herald*, 25 January 1844.
25. Ibid.
26. Among the most prominent trustees and members were Rev. Joseph Verschoyle, Col. A. Knox-Gore, and philanthropist and landlord, George Vaughan Jackson of Carramore, near Cloghans, outside Ballina. When Jackson saw the increasing number and desperation of the poor, he 'broke up his establishment, sold his carriage horses and devoted himself to the destitute'. He immersed himself in working for the distressed in both Ballina and Swinford Poor Law Unions, of both of which he was chairman. He later became chairman of Ennis union and was described as 'exceptional among the government officials in Ennis for the openness of his character and the genuineness of the sympathy he exhibited towards the starving poor'. He died from the fever just two months after arriving in Ennis. See Ciarán Ó Murchadha, *Sable Wings over the Land* (Ennis: Clasp Press, 1998) p. 194; Brendan Hoban, *Ocras, The Great Famine in Killala Diocese, 1845–1852* (Dublin:

Banley House, 2021) p. 146; Brendan Hoban, *On Our Knees, Famine in the Parishes of Killala Diocese* (Dublin: Banley House, 2022) pp 91–92.

27. *Tyrawly Herald,* 25 January 1844. The loans were distributed to 'the industrious poor', including 560 farmers, 260 milk dealers, 143 flax and yarn dealers, 240 hucksters, 121 labourers, 90 nailors, 80 carpenters, 79 shoemakers, etc.
28. Rev. Brabazon Ellis, a clergyman of the Established Church who served in Connemara in the parish of Ballinakill (1831–7) – first in Tully and later in Roundstone – was a founder member in 1836 and secretary of the Connemara Christian Committee. The committee was established to convert Catholics and to support and protect such converts to the Protestant faith. A further intention was to establish a colony on 600 hundred acres of bogland outside Clifden and to drain and divide the land among converts from Catholicism. Kathleen Villiers-Tuthill, *Patient Endurance, The Great Famine in Connemara* (Clifden: Connemara Girl Publications, 1997), p. 132. Ellis, with the support of Bishop Trench, sought to protect former Catholics 'whose Christian courage has induced them to abandon the superstitions of their youth' from the attention of their priests and Ellis clashed with Catholic priests who denounced him from the altar: 'For a long period I stood alone in the struggle with the powers of darkness' (Joseph D'Arcy Sirr, *A Memoir of The Honorable and Most Reverend Power le Poer Trench, last archbishop of Tuam* (Dublin, 1845) pp 634–58.). The model for the colony and its support systems for converted Catholics was similar to what Rev. Edward Nangle established in Achill in 1834, Irene Whelan, Nangle in Gillespie/ Moran, (eds) *A Various Country, Essays in Mayo History, 1500–1900* (Westport: Rev. Brabazon Ellis, a clergyman of the Established Church who served in Connemara in the parish of Ballinakill (1831–7) – first in Tully and later in Roundstone – was a founder member in 1836 and secretary of the Connemara Christian Committee. The committee was established to convert Catholics and to support and protect such converts to the Protestant faith. A further intention was to establish a colony on 600 acres of bogland outside Clifden and to drain and divide the land among converts from Catholicism. Kathleen Villiers-Tuthill, *Patient Endurance, The Great Famine in Connemara* (Clifden: Connemara Girl Publications, 1997), p. 132. Ellis, with the support of Bishop Trench, sought to protect former Catholics 'whose Christian courage has induced them to abandon the superstitions of their youth' from the attention of their priests and Ellis clashed with Catholic priests who denounced him from the altar: 'For a long period I stood alone in the struggle with the powers of darkness'. Joseph D'Arcy Sirr, *A Memoir of The Honorable and Most Reverend Power le Poer Trench, last archbishop of Tuam* (Dublin, 1845) pp 634–58 The model for the colony and its support systems for converted Catholics was similar to what Rev. Edward Nangle established in Achill in 1834. Irene Whelan, Nangle in Gillespie/ Moran (eds) *A Various Country, Essays in Mayo History, 1500–1900* (Westport: *Foilseacháin Náisiúnta Teoranta*, 1987), p. 113.
29. Trinity Archives, File 3207/32, 29 May 1839.
30. Bowen, *Souperism,* p. 220.
31. Trinity Archives, File 3207/60, 11 October 1841. A scroll of the agreement of Ballina parish to employ him at £75 sterling a year to be paid quarterly is in his archives in Trinity College.

32. Trinity Archives, File 3207/32.
33. Leslie/ Crooks, *Clergy*, p. 424.
34. *Christian Examiner*, 1 March 1847.
35. *Tyrawly Herald*, 28 January 1847.
36. *Mayo Constitution*, 2 February 1847.
37. Asenath Nicholson was an American philanthropist who visited Ireland before and during the Famine. A Protestant Congregationalist, she was open to and accepting of all faiths and despised sectarianism of any kind. She had a variety of other interests including moral and social reform and the care of the poor and was an exceptional judge of people's characters and dispositions. For more on Nicholson's role during the Famine see Maureen Murphy, 'Asenath Nicholson: Heroine of Ireland's Great Hunger' in Christine Kinealy, Jason King and Gerard Moran, *Heroes of Ireland's Great Hunger* (Cork University Press, 2021), pp 87–100.
38. Nicholson, *Annals,* pp 124–25.
39. Trinity Archives, File 3207/41, 6 November 1846.
40. Nicholson, *Annals,* p. 215.
41. Elizabeth Kincaid was part of a wider socio-religious relief support system in which several female-run societies (like the Ballina Benevolent Society) comprising wives, sisters and daughters of local clergy and gentry (and exclusively Protestant in their provenance) were part of the Owenmore Society, and effectively contributed to the relief of distress by organising soup kitchens and providing employment for women. The Owenmore Society, so called because it originated in Owenmore House, Moygownagh, was the brainchild of Sydney Francis L'Estrange, wife of Robert Orme. Hoban, *On Our Knees,* pp 571–576.
42. *Tyrawly Herald,* 14 January 1847. Francis Kincaid acknowledged the sum of £10 from the St Jude's Committee in Liverpool, which he handed over to the Benevolent Society. Walter Bourke's wife of the Castle, Killala, adopted the same approach, purchasing flannels and employing women to make petticoats. *Tyrawly Herald,* 28 January 1847.
43. Bowen, *Souperism,* p. 221.
44. An exception was Edward Howley, a magistrate and landlord and chairman of the Ballina Guardians, who personally funded the workhouse when the Provincial Bank of Ireland withdrew its services, and the workhouse was bankrupt with contractors owed £2,000, National Archives of Ireland (NAI), Chief Secretary's Office, Rebellion Papers, 0.8579, Provincial Bank of Ireland to Edward Howley, 1 February 1847. Two weeks later, Howley wrote to the Relief Commissioner, Edward Twistleton, that he was advancing £105 a week from his private resources and though he was prepared, as he wrote, 'to expend the last farthing sooner than let the poor people starve, with 1,235 paupers in the house and as many more seeking entrance and £3,000 in debt, I cannot much longer hold out'. Ibid., 0.3475, Howley to Twistleton, 16.2 1847. Two years later, in 1849, Ballina Union would owe £18,000 with 21,000 people on outdoor relief.
45. Hoban, *On Our Knees,* pp 459–60.
46. *Tyrawly Herald*, 21 January 1847.
47. Trinity Archives, 3207/43, 2 January 1847.

48. Bowen, *Souperism,* p. 221.
49. Kincaid indicated that, as it was 'for special relief', he was handing it over to the 'Ladies of the Ballina Benevolent Society, to be applied by them to the payment of poor women for spinning wool and flax', *Tyrawly Herald,* 14 January 1847.
50. *Tyrawly Herald,* 21 January 1847.
51. Leslie/Crooks, *Clergy,* p. 424; Trinity Archives, File 3207/43; *Mayo Constitution*, 2 February 1847.
52. Nicholson, *Annals,* p. 213.
53. *Tyrawly Herald*, 28 January 1847.
54. Conway was speaking to the *Western People*, 30 January 1892, while celebrating the 50th anniversary of his ordination. Brendan Hoban, *Tracing the Stem, Killala Bishops* (Dublin: Banley House, 2015), p. 110.
55. Society of Friends' Famine Papers, 2/596/19, *Conway to Todhunter*, 8 March 1847.
56. *Tyrawly Herald,* 21 January 1847.
57. NAI, Chief Secretary's Office, Rebellion Papers, 0.718 Minutes, 4 January 1847.
58. Ibid.
59. *Tyrawly Herald*, 4 February 1847.
60. Ibid.
61. Obituary.
62. At the age of.
63. Asenath Nicholson, *Annals,* pp 124–25.
64. Ibid.
65. Joseph Stock was the Protestant bishop of Killala when the French invaded in 1798. He wrote an inside account of what happened in Killala which was regarded as favouring the French and which later militated against his advancement in the Established Church. He was later bishop of Waterford.
66. NAI, Relief Commission Papers, 3/2, Incoming Letters, No. 11529, Mayo, 2/442/5.
67. Ibid, No. 14177, Mayo, 2/442/5.
68. Protestant ministers who held degrees from Trinity College, such as Burrowes, were much more confident and assured in their public role than Maynooth-educated priests.
69. Burrowes was 78-years-old at this time.
70. *Tyrawly Herald*, 24 June 1847.
71. Ibid.
72. *Achill Missionary Herald*, 19 June 1847.
73. *Ballina Chronicle*, 22 August 1849.
74. Trulock was a substantial figure. When the dioceses of Achonry and Killala were amalgamated in 1834, he was appointed vicar general of the united dioceses and immediately indicated that he did not share his bishop's (Power le Poer Trench's) enthusiasm for proselytising. During the Famine, Trulock worked closely with his Catholic counterparts on relief committees. Trulock's contribution took two forms: one, he tried to deal with the immediate distress in Skreen and, two, he wrote letters far and wide soliciting financial help and writing pamphlets (e.g. *Remedies suggested to meet the Present State*

of Ireland) analysing government policies (e.g. on public works schemes and emigration) and suggesting alternatives to public policy. Trulock was regarded as a friend of the poor and was indefatigable in alleviating their sufferings during the Famine years. Having exhausted himself in his service of the distressed, Catholic and Protestant, he died suddenly in September 1847 from an apoplectic fit. He was 55-years-old, Alan Acheson, *A History of the Church of Ireland, 1691–1966* (Columba Press, 1997), p. 190; *Sligo Champion*, 3 October 1847; *Sligo Journal*, 1 October 1847; *Tyrawly Herald*, 30 September 1847.

75. James Collins was appointed Dean of Killala in 1844. He cooperated with Killala PP, Anthony Corcoran, by setting up feeding stations for the starving, keeping order as fever raged, directing sewage disposal and fumigating pest-houses. Corcoran was content to let Collins take a leading role but John Jordan, PP, Kilfian proved less amenable. Thomas Armstrong, *My Life in Connaught*, p. 4
76. St George and Costello, later clashed over allegations of souperism.
77. Little's wife, Jane, helped to tend the soup-kitchen in St John's School with the result she contracted the fever and died on 20 March 1848. *Tyrawly Herald,* 20 March 1848.
78. Stock lived in Belmullet during the Famine years as there was no glebe-house in Kilcommon.
79. An application to the Quakers for relief indicates that Fanny and her mother, Henrietta Marie St George, co-operated in 'directing operations at the soup boilers'. They also organised weaving and spinning employment for the poor.
80. Not without reason, Donal Kerr, the author of *A Nation of Beggars, Priests, People and Politics in Famine Ireland, 1846–1952* (Oxford University Press, 1992), in an instructive understatement, described the Irish Famine period as 'not an ecumenical age'.
81. Because of this ecumenical cooperation, I felt compelled to dedicate my book, *On Our Knees, Famine in the Parishes of Killala Diocese (1845–1852)* to 'the memory of Rev. Francis Kincaid, Ballina and Rev. James Burrowes, Castleconnor, Church of Ireland clergy, who died feeding the hungry of all faiths'. I chose Kincaid and Burrowes as representative figures of an impressive, indeed remarkable, non-sectarian bias among clergy of the Established Church which exemplified such a noteworthy level of Christian witness at a time when the Catholics of Killala diocese were being targeted for conversion by the forces of the Second Reformation. *On Our Knees*, was borrowed (with permission) from the title of the famous painting by the celebrated artist, Hughie O'Donoghue, who had borrowed it from his mother, Sheila Carey, a phrase that was part of her inherited family memory of the Famine, handed down through the generations. 'On Our Knees' evoked not just the terrible reality of hunger but also the response of a people embedded in a faith culture – an incessant harrowing of God in prayer to release the Famine Irish from their agony. The painting was part of the collection in Ireland's Great Hunger Museum at Quinnipiac University in Hamden, Connecticut.
82. Until the passage of the amended Poor Law in August 1847, relief was only permitted to inmates of the workhouses.

CHAPTER TWO

ALEXIS SOYER (1810–1858)

'A feeling heart'

Christine Kinealy

When famine scourged Green Erin's land,
Thy generous heart swift succour plann'd.
And from thy able, willing hand,
Was poured a rich supply.
Ode to M. Soyer. 13 July 1847.[1]

A flamboyant Frenchman, Alexis Soyer, was the *chef de cuisine* at the Reform Club in London. He catered the wedding breakfast for Queen Victoria and hosted a lavish feast for the Pasha of Egypt, and thus he may appear to be an unlikely hero of the Great Hunger in Ireland. Indeed, his appearance in Dublin in early 1847 proved to be contested and controversial. Yet, this kind-hearted culinary artist was responsible for devising a system through which thousands of people were fed daily, his soup often making the difference between life and death in the summer of 'Black '47'. In return, he received neither payment nor official honours. Moreover, starting with Charles Trevelyan's self-serving account of the Great Hunger, published anonymously in 1848, Soyer was largely written out of the historiography.[2] Who was this hero of the Famine and why was his contribution so important—and controversial?

Alexis Benoit Soyer was born on 4 February 1810 in Meaux-en-Brie in France. From the age of 11 he worked in kitchens, achieving the status of head chef by the age of 17.[3] Inevitably, given his ambition, he moved to Paris where he was employed by several leading politicians, gaining a reputation both for his cooking skills and his showmanship. Not only did the July Revolution of 1830 mark the end of Charles X's reign, it prompted Soyer's decision to relocate to London, to a less turbulent political atmosphere.[4] There, he found employment in a number of aristocratic households, commencing with Henry de la Poer Beresford, third Marquis of Waterford, known for his eccentricity and wild pranks.[5] Soyer next worked in Stafford House, home of the wealthy Sunderland family. The matriarch, Harriet, was a friend and confidante of the young Queen Victoria and was at the centre of an influential coterie who championed the abolition of enslavement.[6] She would become a life-long patron of Soyer.[7]

In 1837, at the age of only 27, Soyer was appointed *chef de cuisine* of the newly founded Reform Club in the fashionable Pall Mall area of London. The club had recently been opened as a centre of 'English liberalism' and it was closely associated with the Whig and Liberal parties.[8] Daniel O'Connell, an occasional supporter of the Whig Party, was a founder of the club, although it is likely that his presence was not always welcome.[9] Soyer, whose innovations extended to all aspects of food and kitchen science, immediately helped to redesign the kitchens, in the process making the Reform Club's cooking area a popular tourist destination for the upper classes.[10] The security of his new position meant he was able to propose to a talented and spirited artist, Elizabeth Emma Jones. In 1831, at the height of the campaign to abolish slavery in British colonies, Emma, still only a teenager, had painted 'Two Black Children with a Book', in support of abolition.[11] Emma and Soyer married in the fashionable St George's Church on Hanover Square, Westminster, in April 1837. It was a happy marriage but also a short one, as Emma died, while pregnant, in August 1842.[12]

In addition to his cooking skills, Soyer proved to be both an innovator and an entrepreneur. Not only was he a talented designer of kitchen apparatus, he created sauces and relishes for commercial sale, and was the author of multiple cookbooks, several of which became best sellers.[13] In addition to allowing tours of his model kitchen in the Reform Club, he sold lithographs of it. However, Soyer's indefatigable sense of creativity was never motivated by money, and his trademark generosity meant that his wealth would ebb and flow throughout his life. Soyer's activities, combined with his colourful personality and distinctive style of dress, meant that by the 1840s, his name and his image (always wearing his trade-mark beret) appeared frequently in the British press. He was widely praised for his innovative kitchen, which provided a template for other kitchens to be remodelled in several stately homes and royal palaces, as well as in the exclusive Gresham Club.[14] In 1844, a competition between six leading, but anonymous, 'culinary artists' was held to produce 'the newest, lightest, and most delicate dish'. The winner was Soyer, for which he received a £50 prize.[15] Being in the public eye was not without disadvantages, and could lead to jealousies and animosities. Inevitably, Soyer's flamboyance was mocked. The satirical magazine

Punch suggested that a new society for the Advancement of British Cookery should be formed with Soyer as its President, while one of the branches of studies would be 'MEAT-PIE-OLOGY'.[16] In 1844, Walter Scott, the Secretary of the Reform Club, accused Soyer of extravagance and mismanagement.[17] The matter was widely reported with rumours of Soyer's resignation. The accusation proved to be unfounded, and it was Scott who resigned his position, while Soyer received the unanimous support of the members.[18] For Soyer, it must have been a bitter-sweet reminder that fame came at a price. Regardless, even when parodied, the name of Soyer had come to represent all aspects of cooking in Britain.

In 1845, Soyer turned his hand to writing. His first publication was in French, *Délassements Culinaires* (Culinary Relaxation), which was a mixture of recipes (also called receipts), culinary wisdom, amusing anecdotes, and 'professional chit-chat'.[19] According to one review, 'That ingenious chef de cuisine has blended together poetry, pastry, and politics, with considerable skill'.[20] The following year, Soyer published *The Gastronomic Regenerator*, which included 2,000 recipes.[21] The underlying philosophy was that English cooking could learn from French cuisine, primarily by using a wider variety of vegetables and by utilizing all parts of an animal. Soups or stews (based on the classic *pot-au-feu*) were suggested as an excellent way of using both.[22] Soyer believed that food should be both nutritious and tasty, the latter helped by the addition of herbs and spices, and it should always be pleasing to the eye and the palate.[23] The publication was widely reviewed and praised, with the words 'celebrity', 'genius', immortal', 'peerless', and 'celebrated gastronomic artiste', being used to describe the Frenchman.[24] His acceptance in British high society was noted, with one paper stating that he was 'as great and adept at tickling aristocratic vanity as he is in pleasing the palate'.[25] In July 1846, Soyer again dominated the press for creating, in the Reform Club, a lavish banquet for His Highness, Ibrahim Pasha of Egypt.[26] The visitor was delighted and Soyer 'was highly complimented by his Highness'.[27] In the wake of this sumptuous banquet, which was both a culinary and a diplomatic success, the *London Globe* was moved to write, 'The impression grows on us that the Man of this Age is neither Sir Robert Peel, nor Lord John Russell, nor even Ibrahim Pasha, but Alexis Soyer'.[28] At this stage, Soyer, celebrity chef and creator of opulent concoctions, could hardly have imagined he would find himself in famine-stricken Ireland only a few months later, and that he would be cooking for the starving Irish poor.

Soyer's Soup

The same English newspapers that carried details of Soyer's multiple successes in 1845 and 1846 were reporting on the unfolding crisis in Ireland as two successive failures of the potato crop transitioned into a devastating famine. In the summer of 1846, the Prime Minister, Sir Robert Peel, had resigned and been replaced by Lord John Russell. Public works were the mainstay of relief provided under the new Whig administration.[29] As a system of emergency relief, they were palpably ineffective. At the beginning of 1847, a decision was made to close the public works and, in February, the Temporary Relief Act was rushed through the British parliament. The legislation provided for the opening of a national network of government-run soup kitchens.[30] The kitchens were to be a short-term expedient only, and would close in August, when an extended Irish Poor Law would become responsible for all relief.[31] This programme marked a significant divergence from accepted relief policy as, for the first and only time, the government accepted the much-disliked principle of providing 'gratuitous relief'. The change was not universally liked, with various groups, extending from officials in Westminster and Whitehall to the nationalist press in Ireland, perpetuating the idea that receiving free cooked food was demeaning. In the words of the *Freeman's Journal*, 'the government prefers starving the populace on Soyer soup, to employing them in honourable and useful employment'.[32]

Soup Kitchens, as a medium for feeding large numbers of people in Ireland, were well established by 1847. Their usage was not new—they had been used during the famine of 1739 to 1740 and intermittently since.[33] Following the second failure of the potato crop, soup became a favoured way of feeding large numbers of people efficiently and economically, it being used by the Quakers, the British Relief Association, various religious bodies, by ladies' committees, local gentry, and by individual benefactors, including Father Mathew and Asenath Nicholson. For people used to a nutritious diet of potatoes and buttermilk, inevitably any sudden dietary transition would cause problems. The Indian Corn that had been distributed since spring 1846, for example, had resulted in diarrhoea, pellagra, scurvy, and other diseases associated with a vitamin C deficiency.[34] Similarly, a liquid soup diet, especially if poorly made, could cause bowel problems. Soup, however, provided in government soup kitchens, would be the main diet of over three million Irish people in the summer of 1847.

Soyer's interest in feeding the poor with nutritious soup had been prompted by his witnessing first-hand extreme poverty on the streets of London. The late 1840s had been marked by successive poor harvests, a trade slump, and a credit crunch throughout the whole of Europe.[35] Unemployment was extensive in Britain, partly fuelled by the 'railway mania' of the preceding years and the resultant commercial crisis.[36] During the winter of 1846 and 1847, while catering to the dietary whims of the wealthy and powerful, Soyer had visited institutions that looked after some of the poorest members of society. It led him to conclude that the soup being provided was neither nutritious, palatable, nor economical. He offered to design a special kitchen in which flavoursome soups could be made quickly and cheaply, which would also restore good health.[37] Just as beneficially, Soyer's kitchens could be set up in a field, to allow the poor to be fed who were not in institutions.[38] To promote his ideas, Soyer had written to the London press on 10 and 17 February sharing his ideas, recipes and expertise.[39] His letters were reprinted in several Irish newspapers.[40] In London, his soup cost three farthings to make a quart, but Soyer believed it would be even cheaper outside the capital.[41] He claimed that members of the Reform Club, including Daniel O'Connell, had tasted his new soups and declared them to be delicious.[42] Soyer also offered his services in setting up soup kitchens for no payment, while making a personal donation of £20 to encourage other people to donate to this worthy cause.[43] His actions led to him being praised as a 'public benefactor'.[44]

In the wake of these well-publicised suggestions, a number of soup kitchens in London adopted Soyer's recipes. The most famous was in Leicester Square, close to the headquarters of the Poor Man's Guardian Society. The society's officers were fulsome in praise of this diet and the difference that it made to the recipients:

> With what ravenous appetites did these forlorn, emaciated creatures, devour the long-awaited meal of bread and soup! — the only one, perhaps, which, during the last twenty-four or forty-eight hours, these unfortunates were able to procure! — How changed the countenance, when the appetite had been appeased! — before, — a hungry, wolfish, and half maniacal stare; — afterwards, — a restored, pleasing, and grateful expression.[45]

Several soup committees elsewhere in England adopted these measures, and several even sent delegations to London to meet with Soyer and seek his advice.[46] Within a short space of time, therefore, Soyer had moved from being a celebrated society chef to becoming the authority on feeding the poor. More light-heartedly, during a debate in the House of Commons, one MP, Henry Grattan, suggested that if the Prime Minister resigned, his successor should be Soyer, as the latter would be able to feed the poor of Ireland—something the former had failed to do.[47]

Soyer's first letter to the press had commenced by saying 'Amongst all the terrestrial afflictions which occasionally oppress humanity, famine is the most redoubtable; it is deeply to be regretted that at the present time this evil goddess of terror rides victoriously through the greater part of Europe'. He added: 'Need I say that, though the starvation is continental, Ireland and Scotland are the greatest sufferers of that awful calamity'.[48] At this stage, it is unlikely that Soyer realised that his words would lead him to Dublin. Soyer's intervention, however, into the question of how to feed large numbers of people proved to be perfect timing for the British government, who were about to embark on a major change in relief provision, based on providing the Irish poor with cooked food. The logistics of such a massive undertaking, however, had not been a key concern of policy-makers in London when they decided to, peremptorily, close the public works, leaving the poor without relief except that provided by private philanthropy.

Soyer, understanding the potential of extending his scheme to Ireland, submitted his proposals to the British government. He was asked to show his plans to the Lords of the Treasury—in effect, Charles Trevelyan—who gave his approval. The Board of Works and the Admiralty also supported the scheme being extended across the Irish Sea.[49] Lord Bessborough, the Irish Viceroy, who, together with his colleagues in Dublin Castle were confronted with the day-to-day realities of the suffering of the Irish poor, realized that a replacement for the public works needed to be put in place immediately, or thousands more would die. It fell to Bessborough to ask the Reform Club to allow Soyer a temporary leave of absence. It was approved and only days later, Routh wrote a note to Trevelyan simply stating, 'Soyer is on his way!'[50] According to Soyer, 'Je lui ai soumis mon plan, don't il a approve, et m'invita de me render aupres du vice roi d'irelande'.[51] Consequently, on 20 February, only ten days after Soyer had first written to the London press, a notice appeared in several newspapers:

> We are happy to inform the public that M. Soyer, of the Reform Club, has received instructions from Government to proceed immediately to the Lord-Lieutenant of Ireland, and to submit his plan of a model kitchen for the preparation of soup on a large scale, which, if approved of, will at once be carried into effect, and may be the cause of saving some thousands of poor creatures from death's door for want of proper food.[52]

Within days, Irish newspapers were carrying details of Soyer's visit.[53] The *Freeman's Journal* revealed that he was coming at the behest of the British government to act as the 'superintendent of the soup kitchens about to be established'. They referred to him as the person 'who has recently published some valuable letters in the London journals explanatory of the most expeditious and economic mode of staying the famine in Ireland', adding that he would be bringing models of his 'ingeniously constructed' kitchens and boilers. Soyer was to commence his work in Dublin and then proceed to rural districts with officers from the Board of Works.[54] The *Armagh Guardian*, reprinting a report from a British newspaper, predicted: 'It is confidently anticipated that there will be no more deaths from starvation in Ireland'.[55] Just as positively, William Thackeray, a close friend of Soyer's, wrote in *Punch*, 'M. Soyer deserves to be called the gastronomic regenerator of Ireland. His receipt for cheap soup is the best practical suggestion which has yet been made for that unlucky island'.[56] These early reports augured well for Soyer's visit to Ireland and for the success of his soup kitchens.

Soyer and his trusted assistant, George Warriner, arrived in Dublin on 1 March. For the next few weeks their home would be the fashionable Morrison's Hotel on the corner of Nassau Street and Dawson Street.[57] While travelling to the port of Liverpool, Soyer claimed that he had visited 'every philanthropic and other useful institution, but more especially the domains of that industrial class, the backbone of every free country—the People'.[58] On his first day in Dublin, Soyer shared his plans with the Lord Lieutenant, the Commissariat General, Sir Randolph Routh, and Sir John Burgoyne, the chairman of the Irish Relief Commissioner.[59] According to official reports, 'although they had previously doubted of his plan of relief for the starving Irish, are now convinced and delighted with it'. Consequently, Soyer was given permission to immediately erect a kitchen based on the plans made in London.[60] A few weeks later, however, the Chancellor of the Exchequer, Sir Charles Wood, informed the House of Commons that the Relief Commissioners privately believed Soyer's suggestion 'to be an extremely bad one'.[61] At this stage, there was a backlash against Soyer's soups, so Wood may have been protecting the actions of his government, while simultaneously sacrificing the reputation of the French chef.

Soyer's much-publicized visit to Ireland and his advocacy of a soup diet provoked a lively and, at times, vicious, debate about the efficacy of such a diet. Gravitas was added to the debate surrounding 'Soyer's soup' by the intervention of several medical authorities who contended that their understanding of scientific nutrition was superior to that of a chef. Even before Soyer had set foot in Ireland, an editorial appeared in the influential *Lancet*, which commenced:

> The mass of the poor population of Ireland is in a state of starvation. Gaunt famine, with raging fever at her heels, are marching through the length and breadth of the sister island, and they threaten to extend their fury to this Country ... But parliament and the executive, in the midst of the best intentions, seems to be agitated by a spasmodic feeling of benevolence; at one time adopting public works, at another preaching a poor law—now considering the propriety of granting sixteen millions for railways, and then descending to M. Soyer, the chief cook of the Reform Club,

> with his ubiquitous kitchens and soups, at some three farthings the quart, which is to feed all hungry Ireland.

The remainder of the article was concerned with demonstrating that the latter was 'a soup of pretence' and that 'soup quackery' alone was not sufficient to keep people alive.[62] The *Lancet* article was quoted far and wide in Ireland and was reprinted in newspapers in Australia and Van Dieman's Land (Tasmania).[63] Garnering far less attention, but with a similar intent, was an article in the *Dublin Medical Press* that appeared on 24 March. Again, Soyer and his soup were the target of general Irish dissatisfaction with the actions of the government:

> We have had to complain of the strange policy or oversight which has led to the disregard of medical advice or assistance at this most critical moment, if not to the exclusion of the members of our profession from all official deliberations respecting the health or feeding of the people; but we were not prepared to encounter the monstrous absurdity of bringing over from London a French cook to instruct us as to the nutritive properties and digestibility of articles of diet.[64]

As with the *Lancet,* the lack of nutrition in the soup recipes was criticized, while Soyer was compared to Nero's fiddle, making music as Rome burned—the implication being that Soyer was being manipulated.[65]

The press on both sides of the Irish Sea also entered the debate. An article in the London *Times,* which was reprinted in Ireland, stated: 'Every physician and physiologist knows that the digestive organs in a man are incapable of assimilating sufficient nutriment for health or strength from any liquid diet'. Regarding Soyer's soup diet, the *Times* suggested that the government take this into consideration 'ere they squander more thousands for the unfortunate victims of Irish landlordism'.[66] These comments were in keeping with the newspaper's overt dislike both of government spending and of Irish landlords. In contrast, an editorial in the *Limerick Reporter* fully blamed the British government and its lack of spending, believing that if Ireland had been allowed self-government, the food shortages would not have turned into a famine. The paper disliked the idea of a French chef being sent to make 'a complicated soup', viewing it as reflecting the government's commitment to political economy, rather than saving Irish lives.[67] Elsewhere, disparaging references were made to 'frogs', 'foreigners' and, more pointedly, 'soup-quackery (for it is no less) ... taken by the rich as a salve for their consciences, and with a belief that famine and fever may be kept at bay by M. Soyer and his kettles'.[68] For John MacHale, the nationalist Catholic Archbishop of Tuam, the poor of Ireland were being slowly starved with 'Saxon soup'.[69]

The intervention of these medical men and the more general criticisms of Soyer were, in turn, questioned by diverse sources, including a ladies' journal in England that averred:

> Mr. Alexis Soyer, of the Reform Club, not only subscribed largely towards the relief of the Irish, but offered his plans and his services gratuitously to the Government, with a view to the establishment of soup kitchens in Ireland ... we should infinitely prefer the opinion of one who during thirty years has studied the art of preparing food so as to render it agreeable as well as digestible. Such a man is a practical Liebig.[70]

A further defence of Soyer came from an Irish medical doctor living in Paris, who suggested:

> This man, whose motives were evidently humane and charitable, whose intentions and whose soup were equally irreproachable, was treated by the literati with the utmost ridicule, and this moment when our dear country was suffering under all the horrors of famine![71]

He agreed with Soyer that British and Irish people did not make enough use of vegetables and did not take soup seriously as an item of food. Overall, he judged Soyer's advice to be 'invaluable' regarding soup making and one that could be utilized outside of Ireland.[72]

Undeterred, Soyer followed his usual practice of gaining first-hand experience of the situation. To this end, he visited the Dublin Mendicity Institution to observe soup being prepared and distributed.[73] On 10 March, he visited a soup kitchen located on Winetavern Street which catered for the poor of St Michael's and St John's Parishes. He did not simply come to observe, but assisted in making soup 'in the kindliest manner'. Moreover, his soup was pronounced to be 'excellent and considerably cheaper than that previously manufactured'.[74] Two days later, Soyer made soup in the parochial school in St Anne's Parish.[75] It was described as 'very good to the taste'.[76] Soyer's visit to St Audeon's Parish was similarly successful.[77] In addition to the quality of his soup, he was praised for the speed with which it was prepared—taking only three hours, in contrast to the more traditional 15 to 20 hours.[78] Furthermore, Soyer was personally commended for his tact and helpfulness.[79] On 16 March, Soyer attended the soup kitchen of St Andrew's Parish. There, he met the committee, which included Rev. W. S. Sleater and Rev. William Kerr. Soyer's soup was declared 'excellent' and 'fit for the table of any nobleman in the land'. Moreover, 100 gallons were produced in three bours, thus allowing three distributions daily if required.[80] The committee's cook endorsed the success of Soyer's visit by sending a letter of commendation to the editor of the *Freeman's Journal*.[81] As usual, special praise was reserved for the chef himself: 'All present felt the kindness and courtesy of this gentleman, and bore testimony to the great anxiety which he manifested to afford the fullest information in his power'.[82] It was not just the poor who benefitted. Throughout this period of intense activity, new recipes from Soyer periodically appeared.[83] For St Patrick's Day, Soyer created a special soup, the key flavouring being seaweed or, as it was locally known, 'dillisk'. [84] Soyer claimed its inclusion made the soup 'equal to the great bird's nests soups of China'.[85] One hundred gallons were produced and served in tureens at public gatherings throughout the city, including Dublin Castle, where it was enjoyed by the Lord Lieutenant.[86] It was also fed to diners in hotels throughout the city, including Morrison's Hotel, and, everywhere, it was 'eaten with gusto'.[87]

Soyer was clearly in demand. At a meeting of the Poor Law Guardians of the South Dublin Union, a motion was passed to invite Soyer to join them so that they could discuss his plans for making soup.[88] On 18 March, Soyer visited the workhouse kitchen. Although he declared the soup to be the best that he had tasted in any institution since coming to Dublin, he believed that it was 'over-boiled' and thus had lost its flavour and nutrition. Furthermore, it had taken 16 hours to make, whereas his took two hours. While there, Soyer attempted to make his own soup, but was hampered by the lack of appropriate utensils and the flour being damp. He promised to return the following week.[89] He also recommended that an inspector be appointed to check on the quality of provisions used in all soup kitchens.[90] Soyer's visit was not welcomed by all. Only days later, one guardian, Dr McKeon, criticized Soyer with 'unsparing severity'. He described the soup as 'a perfect humbug ... sour ... not nutritious ... unfit for the consumption of human beings', moreover, 'the sending over of this French cook was a scheme on the part of the Government to direct the attention of the people from their do-nothing policy'.[91] McKeon received no support, so the subject was dropped.[92] These comments, however, prompted Soyer to write to the Dublin press, explaining that although his first visit to the workhouse had not been successful, he had returned and produced his soup in only two hours. In his letter, he thanked the Poor Law Guardians for giving him 'a most flattering reception'.[93] There was a caveat:

> I also, with a smile on my lips, say that one among those gentleman guardians is not a guardian angel; he is known and justly celebrated as doctor in this beautiful city, and although interests himself in my welfare, I cannot say that if I should require his aid, I would place myself in his hands, as I do not like his treatment; but as I have consulted with many since my visit to this country, I have not the least doubt but, that in a short time, I shall number him among my proselytes. [94]

It was a telling insight into Soyer's character, resilience, and self-belief. Nonetheless, questions were being raised about Soyer in the House of Commons, although they focused on the cost, not the quality, of Soyer's project. The House was reminded that Soyer had given his services for free and had raised private subscriptions to help finance his work.[95] More worryingly, while criticisms were overwhelmingly focused on Soyer, a month after the Temporary Relief Act had been passed, no government soup kitchens were in operation.[96]

During his time in Ireland, Soyer published *Soyer's Charitable Cookery or, the Poor Man's Regenerator*.[97] It was 'for the benefit of the labouring, and poor classes of the United Kingdom'. The author explained that, 'one penny out of every book sold will be given to the poor, through the medium of a charitable committee'. The publication had been patronized by 37 'noble and distinguished personages', including the Earl of Bessborough, the Mayor of Dublin, the Duchess of Sutherland, the Duke of Leinster, and the Relief Commissioners, Sir Randolph Routh and Sir John Burgoyne.[98] Not known for his modesty, Soyer explained in the Preface that his recipes 'might prove useful to humanity at large', because they were very cheap and easily made. He believed a good diet was necessary for good health because: 'when entirely deprived of food, the greatest suffering acts upon it, and often makes a thief of an honest man, or a murderer of a civilized Christian ... nature loudly speaks, and a strong appetite never jokes'.[99] The Introduction, entitled, 'Address to the World in General, but to Ireland in Particular', offered a further rationale for his interest: 'You have heard, dear brethren, the distant sounds of distress, misery, and starvation in different parts of the kingdom; whoever has a feeling heart must shed a tear, and pray for the relief of the hungry'.[100]

A Model Kitchen

Soyer's busy schedule, and the ongoing controversy surrounding his work, did not deter him from his main task in hand, namely, to apply his model kitchen plan to the Irish context. To this end, he worked closely with Mr Tonge of Great Britain Street to manufacture the correct utensils and equipment.[101] Soyer's attention to detail was meticulous. The poor were to enter the dining area through a zig-zag passage capable of holding 100 persons. Soyer's explanation of this system was 'to prevent the crowding together of the poor, which causes a propagation of infectious disease'.[102] Food was to be served on long wooden tables, each with white enamel dishes and a metal spoon, attached with a 'neat chain'. Every table had water tins and cloths for cleaning the enamel dishes between servings.[103] On the far side of the kitchen was a bread and biscuit room—both baked in a special cooker designed by Soyer to ensure their freshness. Every person received a quarter of a pound of bread or biscuit on leaving.[104] Soyer believed this food would be more beneficial if eaten later, rather than in haste. As one group departed and the bowls were cleaned, a bell was rung, signalling the next 100 people could enter. This process would take place every six minutes, thus allowing 1,000 people to be fed each hour.[105] Soyer recommended that the soup recipe be changed every day, that all parts of the vegetable be used, and that ingredients should be steam-cooked to allow nutritional values to be retained. A further innovation was that 'portable cooking barrels' would take food to the sick and the aged, and to those living in remote districts. Soyer designed delivery wagons, each containing a stove, to ensure that the soup arrived hot.[106] He explained that, in the past, people had walked miles to get relief, thus adding to their misery.[107] He also recommended that a medical man should be present at every centre to ensure that there was no adulteration of the food.[108] Overall, Soyer's recommendations were thoughtful and thorough, based on the best medical knowledge of the day. Additionally, his concerns were practical and humanitarian, based on compassion towards, rather than condemnation of, the poor.

Upon Soyer agreeing to travel to Ireland, construction had commenced of a temporary structure on the grounds of the Royal Barracks, near to the Phoenix Park. It was to be large enough to accommodate the 'model' soup kitchen created in London.[109] There was delay in its transport, and it was not until mid-March that the kitchen arrived in Dublin and was taken to the specially-erected esplanade.[110] The proposed opening on 27 March, therefore, had to be postponed.[111] Reports of it opening a few days later also proved to be unfounded.[112] At this stage, concerns were being voiced about the slowness in implementing the legislation that had been passed in February. A Treasury directive had required that 20 per cent of all workers be dismissed on 20 March, even though the Soup Kitchen Act was not operative in any Poor Law Union in Ireland. Reports from the countryside stated that workers and their families had 'literally been left to starve'.[113] In these discussions, Soyer's name was frequently invoked, as he was increasingly becoming the scape-goat for the government's inaction.[114] Only a few days later, Burgoyne announced that he would be employing a staff of 110 to oversee the implementation of the Temporary Relief Act, of which 57 were military officers, 26 naval officers, and the remainder civilians. Although he would play no part in this new arrangement, and had given his services for free, Soyer was included in the outcry:

> Of the military gentlemen, 52 are on full pay. The pay and allowance of this new corps, under its distinguished chef de cuisine, are estimated at £2 per diem, or at the rate of £370 a-year each; equal to £736,570 per annum on the whole; or to the maintenance of nearly 100,000 labourers, at a shilling a-day, for the next six months! Nor is it at all improbable that Mr Soyer, and his commissary general, may require reinforcements in the course of summer; so that the economy of the Government seems to consist in laying on with one hand upon the public kitchen whatever they save with the from the public works.[115]

Easter Monday, which fell on 5 April, was the day designated for the opening of the Dublin soup kitchen. To mark the occasion, the Royal Barracks was decorated with flags and ensigns, including the Union flag, while a portrait of Queen Victoria overlooked the kitchen's dining area. Lord Bessborough and his entourage arrived at three o'clock and received a military salute from a guard of honour.[116] Many members of the Irish landed gentry were present, as were several of the city's doctors, including the oculist, William Wilde.[117] Several of the most eminent restauranteurs also attended, including Messrs Hayes, Jude, Radley, Graham, Belanger, and Roch, the *chef de cuisine* in Dublin Castle. An artist from the *Illustrated London News* was in place to sketch the scene.[118] Due to an indisposition, Bessborough was unable to leave his carriage. Nonetheless, soup was delivered to him, which he declared to be delicious and Soyer presented him with a copy of *Charitable Cookery*. Shortly after three o'clock, 100 dignitaries were admitted into the dining area and asked to take their positions at the tables where the bowls were placed. Six different types of soup had been made. After seven or eight minutes this group left and they were replaced by 100 male and female poor from the Mendicity Institution. After Grace had been said by the Very Rev. Dean Tighe, they were served their meal. Upon departing, they were given a biscuit to eat at their leisure. The public were then admitted. At six o'clock, the poor people who had been waiting outside were invited in and supplied with soup. At night-time, the kitchen was illuminated, and so it continued to be an object of attraction during the evening.[119]

Soyer viewed the opening of what he referred to as his 'experiment' as a great success. The kitchen could feed more than 25,000 a day with 'wholesome, nutritious and cheap food'. Days later, the kitchen was purchased by the government to enable it to remain in Dublin. There were plans for others, on the same principle, to be erected elsewhere in Ireland. Moreover, encouraged by his Dublin success, Soyer planned to open a similar kitchen in London, paid for by private subscription.[120] A few days after the grand opening, Soyer left Ireland, although Warriner stayed behind to assist with extending the scheme to other Poor Law Unions. In advance of his departure, a banquet was held at the Freemason's Hall on College Green, hosted by Thomas M. Gresham, owner of the eponymous hotel on Sackville Street. Nearly all the hotel keepers in the city attended. Soyer was thanked for bringing lasting benefit to the poor of Ireland and for 'making soup palatable to every description of the Irish'.[121] He was presented with an elegant snuff box made by Thomas Bennett of Grafton Street.[122] On his return to London, another banquet was given at the London Tavern. Soyer was thanked for his 'disinterested exertions for the relief of the poor in Ireland, and likewise to ameliorate the condition of the destitute in other civilised countries'.[123] In total, 150 people dined at a table service made of gold and silver.[124] The Famine in Ireland must have seemed very far away.

Soyer may have left Ireland, but his colourful presence was not forgotten. He even continued to be commemorated in street ballads, not all of which were flattering.[125] As the General Election approached in summer 1847, Soyer appeared in a satirical political poem, based on the play, *Macbeth*:

> Ancient spring of Ireland's trouble
> Like soup of Soyer—toil and bubble
> Double, double, toil and trouble
> Members spout and agents bubble.[126]

More seriously, Soyer's kitchen and recipes remained at the forefront of dissatisfaction with relief policies. The pomp and spectacle that had attended the opening of the model soup kitchen remained a source of contention, as it was widely regarded as demeaning to the recipients. Several newspapers likened the treatment of the starving people to the handling of animals in a zoo. The committee of the Mendicity Institution even published a resolution condemning 'the unchristian and unnatural exhibition of our poor people at the Soyer Soup Kitchen'.[127] At a meeting of the guardians of the North Dublin Union, Mr Long claimed to be 'mortified' at the 'disgusting exhibition' he had witnessed. He viewed the opening as a degrading display of the people's misery, and suggested that flying a black banner would have been more appropriate than flying the Union flag. The other guardians responded to his comments with cheers of 'hear, hear'.[128] The *Freeman's Journal* echoed these sentiments regarding the display of the British flag, on the grounds that it was 'the emblem that had brought our country to require soup kitchens'.[129] At a meeting convened in Limerick to thank Americans for their sympathy, 'gallant Captain Forbes', who had brought a ship-load of provisions from Boston to Cork, was cheered.[130] Lord George Bentinck was also praised. In contrast, Soyer's name was repeatedly greeted with hisses. He was referred to as 'the turn-spit of the Reform Club', while his soup was described as 'un-nutritious' and 'trash'. It was claimed that while he was in Dublin, he 'lived at Morrisons' Hotel, and drank champagne, ate turtle soup, and drank Maderia there'. The meeting closed with a call for a repeal of the Union.[131]

Despite the attention devoted to the opening of Soyer's model kitchen, the implementation of the Temporary Act proved to be no faster or less bureaucratic than the public works had been. In early April, it was announced that the North Dublin and South Dublin Unions would be the first to offer this new form of relief, despite evidence of need elsewhere in the country.[132] It was not until the end of April that applications to become operative under the Soup Kitchen Act were complete. Out of the 127 Poor Law Unions only three had not applied: they were the Antrim, Belfast, and Newtownards Unions, all in the northeast of the country. In these unions, private, rather than government, soup kitchens continued to provide relief.[133] Yet, by early May, soup kitchens had not opened in many unions. This led the radical English MP, George Poulett Scrope, to ask in the House of Commons on 17 May for a statement on the progress of the act that had been passed on 26 February.[134] It was not until early July that the act was fully operative. At that stage, over three million people were daily receiving free rations of soup and biscuit—an impressive logistical feat. Also, regardless of the delays and other criticisms of Soyer and his soup, mortality did decline in Dublin and elsewhere after April, it having peaked in the first four months of 1847.[135] Ironically, while the soup kitchen controversy continued to rage in Ireland, English newspapers were reporting on the success of soup kitchens in London that had been based on Soyer's principles.[136] The government soup kitchens in Ireland were officially closed in mid-August and an extended Poor Law became responsible for all relief. Even following the closing of the kitchens, Soyer and his soup continued to divide public opinion. Anger was again inflamed following the publication of a letter from Soyer to the London *Times* in September 1847 in which he described how much money his innovations had saved the South Dublin and North Dublin Unions.[137] The letter was widely reprinted.[138] At a meeting of the South Dublin guardians, they agreed that while they wanted to hold on to the kitchen designed by Soyer, it was for the purpose of making bread and other foodstuffs, not soup. Dr McKeon, an erstwhile critic of the chef, dismissively referred to Soyer's letter, accusing him of taking 'the whole and entire credit' for saving the lives of the poor in the preceding months.[139]

In 1848, as revolutions were taking place throughout Europe, an article in the Dublin-based *Pilot* predicted that the age of empire was melting away. Regarding Ireland, the failure of the Union was evident from one million deaths that had occurred in the space of only two years. Soyer was named, and blamed, for starving people 'to death' on his soup.[140] As evictions, emigration and mortality showed no signs of declining in many parts of Ireland, another paper asked:

> Are we to have another year of Soyer soup and Skibbereen corpses, of foreign alms and home extortion, of paupers choking in crammed workhouses, and skeletons ministering at public works, of famine eating the flesh off our bones, and fever rotting the blood in our veins, of ministerial congratulations on our forbearance and the contempt of the world for our cowardice.[141]

In the same week, it was announced in the English press that Soyer had opened a Philanthropic Gallery in London, the proceeds of which were to finance local soup kitchens. He was praised for his 'excellent intent' and his 'excellent soup'.[142] In Ireland, however, references to him were generally pejorative. In 1850, an article entitled 'Horrors of Carlow Workhouse', held the use of vegetable soup by the 'Carlow Soyers' responsible for the high mortality.[143] The following year, the government decided to consolidate all famine 'debts' and make them a charge on the Poor Law. Again, Soyer's name was invoked and partly blamed for the expenditure:

> These rulers during the famine, starved and worked the people of Ireland on strict principles of political economy; Nicholls' tests, McGregor's preventative checks, and Soyer's weak soup and weaker gruel, were all of them administered on these established principles.[144]

Later Life and Legacy

Soyer's activities following his return to London from Ireland, both in and out of the kitchen, continued to fascinate people. In 1848, Thackeray helped to immortalize his friend in the novel, *Vanity Fair*:

> As the immortal Alexis Soyer can make more delicious soup for a half-penny than an ignorant cook can concoct with pounds of vegetables and meat, so a skilful artist will make a few simple and pleasing phrases go farther than ever so much substantial benefit-stock in the hands of a mere bungler.[145]

In 1850, Soyer unexpectedly resigned from the Reform Club.[146] Following this, he was engaged in freelance work that extended from creating popular sauces and relishes to opening 'Soyer's Universal Symposium' at the Great Exhibition in 1851.[147] Some of the Dublin press mocked Soyer's involvement, referring to him as 'King Rolling Pin'.[148]

At the same time, his philanthropic activities continued. Over the Christmas holiday period in 1851, Soyer presided over cooking food for the poor in seasonally-decorated tents in Leicester Square. Over 22,000 people were fed roast beef, herring, pies, potatoes, and plum pudding. They were also given a pint of porter and a bag of biscuits to take home.[149] Again, Soyer gave his services for free.

The commencement of the Crimean War in 1853 proved to be life-changing for Soyer. After a soldier had written to him asking for help in creating recipes that could be used in such circumstances, Soyer, with his usual energy, wrote to the *Times* offering his services gratuitously to assist with creating healthy diets, especially for the wounded.[150] At his own cost, he travelled to Sebastopol. While there, he accompanied Florence Nightingale on many of her travels. During this time, he contracted 'Crimean fever'. Although he recovered, the illness ultimately destroyed his health. Financially also, Soyer suffered. He had been personally invited by Emperor of France, Napoleon III, to oversee food preparations at the 1855 Paris Exhibition. Soyer had agreed to do so, but believed it was his duty to remain in Crimea until the end of the war.[151] When the war ended in February 1856, Soyer travelled through Turkey collecting recipes. Additionally, he wrote a personal recollection of his time in the Crimea. As had been the case in Ireland, Soyer remained engrossed with the challenge of feeding large numbers of people who did not have access to a traditional kitchen. While living in various sites of war, he had devised a 'field' kitchen that he continued to perfect on his return to England.[152] It was based on the travelling food carts that he had devised in Ireland in 1847.[153] On 28 July 1858, Soyer unveiled his mobile kitchen to much acclaim. It would provide a template for armies on the move for the next century. A week after the unveiling, however, Soyer was dead. He was 48-years-old. Despite his long and distinguished career, he did not die a wealthy man.[154] His passing was widely reported in the British press, but less so in Ireland.[155] The *Cork Daily Herald* noted the death of 'poor Soyer', adding that he would be remembered in Ireland 'for his soup kitchens during the Famine'.[156] The obituary in the *Freeman's Journal* made no mention of his time in Ireland but praised his work in the Crimea, commenting that he had 'a kind heart and a lively disposition'.[157] The *Belfast Morning News* did not mention Soyer's time in Ireland either, but stated that he had 'done more than was ever done before in England, to improve and dignify' the benefit of healthy eating amongst middle and poorer classes.[158]

In subsequent decades, Soyer's name was intermittently mentioned, with later generations of chefs clearly appreciating his practical approach to cooking.[159] The Emigration Commissioners recommended to Irish emigrants that his recipes and cooking methods be used on long-distance voyages.[160] During the cholera epidemic of 1884, his chapter on the 'Anti-Cholera Diet', that had been first published in 1853, was widely quoted the Irish and British press.[161] Increasingly, however, his name was linked with the Great Hunger in Ireland. In 1897, the *Enniscorthy Guardian* published a long article on the famine of 1846 and 1847. It included reference to 'Sawyer's, or Soyer's soup', describing it as the 'benevolent invention of a distinguished French chef'.[162] In 1911, Nicholas Soyer, who claimed to be a grandson of Alexis, and had been chef to the Prince of Wales, caused a sensation in Ireland with demonstrations of his 'paper bag cookery'.[163] His illustrious ancestor was recalled for giving the poor of Ireland his 'earnest attention' during the Famine.[164] In 1933, the *Waterford Standard*, which was known for its outspoken and libertarian views, published an extensive article on Soyer and his soup kitchens.[165] The subtitle was 'The man who fed Ireland in 1847'.[166] Soyer was praised for creating a 'a colossal soup kitchen' that could economically feed the starving people. Moreover, he had devised a system of food distribution that provided the poor in the countryside with hot food. According to the writer:

> Soyer's ingenious and successful attempts to combat the Famine in Ireland were recognised by all creeds and classes as well as by the government of the day ... Soyer had in fact become a popular idol owing to his successful efforts in connection with the Irish Famine.[167]

The centenary of the founding of the Reform Club in 1936 inspired a number of retrospectives in which Soyer was inevitably mentioned. According to the *Belfast News-Letter*, Soyer had 'rendered important service as a culinary expert in Ireland during the Famine'.[168]

In 1995, the sesquicentenary of the first appearance of the blight renewed interest in the tragedy. One article stated—incorrectly—that one of the most hated aspects of the workhouses was the 'infamous soup', which it attributed to Soyer.[169] However, a lecture given in September 1995 in Gorey, County Wexford, which was entitled 'Alexis Soyer, chef extraordinaire, and the famine', praised his involvement.[170] In 2004, at a time when soup kitchens were opening in many places to feed the poor and homeless, Soyer's actions were commended in the *Dublin Evening Standard* in an article sub-titled 'He Didn't Make Soup to Conquer'.[171] Clearly, Soyer had remained in the popular memory of the Great Hunger, and was largely remembered in a positive way. For many historians, however, he remained defined by one soup recipe and the spectacle that had accompanied the opening of his model kitchen.[172]

Was Soyer a hero? In life and death his role during the Famine was controversial. Placing his actions in Ireland in 1847 within the larger trajectory of his life, it is hard not to view him as a man who was motivated by humanitarianism, not greed. For his role during the Famine he was openly mocked, parodied, and patronized, and the fact that he was 'fashionable' and 'French' were used to criticize him.[173] Soyer's actions, however, should be judged in the context of both the severity of the suffering of the Irish poor in 1847 and the determination of the government to make all relief an Irish responsibility and an Irish charge. Soyer's time in Ireland was born out of a failure by the British government to provide relief that was timely, appropriate, and effective in saving lives. It fell to a flamboyant Frenchman to devise a system that, at its peak, would feed over three million people each day, and to do so at a minimal cost. Soyer's compassion for the poor, in Ireland and elsewhere, place him amongst the many unsung heroes of the Great Hunger.

NOTES

1. F. Volant and J.R. Warren, *Memoirs of Alexis Soyer* (London: W. Kent, 1859), pp 144–146.
2. Charles Trevelyan, *The Irish Crisis* (London: Longman, Brown, Green & Longmans, 1848). Nor is Soyer mentioned in the memoirs of Sir John Burgoyne, either for his role in the Famine or in the Crimean War. No mention is made of either the Temporary Relief Act or of Soyer in Timothy W. Guinnane and Cormac Ó Gráda, 'Mortality in the North Dublin Union During the Great Famine' (2001). *Discussion Papers*. 837. https://elischolar.library.yale.edu/egcenter-discussion-paper-series/837
3. Ruth Cowen, *Relish: The Extraordinary Life of Alexis Soyer* (London: Weidenfeld & Nicolson, 2019), p. 11.
4. Ibid., pp 15–16.
5. D.G. Hewitt, *10 of Britain's Eccentric Aristocrats.* https://historycollection.com/10-of-britains-eccentric-aristocrats/6/
6. For more on the Stafford House Set and their involvement with abolition see Christine Kinealy, *Black Abolitionists in Ireland,* vols 1 and 2 (London: Routledge, 2020 and 2024).
7. Cowen, *Relish*, pp 19–21.
8. 'The Reform Club'. www.reformclub.com/Home
9. A portrait of O'Connell still adorns the walls of the club by Irish artist, Joseph Patrick Haverty (1794–1864). 'Drawn to the Page', Trinity College Dublin. www.tcd.ie/library/exhibitions/drawn-to-the-page/commemorative.php
10. According to the Reform Club's website, 'The kitchens at the Reform Club were designed in 1838 by the architect Charles Barry in partnership with the exuberantly creative Victorian celebrity chef Alexis Soyer. Soyer's legacy of innovation and culinary excellence continues in today's kitchen'.
11. For decades the provenance of the painting was disputed, and it was the subject of an enquiry in the BBC programme *Fake or Fortune* on 2 September 2018. The experts concluded that Emma was the artist. www.bbc.co.uk/programmes/b0bj6gm7

12. 'Died', *Morning Chronicle*, 2 September 1842; *Morning Herald* (London), 2 September 1842. Emma was buried in Kensal Green, under an elaborate monument designed by Soyer, unveiled in 1844, 'Monument of the late Madame Soyer', *Illustrated London News*, 7 September 1844.
13. 'The Kitchen at the Reform Club', *Age*, 3 July 1842.
14. Ibid.: 'Culinary Intelligence', *Illustrated London News*, 3 December 1842; Ibid., 17 February 1844; 'M. Soyer', *Railway Bell and London Advertiser*, 20 July 1844.
15. 'Culinary Legerdemain', *Sun* (London), 31 August 1844.
16. 'Essence of "Punch". Meeting for the advancement of British cookery', *Dover Telegraph and Cinque Ports General Advertiser*, 12 October 1844.
17. *Weekly Dispatch* (London), 30 June 1844.
18. 'The Reform Club', *Sun*, 3 July 1844; *Evening Mail*, 8 July 1844.
19. Alexis Soyer, *Délassements Culinaires* (London: Simpkin and Marshall, 1845); 'Delassements Culinaires', *Satirist; or, the Censor of the Times*, 21 September 1845; *Morning Advertiser*, 8 September 1845.
20. *Morning Advertiser*, 25 September 1845.
21. Alexis Soyer, *The Gastronomic Regenerator* (London: Simpkin and Marshall. 1846); 'Culinary Relaxations', *The Era*, 7 September 1845.
22. 'Soyer's Cookery.—The Gastronomic Regenerator, a Simplified and Entirely New System of Cookery', *Illustrated London News*, 18 July 1846; 'Gastronomic Regenerator', *Sun*, 20 July 1846.
23. 'The Gastronomic Regenerator', *Morning Post*, 7 July 1846.
24. 'Notices of new books', *Monthly Times*, 25 August 1845; 'A Cook of Genius', *Satirist; or, the Censor of the Times*, 17 August 1845; 'Gastronomic by A. Soyer', *Weekly Dispatch*, 20 December 1846.
25. Ibid.
26. 'Reform Club Dinner to Ibrahim Pasha', *Morning Herald*, 4 July 1846. The dinner was for 150 people and cost £4 4*s* per head.
27. 'Ibrahim Pacha', *Morning Post*, 7 July 1846.
28. *The Globe*, 10 July 1846.
29. For more on Peel's demise, see the chapter by Peter Murphy on Lord George Bentinck.
30. 'An Act for the Temporary Relief of Destitute Persons in Ireland', 10 and 11 Vict. c. 7.
31. Queen's Opening of Parliament, *Hansard*, House of Lords, 19 January 1847, vol. 89 cols 1–5.
32. *Freeman's Journal*, 19 March 1847.
33. Trevelyan, *Irish Crisis*, p. 13.
34. Jonny Geber and Eileen Murphy, 'Scurvy in the Great Irish Famine: Evidence of Vitamin C Deficiency From a Mid–19th Century Skeletal Population' in *American Journal of Physical Anthropology*, 2012, 148 (4), 512–524. Doi: 10.1002/ajpa.22066
35. Eric Vanhaute, Richard Paping, Cormac Ó Gráda, 'The European subsistence crisis of 1845- 1850: A comparative perspective', UCD Centre for Economic Research Working Paper, University College Dublin (2006). https://hdl.handle.net/10197/469

36. James Narron and Donald P. Morgan, 'Crisis Chronicles: Railway Mania, the Hungry Forties, and the Commercial Crisis of 1847'. https://libertystreeteconomics.newyorkfed.org/2015/06/crisis-chronicles-railway-mania-the-hungry-forties-and-the-commercial-crisis-of-1847/
37. 'Very Cheap Soup for the Poor', *Newcastle Courant*, 19 February 1847.
38. 'Distribution of Soup', *Essex Standard*, 19 February 1847. The Irish press following this correspondence: 'Cheap Soups', *Northern Whig*, 23 February 1847.
39. 'Soyer's Kitchens and Soup for the Poor', *Bell's Life in London and Sporting Chronicle*, 14 February 1847; 'M Soyer's soup for the poor', *Sun*, 19 February 1847.
40. 'Mr Soyer's Kitchen and Soup for the Poor', *Freeman's Journal*, 20 February 1847.
41. Alexis Soyer, *Soyer's Charitable Cookery or, the Poor Man's Regenerator* (Dublin: Hodges and Figgis, 1848). There were four farthings in a penny.
42. 'Establishments for Ireland', *Freeman's Journal*, 23 February 1847.
43. 'Distribution of Soup', *Essex Standard*, 19 February 1847.
44. Ibid.
45. William Ellis-Rees, 'The Prince and the Paupers: The Soup Kitchen in Leicester Square' (2019). https://london-overlooked.com/soup-kitchen/
46. 'Soup Committee', *Oxford Chronicle and Reading Gazette*, 20 February 1847; *Lady's Newspaper and Pictorial Times*, 20 February 1847.
47. 'House of Commons', *Morning Post*, 20 February 1847.
48. 'Soyer's kitchen and soup for the poor. To the editor of the Sun', *Sun,* 10 February 1847.
49. Cowen, *Relish*, p. 123.
50. Ibid.
51. Soyer, *Charitable Cookery*, p. 48.
52. *Sun,* 20 February 1847.
53. 'Soup Establishments for Ireland', *Dublin Evening Post*, 23 February 1847.
54. 'Superintendence of the District Soup Kitchens', *Freeman's Journal,* 23 February 1847.
55. 'Soup Establishment from Ireland', from *Sunday Observer* in *Armagh Guardian*, 2 March 1847.
56. Cowen, *Relish*, p. 124.
57. 'A potted history of ... Morrison Chambers'. https://hospicefoundation.ie/other/culture-night-a-potted-history-of-our-home-morrison-chambers/
58. Alixis Soyer, *Soyer's Shilling Cookery for the People* (London: Routledge, 1854), p. 57.
59. 'Sir Randolph Routh', *Douglas Jerrold's Weekly Newspaper,* 6 March 1847; *Dictionary of Irish Biography'. www.dib.ie/biography/routh-sir-randolph-isham-a7819*
60. 'Mr Soyer's Arrival in Dublin', *Hereford Journal*, 10 March 1847.
61. 'Imperial Parliament', *Limerick Reporter*, 26 March 1847.
62. 'The Proposed Relief of Irish Famine by M. Soyer's Soup', *Lancet*, 27 February 1847, vol. 1, p. 232.
63. 'M. Soyer's Soup', *Bury and Norwich Post*, 10 March 1847; 'M. Soyer's Soup for the Irish', *Newry Telegraph*, 15 April 1847; *Kilkenny Journal, and Leinster Commercial and Literary Advertiser*, 17 April 1847. Australian coverage included 'M. Soyer's Soup', *The Sydney Morning*

Herald (from *The Lancet*), 31 August 1847; 'Mr Soyer's Soup', *The Hobart Town Advertiser,* 21 September 1847.

64. 'The Soyer-Soup Relief Measure', *Dublin Medical Press*, 24 March 1847.
65. Ibid.
66. 'Insufficiency of Soup Diet', *Galway Vindicator, and Connaught Advertiser,* 3 March 1847.
67. 'The Present Emergency', *Limerick Reporter*, 2 March 1847.
68. 'State of Ireland', *Bury and Norwich Post*, 10 March 1847.
69. 'The past week', *Cambridge Independent Press,* 27 March 1847.
70. *Lady's Newspaper and Pictorial Times*, 17 April 1847. Justus von Liebig (1803–1873) was a German biological chemist, with an interest in food science.
71. 'The Food Question', *Dublin Evening Post*, 29 June 1847.
72. Ibid.
73. *Worcestershire Chronicle*, 17 March 1847.
74. *Dublin Evening Herald*, 11 March 1847.
75. 'Mr Soyer', *Clare Journal, and Ennis Advertiser*, 18 March 1847.
76. 'Mr Soyer's Soup', *Dublin Evening Herald*, 13 March 1847.
77. *Freeman's Journal*, 20 March 1847.
78. 'Ireland', *Daily News* (London), 19 March 1847.
79. 'Mr Soyer's Soup', *Dublin Evening Herald*, 13 March 1847.
80. 'Mons. Soyer's Food for the Million', *The Era*, 21 March 1847.
81. 'Soyer's Soup. John Radley to Editor', *Freeman's Journal*, 22 March 1847.
82. 'Mons. Soyer's Food for the Million', *The Era*, 21 March 1847.
83. 'Soyer's Cheap Soup', *Lincolnshire Chronicle*, 19 March 1847.
84. Also known as 'dulse', this seaweed is recognized as a rich source of minerals and vitamins, with a high protein content. See 'Irish Seaweeds'. https://irishseaweeds.com/product/dulse-dillisk/
85. 'Soyer's Soup', *Daily News*, 20 March 1847.
86. 'M. Soyer in Dublin', *Saint James's Chronicle*, 20 March 1847.
87. 'Soyer's Soup', *Daily News*, 20 March 1847.
88. 'South Dublin Union', *Freeman's Journal,* 12 March 1847.
89. Ibid., 19 March 1847.
90. Ibid., 'Mr Soyer. South Dublin Union, *Freeman's Journal*, 22 March 1847.
91. 'M. Soyer in Dublin', *Southern Reporter and Cork Commercial Courier*, 1 April 1847. McKeon's criticisms were reprinted in several English newspapers including *Lancaster Gazette*, 3 April 1847.
92. Ibid.
93. A. Soyer, Morrison's Hotel, 27 March 1847 to Editor of *Saunders's News-Letter*, 'South Dublin Union', *Dublin Evening Mail*, 31 March 1847.
94. Ibid.
95. The question was raised by John Collett, MP for Athlone, and a member of the Reform Club, 'Mortality (Ireland)—Defective Returns', *Hansard,* House of Commons, 22 March 1847, vol. 91, cols 302–315.

96. For example, a meeting of Dublin citizens on 22 March called for the Finance Committee formed under the Temporary Relief Act to 'hasten their operations'. The meeting petitioned the Queen for a domestic parliament, 'Meeting of Citizens of Dublin', *Morning Advertiser*, 23 March 1847. Similar concern was expressed in the countryside, 'Distress of People', *Limerick Reporter*, 23 March 1847.
97. Alexis Soyer, *Soyer's Charitable Cookery or, the Poor Man's Regenerator* (Dublin: Hodges and Smith, 1847).
98. Ibid., front matter.
99. Ibid., p. vi.
100. Ibid., p. 7.
101. Cowen, *Relish*, p. 127. Tonge. later Tonge and Taggart Ltd, were a major iron foundry in Dublin. https://glassian.org/Prism/TongeTaggart/index.html
102. Soyer, *Gastronomic*, p. 41.
103. Ibid., p. 40.
104. Ibid., p. 41.
105. Ibid., p. 42.
106. Ibid., pp 42–44.
107. Ibid., p. 45.
108. Ibid., p. 46.
109. 'Mr Soyer and Soup Establishments for Ireland', *Dublin Evening Mail*, 24 February 1847.
110. 'Relief Under New Act', *London Evening Standard*, 23 March 1847.
111. 'M. Soyer's Soup Kitchen', *Illustrated London News*, 27 March 1847.
112. 'The Famine In Ireland', *Morning Post*, 23 March 1847.
113. 'Wholesale Dismissal of the Labourers from the Public Works—consequent distress and tumultuary meetings of the people at Youghal', *Dublin Evening Packet and Correspondent*, 6 April 1847.
114. 'Inhumanity of the Treasury', *Dublin Weekly Register*, 20 March 1847.
115. 'Soyer's Soup for the Irish', *Weekly Dispatch*, 28 March 1847.
116. 'M. Soyer's Model Kitchen', *Dublin Evening Post*, 6 April 1847.
117. 'M Soyer's Model Kitchen', *Dublin Evening Packet and Correspondent,* 6 April 1847.
118. For more on this newspaper see Niamh Ann Kelly, 'James Mahony: *The Illustrated London News*, in Christine Kinealy, Jason King and Gerard Moran (eds), *Heroes of Ireland's Great Hunger* (Cork University Press, 2021), pp 239–260.
119. 'Soyer's Model Soup Kitchen', *Dublin Evening Packet and Correspondent*, 6 April 1847.
120. Alexis Soyer, *Soyer's Charitable Cookery or, the Poor Man's Regenerator* (Dublin: Hodges and Smith, 1848), p. 49.
121. *Westmeath Independent*, 17 April 1847.
122. Cowen, *Relish*, p. 111
123. 'Grand Entertainment to M. Soyer', *Cambridge Chronicle and Journal*, 12 June 1847.
124. Warren, *Memoirs,* p. 111.
125. Ibid., p. 110.
126. 'The Electioneering Cauldron—from *Punch*', *Western Times*, 10 July 1847.

127. 'Soyer's Soup Menagerie. The New Zoological Exhibition', *Limerick Reporter*, 23 April 1847.
128. 'North Dublin Union', *Weekly Freeman's Journal*, 10 April 1847.
129. Cowen, *Relish*, p. 110.
130. For more on Forbes see Catherine Shannon, 'Captain Robert Forbes and his 1847 Voyage of Mercy' in Kinealy, King and Moran, *Heroes,* pp 39–54.
131. 'American Sympathy Meeting', *Cork Examiner*, 23 April 1847.
132. 'Dublin, 5 April', *Express* (London), 7 April 1847.
133. See Christine Kinealy and Trevor Parkhill, *The Famine in Ulster* (Belfast: Ulster Historical Foundation, 1997).
134. 'Temporary Relief (Ireland)', *Hansard,* House of Commons, 17 May 1847, vol. 92, cols 956–961.
135. Guinnane and Ó Gráda, 'Mortality in the North Dublin Union'.
136. The Poor Man's Guardian Society in London were feeding 300 a day. 'Soyer's Soup Kitchen', *Hereford Journal*, 28 April 1847. It had been forced to close in March but Soyer helped it reopen, *Morning Advertiser*, 16 March 1847.
137. In his letter, Soyer claimed that because of his soup kitchen, 'whilst the ratepayers of the North Dublin Union have paid 3s. 4d. in the pound, those of the South Union have only had to pay a 1s. Rate', *Dublin Weekly Nation*, 2 October 1847; *Essex Herald*, 5 October 1847.
138. *Home News for India, China and the Colonies*, 7 October 1847.
139. 'South Dublin Union', *Freeman's Journal*, 1 October 1847.
140. 'Repeal or Republic, to the Statesmen of England', *Pilot,* 26 April 1848.
141. 'The State Trials', *Tablet*, 27 May 1848.
142. The exhibition consisted of almost 150 paintings, predominantly the work of Emma, 'Soyer's Philanthropic Gallery', *Morning Advertiser*, 12 May 1848.
143. 'Horrors of the Carlow Workhouse', *Freeman's Journal*, 17 January 1850.
144. 'The Present Poor Law Taxation', *King's County Chronicle*, 3 September 1851.
145. William Thackery, *Vanity Fair, a Novel Without a Hero* (London: Bradbury & Evans, 1848), p. 161. Throughout the 1840s, Thackery had frequently parodied Soyer in *Punch*.
146. Cowen, *Relish*, pp 150–152.
147. Ibid., pp 215–219.
148. 'King Rolling Pin', *Dublin Weekly Nation*, 24 May 1851.
149. 'Extraordinary Christmas Festival', *Southern Reporter and Cork Commercial Courier*, 1 January 1852.
150. *Dublin Daily Express*, 7 August 1858; *Kilkenny Moderator*, 11 August 1858; *Kerry Evening Post*, 11 August 1858.
151. For Soyer's personal account see, Alexis Soyer, *Soyer's culinary campaign. Being historical reminiscences of the late war* (London: Routledge, 1857).
152. Ibid., pp 212–216.
153. Cowen, *Relish,* pp 316–317.
154. 'Funeral of M. Alexis Soyer', *Birmingham Daily Post*, 13 August 1858.
155. 'Births, Deaths and Marriages', *Examiner*, 7 August 1858; *Dublin Daily Express*, 7 August 1858; *Kilkenny Moderator*, 11 August 1858; *Kerry Evening Post*, 11 August 1858.
156. 'Our London Letter', *Cork Daily Herald,* 14 August 1858.

157. 'Death of M. Soyer', *Freeman's Journal*, 7 August 1858.
158. 'Death of M. Soyer', *Belfast Morning News*, 9 August 1858.
159. The best-selling *Mrs Beeton's Book of Cookery and Household Management*, first published in 1861, leaned heavily on Soyer's methods.
160. Cowen, *Relish*, p. 317.
161. 'The Cholera Ship at Liverpool', *Drogheda Conservative*, 26 July 1884. A diet of rice was recommended.
162. 'The Famine of '46 and '47', *Enniscorthy Guardian,* 16 October 1897. It also appeared in *Cork Examiner*, 17 October 1908; *New Ross Standard*, 30 October 1908; *Wexford People*, 31 October 1908; *Wicklow People*, 31 October 1908.
163. 'The Most Famous Living Chef', *Belfast Telegraph*, 26 October 1911; *Belfast News-Letter,* 14 December 1911; *Lady of the House*, 15 March 1912, included an image of Alexis, 'the grandsire'.
164. 'Paper Bag Cookery', *Evening Irish Times*, 16 October 1911; 'Mr Soyer to revisit Belfast', *Northern Whig*, 13 February 1912.
165. The editor was David Culbert Boyd, a northern Protestant involved in republican activities in 1916. See Anthony Keating, 'Criminal libel, censorship and contempt of court: D.C. Boyd's editorship of the *Waterford Standard*'. https://doras.dcu.ie/24177/1/Keating%20-%20Waterford%20Standard.pdf
166. 'The Irish Famine of 1847' *Waterford Standard*, 11 March 1933.
167. Ibid., 18 March 1933.
168. 'Reform Club Centenary', *Belfast News-Letter*, 26 May 1936.
169. 'As usual, Brussels is to blame', *Irish Independent*, 19 August 1995.
170. 'Top personalities coming for discussion group talks', *Gorey Guardian*, 20 September 1995. The lecturer was Dr Donal Flanagan.
171. 'He did not make soup to conquer. A celebrated French chef set up a successful Dublin soup kitchen during the Famine', *Evening Herald*, 25 September 2004.
172. Early accounts of the Famine generally referred to the government soup kitchens in a negative way, for example, Canon John O'Rourke (1875) pp 220–223 and Cecil Woodham-Smith (1962) pp 178–179. Mary Daly (1986) paid little attention to Temporary Relief Act and did not mention Soyer. The Great Famine Curriculum (New York, 1995) described the soup as 'a joke in Dublin', pp 228–229. www.nysed.gov/sites/default/files/gifcfamnature.pdf
173. 'Scene from the Soup Kitchen', *Limerick Reporter*, 6 April 1847.

CHAPTER THREE

LORD GEORGE BENTINCK (1802–1848)

'feed the starving population'

Peter Murphy

In the annals of legislative bodies in modern Western democracies, it is rare when a legislator is portrayed as heroic. Far more often are the individuals who, while seeking elective office may have noble and lofty goals at the beginning of their political careers, eventually succumb to the desire to retain the power associated with the position, bask in the attendant prestige, and enjoy the perks of the office. However, every so often, a legislator emerged from anonymity and acted uncharacteristically and, occasionally, heroically. Lord George Bentinck, who served in the House of Commons from 1828 until his untimely death in 1848, was one such individual.

In the 1840s, the United Kingdom was governed by a parliament based in London. Members of the Upper Chamber, also known as the House of Lords, consisted of members of the nobility and Anglican Church hierarchy. They were not elected nor was there a term limit.[1] Regarding the House of Commons, despite the 1832 Reform Act, the traditional landed interest remained dominant.[2] Lord George Bentinck had, in his own words, 'sat in eight parliaments without having taken part in any great debate'.[3] It was not until the onset of the Great Famine in 1845 before almost anyone, outside of perhaps of the Palace of Westminster, had heard of him. Ironically, he rose to prominence fighting against the repeal of the Corn Laws, which had been enacted in 1815 and were 'designed to protect English landholders by encouraging the export and limiting the import of corn when prices fell below a fixed point'.[4] The 'Corn Laws' included flour, meal, peas, rye and beans.[5] Bentinck, in opposing repeal, went up against Sir Robert Peel, a fellow Conservative and Prime Minister. The split in the Conservative or Tory Party, as it was colloquially referred to, led to Peel's resignation in 1846. Bentinck became the leader of the Conservative Party, though he was never Prime Minister.

Lord William George Frederick Cavendish-Scott-Bentinck was born in 1802 to William Bentinck, the fourth Duke of Portland, and Henrietta Scott Bentinck. Bentinck's maternal grandfather was the wealthy General John Scott of Fife, who added to his real estate fortune by being a successful gambler. According to one of Bentinck's biographers, Scott was a 'renowned gambler, but unlike so many of his contemporaries, who thought nothing of risking an inheritance or an estate upon the turn of a card, he both made a fortune and retained it'.[6] Lord George, one of five children, was raised and educated privately at the family estate at Welbeck Abbey in Nottinghamshire and at Fullarton House, near Troon, Ayshire, where his father was developing the docks.[7] In 1818, George and his brother John enlisted in the army, but his time in the army was marred by contentious disputes. Captain Ker, Bentinck's superior officer, took exception as to how he was performing regimental duties and for calling him a 'poltroon'. In February 1821, Bentinck was cleared of the charges of inattention to duty and of contemptuous, insubordinate, and disrespectful behavior. Ker was ordered to apologize to Bentinck, which rankled Ker to the point of challenging his former subordinate to a duel in Paris. At that time, Bentinck was serving as an aide to his uncle by marriage, George Canning, the Foreign Secretary and Leader of the House of Commons. Cooler heads prevailed, however, and a tragedy was averted.[8]

Bentinck's focus then turned away from the army and towards horseracing and breeding. His first mount was at the Goodwood meeting in 1824. The *London Courier and Evening Gazette* reported that G. Bentinck was in attendance and was amongst 300 'fashionables' at a luncheon. He was described as 'tall and well-made, both in face and figure a model of manly beauty, quick of eye and of action, he was distinguished by his skill in every kind of sport'.[9] Later, it was reported that Bentinck and a Captain Berkeley rode in a race that was 'prettily contested'. Bentinck won.[10] He was hooked, finding the excitement of racing and gambling irresistible. In a race at the St Leger in 1826, he wagered, and lost, £26,000. His mother and sister helped him pay off the debt. His father was displeased that his son was devoting so much of his time to such a frivolous pursuit. In order to hide his activities from his father, he partnered with his cousin, Charles Greville.[11]

In what appears to be a precursor to his later efforts at reform, Bentinck's love of horseracing led him to work toward changing the nature of the business, eventually becoming senior steward at Goodwood. In this role, he led efforts to reform the sport, including ridding racing of 'dodgy dealings'.[12] Bentinck is credited with introducing the horsebox (a way to transport horses between racetracks), introduced the numbering of horses, and putting an end to prizes being given to judges by winning owners.[13] His innovations were widely respected among horse racing fans and helped to put 'Goodwood at the leading edge of racing, forming the basis of race organization as it is known today'.[14] Benjamin Disraeli, who would become his mentor and ally in the House of Commons, gave Bentinck the sobriquet 'Lord Paramount of the Turf'.[15] Not all agreed. As one historian later wrote, 'To his honor, be it said, he exercised a powerful influence in endeavoring to rid horse-racing of some of its worst features, and incurred the hostility of the cheats and rogues which have at all times been associated with it'.[16] In 1846, after more than two decades of racing, betting, owning and reforming the horseracing industry, Bentinck stunned the Turf world by selling all his horses for a mere pittance, in order to focus on politics. He was walking away from the sport at the height of his success, yet, as Disraeli noted, 'Notwithstanding his mighty stakes and the keenness with which he backed his opinion, no one perhaps ever cared less for money'. Disraeli added that Bentinck 'valued the acquisition of money on the turf, because there it was the test of success. He counted his thousands after a great race as a victorious general counts his cannon and his prisoners'.[17]

In 1828, Lord George Bentinck had entered the world of politics for the first time, running unopposed as the Whig representative for King's Lynn in Norfolk, a seat previously held by a brother and an uncle. The following year, the British parliament passed the Roman Catholic Act (also known as the Catholic Emancipation Act) which Bentinck supported. It allowed Catholics to sit as MPs, to take public office, and to vote. It also enabled Daniel O'Connell, a leader of the Catholic Association, to take a seat in parliament. Disraeli wrote that Bentinck 'would impress on his friends, that if they wished to maintain the territorial constitution of their country, they must allow no sectarian considerations to narrow the basis of sympathy on which it should rest.'[18] However, to appease members of the Protestant ruling class, a large percentage of rural Catholics were simultaneously disenfranchised by another law, the Parliamentary Elections (Ireland) Act 1829, which required owning land worth at least £10 in order to vote.[19] As one newspaper reported, 'One simple act of even handed justice has been done for Ireland, in an hour, what centuries of ingenious but ill directed policy failed to effect'.[20] Bentinck consistently voted in favor of reform bills and, in reply to his critics who had failed to unseat him in the 1832 parliamentary elections, said:

'I have no disposition to crouch in servile obedience to any ministry, nor, on the other hand, to bend to the excitement of wild popular fury, but will endeavour to support such measures as may conduce to the welfare and happiness of the greatest number of people'.[21] Despite his many votes over the years, generally in favour of reform, Bentinck remained silent within parliament. That reticence, however, would change after a decade and a half serving the people of King's Lynn. In 1836, Bentinck switched political affiliation and became a member of the Conservative Party. His switch can be traced to Sir Robert Peel's Tamworth Manifesto, published two years earlier. The manifesto 'set a foundation for a new form of partisan politics and helped to create more rigid political parties built around clearly delineated ideological frameworks'.[22] It also sought to eliminate patronage, privilege and sinecure.[23] The manifesto embodied a new type of politics that attracted Bentinck.

The summer of 1845 in Ireland, as well as much of the rest of the United Kingdom, was colder than normal and unusually wet.[24] These wet conditions were perfect for the spread of the potato blight (*phytophora infestans*) that arrived on Ireland's shores in 1845. The *Gardeners' Chronicle* stated unequivocally that the cause of the blight was 'excessive wet, and a low temperature'.[25] The blight impacted potato crops in other European countries, including Belgium, The Netherlands, northern France and southern England. But unlike in the rural parts of Ireland, these locales had other foods to consume. The earliest warnings of a blight arriving in Ireland were reported in the Irish press. The *Dublin Evening Post* on 9 September 1845: 'Our accounts from the continent are also of a more serious nature. A fortnight ago, the complaints were confined chiefly to Holland and Belgium; now it appears the disease is extending along the seacoast of France, throughout Normandy'.[26] The *Cork Examiner* reported that, 'All that we see, hear, or read of the Potato Crop, convinces us that the extent of injury which has befallen it is in no degree exaggerated, but the contrary, and that there is no present help for it'.[27] The *Irish Railway Gazette* wrote, 'the extent of the potato failure in Ireland has been greatly exaggerated. All authentic accounts report the crop fully one-third above an average'.[28]

One leader who was not sceptical was Sir Robert Peel, who served twice as Prime Minister of the United Kingdom (1834 to 1835 and 1841 to 1846) and was a member of the Conservative Party, as was Lord Bentinck. One of the first steps Peel took was to appoint a scientific committee to Ireland to assess the extent of the shortages. In September 1845, a circular was forwarded to the officers of the constabulary with queries relating to the loss of the potato crop. Secrecy was to be maintained so as not to reveal the true nature of the inquiries.[29] The reports that came back were full of possible theories as to the cause of the blight. Some were quite fanciful, including lightning blasting the crops or in a pitched battle, the Connacht fairies were vanquished, and the northern fairies blighted, or rather carried off, the potatoes.[30] By late October, Peel's three committee members—Robert Kane, John Lindley and Lyon Playfair—arrived in Ireland and were tasked with answering the following three questions:

> 1. What are the best means of preserving the potatoes which are dug up apparently in a sound state?
>
> 2. Whether anything can stop the progress of the disease when it has once seized upon the potato; and if so, to what use potatoes so circumstanced can be applied?
>
> 3. What means can be adopted for securing seed potatoes for next year?[31]

Once Peel received the committee's findings, he secretly ordered £100,000 of maize (Indian corn) and corn meal to be purchased from America, through the agency of Baring Bros & Co., one of the largest London trading houses. Two problems resulted from importing corn: it arrived late (February 1846) due to weather conditions, and it needed to be ground to be edible.[32]

Newspaper reporting, as well as personal accounts, attested to the desperate situation in Ireland during autumn 1845. As early as November 1845, Russell, the leader of the Opposition, penned 'the Edinburgh Letter', to the electors of the City of London, in which he wrote: 'Two evils require your consideration. One of these is the disease in the potatoes, affecting very seriously parts of England and Scotland, and committing fearful ravages in Ireland'.[33] Writing to Sir James Graham, Peel admitted 'The accounts of the state of the potato crop in Ireland are becoming very alarming'. In the same letter, he added what would reflect the attitude of many in England, 'There is such a tendency to exaggeration and inaccuracy in Irish reports, that delay in acting upon them is always desirable'.[34] The Peel government then took the position that the Corn Laws, in place since in 1815, should be repealed. These laws were ostensibly designed to protect farmers in England from cheap imports. Peel offered two proposals: suspension of the Corn Laws, which Peel thought would provide immediate relief to Ireland, or gradual repeal, over a three-year period.[35] Bentinck, along with Disraeli, who were members of the Protectionist wing of the Conservative Party, were strongly opposed to repeal. Peel felt that the bill to repeal the laws should be debated in parliament, recommending that 'a measure insuring final and early adjustment of the question, but less abrupt than immediate and absolute repeal, would be less exposed to the risk of failure in its passage through the two Houses of Parliament'.[36] Bentinck was the final speaker after hours of debate. But he made quite an impression, winning praise as one with a 'master mind'.[37]

Bentinck's arguments against repeal were, typical of his style, well prepared, filled with reams of statistics on prices of agricultural goods, historical references and much else. He noted that there were 2,300,000 destitute people in Ireland, but that repeal 'would not afford any relief' a phrase he used repeatedly. He pointed out that it was not the want of food but the want of money to buy food. He then suggested that, 'the Government may delude the people of Ireland ... by assuring them that a repeal of the Corn Laws would relieve their distress'.[38] One witness to the debates, the diarist who was clerk to the Privy Council, Charles Greville, had quite a different opinion of Bentinck's three-hour speech. He referred to the Lord's 'laborious preparation' and being 'armed at all points with statistical details, wound up the debate in a speech of three hours length'. Greville went on to add that as 'his speech consisted entirely of statistical details, it was, as might have been expected, intolerably tiresome'. He did go on to say that many thought it a 'remarkable performance, exhibited great power of mind, extraordinary self-possession, and clearness'.[39] One reason for his opposition to repeal was that it would lower wages for growers of grain. He cited how wages fell for those in the silk trade 'have been gradually reduced since the alteration of the law from protection to free trade'.[40] Bentinck also leveled personal attacks against Peel, even going so far as to accuse Peel of causing the death of his relative, former Prime Minister George Canning. The Corn Laws were ultimately repealed but Peel's days as Prime Minister were numbered as he had lost the support of much of his own party, many of whom felt he had betrayed them and their party. As it turned out, the repeal of the Corn Laws had negligible impact on the distress in Ireland, as Bentinck so presciently noted.[41] According to Christine Kinealy, 'it had not been the intention of Peel's government to feed the distressed people, but rather to keep the price of food down'.[42] In June 1846, Peel resigned after the Irish Coercion Bill, which he had proposed, was defeated. This affair also led to the split of the Conservative Party and Bentinck's ultimate elevation to leader of the Protectionists. A further result was that Russell became the British Prime Minister.

The crisis in Ireland became worse following the harvest of 1846 as the crops failed again, leading to more Irish dying of starvation and diseases, including dysentery, cholera, and typhus. The British government's relief efforts became even less effective. Food was being exported across the Irish Sea to England from Ireland while literally millions were starving. The economic policies adopted by the Russell government contributed greatly to the suffering. The Irish were widely held in contempt by the British press. The London *Times*, which had a daily circulation far and above any other paper in the British Isles and was no fan of the Irish, said that 'giving charity would only serve to keep Ireland in permanent degradation'.[43]

Charles Trevelyan, the Permanent Secretary at the Treasury and an avowed evangelical, famously told parliament:

> The judgment of God sent the calamity to teach the Irish a lesson. That calamity must not be too much mitigated. The greater evil with which we have to contend is not the physical evil of the famine, but the moral evil of the selfish, perverse, and turbulent character of the Irish people.[44]

Trevelyan was responsible for the distribution of public aid to Ireland and he worked closely with the British Relief Association, which was raising private donations.[45] His micromanagement of aid relief and condescending attitudes towards the Irish is viewed by many historians as a major contributor to the failure of British relief efforts. As he had stated previously, 'any more interference on the part of the government would only end in disappointment' and 'we are acting on our principles rather than yield to the urgency of claims for interference'.[46]

One of the harshest critics of the Whig government's efforts was Lord Bentinck, now leader of the divided Tory Party. His attacks on the new Prime Minister and his party's response to the devastating famine were centered on several issues.[47] Bentinck, along with his ally Disraeli, condemned many of the Whig's policies, including the government's reduction of the size of rations to the Irish poor, leaving food importation to private traders and speculators, and their exaggeration of the quantity of food being imported into Ireland. He and Disraeli also criticized the Whigs for not keeping accurate records of the mortality rates which they felt the government was fully capable of doing.[48] In a scathing denunciation of the government's policies and programmes, Bentinck spoke at length on the 19 January 1847, partly in response to the Queen's speech, which had opened the session. While he acknowledged the monarch's concern for Ireland, he stated that the operation of the Poor Employment Act had not answered any good purposes. Further, he noted that 400,000 persons had been employed in works that had proved to be altogether useless.[49] From public works projects, he moved on to the government's food policies. He sharply criticized their *laissez faire* ideology:

> This political economy of non-interference with the import and retail trade may be good in ordinary times; but in times such as the present, when a calamity unexampled in the history of the world has suddenly fallen upon Ireland ... it was not reasonable to suppose that suddenly merchants and retailers would spring up to supply the extraordinary demands of the people for food.[50]

The government's position on supplying imported food to Ireland was summed up succinctly by Lord Russell a week later when he said, 'it is not the intention of the Government. Having, by the measures which we have introduced, taken steps to facilitate in every way an unchecked importation of food, we think it far better to leave the supplying of the people to private enterprise and to the ordinary trade'.[51] A clearer definition of *laissez faire* economics would be difficult to find.

During the debate, Bentinck introduced a letter he had received from Reverend Townshend, a Protestant clergyman in Skibbereen, one of the most severely impacted areas of Ireland. Townshend wrote:

> ... between the 1st of December and the 1st of January there have been 140 deaths in the workhouse of that town, and the poor starving creatures are entering the workhouse, as they themselves say, 'so that they may be able to die decently under a roof and be sure of coffins'.[52]

Bentinck moved from providing an eyewitness account of the devastation to outlining the inflated costs of food in Ireland, while pointing out that in the ports of London, Liverpool and Glasgow, there were between 300,000 and 400,000 quarters of corn just sitting there. He asked what had 'prevented Ministers from sending any part or all of this food to the west of Ireland, to feed the starving population there?'[53] Bentinck concluded by adding that the Irish landlords should not be saddled 'with such a monstrous expenditure' or be solely responsible for the costs of feeding and employing their tenants as had been suggested by some in the British government and press.[54] As Disraeli, his ally and biographer wrote, Bentinck felt 'that all public works should be reproductive; and in the second, that, under the circumstances, it was the duty of the government not only to employ, but to feed, the people'.[55]

A week later, on 25 January, parliament again met to debate the merits or shortfalls proposed to relieve the distress in Ireland. Russell's government had suggested providing £50,000 for supplying seed for crops. Bentinck responded:

> When the noble Lord spoke of 50,000*l.*, for supplying the want of seed in Ireland ... that it is scarcely sufficient to sow five baronies in Ireland; about as much as would sow 25,000 acres of oats, or what might sow about 5,000 acres of potatoes. I am afraid, in the present state of matters in Ireland, that a grant of £50,000 will be about like doing nothing at all.

He then moved on to the subject of public works, stating that there was one safe manner of employing capital—the construction of railways. He also mentioned the issue of emigration, which some landlords and others were promoting to relieve the distress in Ireland. He posed the question:

> Who, Sir, are those who do emigrate? They are not the weak, the feeble, the inefficient, and the unenterprising: no; but it is the very bone and sinew of the country

> that are taken out of it. Instead of the country being thus made richer, it is rendered poorer — instead of being made more powerful, it is rendered weaker.[56]

Bentinck's words may have caused consternation within the British parliament, but within Ireland, he was attracting widespread praise. The *Cork Examiner* praised Bentinck on the grounds that he 'would in the first place feed the Irish people at any cost to the treasury while the right trusty Whig ... sees them dropping into their premature graves with the apathy of a stoic, and the cruel heartlessness of an implacable foe to the human race'.[57] At the end of January, a meeting of landed proprietors, and clergymen of the Established and Roman Catholic Churches, held in Castlebar in County Mayo to propose opposing any resolutions put forth by Russell or anyone else until sufficient amounts of food were sent into the country, praised Bentinck for his 'distinguished services in opposing the "fraudulent profits" of merchants importing food'.[58] The meeting closed by thanking Bentinck 'for the admirable manner in which he exposed the fraudulent profits upon food imported for a starving people'.[59]

On 4 February 1847, Bentinck rose and gave an impassioned plea to parliament for the starving people of Ireland. The speech centered around his proposal to introduce a bill 'to stimulate the prompt and profitable employment of the people by the encouragement of railways in Ireland'.[60] Two nights previously, Bentinck and the Irish members of parliament had met in the Old Palace-Yard at Westminster to discuss his proposal to promote employment in Ireland.[61] As the *Manchester Courier* reported, Bentinck 'expressed the pleasure it would give him to explain the nature of his scheme, and to obtain the benefit of such suggestions as honourable members connected with Ireland might have to offer upon the subject'.[62] The meeting was well attended and included many of the leading members of the Irish contingent in parliament. As one historian noted, Bentinck's 'exordium was solemn and earnest, and he seemed much impressed with the importance and magnitude of the subject with which he was about to deal'.[63] Bentinck began his speech with a trait uncharacteristic of politicians: humility. He spoke at length, describing the 'distress, disease and scarcity of food which prevailed at the present to such an appalling extent'.[64] He admitted that he did not 'feel any want of confidence in the intrinsic value of the measure ... but because I fear, lest through the feebleness of the advocate'. He went on to say that if his measure has nothing good in it, or if it was contrary to sound policy, then 'it is my privilege, as the leader of a great party, to claim for myself the right to incur the exclusive blame and to bear the undivided responsibility'.[65] Bentinck pointed out that public works programmes had been variously described as 'works worse than idleness;' and 'public follies', while the Inspector General of the

Government himself had admitted the 'works which will answer no other purpose than that of obstructing the public conveyances'.[66] Nonetheless, there were '500,000 able-bodied persons in Ireland living upon the funds of the State ... commanded by a staff of 11,587 persons'.[67] Bentinck pointed out that in the early 1840s England had experienced 'great distress and difficulty', and some ascribed the country's economic recovery to such measures as a reduction in the cotton duty or the importation of 27,000 head of cattle. Bentinck ascribed the economic rebound to the railway construction throughout the country. He went on to say that more than 2,600 miles of railways had been constructed in England and Scotland and another 5,400 were planned due to recent acts in parliament. For Bentinck:

> Unquestionably it was the railway enterprise which then began to prevail that was the cause of this national renovation. Suddenly, and for several years, an additional sum of thirteen millions of pounds sterling a year was spent in the wages of our native industry.[68]

As the *Illustrated London News* pointed out, Bentinck knew that the construction of railroads in England had 'given employment to hundreds and thousands, who, previous to their introduction, were inmates of workhouses; and he saw no reason why the miseries of Ireland should not be overcome by giving a stimulus to the labours of the people'.[69] In Ireland, only 123 miles had been completed, even though legislation had been passed for another 1,523 miles. The increase in rail lines would reduce the costs of moving goods, allow greater access to items that were imported, increase the demand for iron and steel, and help develop coastal towns. Railway jobs paid well so workers and their families would have more to spend, increasing demand for consumer items.[70] Bentinck compared the cost of building railways in various parts of the United Kingdom, using detailed statistics to buttress his argument. In his speech, he pointed out that support expanding railway construction throughout Ireland came, not unsurprising, from the head of one of the largest rail companies in Ireland. The chairman of the Great Southern and Western Railway, George Carr, on 22 May 1846, had written to Sir Robert Peel, referring to the 'very distressed' state of the country, stating that the contractors 'would undertake to give immediate employment to many thousands in distress, now destitute and unemployed'.[71] Bentinck cited this letter and another from Carr to the Exchequer Loan Commissioners in Ireland in which he warned that 'there appears no way of averting an impending calamity, but by giving full and active employment to the peasantry'.[72]

Bentinck's proposal explained in meticulous detail the costs and funding of the railway proposal. He spoke of how much money the government had invested overseas with little being repaid. He pointed out that, in 1833, £20,000,000 had been provided to compensate slave owners.[73] He added there were many other examples of the government sending funds out of the country, yet they were reluctant to invest in Ireland for fear that it would never be repaid.[74] Bentinck's bill asked the government to pledge its credit or guarantee a loan to Ireland of £16,000,000 over four years, to be repaid over 30 years at an interest rate of 3 1/2 per cent per annum. He calculated that approximately 100,000 persons would be employed. With the average household presumed to be 5.5 persons, this proposal would provide a meaningful and sustainable income for 550,000 persons for four years. The workers were to be 'paid weekly in cash, and decent, suitable dwellings were to be constructed for them along each line'.[75] Bentinck closed his speech with a solemn pledge to 'answer for the loyalty and the honour of the Irish people' and hoping he could help to ensure 'their wants fulfilled, their wishes gratified, their warm sympathies and grateful hearts not to sever, but to cement, the union with England'.[76] In a lengthy commentary on the Railways Bill, the London newspaper, the *Sun*, came out forcefully in favour of Bentinck's proposal. The paper stressed 'that no proposition is made to the people of England to part with one sixpence of their property, in order to make a bold and final endeavour towards the recovery of their brethren in the sister island'. It went on to say that the 'population look to the State for some provision for the future—some permanent and settled mode of earning a livelihood apart from the miserable and insufficient methods of the past'. The article concluded by suggesting that Bentinck had made the boldest, and best, step yet taken for Ireland's recovery and improvement.[77]

Bentinck's empathy towards the Irish people was further expressed when delivering a 'panegyric on the character of the Irish people', in the House of Commons, during which he:

> eulogised their patience amidst the most direful suffering, and concluded by saying, that if by his measure he could fill their bellies with good beef and mutton, and their cottages with fine wheat and sound beer, and their pockets with English gold to purchase the blankets of Wiltshire, the fustians of Manchester, and the cotton prints of Stockport, he, though a Saxon, would answer with his head for their loyalty, and would lead them, through their warm hearts and sympathies, not to sever but to cement the union of Ireland with England.[78]

Disraeli said of his speech that he treated the details 'with so much dexterity that he commanded during the whole time (more than two hours) the unbroken attention of his audience'.[79]

After Bentinck sat down, Lord Russell, the Prime Minister and leader of the Whig Party, spoke. He opened by praising his 'noble Friend in his [Bentinck's] ability in forming his plan and explaining it to the House—to the zeal which he has shown for the benefit of the people of Ireland'. He then talked about a similar plan, yet different in its financial structure, to build railways in Ireland put forth several years previously by Lord Morpeth. His objections to Bentinck's bill were many, but primarily, 'I should say that it is not advisable for Her Majesty's Government to step out of its usual course to interfere with the general application of capital to railways, and to favour one set of companies having set on foot particular railways, rather than another'. Another objection was 'the application of a large sum of money from the Treasury could best relieve those who were immediately oppressed by destitution'. He added, 'what is necessary for them is food'.[80] This statement was clearly a justification of the about to be opened soup kitchens.[81] Russell also felt that much of the £16,000,000 would go in the pockets of the railway companies and not to the workers who needed it most. While saying he did not oppose the introduction of the bill, he tempered this by adding, 'but with the distinct understanding that it was one which the Government could not allow to proceed beyond the first reading'.[82] Russell went so far as to threaten to resign if the Railroad Bill was passed, a not infrequent tactic in parliamentary history.[83] On 11 February, a meeting was held at Lord Russell's house with the Irish members to discuss Bentinck's measure. According to reports from the meeting, Russell 'stated that in the event of there being a majority in favour of the proposition ... it was the determination of himself and his colleagues to resign immediately'.[84] The irony of Russell's opposition was that, as recently as December 1846, he had written to Charles Wood, the Chancellor of the Exchequer, opining that, 'Of all public works none are as useful as railroads, and I trust we shall come to an understanding with the Companies'.[85]

Despite Russell's objections to a second reading of the bill, one did occur, as Bentinck had carefully and eloquently taken apart the objections put forth by opponents of his railway scheme. Though many members indicated support, when the vote came, the nays won overwhelmingly by 332 to 118, and Bentinck's efforts went for naught. The *Kerry Evening Post* attributed this opposition to the British government's 'inveterate hatred towards Ireland'.[86] There were, however, several conditions that made investors and the Russell government reluctant to commit large sums of money or credit for large-scale rail construction in Ireland. A financial crisis in Britain and a severely distressed economy in Ireland were given as mitigating factors in rejecting the bill.[87] Additionally, the Russell government had plans to reclaim thousands of acres of wasteland and felt that this was a better use of funds. One of the sad ironies of

Bentinck's defeat was the number of Irish members who voted against the measure. As the *Penzance Gazette* noted, 'the Irish members, with the proverbial nationality of blundering, having proved their unanimity by dividing, almost equally, for and against the measure, with every variety of excuse, reason and unreason, threatening and praying, complaint, praise and anathema'.[88] Bentinck would later pen an open letter explaining:

> It was not so much through the hostility of the English members as through the desertion and hostility of the Irish members … Out of 105 representatives which Ireland possesses, 28 only…would vote for that loan. Two-thirds of the Irish members present declined the measure—the rest took care to be *non est inventus* at the division, which was the hour of Ireland's need.[89]

The *Cork Examiner* reported on a meeting in April in Limerick to thank America for her aid during the Famine, especially compared to the efforts by the government. It was noted that the best proposal so far had been Lord Bentinck's railroad scheme, which would have provided employment to thousands, 'hindered the emigration of our healthy stalwart Irishmen' and given 'spirit to the faltering poor'. But the scheme had been rejected and 'trampled on by the British parliament'.[90] Bentinck's speech defending his bill was also commended, with one newspaper noting that 'it is impossible to bestow too much or too high praise upon the speech of Lord George Bentinck … it was spoken in a spirit worthy of the best days of British statesmanship'.[91]

Though Lord Bentinck had seen his Railway Bill suffer an overwhelming defeat, he had other concerns regarding Ireland and the tragedy that was unfolding. The British government had no idea of how many people were perishing in Ireland, let alone what exactly was causing deaths—whether starvation or a myriad of diseases. Bentinck, supported by Disraeli, moved for a comparative return of the number of deaths which had occurred in each parish. He responded to the objection that there was no compulsory power to ensure the compilation of such returns by the clergy by pointing out that between 1841 and 1843, clergy had been asked to submit a return of the numbers of illegitimate children and no objections had been made to furnishing the same.[92] While the death totals had increased dramatically towards the end of 1846, 1847 would come to be known as 'Black '47', the year of the greatest number of deaths.[93] Russell remained adamant that 'there had never been known a pressure of business so severe as that which now unhappily prevailed in the offices connected with the Government … the subordinate officers of the Government had already much more to get through than it was practicable for them to accomplish.' Disraeli replied that if returns were to be requested for the quantities of pigs and poultry consumed within a given time, there would not be the least objection raised to any such return.[94]

Bentinck pointed out it was an incorrect assumption that the clergy could not provide the number of deaths, citing a letter from John MacHale, Archbishop of Tuam, who wrote 'that in his Diocese, he could have the required information furnished'.[95] Bentinck repeatedly asked for a circular to be sent to the Roman Catholic clergy of Ireland for a comparative return of the mortality.[96] The *London Evening Standard* pointed out that 'it seems strange that the Board of Works, with its extraordinary staff expenditure of no less than £600,000 per annum, cannot furnish the information demanded'. The *Standard* went on to say that Lord Bentinck's demands were 'made with warmth' but they were resented by the members of the ministerial party. The paper added that the ruling party, the Whigs, 'have failed, and failed to an extent that they are afraid to confess to themselves much more to the public'. The principal cause of failure, the paper went on to say, was the use of private enterprise to supply food to the hungry and the subsequent rise in prices that no poor person could afford. An Irish newspaper, the *Northern Whig*, provided a quite distinct perspective on Bentinck's speech, writing that 'Lord George furiously assailed Ministers, as if they were careless about the loss of life, in Ireland.' He had pointed out that:

> tens of thousands, hundreds of thousands of deaths—but they could not learn, from the Government, how many, for there was one point upon which the Irish Government were totally ignorant, or which they concealed, which was the mortality which had occurred, during their administration of Irish affairs.

Bentinck had again attacked the *laissez faire* economic philosophy of the government:

> They know the people have been dying by the thousands; and I dare them to inquire what has been the number of those who have died, through their mismanagement, by their principles of free trade. Yes, free trade, free trade in the lives of the Irish people—leaving the people to take care of themselves, when Providence has swept away their food from the face of the earth—leaving them to take care of themselves, in a country where there were no stores, nor mills, nor granaries.[97]

Clearly, Bentinck simply could not accept that the people of Ireland would be allowed to die without any record of their deaths being taken. He felt that it was a matter of far too great importance, and too deep interest, for the House and the country to be left in ignorance upon it.[98]

In late March, Lord Bentinck again decried the inadequate and inefficient supplying of food to Ireland. He compared Peel's government, that had brought food into Ireland, with Russell's government, which refrained from interfering with the operations of the private speculators.[99] He questioned the government's reduction of daily rations, the *Times* reporting that they had been 'diminished to half a pound of bread per diem?'[100] Bentinck asked Henry Labouchere, Chief Secretary for Ireland, if he thought that constituted sufficient rations for working men?[101] In another speech in parliament, Bentinck criticized government relief efforts. It had been the original intention of the government to advance £50,000 for seed but, at the eleventh hour, had only provided 'green crop seed', not corn seed, 'which the farmers will not be able to avail themselves till the summertime'. Furthermore, while 50,000 tons of provisions had come into Limerick, 30,000 quarters of grain had been exported from the same port. In the meantime, while speculators were importing and exporting, 200,000 Irish people perished. Bentinck compared the parsimonious response of the government to the generosity of outsiders: 'If the Government had but one-tenth of the sympathy shown in Boston by the Americans for the starving people of Ireland, all this food might have been supplied at least six months ago'. He concluded by directly confronting the government: 'I think, under these circumstances, the Right Hon. Gentleman, the Chief Secretary for Ireland, has little cause to congratulate himself, especially when he reflects on the hundreds of thousands of persons who died under his administration of affairs in Ireland'.[102]

Bentinck continued to lead the Protectionists until February 1848 when he resigned following the defeat of the Jewish Emancipation Bill.[103] He continued to be an outspoken critic of the Whig government, even challenging the Chancellor of the Exchequer for providing the parliament with inaccurate information.[104] But like many others who attempted to do something practical to help the Irish poor, he was ultimately disappointed. When thanked by the Mayor of Cork for his interventions, he responded, 'the warm-hearted thanks I daily receive from the Irish people, I am one-hundredth-fold repaid for my feeble, and alas, I fear, futile efforts to serve the Irish nation'.[105]

Lord Bentinck's career could be likened to a shooting star. Out of the darkness of years of relative obscurity and total silence, he flashed brightly across the political landscape, and, then, suddenly, he was gone. In September 1848, aged 46, he was found dead, apparently of a heart attack, near to his father's home at Welbeck Abbey. As Disraeli wrote some years later, 'So much was never done so unexpectedly by any public man in the same space of time'. Disraeli explained that Bentinck had rallied a great party that seemed hopelessly routed; he had established parliamentary discipline; proved himself a master of detail; and addressed economic issues in several areas.[106] Even the *Times* of London, no fan of Bentinck, called him a 'political moralist, not a statesman' adding that he was 'Young, energetic, confident, hopeful, persevering, full of indignation, opening up new quarrels and provoking new antagonisms every day'. Poignantly, they pointed out that he was just commencing, 'a long and vigorous career'.[107] A number of reports of his death mentioned his volatile temperament, but also his devotion to principles and his lack of desire to lead a party, though he did so for two years. One paper expressed the opinion that 'many of his political opinions and leanings indicated an essentially generous nature'.[108] Ireland was a beneficiary of his generosity. During the first two years of the Famine, Bentinck subscribed upwards of £1,000 for the relief of the distressed Irish.[109] Aware that the distress extended beyond Ireland, he donated £300 to Rev. Hugh M'Neile in Liverpool, for the relief of the distressed Irish and Scotch in the city.[110] Clearly, Bentinck did far more to try to help than simply donate funds. He battled an entrenched British antipathy towards Ireland and its people for more than two years to provide solutions to the tragedy that engulfed the island. An Irish historian, writing three-quarters of a century later, said of Ireland's gratitude:

> It is a pity that noble-hearted Englishman, Lord George Bentinck, did not live long enough to see how enduring the gratitude of the Irish people has been for the friendly and bounteous hand he endeavoured to stretch out to them, in their hour of sorest need. Yet that gratitude still survives, nor is it likely soon to die out amongst a people noted for warm hearts and long memories.[111]

NOTES

1. Samuel Young served in the House of Commons until aged 96. The Right Honorable Lord Shinwell was 101 when he died while in the House of Lords.
2. David F. Krein, 'The Great Landowners in the House of Commons, 1833–85' (2013). https://doi.org/10.1111/j.1750-0206.2013.00311.x
3. Benjamin Disraeli, *Lord George Bentinck: A Political Biography* (London: Colburn and Co., 1852), p. 1.
4. David Cody, *The Victorian Web: Literature, History, and Culture in the Age of Victoria* (Hartwick College, 1987).
5. See 'An Act to amend the Laws now in force for regulating the Importation of Corn' (23 March 1815).
6. Michael Seth-Smith, *Lord Paramount of the Turf: Lord George Bentinck, 1802–1848* (London: Faber and Faber, 1971), p. 17.
7. Cavendish Bentinck, 'Lord William George Frederick, 1802–1848', *The History of Parliament Trust*. www.historyofparliamentonline.org/volume/1820-1832/member/cavendish-bentinck-lord-william-1802-1848
8. Ibid. Also discussed in Seth-Smith, pp 19–20. A 'poltroon' is a derogatory term meaning 'spiritless coward'. Ker was later forced to either resign his commission at half-pay or be court-martialled. He chose the former and died of cholera soon after.
9. William Hunt, *Dictionary of National Biography, 1885–1900*, vol. 4 (1885).
10. *London Courier and Evening Gazette*, 18 October 1824.

11. Seth-Smith, *Palmerston,* p. 22.
12. Hilly Sloan, *The History Guide.* https://thehistoryguide.co.uk/a-few-words-about-lord-george-bentinck/.
13. www.thoroughbredracing.com/articles/4692/why-racing-owes-such-enormous-debt-these-four-men/.
14. www.goodwood.com/horseracing/history/.
15. Disraeli, *Bentinck,* p. 348.
16. Charles J. Archard, *The Portland Peerage Romance* (London: Greening & Co., 1907).
17. Disraeli, *Bentinck,* p. 348.
18. Ibid., p. 139.
19. Parliamentary Elections (Ireland) Act 1829. Statutes of the United Kingdom of Great Britain and Ireland (London: His Majesty's Statute and Law Printers, 1829).
20. *Southern Reporter and Cork Commercial Courier*, 23 April 1829.
21. *Norfolk Chronicle*, 15 December 1832.
22. Jonathan J. Hedeen, *Tamworth Conservatism and The Repeal of The Corn Laws: The Foundation of Modern Conservative Political Discourse* (Master's Thesis, University of North Dakota, 2015), p. 5.
23. Norman Gash, *Sir Robert Peel the Life of after 1830* (Harlow: Longman Group, 1986, 2nd ed.), p. 130.
24. 'Weather in History, 1800 to 1849'. https://premium.weatherweb.net/weather-in-history-1800-to-1849-ad/.
25. *The Gardeners' Chronicle*, 30 August 1845.
26. *Dublin Evening Post*, 9 September 1845.
27. *Cork Examiner*, 10 September 1845. Several Irish and English newspapers accounts were virtually identical suggesting that they borrowed from the same article.
28. *Irish Railway News*, 29 November 1845. Quoted in Christine Kinealy, *Charity and the Great Hunger in Ireland* (London: Bloomsbury, 2014), p. 22.
29. Thomas P. O'Neill, 'The scientific investigation of the failure of the potato crop in Ireland, 1845–6', *Irish Historical Studies*, vol. 5, no. 18, 1946, pp 123–38; National Archives, Ireland, Relief Commission Papers, Constables' Reports, IA. 50. 73.
30. O'Neill, 'Scientific investigation', p. 126.
31. Lord Heytesbury to Sir Robert Peel, 24 October 1845, Sir Robert Peel, *Memoirs*, vol. ii (London: John Murray, 1857), p. 133.
32. Christine Kinealy, *This Great Calamity. The Irish Famine 1845–52* (Dublin: Gill & Macmillan, 1994), pp 46–47.
33. Russell was in Edinburgh, receiving the Freedom of the City. The letter was dated 22 November 1845, *Sun* (London), 26 November 1845.
34. Charles S. Parker (ed.), *Sir Robert Peel From His Private Papers* (London: John Murray, 1899), p. 223.
35. Betty Kemp, 'Reflections on the Repeal of the Corn Laws', *Victorian Studies,* 5, no. 3 (1962), 189–204. http://www.jstor.org/stable/3825322. Kemp's article provides an in-depth reflection on the Repeal process, especially Peel's thinking and approach.

36. Peel, *Memoirs*, p. 247.
37. *Devizes and Wiltshire Gazette*, 9 April 1846.
38. *Hansard*, House of Commons Debates, 24 April 1846, vol. 85, cols 985–992.
39. Charles Greville, *The Greville Memoirs. A Journal of the Reign of Queen Victoria From 1837–1852* (New York: D. Appleton and Company, 1885), p. 101. Apparently, Queen Victoria was appalled when Greville's memoirs were published posthumously, feeling that his portrayals of royalty were reprehensible. Greville, though he was not close to Bentinck, was his cousin.
40. *Hansard*, 16 March 1846, col. 1093.
41. Christine Kinealy, 'Peel, Rotten Potatoes and Providence: the Repeal of the Corn Laws and the Irish Famine' in Andrew Marrison (ed.), *Free Trade and its Reception 1815–1960. Freedom and Trade*, vol. 1 (London: Routledge, 1998).
42. Kinealy, *Calamity*, p. 74.
43. *Times*, 12 October 1847. Quoted in Kinealy, *Charity*, p. 7.
44. Jennifer Hart, 'Sir Charles Trevelyan at the Treasury', in *The English Historical Review*, January 1960, vol. 75, no. 294, pp 92- 110, p. 99.
45. Peter Murphy, 'Jews and the Great Famine: A link with humanity', in Kinealy, King, Moran, *More Heroes*, pp 201–217.
46. Public Works, Ireland, 'Seventeenth Report from the Board of Public Works' in Sessional Papers 1846, vol. xxiii, pp 489, 497–498.
47. Lord Russell served twice as Prime Minister, from 30 June 1846 to 21 February 1852, and from 29 October 1865 to 26 June 1866.
48. Christine Kinealy, *The Great Irish Famine. Impact, Ideology and Rebellion* (Hampshire: Palgrave, 2002), p. 49.
49. *Hansard*, Debates, 19 January 1847, vol. 89, col. 102.
50. Ibid.
51. Ibid., *Hansard*, Debates, 25 January 1847, vol. 89, col. 460.
52. Ibid.
53. *Hansard,* Debates, 19 January 1847, vol. 89, cols 103–104.
54. Ibid., col. 109.
55. Disraeli, *Bentinck,* p. 359.
56. Ibid., 25 January 1847, vol. 89, cols 477–479.
57. *Cork Examiner*, 1 February 1847.
58. *Northern Whig*, 2 February 1847.
59. *Hereford Journal*, 3 February 1847.
60. *Hansard*, Debates, 4 February 1847, col. 89.
61. *Gloucester Journal*, 6 February 1847.
62. *Manchester Courier*, 6 February 1847.
63. John O'Rourke, *The History of The Great Famine of 1847* (Dublin: James Duffy and Co., 1902), p. 338.
64. *Freeman's Journal*, 6 February 1847.
65. *Hansard*, Debates, 4 February 1847, vol. 89, col. 774.
66. Ibid., col. 775. Also recounted in Disraeli, p. 373.

67. Ibid.
68. Disraeli, *Bentinck,* p. 339.
69. *Illustrated London News*, 6 February 1847.
70. Within months of Bentinck's speech, the railway industry and the shares of rail companies experienced a massive devaluation. See Gareth Campbell and John D. Turner, 'Managerial failure in mid-Victorian Britain: Corporate expansion during a promotion boom', *Business History,* 2015, 57:8, 1248–1276.
71. George Carr to Sir Robert Peel, 22 May 1846, *The Sessional Papers of The House of Lords* (London: 1846), vol. x., pp 318–319.
72. Ibid., Mr. George Carr to J.S. Brickwood, Loan Commissioners, 7 May 1846, p. 319.
73. O'Rourke, *Great Famine of 1847,* p. 342.
74. *Hansard,* Debates, 4 February 1847, vol. 89, col. 795.
75. Ibid., p. 342.
76. *Hansard,* Debates, 4 February 1847, vol. 89, col. 801.
77. *Sun* (London), 6 February 1847.
78. *Annual Register or A View of the History of the History and Politics of the Year 1847*, p. 58.
79. Disraeli, *Bentinck,* p. 373.
80. *Hansard,* Debates, 4 February 1847, vol. 89, cols. 802–808.
81. See chapter on Alexis Soyer.
82. *Dublin Evening Post*, 6 February 1847.
83. Stuart J. Reid, *Lord John Russell* (New York: Harper & Brothers, 1895), p. 150.
84. *York Herald*, 13 February 1847.
85. Russell to Wood, 26 December 1846, G.P. Gooch, *Later Correspondence of Lord John Russell, 1840–1878*, vol. 1 (London: Longmans, Greens and Co., 1925), p. 166.
86. *Kerry Evening Post*, 24 February 1847.
87. For a detailed overview of railroad construction in Ireland see Joseph Lee, 'The provision of capital for early Irish railways, 1830–53', *Irish Historical Studies*, 16, no. 61 (1968), pp 33–63.
88. *Penzance Gazette*, 24 February 1847.
89. Letter from Lord Bentinck dated 6 September, *Brighton Gazette*, 14 September 1848.
90. *Cork Examiner*, 23 April 1847.
91. *West Kent Guardian*, 3 April 1847.
92. *Limerick Reporter*, 16 March 1847.
93. For a mathematical study of death rates during the period 1846–51, see S.H. Cousens, 'Regional death rates in Ireland during the Great Famine, from 1846 to 1851', *Population Studies,* 14, no. 1 (1960), pp 55–74. https://doi.org/10.2307/2172043. Emigration reached over 215,000 in 1847 and totalled more than 960,000 during the Famine years according to the Census Commissioners (1851), which were deemed to be reliable by the House of Commons in 1856.
94. *Hansard,* Debates, 29 March 1847, vol. 91, col. 574.
95. *Northern Whig*, 1 April 1847.
96. *Hansard*, Debates, 29 March 1847, vol. 91, col. 572.
97. *London Evening Standard*, 30 March 1847.

98. *Hansard*, Debates, 11 March 1847, vol. 90 col. 1149.
99. Ibid., 22 March 1847, vol. 91, col. 306.
100. Ibid., 23 March 1847, vol. 91, col. 337.
101. *Weekly Freeman's Journal*, 27 March 1847.
102. *Hansard*, Debates, 25 March 1847, vol. 91, col. 380–381.
103. *Dublin Weekly Nation*, 22 January 1848; *Dublin Evening Packet and Correspondent*, 10 February 1848.
104. *Armagh Guardian*, 7 August 1848.
105. *Times,* 12 March 1847.
106. Disraeli, *Bentinck*, pp 332–333.
107. *Times*, 23 September 1847.
108. *Caledonian Mercury*, 25 September 1848.
109. *Cork Examiner*, 27 September 1848.
110. *Limerick Chronicle*, 23 January 1847.
111. O'Rourke, *Great Famine of 1847,* pp 362–363.

CHAPTER FOUR

FROM FAMINE IRELAND TO PROSPERITY IN CANADA

John Robert Godley (1810–1861) and his Colonization Project

Gerard Moran

Until recently, the deeds and exhortations of whose who provided assistance and aid to the starving Irish during the Great Hunger have been marginalized or forgotten.[1] While the work of the Society of Friends and individuals such as Asenath Nicholson have been well documented, the contributions of others have been largely ignored or relegated to a footnote in the historiography of the period. Many worked at a local level, such as clergymen, doctors and landowners, but others took a more holistic approach in the attempts to provide food, relief and, in some cases, an escape from starvation and destitution. Intervention during periods of crises takes two forms: providing immediate relief by distributing food, or securing a more long-term solution to the problem. During the Great Hunger, the main intervention by heroes was through the distribution of food, but others advocated a more radical approach through the removal of the surplus and starving population to the colonies, which had the dual benefit of taking people out of Ireland who did not have resources to support themselves, and sending them to Canada, Australia and South Africa where there was a demand for labour. Among those to the forefront in advocating this approach was John Robert Godley.

Godley was born in 1814, the eldest child of the landowner, John Godley, who had estates in counties Leitrim and Meath. In 1840 he became agent for his father's properties. Godley was an advocate of assisted emigration long before the potato failed. In 1842 he had travelled throughout Canada and the United States and, on his return, published *Letters from America,* in which he was not entirely complimentary of life and government, especially in the United States. He saw in Canada the material advantages of self-government and benefits of systematic colonization. Godley assessed suitable locations for Irish emigrants, visiting Peterborough, Ontario to see at first-hand how the Irish settlers who had been assisted by the British government from the Blackwater region of north Munster between 1823 and 1825 had fared. He was impressed with how they had progressed. By the 1840s, the settlers in Peterborough were exporting large quantities of grain, flour, pork and potash and it was estimated that they had paid the fares of 13,000 people in Ireland to join them in Canada.[2] In addition to Peterborough, Godley also visited the Irish communities in the Rideau Valley to ascertain how they were progressing. On returning to Ireland, he spent the following three years advocating for Irish emigrants to be sent to Canada through speeches and publications. According to Godley, his father had assisted tenants from his properties to emigrate, but he did not say how many. However, Godley was adamant that the vast majority of Irish landowners were not in a position to provide this assistance and that it could only be undertaken with government help.[3] Godley's visit to Canada in 1842 had taken place at a time when Ireland was not facing the crisis that it encountered three years later, but he was aware of the underlying problems that Ireland had endured since the Napoleonic Wars came to an end in 1815 and that a solution was required.

Throughout the nineteenth century the advantages and benefits of colonization were constantly advocated and, on occasions, given serious consideration as a solution to the perennial problems of famine and population congestion. A number of colonization schemes to Canada and the United States were implemented during the century. In the immediate aftermath of the Napoleonic Wars, several emigration schemes from Ireland were suggested, including a proposal to send 2,000 Irish emigrants to the Rideau Lakes region of Canada.[4] It was felt that colonization was the solution to the massive under-employment that affected large sections of the Irish population. Aubrey de Vere, a landowner from County Limerick, told the Select Committee of Colonization in 1847 that the tranquillity of most regions in Ireland had broken down because crimes were being committed by people who had no work, while George Knox, the local land agent for the Crown estate in Ballykilcline, County Roscommon, said that tenants on the property 'are the most lawless and violent set of people in the County Roscommon' because they had little to do.[5] It was argued in some quarters that the large surplus population contributed to economic stagnation and social unrest, and the export of these people could minimize these problems.

The only major colonization scheme from Ireland that took place in the decades leading up to the Great Hunger was that by Peter Robinson, which was funded by the British government. After this the government refused to provide the finances because of the expenditure involved in the Robinson scheme. Godley himself felt that the Robinson scheme had cost too much and could have been done cheaper.[6] His memorial put colonization as a solution to famine and starvation back on the agenda. The government's agreement to establish a select committee to inquire into the proposal indicated that it had many supporters who considered it as an important component to deal with the crisis that Ireland encountered in the late 1840s.

It was inevitable that emigration to the colonies would become a major issue when the potato failed in 1845. Landowners such as Col. George Wyndham had suggested to the Famine Relief Committee that a system of regulated migration be introduced that would involve the government, landowners and the colonial authorities with each contributing to the cost of the exercise. However, it was not until Godley's memorial was published that the issue of colonization gained traction. Godley and the other signatories were indicating that they regarded colonization and assisted emigration as a practical remedy to the crisis in Ireland and it indicated how an influential section of Irish society was looking at various possibilities to counteract the problems of death, starvation and famine. Many of them were critical and unimpressed with the government's response to the crisis, in particular, the manner in which Irish landowners were expected to fund relief operations. Godley also wished to open the debate on the principle of colonization as an immediate solution to the calamity facing Ireland. He and the other signatories argued that emigration should be combined with other remedial measures to alleviate the starvation and destitution. Godley believed that the government had a responsibility to Ireland and that this could be discharged by helping the destitute in Ireland or by transferring a large section of the population to Canada; the expenditure on Irish settlement in the colony would be the best option as it would involve a once off commitment.[7] In his evidence to the Select Committee on Colonization in June 1847, Godley agreed that the emigration should target those parts of Ireland that were overpopulated and which had an oversupply of labour, as with the western seaboard.[8] This would create a greater demand for those who remained in Ireland with higher wages which would let labourers live in relative comfort. Godley and the others maintained that unless the surplus population was sent to the colonies where there was a demand for labour and the resources to absorb them, they would inevitably migrate to Britain and put pressure on resources there.[9] He argued that the cost of keeping a pauper in the workhouse was greater than that involved in assisting them to emigrate, stating, 'If they went there, there would be an end of the expense of their support'.[10]

The failure of the potato crop in 1845 meant that the implementation of a radical plan was imperative to counteract famine and starvation. Godley was aware of what was happening in the country, having been appointed High Sheriff of Leitrim and Deputy Lieutenant for the county and, in the following year, a magistrate, grand juror and Poor Law Guardian. In his evidence to the Devon Commission, given in January 1845, he had suggested that the only way for emigration to be successful was for the imperial government to finance the passage of people to Canada and for landowners to purchase property in the colony where the emigrants would settle.[11] Although the Poor Law had limited powers to fund assisted emigration, Godley had become disillusioned with it, as it had failed to have any meaningful impact in combatting destitution and the ravages of famine. He opposed the principle of public works arguing that the surplus population would remain and would have to be supported when the next famine came; therefore, colonization to the colonies was the only solution to Ireland's underlying problems.[12] Godley argued that the social conditions in the country would not be helped by 'unaided emigration', but that a more structured approach was required as it would otherwise result in an unbalanced population that would remain permanently destitute.[13]

In March 1847, Godley presented a memorial to the Prime Minister, Lord John Russell, promoting assisted emigration as a panacea to the crisis with the potato. It was signed by 83 noblemen, gentlemen, MPs and landed proprietors. The memorial was based on Godley's pamphlet on colonization and was forwarded to all newspapers, landowners and gentry who might support such a proposal. The signatories included the Church of Ireland Archbishop of Dublin, Richard Whately; Lords Ormonde, Sligo, Lucan, Clanricarde, Adare and Clonbrock. Among the 21 MPs who supported the memorial were Maurice O'Connell, Sir Colman O'Loughlin and William Smith O'Brien, all of whom were Repealers.[14] Many of the landowners who signed the petition were engaged in assisting tenants from their estates to emigrate including Col. Wyndham in County Clare, Lord Ormonde in County Kilkenny and Lord Monteagle in County Limerick.[15] Monteagle had served as Chancellor of the Exchequer between 1835 and 1839 and in October 1845 had warned Sir Robert Peel's government of the impending disaster in Ireland. He urged that emigration be considered as a relief measure and had provided suggestions as to how it could be financed.[16] In his evidence to the Select Committee of the House of Lords on Colonization from Ireland in June 1847, Godley gave an account of the problems, both immediate and long-term, that he witnessed in Ireland, in particular in his home base in County

Leitrim. He indicated that a long-term solution was required, otherwise famine and destitution would continue, stating, 'I think that the calamity is very likely to occur again and again; if it does not occur at once, some similar analogous calamity issue to bring about a crisis such as has been produced this last year'.[17]

While hundreds of thousands left Ireland during the Great Hunger, it was largely unstructured and unplanned, a desperate attempt to escape famine and starvation. The majority of emigrants who arrived in North America and Britain brought little with them except disease and they were destitute. Inevitably, the host communities were hostile towards these new arrivals. Even most of the schemes put in place by landlords did not have structures for assisting the emigrants when they disembarked at the North American ports.[18] Godley was proposing a different approach: the plan was to provide for the emigrants in North America. Godley's memorial proposed that two million people would be assisted from Ireland over a three-year period, the government providing part of the passage fare, with landlords, emigrants and families contributing the rest. Canada was the preferred destination for the colonization because it was 'the nearest place to Ireland offering room for a great migration', and it had the lowest passage costs. Godley wanted the Irish to settle in one country and not be spread over a number of locations, as it was claimed the dispersal would result in them losing their identity and nationality. Settlement would be in the St Lawrence region which already had a large, well-established Irish community. People would be transported from small village communities in Ireland led by their priests. An incorporated company, called the Irish Canada Company, would manage the scheme and be subject to rules laid down by parliament. It would receive a fixed sum per person to be used for building roads, schools and other works. The colonization would be financed by extending the English property tax to Ireland which would generate £9 million over a three-to-four-year period. It was envisaged that the emigrants would contribute towards their passage fares.[19] In the covering letter to Lord John Russell, Godley and some of the signatories argued that urgent action was imperative and state involvement needed as the alternative was that thousands of people would die.

In his evidence to the Select Committee on Colonization Godley reaffirmed his view that emigration was necessary, warning that the coming winter would be worse than the previous one with higher mortality levels as the people could not be supported by the produce from the land. He added, 'I do not think that this year the extent of [potato] production will enable it to be resumed as the staple food of the people'.[20] Godley also called for farmers to be educated so that they could produce crops other than potatoes. The main thrust of the memorial and his evidence to the select committee was that only when the population was greatly reduced, either through death or emigration, would prosperity be restored to Ireland. He explained, 'We are persuaded that emigration alone, on whatever scale, and however admirably conducted, would not merely fail to remedy the social ills of Ireland, but would be quite fruitless for the people'.[21]

Godley's colonization proposal was largely a knee-jerk reaction to the immediate crisis that he saw looming before the advent of 'Black '47'. While he had a good overview of what should be put in place, it was vague on specifics such as who would co-ordinate the travel between Ireland and Canada, who would select the emigrants to be sent, etc. He had hoped that the British government and the colonial authorities would provide this, but it was clear from the outset that this was not going to happen. However, he was certain that the success of colonization depended on the active engagement of the Catholic clergy. Godley contended that clerical involvement was important, stating, 'It is notorious all over the continent of America that they feel deeply and complain loudly that they have not access to the means of religious instruction, except in the larger towns'.[22] An endowment would be established which would pay those priests who left with the emigrants for Canada. The clergy would initially be the leaders of the emigrant groups, but Godley felt over time a middle and upper class would emerge in these communities who would assume the leadership role. Godley believed the priests would play an important role in encouraging their parishioners to emigrate if they accompanied them across the Atlantic. The inclusion of the priests would also ensure that lawlessness and crime would be greatly reduced in Canada.

Unlike other calls for assisted emigration during the Great Hunger, the Godley memorial stimulated interest in Britain, Ireland and the colonies. While a number of influential landowners in Ireland supported the memorial, more significantly, cabinet ministers such as Earl Grey and the head of the British Treasury, Charles Trevelyan, saw merits in the proposal, although they were not prepared to give it full commitment. Letters of support came from Australia, Canada and the United States, stating that the new settlers would be welcome in these countries as there was a great demand for labour. Godley hoped that other government ministers such as Lord Palmerston, Lord Clanricarde and Thomas Reddington, who all owned property in Ireland, would publicly endorse the scheme as they had previously advocated colonization as a solution to Irish problems.

Godley's proposal was promoted by a number of MPs in parliament during the spring and summer of 1847, who suggested that, at the very least, the Landed Emigration Commissioners be given more support to encourage emigration from Ireland to the colonies. He also attempted to promote colonization by standing as a Conservative candidate for County Leitrim in the 1847 general election, but he failed to get elected because of opposition from the local clergy as he contested it as a Conservative. While Sir Robert Peel, the former Prime Minister, favoured colonization, he felt that the Godley proposal was too ambitious and the arrival of such vast numbers would create problems for Canada. Instead, he advocated that a smaller scheme, comprising of 300,000 people, be sent from Ireland to the colony.[23] A cohort of Irish MPs, calling themselves the Council of National Distress and National Safety, under the chairmanship of Henry Grattan, passed a resolution in November 1847 about the state of the country. They stated that as there was a great desire for emigration in many parts of the country, 'it is the duty of government to make such arrangements as shall cause it to be a means of relief to the destitute population'.[24]

Godley also attempted to secure support from nationalist leaders in Ireland. John O'Connell was informed that the choice for the people was emigration or death, and the situation would continue to be as bad in 1848 unless drastic action was taken. O'Connell refused to be swayed by the argument. Instead, he called for the government money to be diverted for land reclamation.[25] Nationalists, like O'Connell, saw colonization as a threat and opposed the principle itself fearing that the government would use it as an alternative to providing direct relief. They claimed that the Russell administration wanted to transport the population of Ireland to British North America. During this period, a Vagrancy Bill was being debated in the House of Commons and nationalists maintained that these poor 'vagrants would be taken by Mr. Godley and brought to Canada'.[26] Godley's proposal was also condemned by the Irish Confederation, a nationalist organisation founded in January 1847 by the Young Irelanders, who maintained that Ireland had the ability to feed its population and did not need to export its people to another country.[27] Irish nationalists attacked Godley's memorial because he was viewed as an imperialist whose only objective was to bring benefits to the empire and not to Ireland. The only nationalist leader to publicly support Godley's colonization scheme was William Smith O'Brien, MP for County Limerick and a landowner. As early as January 1847, he made his views known on assisted emigration and called on Irish landowners to fund such schemes, with the government providing the passage fares and land for the new settlers in the colonies.[28] Smith O'Brien argued that the colonization would have to be planned and organized in such a way that only those with the ability to succeed should be assisted.[29]

The reaction in Ireland to Godley's attempts to deal with the famine crisis can be seen from the national and local press. Most of the nationalist newspapers condemned the scheme, although some were more hostile than others. The *Limerick and Clare Examiner* was prepared to give qualified support for the colonization proposal provided it was properly conducted and organized as it would 'avoid periodic visitations of famine and pestilence'; while in June 1847 the *Freeman's Journal* suggested that the proposal be given a fair hearing.[30] The *Kilkenny Journal* was also prepared to examine the scheme on its merits, arguing that it would give people a chance of bettering themselves in the colonies rather than ending up in the workhouse, but warned that such emigration was not to be compulsory.[31] However, the majority of the nationalist newspapers condemned Godley's proposal with the *Galway Vindicator* maintaining that 'In truth the whole thing is only an effort to relieve the Irish landowners of any motive whatever to promote the improvement of the country'. The *Nation* described the scheme as a new form of '"To Hell or to Connaught"—to Canada or the grave', and added that if the government was prepared to spend money on such schemes, why could it not use the funds to help the Irish remain in Ireland?[32] The *Nation* reprinted a report from Sir John Harvey of Halifax, Nova Scotia, to show that conditions in British North America were not suitable for Irish emigrants for 'extreme privation and misery could prevail' as there was little employment available.[33] This was at a time when there was a famine in Nova Scotia.[34]

Godley's colonization plan's success in Ireland was dependent on the support and participation of the Catholic clergy, but soon ran into difficulties from members of the church hierarchy. Godley wrote to the bishops to drum up support from the outset stating that it would be a Catholic colonization scheme with priests accompanying the emigrants and helping the settlers establish themselves in Canada. In early April 1847, the Bishop of Killala, Thomas Feeney, informed Godley the emigration was not the panacea to Ireland's problems but would send 'the bone and sinew' from the country 'and would leave nothing behind but a large inert mass of wretched paupers, incapable of cultivating the soil'. Feeney continued that it would be better if Godley's committee could persuade Lord John Russell to abandon his policies of political economy and help Ireland.[35] Bishop Edward Maginn of Derry told him that landowners were the cause of Ireland's problems and they were now proposing to send the Irish people and their clergy to Canada.[36] If the Irish had to leave their country, Maginn preferred that they emigrate to 'the land of the brave and home of the free'. He was very critical of Morgan O'Connell for allowing his name to be associated with the project for such people were 'devoid of patriotism'.[37] The Catholic clergy of Tuam, headed by Archbishop John MacHale, condemned the proposal, describing the scheme as just another government attempt to divert attention from the real problems that Ireland faced and called it 'treachery'.[38] Prior to this, the Catholic bishops had not defined their position on emigration. Many bishops saw inherent dangers in emigration that would destroy the religious well-being of their parishioners who left, while it would have negative financial repercussions for their dioceses and parishes.

Although the Catholic bishops publicly opposed and condemned the colonization proposal, Godley himself maintained that many priests had contacted him encouraging him to proceed.[39] This pattern was reflected throughout the nineteenth century: members of the hierarchy condemned emigration, in particular when the British government was involved, but the parochial clergy often took an opposing view.[40] Even during the Great Hunger priests like Father John O'Sullivan of Kenmare[41] and Father Thomas Hore in Wicklow not only called for the people to emigrate and leave behind famine and destitution, but in some cases, as with Hore, accompanied them to North America.[42] Father James Berry of Easthill told the Devon Commission in 1844 that if assisted emigration to the colonies was available, the people would leave for they had been told by friends and relations who were already in North America, 'that there was no tyranny, no oppression from landlords and no taxes' to be paid.[43] Father Salmon of Grazbo told T.M. Ray of the Repeal Association that tenants had not been forced to leave the Wandesforde estate in County Kilkenny, but the landlord gave them the opportunity to emigrate as they had no employment.[44] Father Malachy Duggan, PP of Moytra and Kilballyowen in west Clare, felt that the people would have to be helped to emigrate to another country as they had nothing and were 'flocking to every door, craving for something to eat to prolong life, even for a few hours'.[45]

While there were supporters and opponents to Godley's colonization proposal, it nevertheless provoked a major debate on emigration as a remedy to the problems facing Ireland during the Great Hunger. From the correspondence received by Lord Monteagle and others, it is clear that emigration as envisaged by Godley was being given serious consideration.[46] Initially, the Russell administration adopted a cautious approach to the memorial with government members stating officially that no decision had been made, while in private, officials like Sir George Grey, the Home Secretary, told the Earl of Elgin and Kincardine, Governor General of Canada, that the memorial had 'considerable vagueness and obscurity, and an absence of detail'.[47] Russell eventually capitulated and agreed to the establishment of a select committee on colonization from Ireland because of the relentless pressure from Irish MPs. However, it was evident that the government felt its conclusions would only reinforce its approach to assisted emigration.[48] The select committee was established on 1 June 1847 and had general cross-party support, including from Sir Robert Peel and the Repeal MP, Morgan O'Connell, nephew of Daniel.[49] Russell only agreed to its establishment after a meeting in late April 1847 with a group of Irish parliamentarians along with the Irish Colonization Committee. The select committee was more a sop to placate influential individuals in British society and did not mean that the government was committed to financing the colonization proposal.

Parliamentary select committees, along with parliamentary commissions, were parliament's way of being informed about important issues which came up for discussion before the House of Lords and House of Commons. Select committees were composed of small groups of parliamentarians as it was felt they could deliberate more effectively and more expeditiously than the whole house. In the early nineteenth century, select committees were the principal means by which parliament conducted investigations that it felt it had to be informed on. The committees collected evidence, examined witnesses, and prepared reports which were then presented to parliament. Even if the work of the select committee was not completed by the end of the parliamentary session, it still had to report to the house: this was why the Select Committee on Colonization from Ireland issued four reports. The committees could only be in operation when parliament was in session and this limited their usefulness as the report often dragged on into the next parliamentary session. Whereas select committees only comprised members of parliament, royal commissions like the Devon Commission, included people with no connection with politics but who were regarded as experts in the subject area that was under investigation. Select committees, like that on colonization from Ireland, provide the historian and researcher with much information on conditions in Ireland, especially on events during the Great Hunger. They are also a valuable guide as to trends and contemporary opinions within committees, while the minutes of evidence are a major font of information and detail. The objectives of the committee on colonization during the Great Hunger were clear:

> [to] ... consider of the means by which colonization may be made subsidiary to other measures for the improvement of the social conditions of Ireland, and by which with full regards to the interests of the colonies themselves, the comfort and prosperity of those who emigrate may be effectively promoted...

Lord Monteagle, an Irish landlord, was appointed chairman of the Select Committee on Colonization, a prudent choice given his involvement with John Godley in the assisted emigration campaign. Monteagle had played a major role in securing many of the signatures for the memorial. As a former Chancellor of the Exchequer, he commanded respect and authority not only in Britain, but in the colonies. Monteagle had been active in assisting tenants from his County Limerick estate to move to Australia in the 1830s and early 1840s.[50] His involvement with the select committee ensured that those with an expert knowledge of immigration in the colonies were prepared to give evidence and provide the parliamentarians with relevant information. Among those who gave evidence were T.F. Elliot, who had been appointed Agent General for Emigration in 1837 and, in 1847, was chairman of the Colonial Land and Emigration Board; M.H. Perley, Emigration Agent at the port of Saint John, New Brunswick; Rear Admiral Henry Prescott, Governor of Newfoundland between 1834 and 1841; and Charles Rubidge, a member of Her Majesty's Naval Service who had been heavily involved in the settlement of the Peter Robinson emigrants in Peterborough. Among the witnesses from Ireland who gave evidence were the landlords, Francis Spaight, Sir Robert Gore Booth, Aubrey de Vere and the land agents Joseph Kincaid and J. B. Brydone, who had assisted families to leave from Irish estates. Other Irish contributors were Father Theodore Mathew, the temperance priest; Captain Thomas Larcom, director of the Irish Ordinance Survey between 1842 and 1845 and Commissioner of the Irish Census in 1841 and who had an extensive knowledge of Ireland; and John Robert Godley. Fifty-four witnesses gave evidence on conditions in Ireland, the prospects for Irish emigrants in the colonies, the amount of land available for settlement, employment prospects, etc. However, as witnesses were obliged to travel to London for select committees, no evidence was gathered from people who wanted to leave for the colonies or from clergymen who opposed the emigration proposal.

As a result of Godley's endeavours, the select committee, or 'the Godley Committee on Colonization', is an important source for the study of emigration during the Great Hunger as it covers over 1,600 pages of evidence and includes an appendix. However, it did not accomplish the primary objective of making the case for the introduction of a major colonization scheme from Ireland to counteract the ravages of famine, starvation and death. The principal reason was that it took too long to establish the committee and issue the results of its proceedings; consequently, the impetus for a government-sponsored emigration scheme was lost. Moreover, 1848 would have been the earliest period that any of its recommendations could be operational. By this stage, landowners who had waited and hoped for government intervention had lost patience and were resorting to their own methods to clear their estates of their surplus populations and, in some instances included sending tenants to North America.[51] At the same time, voluntary emigration was in full flight and state assistance no longer appeared to be required. This was much to the regret of Godley and some of the other signatories to the memorial such as Monteagle, who argued that voluntary emigration was not the solution to the crisis in Ireland, for the best and those with the financial resources were more likely to leave and this would have a disastrous impact for the country in the future. Monteagle maintained that assisted emigration would be more beneficial, as those who left would remit money back to Ireland and assist others to leave, as had been the case with the Peter Robinson scheme.[52]

The government was not convinced by the arguments advanced by Godley and the recommendations put forward by the select committee regarding colonization. Lord John Russell maintained that such a large scale emigration scheme to Canada was not practical because of the numbers involved and the colony would be unable to absorb such a massive influx of settlers.[53] The government's attitude was summed up by Sir Charles Wood, Chancellor of the Exchequer, to Monteagle when he said that the more he saw regarding government involvement, the less he felt disposed to it.[54] Other ministers expressed similar sentiments: Lord Lansdowne believed that assisted passage would not benefit the country permanently, for those places where the poor were removed from would be filled by other paupers if assisted emigration was introduced and the people would end up in the United States where they would be a nation-in-exile with strong anti-English feelings.[55]

It was only natural that Godley, Monteagle and others were hugely disappointed with the government's reaction to the colonization proposal as they regarded it as a fundamental part of famine relief policy. Monteagle rebuked the government, and in particular Sir Charles Trevelyan, the Assistant Chief Secretary to the Treasury who oversaw relief programmes in Ireland, because of his refusal to even consider the colonization proposal.[56] Nonetheless, assisted emigration was already taking place from the Crown estates in Ballykilcline with government assistance and the tenants being sent to North America.[57] The major problem with Godley's proposal was the expense involved, for it had not been properly costed. Given the government's reluctance to spend large sums of money during the Great Hunger, it was unlikely that it would finance the emigration of large numbers of destitute Irish to the colonies. Aspects of Godley's proposals indicated that heavy expenditure would be required: a separate Irish agency would be based in Cork that would be independent of the Imperial Emigration Board and would encourage emigration from Ireland. Landlords would have to contribute funds if their estates benefited from the exodus, but many landed proprietors were in severe financial difficulties by 1848 as they were receiving little or no rents from their Irish estates.[58] It was also suggested that landowners who sent their tenants to the colonies would apply for funding to the Irish Emigration Agency. No definite estimates were provided as to the overall cost and of who would fund the scheme. Given the nebulous approach to costings, it was not surprising that the government, and particularly the Treasury, were not enthusiastic about financing the scheme. Godley's proposal presupposed that the emigrants would contribute funds towards the passage fare, or that friends and relatives would provide the additional money required. It failed to realise that by early 1847 most people were unable to pay their rent, let along contribute towards their passage fares across the Atlantic.

Godley's colonization proposal had its best chance of success in 1846 and early 1847 when the memorial was first published. Many landowners indicated they were prepared to engage with the scheme, but initiative, leadership, commitment, and, most of all, government funding was required. The government was reticent to support such a venture fearing that the introduction of a free passage scheme would result in all tenants wanting to be sent, including those who could afford to pay their own passage fares.[59] With the government refusing to become involved, landlord enthusiasm for Godley's vision waned and many landowners were not in a position to provide the necessary resources for it to take place. The government was not opposed to people leaving for the colonies and in some quarters saw the exodus as having a beneficial impact for Ireland as it would result in the country's resources being able to support a reduced population, but it was not prepared to provide the funding for large numbers to leave.

The government's failure to support Godley's plan did not deter him or his supporters who continued with the campaign. Godley himself continued to advocate for emigration to the colonies for the rest of his life and was persuaded by the New Zealand Company to establish a colony at Lyttelton (Port Cooper). In Ireland, a private company, the Irish Colonization Fund, was established, whose aim was to promote the colonization principle. It had three main functions: first, to collect and provide the best information that could be obtained in Ireland and the colonies for colonization; second, to investigate all questions relating to the colonies which would be brought before parliament; third, to use every effort and means to put into effect the colonization programme.[60] However, in the late 1840s there was little chance of securing private money for its proposals either from landowners or potential emigrants, and the Fund disappeared without achieving its aims.

There is little doubt that a large colonization scheme as envisaged by Godley was not practical as the transfer of large numbers of Irish people to Canada and Australia would have created logistical problems for the host countries. Sir Randolph Routh, chairman of the Government Relief Committee, questioned the wisdom of transferring two million people to Canada over a short time period, arguing that the country could not absorb such numbers. Routh felt there was not enough land in Upper and Lower Canada, and the forests would have to be cleared and the people supported for the first year, all of which would entail an exorbitant cost.[61] Despite the failure of his colonization proposal to Canada, Godley remained a staunch advocate of the principle throughout the rest of his life. As a result of his campaign during the Great Hunger he gained a reputation which resulted in him establishing the Canterbury Association in early 1848 along with Edward Gibbon Wakefield who was also an advocate of colonization. Their plan was to purchase 300,000 acres in New Zealand for settlement of members of the Church of England who would be selected from all ranks of society. For Godley, colonization was more important than unplanned emigration. Many of the ideas that he had proposed for his Irish memorial were incorporated in this project which was to be based in Canterbury. He agreed to act as leader of the colony in the absence of religious leaders and so, in effect, became governor of the settlement when he arrived there in 1849. It was as a result of his lobbying that Canterbury became a self-governing province as Godley was adamant that imperial interference in the region should be kept to a minimum. However, the settlement soon encountered financial problems and Godley became increasingly frustrated with interference from London. In December 1852, Godley returned to London and was appointed Commissioner for Income Tax in Ireland. He became agent for the province of Canterbury in 1854 and between 1857 and 1861 served as Under Secretary for War. He also wrote for the *Spectator*, mainly advocating for colonization which he remained a firm advocate of. He died in London in November 1861. Godley was regarded as the founder of Christchurch in New Zealand and a statue was erected to him in the city in 1867.

The colonization ideal did not disappear when the Great Hunger ended in the early 1850s. While the Great Famine is the defining watershed event in nineteenth century Ireland, the country continued to experience famines and subsistence crises for the next 70 years, often requiring public and international intervention. These were the result of over population and a continuing dependence on the potato in the poorest parts of the country, mainly along the western seaboard. During the 'Forgotten Famine' of 1879 to 1881, over one million people were kept alive by private relief organisations and the international community. Colonization and assisted emigration were once again proposed as a remedy for Ireland's problems.[62] It resulted in assisted emigration schemes being put in place by Father James Nugent, John Sweetman and James Hack Tuke.[63] They were following John Robert Godley's approach during the Great Hunger. Godley thus was more of an influencer than an achiever, and his endeavours to provide a solution to the calamity of the Great Hunger should not be forgotten.

NOTES

1. For the attempts to redress this see Christine Kinealy, Jason King and Gerard Moran (eds), *Heroes of Ireland's Great Hunger* (Cork University Press, 2021); Kinealy, King & Moran (eds), *More Heroes of Ireland's Great* Hunger (Cork University Press, 2022).
2. *Report from the Select Committee of the House of Lords on Colonization from Ireland; together with the Minutes of Evidence,* HC 1847 (737), vi, p. 277, qs 2683–4.
3. Ibid., pp 177–8, qs 1717–8.
4. H.J.M. Johnson, *British Emigration Policy, 1815–1830: Shovelling Out Paupers* (Oxford University Press, 1972), pp 28–29.
5. *Report from the Select Committee on Colonization*, pp 533–4, qs 4840–4: Robert Scally, *The End of Hidden Ireland: Rebellion, Famine and Emigration* (New York: Oxford University Press, 1995), p. 65.
6. *Report from the Select Committee on Colonization*, p. 179, q. 1737. For the Peter Robinson scheme see Wendy Cameron, 'Selecting Peter Robinson's emigrants', *Histoire Sociale/ Social History*, 9:17 (May 1976); Peter Pammett, 'Assisted Emigration from Ireland to Upper Canada under Peter Robinson in 1825', *Ontario Historical Society Papers and Reports,* 31 (1936); Donal MacKay, *Flight from Famine: The Coming of the Irish to* Canada (Toronto: McClelland & Steward Inc., 1990), pp 59–64.
7. *Limerick and Clare Examiner*, 28 April, 1 May 1847; *Nation*, 1 May 1847.
8. *Report from the Select Committee on Colonization*, p. 175, q. 1693.
9. Ibid., p. 176, qs 1709–10.
10. Ibid., p. 183, q. 1780.
11. *Appendix to Minutes of Evidence before the Select Committee on Colonization from Ireland*, HC 1847–8 (737-ii), xl, p. 150, q. 37.
12. Godley to Lord Monteagle, 22 March 1847 (NLI, MS 13,000/2/25, Monteagle Papers); J.R. Godley, *Observations on the Irish Poor Law* (1847), pp 1–32.
13. *Report from the Select Committee on Colonization*, pp 173–4, q. 1675.
14. Ibid., p. 168; David Fitzpatrick, 'Emigration, 1801–70' in W.E. Vaughan (ed.), *A New History of Ireland*, v: Ireland under the Union, i, 1801–70 (Oxford University Press, 1989), pp 576–7; Marianne O'Gallagher & R.M. Dompierre, *Eyewitness Grosse Isle, 1847* (Quebec: Livres Carraig Books, 1995), p. 38; *Kilkenny Journal*, 7 April 1847.
15. See Gerard Moran, *Sending Out Ireland's Poor: Assisted Emigration to North America in the Nineteenth Century* (Dublin: Four Courts Press, 2004), pp 36–39; Fitzpatrick, 'Emigration', p. 586.
16. Letters of Monteagle to Sir Robert Peel, 24 October and 21 November 1845 (NLI, MS 13,400/2/16, Monteagle Papers).
17. Ibid., p. 172, q. 1657.
18. See Moran, *Sending Out Ireland's Poor*, pp 97–116; Tyler Anbinder, 'Lord Palmerston and the Irish Famine emigration', *Historical Journal*, 44;2 (2001); Thomas Power, 'The Palmerston estate in Co. Sligo: improvement and assisted emigration' in Patrick Duffy and Gerard Moran (eds), *To and From Ireland: Planned Emigration Schemes: c.1600–2000* (Dublin: Geography Publications, 2004).

19. *Sydney Morning Chronical*, 7 April 1847, copy in Monteagle Papers (NLI, MS 13,400/2/37, Monteagle Papers); *Limerick and Clare Examiner*, 21 February 1847; *Sligo Journal*, 9 April 1847; Peter Gray, *Famine, Land and Politics: British Government and Irish Society, 1843–50* (Dublin: Irish Academic Press, 1999), pp 300–301.
20. *Report from the Select Committee on Colonization*, p. 171, q. 1653.
21. Copy of the Memorial addressed by the Noblemen, Gentlemen and Landed Proprietors to Lord John Russell, First Lord of the Treasury, 23 March 1847 in *Appendix to Minutes of Evidence before the Select Committee on Colonization from Ireland*, HC 1847–8 (737-ii), xl, p. 202.
22. *Report of the Select Committee on Colonization*, p. 186, q. 1816.
23. *Nation*, 13 March 1847; *Limerick and Clare Examiner*, 5 June 1847.
24. *Limerick and Clare Examiner*, 20 November 1847; see also *Sligo Journal*, 15 January 1847.
25. *Nation*, 24 April 1847.
26. Ibid.
27. Ibid., 9 January 1847.
28. *Limerick and Clare Examiner*, 20 March 1847.
29. Ibid., 13 January 1847.
30. Ibid., 7 April 1847; Oliver MacDonagh, 'The Irish clergy and emigration during the Great Famine', *Irish Historical Studies*, v (1946–7), p. 290.
31. *Kilkenny Journal,* 7 April 1847.
32. *Galway Vindicator*, 9 June 1847; *Nation*, 3 and 17 April 1847.
33. *Nation*, 24 April 1847.
34. For the famine in Nova Scotia in 1847 see Mark McGowan, 'A tale of two famines: famine memory in Nova Scotia' in Patrick Fitzgerald, Christine Kinealy & Gerard Moran (eds), *Irish Hunger and Migration: Myth, Memory and Memorization* (Hamden: Quinnipiac University Press, 2015), pp 57–68.
35. *Nation*, 24 April 1847; *Kilkenny Journal,* 24 April 1847.
36. For more on Bishop Maginn's role see Turlough McConnell, 'Edward Maginn of Derry and Donegal: bishops, rebels and contagions', in Kinealy, King and Moran, *Heroes of Great Hunger,* pp 179–190.
37. *Kilkenny Journal,* 28 April 1847.
38. Ibid., 17 April 1847; *Kilkenny Journal*, 17 April 1847; MacDonagh, 'Irish Catholic clergy and emigration', p. 272.
39. *Report from the Select Committee on Colonization*, p. 188, q. 1845.
40. For the attitudes of the hierarchy and clergy towards emigration in the nineteenth century see Gerard Moran, *Fleeing from Famine in Connemara: James Hack Tuke and his Assisted Emigration scheme in the 1880s* (Dublin: Four Courts Press, 2018).
41. For more on Father O'Sullivan see, Colum Kenny, 'John of Kenmare: Father John O'Sullivan' in Kinealy, Moran and King, *More Heroes,* pp 21–38.
42. For the Hore emigration scheme see Seamus de Val, 'Fr Thomas Hore and the 1850 migration', *The Past,* 21 (Wexford, 1998); Jim Rees, *A Farwell to Famine* (Arklow Enterprise Centre, 1994).

43. *Evidence before Her Majesty's Commissioners of Inquiry into the state of the Law and Practice in respect to the occupation of land in Ireland* (Devon Commission), part II, HC 1845 (616), xx, p. 959, q. 46.
44. Father Salmon to T.M. Ray, 18 April 1844 (NLI, MS 49,683, Wandesforde Papers).
45. Donal A. Kerr, *'A Nation of Beggars?': Priests, People and Politics in Famine Ireland, 1846–52* (Oxford University Press, 1994), pp 297–9.
46. See letter of R. Bourke to Monteagle, undated (NLI, MS 13,400/4, Monteagle Papers).
47. *Nation*, 17 April 1847; Earl Grey to Earl Elgin, 1 April 1847 in *Further Papers in relation to Emigration to the British Provinces in North America*, HC 1847 (824), xxxix, p. 8.
48. Oliver MacDonagh, 'Irish emigration to the United States of America and the British Colonies during the Famine' in R. Dudley Edwards and T. Desmond Williams (eds), *The Great Irish Famine: Studies in Irish History, 1845–52* (1956, reprint, Dublin: Lilliput Press, 1994), pp 318–9.
49. *Nation*, 5 June 1847.
50. For Monteagle's role in assisting tenants from his estate to emigrate to Australia see Christopher O'Mahony and Valerie Thompson, *Poverty and Promise: The Monteagle Emigrants, 1835–58* (Darlington: Crossing Press, 1994).
51. See the emigration from the Gore Booth estate in County Sligo, Gerard Moran, *Sir Robert Gore Booth and his Landed Estate in County Sligo: Land, Famine, Emigration and Politics* (Dublin: Four Courts Press, 2006), chapter 3.
52. *Nation*, 12 June 1847.
53. Remarks on colonization memorial, undated (NLI, MS 13,400 (2), Monteagle Papers).
54. Charles Wood to Monteagle, 22 November 1848 (NLI, MS 13,400 (2), Monteagle Papers).
55. Lansdowne to Monteagle, 21 October 1848 (NLI, MS 13,400/ii/52, Monteagle Papers).
56. Charles Trevelyan to Monteagle, 14 February 1848 (NLI, MS 13,400/i/23, Monteagle Papers).
57. For information on emigration from Ballykilcline, see Scally, *End of Hidden Ireland*.
58. See Moran, *Gore Booth and his Landed Estate*, pp 46–8.
59. *Report of the Select Committee on Colonization*, p. 537, q. 1486.
60. *Sligo Journal*, 2 June 1847; *Nation*, 19 June 1847; John Robert Godley to Monteagle, 29 April 1847 (NLI, MS 13,400/ii/42, Monteagle Papers).
61. Sir R. Routh to Sir Charles Trevelyan, 11 May 1847 in *Appendix to Minutes before the Select Committee on Colonization*, pp 34–5.
62. For the crisis in this period see Gerard Moran, 'From Great Famine to Forgotten Famine: the crisis of 1879–81" in Fitzgerald, Kinealy & Moran (eds), *Irish Hunger and Migration;* Idem, '"Near famine': The Roman Catholic Church and the subsistence crisis of 1879–81', *Studia Hibernia* (2004); idem, 'Uncovering the "Forgotten Famine" of 1879–81 in the west of Ireland: Food shortages and distress', *Journal of the Galway Archaeological and Historical Society*, 72 (2002); idem, '"Giving a helping hand": International charity during the Forgotten Famine of 1879–81', *New Hibernia Review*, 24:2 (Summer, 2020).
63. For the Nugent Scheme see Bridget Conneely, *Forgetting Ireland : Uncovering a Family's Secret History* (St. Paul: Borealis Books, 2003; Jane Kennedy, 'The Connemara: despair in the heartland', in Christine Kinealy and Gerard Moran (eds), *Irish Famines before and after*

the Great Hunger (Hamden: Quinnipiac University Press, 2020); for the John Sweetman Scheme see, Malcolm Campbell, 'Immigrants on the land: Irish rural settlement in Minnesota and New South Wales, 1830–1890', *New Hibernia Review* (Spring 1988); for the James Hack Tuke Scheme see Gerard Moran, *Fleeing from Famine in Connemara*; idem, 'From poverty to posterity: The Tuke Committee assisted emigrants in Minnesota, 1882–1884', *New Hibernia Review,* 26:3 (Fall, 2020).

CHAPTER FIVE

GEORGE HENRY MOORE (1810–1870)

Politics and Benevolence during the Great Famine

Fiona White

Moore Hall, County Mayo, was one of around 7,000 landed estates in nineteenth-century Ireland. The house was occupied continuously from 1795 until 1910. For 13 years only, it was unoccupied by the Moore family and then eventually destroyed by fire in 1923 during the Civil War. It witnessed its most stable period under the proprietorship of George Henry Moore, a respected landlord and illustrious statesman. Using several different historical sources, including letters, family memoirs and newspapers, this chapter investigates Moore's benevolence and political activity during the Great Famine of the 1840s, while also setting the scene of his interesting and varied life as a younger man with few responsibilities.

Moore Hall is situated on the banks of Lough Carra, built by George Moore of Alicante between 1792 and 1795. He made his fortune in the 1780s in Alicante, Spain in the wine and grain trade.[1] With the passing of the Acts of Relief in Ireland, which allowed Roman Catholics to inherit and purchase land, Moore returned and built Moore Hall. George Moore of Alicante had four sons, all educated in the finest Catholic schools abroad. His eldest son, the unfortunate John Moore, became embroiled in the 1798 conflict in County Mayo and received the title, President of the Republic of Connacht from the general of the French forces, Jean-Joseph Humbert. John was later arrested and tried by the English forces and died in captivity in Waterford.[2] Shortly after his son's death, George Moore of Alicante also died. His successor was his second son, also named George, who was known as 'the Historian'. With more ability and stability George Moore, 'the Historian', took over the running of Moore Hall. He was a scholar and Whig historian and, unlike his brother, supported the 1800 union with Britain. He married Louisa Browne of Westport House, also in County Mayo.

There were three sons of the marriage of George 'the Historian' and Louisa, namely, George Henry, John, and Augustus. Both John and Augustus would die as a result of falls from horses. George Henry was sent to Oscott College, a Catholic school near Birmingham, to be educated, a common practice of the Irish gentry at this time.[3] His father and mother hoped that, on leaving Cambridge, he would return to Ireland and become a resident and improving landlord. George Moore, George Henry's father, soon realised that George Henry's prospects were poor and he handed over the decision-making on his son's future to his wife Louisa. The mother and son had a strong relationship but fought as fiercely as they loved. The fact is that George Henry had learned little at Cambridge, except skill at billiards. He emerged as an affable young extrovert who preferred horse racing, hunting, and gambling to more scholarly pursuits.[4] It was decided to bring him home to Moore Hall, but there, he became immersed in horses, hounds, racing, and duelling: 'If the acquaintances he made in Cambridge were bad, the sporting squireens of Mayo were worse companions, and it was thought wiser to send him to study law in London'.[5]

It was during this period that the Moores became friendly with Maria Edgeworth, the prolific Irish novelist. The Moores met Edgeworth through a mutual friend, Charles Strickland of Lough Glynn in Roscommon. Maria and Louisa became lifelong friends. Maria admired George 'The Historian', especially Moore's works on the French Revolution and his *History of the British Revolution*. She wrote to a friend: 'They are not of the poet's race of Moores, but of more ancient and aristocratic lineage'.[6] The letters between the two women demonstrate a strong friendship and deep mutual admiration. For the liberal-minded Moores, Maria was a recognised authority on education, and Louisa Moore hastened to confide in Maria her griefs and anxieties concerning her sons, George Henry and Augustus, both of whom had been brilliant schoolboys but were now running wild. Maria's letters to Moore Hall therefore consisted largely of advice and sympathy. She assured the anxious mother that the young men would not always prefer a racehorse to Pegasus and the *Racing Calendar* to transcendental mathematics.[7]

George Henry and Augustus Moore were quickly noted for their skill as horse riders and horse breeders and Moore Hall became a centre of equine activity.

Castlebar was the main centre of horse racing in Mayo, which was a highly popular social event among the landed classes. The races were held at Breaffy outside the town and were second in Connacht only to the Galway Races. They were attended by the distinguished families of the county such as the Knoxes and Gores, but the Moores of Moore Hall were the most prominent, known especially for the training of racehorses and hunters. Maria Edgeworth in a letter to Louisa also commented on horse racing:

> The account you give of your sons being so carried out of the course of science and literature by the horse fever, I would deplore, but that I am convinced it will soon come to a crisis with such men, and that it is a disease which they will have but once in their lives ... I wish them well through it and well married all in good time.[8]

George Henry was sent to London to study law, but he fell heavily in debt. Racing and hunting filled his life, but they were impossible on an allowance of £400 a year. In one incident, his mother had to pay off a bond to a very unsavoury character to whom George Henry had promised a horse. She sent agitated messages both to her lawyer and her banker in London, saying that he must come home at once. The former responded:

> My dear Mrs Moore, I have been directed to send off your son directly, and to arrange as best I can his affairs here. We must cut the knot and he must return to you and I hope learn wisdom by reflection. He appears to me not to have an idea of the value of money and from all I see if left here will soon run into debt again without really finding out that he is doing anything outrageous.[9]

George Henry was also involved romantically with a well-known married socialite from Cheltenham, much to his mother's dismay. As a result of this affair, his mounting debts and constant pressure from his mother to return to County Mayo, George Henry felt the time was right to travel abroad and, from 1834 to 1839, he journeyed through Russia, the Caucasus, Persia, Syria, Egypt, and Greece, drawing ruins, sketching camels and Syrian girls, and writing memoirs as he went along. George Henry even provided a vivid description of a peasant's Russian wedding which was invaluable as little was known of the ethnography of the region near the Caucasus at the time:

> The feasting now begins; the brandy circulates, mirth and gladness crown the board; the music strikes up, the song goes round, the jest and the double entente are flung from side to side; youths laugh and maidens blush, and the hearts of all beats high with mirth and strong spirits.[10]

Furthermore, George Henry was one of the first to explore, survey and sound the Dead Sea, which had, up until this point, baffled the efforts of other travellers, owing to the harsh climate and marauding Arabs.[11]

In 1837, George Henry Moore returned home, and devoted himself to hunting and racing, becoming the best steeplechase rider of his day. But there was still a cultured side to him. He divided his time between 'the season' in London and his beloved horses in Ireland.[12] George Henry accumulated as many books as his father, so much so, that the library at Moore Hall had to be extended. Horses, however, would dominate his life, along with that of his brother Augustus. The brothers were noted for their 'neck-or-nothing' riding across country in 'pounding matches'.[13] Leading this dare-devil sort of life, it is no wonder that he was occasionally involved in serious quarrels and duelling adventures. In 1839, duelling was still common in Ireland. Though it had ceased to be the glaring abuse of former years, it was still an option to settle arguments in the early nineteenth century. On one occasion, George Moore had a quarrel about a horse with a certain Joe MacDonnell—'Big Joe' or 'Joe More'—as he was called; this Joe More was noted not only as a big man, but also as the biggest punch-drinker of his time; he was what was called a 20-tumbler man. Maurice Moore noted that: 'In Mayo, strange as it may seem, a man's popularity depended very much on the number of tumblers of punch he could drink at a sitting'. Joe More MacDonnell, therefore, was a popular man.[14]

George Moore was not a fighting man, however, and so he sent to County Clare for an experienced duellist named The O'Gorman Mahon to get him out of trouble. In endeavouring to do this, a number of letters passed, which fell into the hands of a Mayo newspaper and made matters worse. Consequently, O'Gorman Mahon himself received a challenge from Moore, while MacDonnell received a challenge from Augustus Moore, George Henry's brother.[15] Augustus stated that he had sent the challenge to MacDonnell on the grounds that the latter had insulted his father in one of the published letters by referring to 'the family arrangements' at Moore Hall; this, MacDonnell pleaded later on, when he took an action against Augustus for criminal libel, was merely an allusion to the well-known fact that, owing to the grave bodily infirmity of Mr Moore, Mrs Moore had for years almost exclusively managed the affairs of the family.[16] The quarrel with MacDonnell and Mahon fizzled out in a Dublin law court and involved no duelling. Mrs Moore was pitied all around her, especially by Maria Edgeworth, who wrote:

> You must have suffered dreadful suspense during the whole of that long protracted correspondence about the duel and I can only conceive that with your strong feeling

> and affection for your son that affair must really have made you ten years older in health, strength and looks.[17]

Maurice Moore said of his father's temperament regarding the incident: 'It will be understood from these incidents the sort of strong, active character George Henry Moore possessed, in violent contrast to that of his quiet literary father. He turned more readily to the pistol than the pen in a quarrel'.[18] Circumstances in his life, however, were to bring more responsibility to George Henry's shoulders and, with it, a change in his nature.

Three events would change the course of George Henry's life considerably. Firstly, the death of his father; secondly, the death of his brother, Augustus; and thirdly, the occurrence of the Great Famine. In September 1840, George Moore, 'the Historian', died. The bulk of the income from the Moore property in land was now George Henry's, but there were many charges on the inheritance. In anticipation of his inheritance, George Henry had taken out numerous mortgages.[19] Once again, George Henry was happy to leave the figures and accounts to his mother, particularly the administration of his father's will. The brothers ran with a very illustrious horse-set that included fellow Irishmen, Lord Waterford and Christopher St George. A tragic setback and certainly the incident which changed the trajectory of George Henry's life was the death of his brother, Augustus. Augustus died after injuries received whilst riding 'Mickey Free' at Liverpool in 1845.[20] George Henry's passion for racing continued, but he sold a lot of his horses and curbed his gambling. Edgeworth wrote to Louisa after Augustus' death, again providing a proxy view of what was happening in the Moore family:

> But truth I do pity George; we know how fond they were of each other; but I have no doubt that such a great shock, instead of being permanently weakening as sorrow sometimes is to the mind, will be serviceable and strengthening and consolidating to his character. He will turn more to quiet literary pursuits, and he will feel in them, along with resource against sorrow, something congenial to his hereditary nature and pleasing and comforting to his mother. His higher nature, his superior tastes and abilities will come out. You will pardon me for this prophecy. I am an old woman.[21]

She was correct; his brother's death and the catastrophe that now overwhelmed the country called George Henry to a sense of duty.

Documentary sources in the Valuation Office, the Land Commission, and the National Library—all in Dublin—provide a clear picture of the structure and management of much of the Moore estate under George Henry's proprietorship.[22] The Moores owned over 12,000 acres near Ballintubber, Partry and Ballcally.[23] Agricultural land on the Ballintubber estate, close to Moore Hall, fell into the categories of arable, pasture and mountain-commonage. The quality of the land, according to the Field Valuations of 1843, varied from poor mica-slate soil to rather good arable.[24] Land on the estates was let by the Moores either directly to a tenant or to a sub-tenant via a middleman. An agent, William Mullowney, was employed to oversee the running of the estate, combining his duty with those of butler and steward.[25] Tenants included cottiers who paid their rents with their labour, tenant farmers who paid rent either in cash or in kind, and graziers who rented pasture for their cattle. There was also a full staff employed at the house.[26]

Rack-renting was a common phenomenon in mid-nineteenth century Ireland and this most certainly happened at Moore Hall. Looking at the holdings of three middlemen, namely, Malachy Tuohy, Peter Tuohy, and Mr Cheevers, it would seem that they were sub-letting their holdings at between two and three times the rent paid by them to George Henry Moore. The power of the Tuohys stemmed in part from the long leases they had been given, they had secured a lease for lands of Kiltarsaghaun for a period of four lives. Griffith's Valuation shows that Tuohy's property was recorded at a very low value (ten shillings) despite having a large quantity of land (30 acres). A valuation officer prior to the Famine judged that rent for portions of the Ballintubber townland were 'greatly too high', prompting him to conclude that Mr Moore was a rackrent landlord.[27] It can be argued that it was the middlemen who were driving up the rent. Edgeworth, in a letter to Louisa Moore wrote: '40gns taken from these wretched tenants it is beyond anything my wickedest imagination could have conceived for a bad Irish agent'.[28] Despite the rent levels in the early 1840s, there is no evidence that George Henry evicted any of his tenants for non-payment. During the later life of George Henry and that of his sons rent levels on the estate fell generally, which indicates that they had addressed the rack-rent issue.

Grazing was a highly emotive national issue at this time, when it was becoming an increasingly attractive financial proposition for large farmers in the wake of the Repeal of the Corn Laws in 1846. Extensive grazing reduced employment and forced the eviction of smallholders to make way for cattle.[29] Large-scale clearances were common in the east of Ireland. Moore Hall included a livestock farm and when George Henry took over the management of the estate, cattle and sheep produced an expected turnover of £1,500 per annum.[30] It seems, however, that Moore could have yielded much more profit if other parts of the Ballintubber estate had been let out as grassland, consequently the Ballintubber estate in particular saw no mass clearance of tenantry for cattle despite the financial benefits such an action would have brought for George Henry.

During the period 1840–1845 no forceful measures to improve the condition of his estate were taken by George Henry. He did, however, respond to the distress experienced amongst his tenants, particularly around the Ballybanaun and Partry estate, by sending donations as early as July 1842.[31] When the potato blight came to County Mayo in 1845, it hit hard. The population decline overall for the country during the Famine was about 20 per cent, but, in Mayo, the population fell by 29 per cent, from 388,887 to 274,830 due to death and emigration.[32] The parish priest of Carnacon, Father J. Browne, wrote the following to George Henry:

> On my way to Castlebar yesterday, I saw numbers of young people in the fields scraping up the earth in search of roots. Oh, my dear Mr Moore, I know how tender-hearted you are, and how much affected by the ruin and destruction of the people. The poor law is wholly inapplicable to this terrible disaster. I was in the Board Room at the Castlebar workhouse; there were outside about two thousand starving creatures crying out for food, some of whom had been there the day and night before, under rain and storm. The guardians had not a shilling to purchase meal.[33]

The Famine was particularly bad in County Mayo because of the power of the 'middlemen', the dependency on the potato and the unsustainable small holdings. A lack of industry in the region and alternative food supply ensured that Mayo, as well as most of the counties on the western peninsula of Ireland, suffered the greatest. Father Browne also recorded in April 1847 that of the 1,600 houses standing in 1844 at least 800 had been levelled, 3,000 lives had been lost, and 500 persons had fled to either America or England. Four thousand people remained, and some families had been forced to pawn their clothes to buy seed in a desperate bid to plant the land and feed themselves.[34]

The areas referred to included parts of George Henry Moore's estates. Local landlords received much criticism from Father Brown and other local priests for their lack of response. George Henry seems to be the exception. He chaired two relief committees at Ballintubber and Partry and was actively involved in the management of relief measures.[35] George Henry found that the lists and estimates which the committee for the electoral division of Ballintubber sent to the Finance Committee at Castlebar were considered excessive. The Finance Committee at Castlebar reduced the estimates of the local committee by nearly 1,000 daily rations, which meant that the destitute population of the district of Ballintubber were receiving only five days' provision in the week. The Finance Committee were using the census of 1841 to calculate the population of Ballintubber which was not a true reflection of the population of the district in 1846. George Henry wrote to Sir John Burgoyne, the chairman of the Board of Temporary Relief Commissioners, about the situation:

> I found the whole destitute population of the district receiving little more than five days' provision in the week and living for two days each week literally without food ... The consequence of this has been that fever, dysentery and swelling in the feet, from which until lately, this district has been comparatively free, has increased to a fearful extent and is still increasing. The ground upon which the Finance Committee acted in this summary manner was the census of 1841, which, if it exhibited a true statement of the population of the present day, would certainly afford them considerable foundation for such a proceeding ... the census of 1841 is no evidence whatever of the present state of the population; it has increased in many places twenty and thirty per cent since then ... I am sure it is not your wish, nor that of the Government, that a destitute population of upwards of five thousand persons should pass two days every week without food.[36]

George Henry also disclosed that there had been no aid provided for three weeks to the Partry Relief Committee from the Finance Committee of the Castlebar district or from the commissioners in Dublin. Like the Ballintubber district, the relief estimates for Partry were based on the 1841 census. George Henry explained to Burgoyne:

> It is true that the estimates at Partry are very large, and exceed the whole population according to the census of 1841, but in this district the population has increased enormously since then. Independent of the natural annual increase, large settlements have been made in the mountainous parts, and so poor are the inhabitants that I am convinced that it would be impossible to strike off three per cent of the entire population. I have myself a farm worth about £300 a year in this electoral division, and I have not only not received, but I have not asked for a farthing of rent during the whole of the last year.[37]

The letter demonstrated that, as chairman of two relief committees, George Henry had to ascertain the needs of the districts under his charge, ensure that works were commenced where required, and provide accurate lists of the workers. Names of those who had died or were absent had to be struck off the roll. George Henry was responsible for two parishes with thousands of inhabitants, but continued to organise and regulate relief to the best of his ability. The work was difficult and often held up due to bureaucracy.

A notably generous act on behalf of George Henry was the provision of funds as a result of a win by one of his horses. *Coranna* was a horse who he had entered in association with Lord Waterford in the Chester Cup in May 1846. Much of the money he won went on settling his debts, but he sent £1,000 to his mother at Moore Hall with instructions for its distribution. He wanted £500 to be used to finance relief works, while the balance was to be distributed in charity to the very poorest because he believed that the 'horses would gallop all the faster with the blessings of the poor'.[38] Father Michael Heaney, Parish Priest of Mayo Abbey, mentioned that every widow on George Henry's property received a milch cow, land was free to tenants who paid under £5 in rent, and relief was given to others paying up to £20 in rent.[39] Unfortunately, despite his best intentions, the distribution of relief was not trouble free. George Henry's mother, Louisa, who had been placed in charge of the fund from the *Coranna* win, found herself in dispute with local priests who prompted tenants to refuse to work except for double wages in the Ballybanaun area. George Henry wrote to his mother to suspend all relief to this region until he returned from England. In this instance, both parties were doing what they felt was best for the tenants, but there were other less scrupulous individuals prepared to profit from the crisis, for example, one Tom Lawless was convicted of using false weights when selling flour and meal.[40]

For George Henry, and his neighbour, friend and relative, the Marquis of Sligo, the recurrence of famines in Ireland required a longer-term solution that placed Irish interests at its centre. In early January 1847, they issued a number of resolutions, and called on Irish MPs and landowners to support them in forming an 'Irish Party'. They explained:

> That at this awful period of national calamity it becomes the first duty of every Irishman to devote his undivided efforts to the interests of Ireland; and that neither politics, parties, nor personal prejudices should influence his mind in the discharge of such a duty ... That if the necessity of joint and united action be urgent and important to Ireland, under ordinary circumstances, it at this moment becomes imperative and vital, as not only the future fortunes, but the present lives of millions, may depend on our exertions, and that dissension at such an hour is not only a reproach, but a crime.

Meetings were to be convened throughout Ireland, mostly chaired by Sligo.[41] Regardless of widespread support, ultimately, the proposal did not come to fruition. Nonetheless, it revealed how two young landowners in one of the most distressed counties in Ireland were seeking a more permanent solution to Ireland's poverty. Only a few weeks later, George Henry chaired a meeting in Castlebar in which Archbishop John MacHale was the main speaker. MacHale denounced the government for not doing more to help the Irish poor and rescuing them from 'the jaws of famine'.[42] In contrast, during the meeting a resolution was passed thanking Lord George Bentinck for his efforts on behalf of Ireland.[43]

As chairman of two relief committees, George Henry often contacted the Lord Lieutenant in Dublin describing the situation in his committee's region. He wrote the following on 21 January 1847:

> Able-bodied men can no longer obtain two quarts of meal for a day's work, which has to be divided amongst six individuals ...We have sent from this house several times to Westport within the last fortnight without being able to procure meal. The merchants in this county ... are apprehensive that the enormous profits they have been making will soon be interfered with ... There is a necessity of having provisions in government depots, sold to the people at a reasonable price ... If not done, serious and alarming outbreaks are likely to take place. A meeting which will be attended by enormous crowds of people has been convened for Monday next.[44]

George Henry also helped to finance the voyage of the *Martha Washington*.[45] This vessel shipped a large cargo of foodstuffs from New Orleans to Westport Quay in June 1847 and was financed by a trio of Mayo landlords; Lord Sligo, Sir Richard Blosse and George Henry Moore. Flour and meal imported were sold to famine-stricken tenants at highly subsidised rates, the deficit being met by the three landlords. Moreover, it was not only the tenants of these three men who benefitted. Anybody in need could purchase the food, as the main purpose was to bring down food prices in County Mayo.[46] The venture required £10,000 in capital and incurred an overall loss of £4,800. Maurice Moore estimated George Henry's deficit share to be approximately £900.[47]

Despite his request to suspend all relief to the region, there is no doubt that George Henry felt genuine distress about the effects the Famine was having on his tenants. Edgeworth's philosophy differed greatly to Moore's.[48] She wrote to Louisa in 1847: 'I do not quite agree with Mr Moore in his anger against the English government for their conduct towards Ireland through these late distresses'. Edgeworth's belief was despite 'plenty' of mistakes made by the Peel and Russell's administrations, 'they have meant well for Ireland'.[49] Her own views about the Famine were laid out in the letter:

> The conduct of Irish proprietors during these distresses must convince England as it has convinced the Irish of their good will by their good deeds ... I see also that the feeling excited in England by Irish distress still more than the munificent contributions they have made towards the relief of our poor has created gratitude and has counteracted that mischievous spirit of national hatred which O'Connell (Peace to his too clever undisciplined soul!) raised between the Irish and the Sassenach. I am persuaded that the Union between the two countries will be more strongly cemented now than it has yet ever been. The edges have been washed clean and the asperities cleared away and simply by the cohesion and happy contiguity they will fit and stick together solidly—permanently.[50]

This was certainly in contrast with Moore's views about the Union with Britain and the views of other contemporaries writing about the Famine, in particular Elizabeth Smith,[51] who by the late 1840s believed in the need of some form of Repeal.[52]

As a result of the Famine, heavy Poor Law rates and his general philanthropy, George Henry was forced to put his heavily indebted estate in chancery. It was because of the ever-increasing debts of landlords like George Henry that the government decided to pass the Encumbered Estates Act in 1848.[53] Moore was one of many landlords who had to sell off parts of their estates. From the large estate of Ballintubber and Ballybanaun Mountain, a total of 9,000 acres of land were sold off in two lots in the Landed Estates Court in July 1854.[54] George Henry obtained a loan and bought back the Ballintubber estate of approximately 6,000 acres, but the Ballybanaun Mountain portion of the estate was bought by Bishop Thomas Plunket, the Church of Ireland Bishop of Tuam, Achonry and Killala.[55] In the same year Plunket had also acquired land in the region from Sir Robert Blosse so that his overall property was just over 10,000 acres.[56] Before selling the land to Plunket in 1854, this part of the estate had been in receivership.[57] Evictions took place on the Moore property during the early 1850s, effected by the receiver.[58] Such a circumstance was not favourable for the creation of a passive tenantry.

The local priests accused Bishop Plunket of being a proselytiser and evicting Catholic tenants and replacing them with Protestants. Plunket denied that the evictions were part of a proselytising scheme and argued that they were purely the legal clearance of Chancery Court tenants and squatters.[59] George Henry gave the evicted tenants land on his own estate, dividing some large grazing farms among them, and some, he took into his own demesne.[60] This would create further problems on Moore's estate which was already heavily sub-divided, something his cousin, Lord Sligo of Westport House, continued to pressure him about.[61] Sligo wrote to Moore: 'In my heart's belief you and Sir Samuel do more (to) ruin and injure and persecute and exterminate your tenants than any (other) man in Mayo'.[62] Sligo was referring to the fact that both Moore and Sir Samuel O'Malley initially refused to evict for non-payment of rent. O'Malley was eventually forced to evict on a large scale.[63]

During the Famine years, George Henry embarked on a political career. He lost the March 1846 by-election but succeeded in being elected MP for Mayo during the 1847 general election. In 1846, Moore issued his own manifesto in which he said:

> My principles are those of civil and religious liberty in its broadest and most extended sense; and, should I have the honour of being chosen your Representative, I trust I shall be found always watchful and zealous in their defence. The causes which have hitherto contributed to deprive this island of her share in the general prosperity of the Empire, shall constantly engage my most anxious attention originating as they do in a system of unjust, unequal and ignorant legislation, which has for so long oppressed us, and for which the English Government owes this country

> not only her best exertions for the future, but reparation for the past ... I shall always regard the interests of Ireland as paramount to every other consideration. Her enemies shall be my enemies, and her friends my friends.[64]

The by-election of 1846 was eagerly followed by the Mayo gentry. The Dowager Lady Sligo wrote the following to George Hildebrand, the estate agent at Westport House:

> You will have heard that Mr. Geoffrey Browne is going to stand for Mayo, either he or Mr. George Moore must give way to the others—they must settle that between them ... I should think the one who decides on standing will be returned against the repeal candidate ... I cannot believe that Mr. George Higgins will have the repeal interest ... Mr. McDonnell is more likely.[65]

In Whitehall, Moore was described by Michael J. Whitty, the parliamentary critic, as: 'a very clever man, full of thought and very fluent, but he will say what he thinks',[66] while the London *Times* described him as: 'Wolf Dog Moore, the Tender-Hearted Turfman'.[67] At a Dublin convention of Liberal MPs, he proposed that all Irish MPs should take a pledge to cooperate closely on matters of particular importance for Ireland; the proposal made little immediate impact. He introduced this idea again in 1851, when he became the spokesman in parliament for Irish Catholics' opposition to the Ecclesiastical Titles Act. Moore took a leading role in establishing the Catholic Defence Association which opposed this act and helped to establish 'The Friends of Religious Freedom and Equality', which called for the disestablishment of the Church of Ireland.[68]

With Charles Gavan Duffy, George Henry played a key role in 1850 and 1851 in compelling all MPs who supported the Tenant League to take a pledge not to accept government offices until the league's demands were met. George Henry used two platforms—religious inequality and the land question—to unite Irish liberals and Catholic MPs under one movement. One could say that he was responsible for formulating 'independent opposition', which became the backbone of this loosely-based independent party in the 1850s. He openly attacked former associates William Keogh and John Sadlier when they reneged on their pledges and accepted government positions. George Henry's support for the Tenant League made him unpopular among the landed elite in Mayo, especially his erstwhile partner, Lord Sligo, but he was returned as one of the MPs for Mayo. In the 1857 general election, George Henry was re-elected for Mayo, but was unseated on the grounds of undue clerical influence being used against his Tory rival. In the 1859 general election, George Henry and other independents supported the Tory government of Lord Derby to show their irritation with the Palmerstonian liberals. The Tories went on to win a majority of Irish parliamentary seats.[69] Following his departure from parliament and with a reduction in public involvement, George Henry began once again to spend more time at Moore Hall with his wife Mary (whom he had married in 1851, the daughter of Mark Blake of nearby Ballinafad House) and his children (George, Maurice, Augustus, Nina, and Julian). Louisa, his mother, was pleased that George Henry was now taking responsibility for his estate and had engaged in a successful parliamentary career. He also became Deputy Lieutenant in 1862 and served as High Sheriff of County Mayo for a short time during the same decade.[70] Shortly after George Henry's marriage, Louisa Moore, then only 60 years of age, met with an accident and she died in 1861.

George Henry had opposed the Young Irelanders during the 1840s but, as the Famine progressed, he softened and expressed his support for the establishment of a nationalist-orientated party. At the least, he flirted with Fenianism. According to John Devoy, George Henry was asked to join the Irish Republican Brotherhood (IRB) by Jeremiah O'Donovan Rossa in 1864. He refused to support the National Association of Ireland because it was virtually controlled by Archbishop Paul Cullen.[71] This caused George Henry to become politically marginalised.[72] Supported by his great friend, Archbishop John MacHale, George Henry decided to run for Mayo in the 1868 general election on a ticket of tenant rights and amnesty for Fenian prisoners. He succeeded and began conferring regularly with IRB leaders throughout the following year. A talented and lively speaker, on election he became the most enthusiastic champion of the amnesty cause in parliament, endearing him to a new, young IRB leadership. George Henry was returned for the last time as MP for Mayo along with Lord Bingham in 1868.[73] Concluding a letter to A.M. Sullivan after the election, he expressed his views of the political future saying that: 'The landlords must surrender their feudal claims at discretion. We have a different people to fight with now from those of twenty years ago; accept this as fact'.[74]

Throughout 1869, George Moore began conferring regularly with some IRB/Fenian leaders against the hostility of the Roman Catholic Church. Cardinal Newman's associate, Bishop Moriarty of Kerry, declared that: 'hell would not be hot enough nor eternity long enough for a Fenian'.[75] In common with John O'Connor Power and moderate IRB leaders, Moore apparently desired some form of alliance between the Fenians and MPs, with a view to forming a new public movement. As he was still committed to an essentially Catholic-Whig political agenda, however, it is improbable that Moore ever became a member of the IRB or seriously worked with it on any basis other than promoting the amnesty agitation. Moore's personal loss was as great as his political success.[76] The power of the landlords had certainly been curtailed but these individuals had been his own personal friends, and many (particularly Lord Sligo) bitterly resented his interference and made the quarrel personal. The correspondence between these two friends shows their gradual alienation. Lord Sligo wrote to George Henry on 15August 1868: 'My Dear George, I cannot deny I wish most sincerely that I could, as you, have seen our friendship decaying'.[77]

The last few years of Moore's life were clouded with bitter rent disputes on his estate. Father Patrick Lavelle, a well-known Mayo man and nationalist priest, arbitrated on several occasions for Moore while he was absent due to his political career, but on receiving the following letter Moore returned home to settle the rent disputes: 'Important-Caution. Notice is hereby given that any person who pays rent to landlords, agents or bailiffs above the ordnance valuation will at his peril mark the consequences. By order. Signed Rory'.[78] Moore refused to be blackmailed and warned that he would evict those refusing to pay their rent:

> If it is supposed that because I advocate the rights of the tenants, I am to surrender my own rights as a landlord; if it is suspected that I am so enamoured of a seat in Parliament that I am ready to surrender my own self-respect rather than imperil its possession; if it is hoped that because I alone of all the landlords in the parish of Ballintubber have not cleared the estate, the people are to send me to gaol ... I am determined to vindicate my own rights without fear of flinching, and if it be necessary to evict every tenant who refuses to pay his rent in full.[79]

Moore arrived on Good Friday, 1870 at Moore Hall, demonstrating much fatigue and exhaustion. He wrote to his wife:

> Found the place looking well, considering that the trees are not yet in leaf. The climate and air are delicious, and it seems to me as if it were 'good for us to be here', and that if we could build tabernacles for ourselves in this world, we could find a paradise for ourselves here.[80]

He died the following Tuesday. The doctor diagnosed apoplexy. Father Lavelle said that he died from heartbreak, and his son and biographer Maurice Moore agreed. However, his other son, the novelist George Augustus Moore, in a preface to Maurice's biography, expressed the belief that his father had committed suicide and died like an old Roman.[81] The Irish papers came out the next day with a black border, while even the English newspapers paid tribute to his talents and his integrity. The following tributes were amongst those made:

> He was signally remarkable for his earnest and impassioned eloquence, and for great capacities as a debater, very often and recently illustrated in the part which he took in the great measures before Parliament. He was also eminently distinguished as an eloquent, ready, and accomplished scholar.[82]

> Moore Hall was indeed a fitting retreat for one so rarely gifted as George Henry Moore, whose refined tastes and varied accomplishments are well illustrated in the interior of the family mansion, where he was so long the generous, courteous, and hospitable host, and the life and soul of the circle in which he was wont to display the knowledge which he had acquired by study and travel, and the great social virtues for which he was eminently distinguished...the poor deplored him as a lost friend, and one who was heart and soul in their interest, and the stern and uncompromising foe to their enemies and oppressors.[83]

George Henry's political friends wanted to give him a public funeral in Glasnevin Cemetery in Dublin, but his family desired that he should be buried in the family tomb at Kiltoom, Moore Hall.[84] Isaac Butt organised a gathering on the Green at Harold's Cross on Sunday, 24 April, to express the widespread and sincere grief for George Henry's death. The city trades and their standards were displayed, with Butt addressing the crowd: 'Fellow countrymen, we are assembled on a very solemn occasion, to do mournful honour to the memory of a departed patriot, one of the men whom Ireland could ill spare'.[85] There were many mourners at his funeral, but some of the Mayo gentry did not attend because of his nationalist politics. Father Lavelle said at his funeral: 'the poor deplored him as a lost friend [,] one who was heart and soul in their interests and the stern and uncompromising foe to their enemies and oppressors'.[86]

George Henry Moore, during his political career, had come into conflict with three great forces which seemed to impede his fight for religious freedom and tenant prosperity. He attacked successively political corruption, ecclesiastical tyranny and landlord domination, and though the struggle was long and severe, he had in each case, met with some successes in his fight against misgovernment. He enjoyed life, was a devoted family man, a horse lover, and always demonstrated empathy and fairness towards his tenants. George Henry had changed considerably from his time as a young man, concerned with racing, gambling and women—interests that had caused his mother some consternation and worry. In time, and with increased responsibility, he came to embrace the dignity of his position and to behave benevolently and responsibly towards his tenants and on behalf of his family, especially during the Famine.

George Henry's son, George Augustus, a controversial but successful novelist, took over the estate in 1870 but had little interest in it. His brother, Col. Maurice Moore, who would become a senator in the Free State, managed it to the best of his ability. The house was eventually burned in 1923 by Anti-Treaty forces and, with it, much of the material culture associated with the family.[87] The irony lies in the fact that more than a century later, a monument was erected near the estate at Kiltoom acknowledging the charitable work that George Henry had carried out during the Famine. The plaque reads: 'Kiltoom/Burial place of the/Moores of Moore Hall/this Catholic patriot/family is honoured for/their Famine relief/and their refusal to/barter principles for/English gold. Erected by Ballyglass Co/Old I.R.A. 1964'. Despite his controversial beliefs, there is no doubt that, by his actions, George Henry Moore fulfilled the family motto: 'Fortis Cadere Cedere Non Potest' (He who proceeds with courage shall not fail).

NOTES

1. J. Hone, *The Moores of Moore Hall* (London: Jonathan Cape, 1939) p. 21.
2. G. Freyer and S. Mulloy, 'The Unfortunate John Moore', *Cathair Na Mart—Journal of Westport Historical Society,* vol. 4, no. 1 (1984), pp 51–68.
3. Hone, *The Moores of Moorehall*, p. 4.
4. Ibid., p. 93.
5. M. Moore, *An Irish Gentleman, George Henry Moore: His Travel, His Racing, His Politics* (London: Laurie, 1913), p. 8.
6. Maria Edgeworth was referring to Thomas Moore, poet, singer and songwriter and who was still living. He died in 1852. J. Hone, 'Maria Edgeworth and the Moores of Moore Hall' in *New Statesmen and Nation* (3 April 1937), pp 553–554. National Library of Ireland, hereafter NLI, MS 495.
7. Ibid.
8. 'Letter from Maria Edgeworth to Mrs Louisa Moore, 17 May 1841', Letter (Dublin), NLI, Typescript copies of letters of Maria Edgeworth, mainly to Mrs Moore, 1835–1849, Letter, MS_UR_029819.
9. Hone, *The Moores of Moore Hall*, p. 93.
10. Ibid., p. 29.
11. H. Goren, *Dead Sea Level: Science, Exploration and Imperial Interests in the Near East* (London: I.B. Tauris, 2011) p. 178.
12. Hone, *The Moores of Moore Hall*, p. 88.
13. 'Pounding matches' where the participants, accompanied by their grooms, had to follow the leader over any selected obstacle or admit defeat. Hone, *The Moores of Moorehall*, p. 91.
14. Moore, *An Irish Gentleman,* p. 74.
15. C.L. Kirwan, 'Affair of Honor', *Connaught Telegraph*, 3 April 1839.
16. Hone, *The Moores of Moore Hall*, p. 94.
17. 'Letter from Maria Edgeworth to Mrs Louisa Moore, 8 April 1839', Letter (Dublin), NLI, Typescript copies of letters of Maria Edgeworth, mainly to Mrs. Moore, 1835–1849, MS_UR_029819.
18. Moore, *An Irish Gentleman*, pp 34–45.
19. Hone, *The Moores of Moore Hall*, p. 101.
20. Moore, *An Irish Gentleman,* p. 102. The actual whereabouts of Augustus' death has been disputed, see Coranna of Moore Hall, 'What really happened to Augustus Moore?' *https://corannaofmoorehall.weebly.com/augustus-moore.html*

21. 'Letter from Maria Edgeworth to Mrs Louisa Moore, 15 April 1845', Letter (Dublin) (NLI, Typescript copies of letters of Maria Edgeworth, mainly to Mrs. Moore, 1835–1849), MS_UR_029819.
22. D. Barr, 'George Henry Moore and his tenants, 1840–1870', *Cathair na Mart,* vol. 8, no. 1 (1988) pp 66–79.
23. Local Government Board for Ireland, *Land Owners in Ireland, Return of Owners of Land of One Acre and Upwards*, vol. 80 (HMSO, 1876). *www.dippam.ac.uk/eppi/documents/16252/eppi_pages/194427*
24. Ordnance Survey Field Name Books of the County of Mayo, 1838, Book 14, Parish of Ballintober, 430.
25. G. Moore, *Hail and Farewell!: Ave. Salve. Vale.* ed. R. Allen-Cave (Gerards Cross: Colin Smythe Limited, 1985), p. 731.
26. Ibid., p. 742.
27. Valuation Lists, no. 4, Co. Mayo. Vol 1, 1858–1883 cited in Barr, 'George Henry Moore and his tenants', p. 71.
28. 'Letter from Maria Edgeworth to Mrs Louisa Moore, 12 October 1841 to 17 May 1841', Letter (Dublin), NLI, Typescript copies of letters of Maria Edgeworth, mainly to Mrs Moore, 1835–1849, Letter, MS_UR_029819.
29. Stephan Heblich, Stephen J. Redding and Yanos Zylberberg, 'The Distributional Consequences of Trade: Evidence from the Repeal of the Corn Laws' (2022). www.princeton.edu/-reddings/papers/LLCL.pdf
30. Barr, 'George Henry Moore and his Tenants', p.71.
31. I. Hamrock, *The Famine in Mayo* (Castlebar: Mayo County Library, 1998) p. 9.
32. Ibid.
33. Moore, *An Irish Gentleman,* p. 119.
34. Letter written by Father Browne to *The Tablet* dated 6 April 1847 communicating the 'awful destitution in Mayo' cited in Barr, 'George Henry Moore and his tenants', p. 71.
35. 'Letter from the Partry Relief Committee to George Henry Moore 12 July 1847', Letter (Dublin), NLI, 11 volumes of correspondence of George Henry Moore re administration of his estates and other family, financial and political matters 1826–1870. MS 889–899, MS 890, no. 158.
36. Moore, *An Irish Gentleman*, p.122.
37. Ibid., pp 122–121.
38. Hone, *The Moores of Moore Hall*, p. 138.
39. Barr, 'George Henry Moore and his tenants', p. 71.
40. Ibid., pp 72–73.
41. 'The New Irish Party', *Sun*, 15 January 1847.
42. 'A Broad Hint to Government', *Bradford Observer,* 4 February 1847.
43. See chapter by Peter Murphy.
44. Cited in L. Swords, *In Their Own Words: The Famine in North Connacht 1845–1849* (Dublin: The Columba Press, 1999), p. 117.
45. Letter (Dublin) (NLI, 11 volumes of correspondence of George Henry Moore regarding

the administration of his estates and other family, financial and political matters 1826–1870. MSS 889–899 MSS 890, No. 152.

46. 'Food', *Freeman's Journal*, 2 July 1847.
47. Moore, *An Irish Gentleman*, p. 125.
48. For more on Edgeworth's role during the Great Hunger see Christine Kinealy, *Charity and the Great Hunger. The Kindness of Strangers* (London: Bloomsbury, 2013), pp 156–158.
49. 'Letter from Maria Edgeworth to Mrs Louisa Moore, 30 July 1847, Letter (Dublin) NLI, Typescript copies of letters of Maria Edgeworth, mainly to Mrs Moore, 1835–1849, Letter, MS_UR_029819.
50. 'Letter from Maria Edgeworth to Mrs Louisa Moore, 30 July 1847, Letter (Dublin), NLI', Typescript copies of letters of Maria Edgeworth, mainly to Mrs Moore, 1835–1849, Letter, MS_UR_029819.
51. Elizabeth Smith was mistress of Baltyboys estate in Co. Wicklow. She kept a meticulous record of all aspects of the Great Famine. J.K. TeBrake, 'Personal narratives as historical sources: the journal of Elizabeth Smith 1840–1850 (3:1) *History Ireland*, 1, no.3 (Spring, 1995).
52. M. Kelleher, 'Philosophick View?: Maria Edgeworth and the Great Famine', in G. Cusack and S. Goss (eds) *Hungry Words: Images of Famine in the Irish Canon* (Dublin: Irish Academic Press, 2006), p. 60.
53. J.S. Donnelly Jr, 'The administration of relief, 1847–51', *A New History of Ireland V Ireland Under the Union, 1801–1870,* W. Vaughan (ed.) (Oxford University Press, 1989), pp 294–306.
54. Landed Estates Court Rental, 1850–1885.
55. Moore obtained the loan of £20,300 from the Scottish investment company. The Ballybanaun Mountain portion of the estate consisted of 2,440 acres and had an annual rental of £254/6/4. Gerard Moran, *The Mayo Evictions of 1860: Patrick Lavelle and the 'War' in Partry,* (Contae Mhaigh Eo: Foilseacháin Náisiúnta Teoranta, 1986) p. 32.
56. The townlands concerned were Gorteenmore, Gortfree, Carheen, Treanlaur, Glenagh-shleeny, Ballybanaun, Derryveeney and Shanvallyard. Moran, *The Mayo Evictions of 1860,* p. 32.
57. The receivership of the property fell to James Ruttledge who had been convicted of giving false measure in relief meal during the Famine. P.G. Lane 'Lord Plunkett and the Party Mountains: a case study of 1850s landlordism', *Journal of the Galway Archaeological and Historical Society* 46 (1994), pp 156–172.
58. Ibid.
59. *Mayo Constitution* 21 November 1854. Letter written by Father Ward to the newspaper.
60. Moore, *An Irish Gentleman*, p. 132.
61. For more on the role of Lady Sligo and her son during the Great Hunger see, Sandy Letourneau O'Hare, 'Lady Sligo of Westport House: "she rolled up her linen sleeves"', in Christine Kinealy, Jason King and Gerard Moran (eds), *Heroes of Ireland's Great Hunger* (Cork University Press, 2021), pp 57–70.
62. Hone, *The Moores of Moore Hall*, pp 158–160.
63. Ibid., p. 159.
64. 'To the Independent Electors of County Mayo', *Mayo Constitution*, 3 March 1846.

65. H. Catherine Sligo to George Hildebrand, n.d. (Arnold Bernhard Library, Quinnipiac University, Lady Sligo Letters, Folder 51). 15 February [1846]. I am grateful to librarian, Robert Young, for accessing these documents on my behalf.
66. Moore, *An Irish Gentleman*, p. 158.
67. Hone, *The Moores of Moore Hall*, p. 149.
68. J.H. Whyte, *The Independent Irish Party 1850–1859* (Oxford University Press, 1958) pp 121–122.
69. Hone, *The Moores of Moore Hall*, pp 160–161.
70. Deputy Lieutenants (D.L.) were empowered to embody militia regiments.
71. K. Waldron, *The Archbishops of Tuam 1700–2000* (Galway: Nordlaw Books, 2008), p. 51.
72. Hone, *The Moores of Moore Hall*, pp 169–170.
73. Ibid., p. 177.
74. Ibid., p. 171.
75. O.P. Rafferty, 'The Catholic Church and Fenianism', *History Ireland* 16, no. 6 (Nov/Dec 2008), p. 33.
76. Moore, *An Irish Gentleman*, p. 327.
77. Ibid., p. 330.
78. J.F. Quinn, 'The Moores of Moore Hall', serialised in the *Western People* (beginning 28 January 1933).
79. Moore, *An Irish Gentleman*, p. 373.
80. Ibid., p. 375.
81. Ibid., p. 337.
82. *Tuam Hearld*, 23 April 1870.
83. *Freeman's Journal*, 25 April 1870.
84. Moore, *An Irish Gentleman*, p. 377.
85. 'The Meeting at Harold's Cross', *Freeman's Journal*, 25 April 1870.
86. Ibid.
87. The National Library, Ireland, holds a telegram, dated 1 February 1923, saying the house had been burned to the ground 'and nothing was saved', Colonel Maurice Moore Papers. https://catalogue.nli.ie/Record/vtls000513351

CHAPTER SIX

FRANCES ANNE, THIRD MARCHIONESS OF LONDONDERRY (1800–1865)

Feudal Lady of the Soil

Anthony Russell

Aristocratic wives, like Frances Anne, Third Marchioness of Londonderry 'were not recorded in mainstream histories of the nineteenth and early twentieth centuries'.[1] Within marriage, their role was maternal, supportive, social, and charitable. Although some worked, 'by distinctly personal means', to influence decision making and promote the family's prospects, they were excluded from overt participation in politics and industry; rather, they were subsumed into their husbands' historical narratives and subsequently forgotten.[2]

This changed for the Third Marchioness of Londonderry when, in 1958, Edith, Seventh Marchioness of Londonderry, aware that nothing had been written about her predecessor, whom she thought 'immeasurably ahead of her times',[3] published the life story of Frances Anne, Third Marchioness of Londonderry.[4] This surprisingly honest, familial account tells of family feuds, foreign travel, diplomatic influence, mutual 'courtly love' for Russian Tsar Alexander, and intimate, platonic, and political letters exchanged with Benjamin Disraeli. Such activities were probably not that unusual for a wealthy, well-connected woman, but Frances Anne was not a typical aristocratic wife. An improving landlord in her own right, she was an industrialist who developed collieries, built railways, bridges, kilns, blast furnaces, towns, and ports. Carnlough was a poor village, with a small quay, that had been 'for some years in a state of dilapidation' when, in 1834, Frances Anne inherited it from her mother Anne Catherine, Countess of Antrim. Frances Anne turned that small Irish quay into an industrial harbour.[5] Along with Carnlough, Frances Anne inherited 24 townlands,[6] in the Baronies of Lower Glenarm, Upper Glenarm, and Kilconway.[7] Her townlands, consisting of 9,800 acres, less than 20 per cent of her mother's estate, were non-contiguous. Had she been born a boy she would have inherited all her mother's land.[8] As it was, prior to the 1882 Married Women's Property Act, her inheritances, at the time of her 1819 marriage and subsequently, belonged to her husband, Charles Stewart, Third Marquess of Londonderry.[9] In 1845, when the potato blight arrived, Frances Anne, with her husband's approbation, was effectively the landlord of his Antrim properties.

Frances Anne's autobiography, 'souvenirs of a long, brilliant existence',[10] dated 27 December 1848, written in middle age, and intended solely for her children, tells of her childhood misery. Her father, Sir Henry Vane, inherited Wynyard House, and collieries in County Durham. He was, 'Young, rich and the handsomest man almost ever seen. It is not surprising he was generally admired and run after'.[11] The one who caught him was the 18-year-old, Anne Catherine, Countess of Antrim; despite 'infinite pains being taken by every member of my mother's family to prevent her getting acquainted with my father'.[12] They were married on 25 April 1799. When Frances Anne was born on 17 January 1800, her parents were disappointed she was not a boy. Thereafter, their unhappy daughter observed the marriage of an 'ill-suited pair'.[13] Her father neglected his wife,[14] but Frances Anne thought her mother remained fond of and in awe of her husband. Frances Anne remained an only child and endured cruelty. 'Never was a child so harshly treated as I was by Father, Mother and Governess. I met with nothing but cuffs and abuse'.[15] At 10, she caught scarlet fever. This was the only recollection she had 'of parental kindness ... my father and mother watched over me unwearied night and day'.[16] However, when she complained that, 'Papa has no business cutting down a tree here, everything is mine' she was beaten, and her toy taken away.[17] If this incident suggested a sense of entitlement, her response also gave notice of a future concern for the children of both pitmen in Durham and tenants in Antrim. 'The only good effect of this mode of treatment was to make me determine never to strike or terrify a child'.[18] This determination promoted schools and children's welfare during the Great Famine. In the 'Londonderry Arms' in Carnlough, her portrait declares, 'She championed Childhood'.

Frances Anne's father died when she was 13 years old and she 'felt his death far more than anyone imagined for he had always shown me far more affection than my mother. He never beat or scolded me but at her instigation'.[19] Her world was suddenly very different. 'The Cuffed Child ... was now an immense heiress. Everyone's manner changed'.[20] Through her teenage years suitors appeared seeking to marry the beautiful young heiress. They were all rejected until the night of 3 February 1818, at her mother's house in London, when she first met Charles Stewart, the British Ambassador to Austria and half-brother to Lord Castlereagh, the Foreign Secretary.[21] When asked by her mother what she thought of Charles Stewart, Frances Anne replied, 'not much'. Despite this first impression, Frances Anne, 'began to feel restless and discontented and more interested about him'.[22] They married on 3 April 1819.

Robert Stewart was 'the only son of Robert Stewart, First Marquess of Londonderry, by his second wife, Lady Frances Pratt'.[23] A brave decorated hussar, he served as Adjutant General to the future Duke of Wellington.[24] At 26, he had married Lady Catherine Bligh, daughter of the Earl of Darnley, with whom he had one son, Frederick. In 1812, after eight years of marriage, Catherine died from a complication following minor surgery.[25] Thus, Frances Anne married a widower, twice her age, and until she had her own children, she was uncomfortable when people told stories of her husband's earlier attachments.[26] However, her brother-in-law, the Foreign Secretary, thought her intelligent and with a 'great deal of decision and character'.[27] These were attributes that she would display as an industrialist and landlord in Durham and Ireland. Frances Anne, 'was now an assured young woman whose inherent belief in her own importance eased her into her new station'.[28] Confidence in her station, her aristocratic status, was something Frances Anne carried into her future and onto the famine-struck townlands of Antrim.

The Third Marchioness of Londonderry who, in middle age, corresponded with land agents about pig styes above Carnlough, in the early years of her marriage was the beautiful, confident, young woman who exchanged letters with the Russian Tsar, Alexander. She made such an impression that she noted in her autobiography: 'He told me that for ten years he had lived like a hermit without the least feeling for any woman until his attachment for me. This conversation was romantic, enthusiastic, and beautiful'.[29] This relationship, probably platonic, and mixing with European leaders, 'certainly shaped her ambition'.[30] Frances Anne wished to return to London, to be near the seat of British power. This desire was aided by unforeseen events. On the 12 August 1822, Lord Castlereagh died by suicide, without a son, and Charles Stewart became the Third Marquess of Londonderry. Francis Anne became the Third Marchioness. Charles resigned from his diplomatic position, and they travelled back to the newly acquired Holdernesse House in London. In a letter to her mother the

Third Marchioness revealed her political ambition for her husband. 'As soon as he arrives in England, he must collect all his friends round him, and endeavour to form a formidable party'.[31]

Inheriting the title fuelled Lord and Lady Londonderry's ambition and, although they were government supporters, they resented both Lord Castlereagh's successor, Viscount Canning, and the fact that Charles was not given control of the Derry Militia.[32] In the House of Lords, because of this resentment, the Third Marquess of Londonderry did not manage to form a party, nor did he gain a position in government. However, Frances Anne became a formidable society hostess; perhaps too formidable. Referring to 'great assemblies at Holdernesse House', Edith, Marchioness of Londonderry, quoted the historian Sir Archibald Alison: 'At receptions in her own house her manner was polite and high bred but frigid such as invariably inspired awe'. When guests saw her, 'seated in her grandeur' they turned away rather than 'pass through perilous straits'.[33] These were the perilous straits her Antrim agent, John Lanktree, would later fail to navigate. The 'high bred' Third Marchioness did not expect her decisions to be questioned. Frances Anne 'was devoted to' and supported her husband.[34] Except for Mount Stewart in County Down, which he later inherited from his half-brother, Charles Stewart's estates, houses and industries had passed into his ownership when he married Frances Anne. However, 'this property reverted back to the wife if her husband died first', as would happen on 16 March 1854.[35]

In their management of the Durham collieries and Irish estates the Londonderrys, instinctively, practised entrepreneurial paternalism. Entrepreneurial paternalists provided jobs, housing and, in the Londonderrys' pit villages, free healthcare and education. However, there was 'as much, if not more, emphasis on the maintenance of standards and strict, authoritarian and all pervasive control as there was on the more humanitarian aspects of paternalism'.[36] Keith Wilson suggested 'the paternalists of the 1840s were similar to certain multinational corporations of today—comforting to be with so long as desires for independence are crushed ... and extremely unpleasant to fall foul of'.[37] This draconian side of paternalism was evident when Lord Londonderry opposed two reforming pieces of legislation, casting a shadow on the Marchioness's claim to heroic status and her care of children. The 1832 Reform Act increased the size of the male-only, qualifying electorate by nearly 50 per cent. The Third Marquess of Londonderry was bitterly opposed. He saw the reform as a threat to his influence over parliamentary constituencies in County Durham. In the event, the reform no more than 'dented' that influence but his opposition marked him as a reactionary and as a political dinosaur, supported by his wife.[38]

Even more reprehensively perhaps, 'In 1842 a report by a Royal Commission on the employment of women and children in mines caused widespread public dismay at the depths of human degradation that were revealed'.[39] Following publication, the 1842 Mines and Collieries Act was passed, despite the Third Marquess of Londonderry leading the opposition in the House of Lords. The act banned all women from the mines and children aged under 10. Before the act was passed it was common for children, 8 and younger, to be used in seams too small for adult labour. The act also introduced inspections which were an anathema to the Londonderrys.[40] 'Lord Londonderry and his wife held the view, that as their mines were well run ... any interference by the state was unnecessary and undesirable'.[41] They had a clear view of their own superiority—something identified by the *Morning Chronicle* which launched a scathing, mocking attack. Londonderry had an intellect, 'vastly in advance of the rest of the world'. He was such a 'stupendous character' that must be right; and the 'evil men', 'the pygmies' and 'minnows' who wanted to make conditions better in the collieries, must be wrong.[42] Thus, at the time of 1842 Mines and Collieries Act, the 'cuffed child' could not yet aspire to heroic status.

Unsuccessful in politics, the Londonderrys were more successful in industry. Around Wynyard, Frances Anne's childhood estate, they developed their collieries and associated infrastructure. In 1821, Frances Anne was the 'second largest exporter of coal' from the River Wear, but at a cost of £10,000 per year.[43] To cut this cost, Charles Stewart wrote to his half-brother, Lord Castlereagh, proposing that he, Charles, buy the manor at Seaham, build a harbour there, and construct a railway along the four miles from the collieries. Castlereagh agreed and a portion of the £63,000 was raised on the Mount Stewart estate in County Down.[44] In her autobiography Frances Anne recorded her first visits to their new property at Seaham and her first visit to her husband's family's home at Mount Stewart. Dated September 1823: 'We returned to Wynyard for a week and then went to Seaham. We had bought this estate with the ultimate view of making a harbour and were much pleased with it.' They left Seaham for Mount Stewart which she 'had never seen'. It was in such a terrible state, 'we only remained to give orders and then proceeded to Mama at Glenarm'.[45] Frances Anne's paternalism was flattered by their reception in Glenarm. 'We were received with great enthusiasm, bonfires blazed on all the hills ... The horses were taken from the carriage and we were dragged 2 miles by the people'.[46] In January 1845 Frances Anne hosted a dinner in Seaham to celebrate the new harbour extensions.[47] With the export of coal generating £5000 per annum, it was a success story; a model Frances Anne would use, during the Great Famine, for exporting limestone along a railway line to a new harbour in Carnlough.[48]

Although it was 1834, when Frances Anne inherited her distributed townlands from her mother, her travels, her involvement in London's social and political life, and her management of her industrial enterprises in Durham left little time, or desire, to become involved in farming in the isolated Glens of Antrim. From 1837 to 1843 she left that to a land agent, Thomas Davidson. Davidson was also the agent for Frances Anne's stepfather, Edmund McDonald at Glenarm.[49] To London society's great surprise, four years after the death of her husband, in June 1817, Anne Catherine, Countess of Antrim, married Edmund Phelps, a music teacher and secretary to Lord Burghersh.[50] Although 'his birth was as low as possible', he changed his name to McDonald.[51]

On 1 April 1844, the Devon Commission, enquiring into the occupation and use of the land in Ireland, visited Larne to collect evidence. Thomas Davidson, a land agent, was the only one to answer questions on the Barony of Lower Glenarm, where most of Frances Anne's townlands were located. Probably because he had been replaced by John Lanktree, he did not mention Lord Londonderry as a landlord. In providing an overview of Lower Glenarm, Davidson's evidence was positive: 'Of late there were considerable improvements going on in agriculture', especially on larger farms but also on smaller farms.[52] McDonald of Glenarm Castle received praise for supporting a model farm at Larne national school. Improvement was associated with a new coastal road reducing isolation, 'with the ten-mile stage to Glenarm' already completed.[53] Unusual for evidence given to the Devon Commission, speaking about the labouring class Davidson was optimistic. The lime works at Glenarm, 'provided employment for a great number of hands...the coast road meant labour here is in greater demand than it was'.[54] Further evidence of the work available for labourers was that 'the con-acre system is a thing we do not know in this county'.[55] Conacre was where a landless labourer rented a small patch of land, for a short period of time, from a tenant farmer. The labourer grew potatoes for subsistence and in return worked for the farmer. However, the rent was nominal and usually no money changes hands. The labourer had no security. When the commission asked, 'Have you, speaking generally, over the district, a class of labourers contradistinguished from small farmers?' Davidson identified another class, the cottiers. Like labourers, they held a small plot of land in return for labour, but they had a certain, unwritten, security. He commented, 'these subtenants or cottiers usually do not pay their rent in cash but in labour'. As he dealt with tenants, he did not know how many subtenants or cottiers rented land from tenants. 'Yes, I found where a lease expired of old standing, I had a population to deal with very embarrassing ... persons with cot-takes and small gardens and little privileges about the place'.[56] Davidson had identified the most vulnerable; those likely to suffer most from a failure of the potato crop. Davidson also expressed concern for the very small tenant farmers, who might well have cottiers below them. In a rhetorical question he asked, 'When a bad year arises, the whole produce of the farm barely suffices for the maintenance of the family; how then, or from what other source is rent to be met or provided for?'[57] He would not have long to wait for the answer. Bad years were ahead, in Frances Anne's more isolated townlands on the slopes of the Antrim Plateau.

The departure of Thomas Davidson and the arrival of John Lanktree marked Frances Anne's involvement with, and concern for, Carnlough and her townlands in Antrim. Although, upon marriage, all her possessions became the property of her husband it was she who managed the Antrim Estate, and it was she Lanktree reported to. His initial 1844 report began with 'My Lord', thereafter his reports and letters began with 'Madam'.[58] Lanktree had originally worked for Lord Londonderry on the Mount Stewart Estate, under John Andrews. Like Andrews he believed in paternalism. Like Andrews, he thought the best future for the estate lay in encouraging tenants to improve their farms. Like Andrews, he became a tenant on the estate he managed.[59] Unlike Andrews, this would bring him into conflict with his landlord, the Third Marchioness of Londonderry. However, when appointed in 1843, their relationship began well. In January 1844, in response to descriptions of need in the townland of Stoney Hill, the Marchioness funded a soup kitchen and even provided the recipe.[60] That year, Lanktree provided his first report on the state of her County Antrim townlands. As with the Devon Commission's, Lanktree's report established the situation before the failure of the potato, but with the focus on Frances Anne's townlands. They were widely dispersed. Ballymacaldrack was situated to the west of Carnlough, well inland from the glens and included the 215m high Long Mountain. Although the estate was unimproved, this townland was the only one giving the agent cause for concern, regarding arrears. Tenants in Ballymacaldrack complained rents were too high and, surprisingly, Lanktree was inclined to agree. Drumcrow, also on higher ground to the west of the coast, was different. Here, Lanktree recorded considerable improvement and to encourage further improvements, he had given a grant of lime, equivalent to a 10 per cent rent abatement. To further encourage the estate's tenants, he reclaimed 40 acres of wasteland, to demonstrate what could be achieved.[61] In Ardclinis parish, rundale still existed. Davidson, when asked by the Devon Commission about rundale replied, 'No; we found a good deal of it some years ago ... we have got it done away'.[62] In rundale, people lived in a clachan, an agricultural village without a church, shops, or services. The land around the clachan was divided into strips, without fences, and each family had strips of good and poor ground which were rotated annually. It was regarded as a fair system that developed a strong sense of community. Landlords disliked rundale because only the land close to the village, the infield, was worked intensively. The outfield, regardless of fertility, was common, extensive pasture. For efficiency, agents, like Davidson, destroyed rundale and placed the individual farmer in the centre of the farm. This increased productivity. Not surprisingly, therefore, in his 1844 report Lanktree wrote that in Ardclinis parish, he was surveying with the aim of providing leases for individual farmers. A side effect of this proposed improvement was landless labourers. In the following years, the removal of two clachans near Garron Point on Frances Anne's orders, would cast another shadow on her legacy.[63] Following receipt of the 1844 report the Third Marchioness's interest in her Antrim townlands increased and the 1845 report made references to how she funded various projects, evidence of that interest.

Lanktree began his second report by thanking her ladyship for often asking about the condition of the tenantry and enabling him to 'respond to every case of urgent distress by a large donation of money', including funding the purchase of 100 pairs of blankets, which he had distributed.[64] Lanktree included a description and full assessment of the housing stock on the Antrim Estate; summarised in Table 1.

Table 1: Lanktree's Description of House Type on the Antrim Estate 1845

Type	Number	The Agent's Comments
1	12	Might be considered good - yet good is only to be taken in a comparative sense
2	103	Middling - capable of being made moderately decent with some small outlay and repairs
3	60	A shade better - not absolutely wretched - but better to rebuild than repair
4	83	Most wretched - filthy and smoky - badly thatched - poorly built, inhabited by families and stock - need to be tumbled
Total	258	

Source: Lanktree's Antrim Estate Report

Lanktree's assessment was of a very poor housing stock. Only two farmhouses out of the 258 had a sitting room or parlour. Frances Anne reacted immediately. She provided £100 of assistance for those, 'who would improve their dwelling by replacing thatch with slate ...and build comfortable pig houses', which were almost unknown on the estate. Lanktree wrote that this 'announcement was received with pleasure and the work of improvement begun'.[65] However, like Davidson before him, Lanktree and the Third Marchioness had very little knowledge of the cottiers, who held a position below the tenants. Their cabins were not included in his survey. Nor would they be eligible for house improvement assistance.

Lanktree was pleased to report that 27 of the most wretched cabins had been thrown down and 20 new houses were substantially built and roofed with slates. Nineteen pig houses had been built with paved yards. Other assisted improvements included drainage and fencing. A clachan at Garron Point was removed and 'replaced by six new houses of excellent craftmanship'.[66] Lanktree praised the Third Marchioness. Her Ladyship's paternalism was promoting permanent improvement 'and civilisation of the tenantry'. Moreover, 'it appears that one year of your ladyship's beneficent encouragement has swept away one fifth of the domestic misery on the estate'. The total cost of the above was listed at £1,137–0–0.[67] Her Ladyship's action was motivating tenants and improving lives; but there were those who were displaced or, as a class, ignored.

One group not ignored were the tenants in Ballymacaldrack, identified in the previous report as complaining. The Londonderrys responded immediately and reduced rents. Something the Marquess was loath to do on his Mount Stewart estate, suggesting the decision may have been his wife's. Lanktree noted, 'a new spirit was diffused throughout the whole district'.[68] From Frances Anne's perspective paternalism was working, improvement was happening, and as shown in Table 2, between 1842 and 1844, arrears were falling, rents were rising.

Table 2: Arrears And Rent 1842-1844

Year	Arrears	Rent
1842	£914-13-5	£2,610-13-0
1843	£547-19-9	£2,687-6-0
1844	£312-6-7	£2,763-4-11

Source: Lanktree's Antrim Estate Report

The Third Marchioness was proving to be an involved, improving landlord. Alas, the tenor of the report changed with mention of the arrival of the potato blight: 'a strange disease hitherto unknown to agriculturalists ... has been prevalent throughout the whole estate'. Lanktree was mystified but he was in no doubt where the impact would be felt most—among 'the poor tenantry on the mountain'. They would be subjected to 'great privations'.[69]

In October 1845, Frances Anne funded another soup kitchen but, perhaps due to the remote location of widely distributed townlands, making travel a hardship, 'the tenants not being disposed to avail themselves'. It was discontinued after a seven to eight weeks' trial. Perhaps the tenants were too ill to travel: 'fever is rather on the increase in the district and very fatal considering the number of cases'.[70] Frances Anne read Lanktree's letters and reports very carefully, with 'hand-written annotations' proving 'her control of the minutia of estate management'.[71] She was no longer a remote disinterested traveller in foreign lands. In 1846, following the second failure of the potato, and against Lanktree's advice, Lord and Lady Londonderry, decided to travel into their Antrim townlands. In remote Ballymacaldrack, they received an address from their tenants. It was a mixture of standard praise, thinly disguised blame, and pleading. After praising Lord Londonderry's military courage, the address continued: 'We were long neglected in this remote region—our former landlords little dreamed of cherishing their lowly tenants. We were little assisted even by their agents except for purposes of oppression'.[72] Strong words, especially since the distant Londonderrys had been their landlord for the previous 13 years. However, the tone changed: '... a new era has dawned upon us. Your Lordship's and Ladyship's wishes are carried into effect by an agent who has our real interest at heart and under his active administration we have been stimulated to greater exertions'. Frances Anne must have noted that the praise was directed more at the agent than the landlord. Lanktree was their hero. There followed a description of the tenants' trauma: 'Our potato crop—the sole sustenance of ourselves and our children has been totally blighted ... and how we shall pass through the coming season or make up our rents is known only to God'. The address, skilfully fashioned within the terms of a paternal relationship, finished with a plea: 'but we know that we are cared for by him (Divine Providence) and by you both—and we submit ourselves to your careful consideration'.[73]

In his report to Frances Anne, recalling the event, Lanktree mentioned the hearty welcome and blazing bonfires, and pointed out that the tenants' address was 'their own genuine production'. He included his lordship's 'admirable reply' which praised her ladyship's concern and kindness. In his address, Londonderry reminded the tenants that those dependent upon the potato, 'which had wholly failed', had been given full rent relief. Since he refused to reduce rents in Down, believing 'he set his rent for good and bad seasons', credit for this full relief should probably go to Frances Anne.[74] The paternal Lord Londonderry ended by telling his tenants that Providence had placed them under his care and those who 'are really unable to support their families and themselves' would be helped by the agent. Frances Anne continued to set relief work for John Lanktree, ask questions, and follow up on progress. On 8 March 1847, Lanktree replied, 'I received your Ladyship's favour this afternoon but could not sooner than this day have written satisfactorily on almost any of the points required by your Ladyship'.[75] In this letter he wrote that he had set up the Glencloy Relief Committee and made the Rev. Waddle the Treasurer

To ascertain need, Mrs Waddle and Lanktree's daughter visited 'almost every cabin in the district'. In over nine townlands they identified 210 people who were destitute. Typical of those in need was William Glynn, a labourer, his wife, and five children: 'The children, wasted by disease and famine, sat close to the sods which formed the back of the fire. They looked like living skeletons. They had but one bed for the whole family. Destitute'.[76] It was the townlands on the mountain sides that suffered most. Lanktree added his own evidence of misery. Hugh Gillan died from starvation in Ballymacaldrack. When the agent last visited his small farm, the family was in in great poverty. The six children, all girls, had hardly any clothes.[77] The ladies on the committee trained and engaged females in 30 families in knitting, and 50 tenants received weekly assistance. Corn was distributed to those who had consumed their grain. Carrot and parsnip seeds were distributed to all. Because of her ladyship's efforts the Glencloy Committee was able to address every case of distress. However, in some isolated townlands, small tenant farmers and cottiers were beyond the reach of the Glencloy Committee.

Lanktree was sorry to report that he 'was not able to keep up the finances of the estate this year—the receipts being only £2,100', meaning it was down a quarter.[78] When presenting news of the receipts, Lanktree referred to Francis Anne as a 'distinguished friend of Ireland' and that is how the Third Marchioness of Londonderry appeared in 1847 when she and the Third Marquess hosted a Grand Military Bazaar in Regent's Park Barracks for the distressed Irish. Queen Victoria attended. Frances Anne's aristocratic status and her interaction with the distressed Irish landscape were to interlock above Garron Point. Lanktree's 1848 report to the Third Marchioness mentioned two building projects at Garron Point. It began with drawings of a new national school erected 'A. D. 1848', erected at a cost of £120. The report mentioned an annual grant from her ladyship for the education of young girls. Also, on 20 October 1848, there was an application from the Marchioness of Londonderry to the Commissioners of Education in Dublin for 'two school rooms' in Carnlough and 'a model farm' at 'the very considerable cost' of 'about £100 to £150'.[79] For such initiatives Frances Anne, the 'cuffed child', is today remembered in the Lady Londonderry Room in the Londonderry Arms.

For Lanktree, the second building project above Garron Point was the great event of the year. It was, 'the commencement of Garron Tower of which your Ladyship laid the foundation stone on the 24th Day of February'.[80] The Marchioness was building a palatial summer house, on a landscape suffering from famine. However, Lanktree's 1848 report also mentioned Frances Anne's concern for her tenants and improvements evident in the townlands. The Clothing Society addressed an existential need, he and members of the Relief Committee identified in visits to wretched cabins. In his report, he interpreted the fact that clothing would no longer be given out gratuitously, but sold at two-thirds of the original cost, as evidence of an improving situation.[81] Drainage work and reclaiming the land was proceeding, encouraged by free grants of lime from the new kiln in Carnlough. Some improving tenants were applying for extended leases. He advised they receive longer leases as 'a shorter lease ... would not be satisfactory to tenants who have been involved in building and agricultural improvements'.[82] However, the above optimism, like the paternalism from which it grew, had social and geographic parameters. Those who could not afford to buy clothing or leases continued to suffer. They suffered in remote areas, like Ballymacaldrack, from where people emigrated. Some emigrants from Ballymacaldrack were on the unfortunate *Exmouth*, which 'driven by a storm on the rocky coast of one of the Scottish Isles, went to the bottom and left not one passenger of hundreds to tell the tale'.[83]

Undoubtedly, Lanktree worked hard to relieve distress, but he also welcomed winnowing by the famine. His first responsibility was the prosperity of the estate: 'Generally speaking these thinnings were for good—they enlarged some farms in the hands of better labourers than the emigrants had been—and if many more should go away—it will all be better for the estate'. All the better because, 'without the potato crop it is quite impossible for small farmers to live and pay rent especially, on poor soils'.[84] Those contributing directly to the estate could expect support, education, and rewards, like free lime and long leases. Those not contributing would receive limited charity and a wish they be gone. Limited charity was the preferred option because paternalists, like the Londonderrys, 'believed the bible when it said the poor shall never cease out of the land…The cutting edge of destitution could be blunted by charity but not removed'.[85]

At the laying of the foundation stone for Garron Tower, Lord Londonderry said it was evidence of Lady Londonderry's desire to have time with her tenantry, and to 'spend among them part of the income she derived from their industrious labour'.[86] He ended by describing his wife as 'the lady of the soil', presumably in recognition of her deep McDonald family roots and dynastic authority. Benjamin Disraeli, in letters to Frances Anne, referring to the Tower of Garron described Frances Anne as a 'feudal princess' and a 'true Lady Chatelaine'.[87] For the Third Marchioness, her wealth, her high place in a God-given, paternalistic hierarchy, bestowed responsibilities. Just as children 'are dependent upon their, parents so also are labourers, servants, tenant farmers, curates dependent upon those of a higher rank'.[88] Those tenants who had worked on the building would receive rent relief. When completed, Garron Tower would create jobs and a need for services, especially for females, something Lanktree approved of and referred to.[89] He assured the Marchioness that those occupying the land where she was building would not 'make any obstacle to the work'. The son of one of the tenant farmers already worked for her at Seaham and both McAlister and Mulvenna would be happy to sell their leases, which they could do under tenant right.[90]

In the foreword to *Garron Tower* by Paul Magill, Cahal Dallat viewed this response simply as acquiescence on the tenants' part and a selfish exercise of feudal power on hers. 'To further please her, the agent made light of the distress of poor farmers who had been displaced in order that the project could go ahead'.[91] Magill pointed out that the poor farmers included 102 people in two clachans. Magill also noted how, by 1850, Lanktree's roles as tenant and agent meant that he too would leave the estate. As a tenant he fell into arrears with his rent and made an appeal for a 'reduction in rent on the estate'. Lady Londonderry's response was unsympathetic. She wrote, 'Lanktree's principle seems to be that tenants should have the land as a free gift and pay no rent'.[92] In replying, the agent stepped outside their paternalist relationship: 'The advice that I have given would be supported by everyone who knows the actual state of the country'.[93] Accusing Frances Anne of ignorance was too much and, in 1850, as the Famine ended in parts of the country, Lanktree was dismissed. Casement, however, has suggested that 'embezzlement of almost one thousand pounds' was the reason the Third Marchioness dismissed her land agent.[94]

Lanktree was replaced by Richard Wilson, who in his 1856 report complained, as Lanktree had done before him, about small farm size, arrears and how difficult it was to introduce agriculture reforms.[95] Wilson referred to some rural improvement, but effective change, both urban and industrial, was focused on Carnlough. In the developing town there were new houses for labourers, bathing lodges for the better off, the Londonderry Arms Hotel, a reading room, a savings bank, a school, an agricultural college, a lime kiln, a railway to the limestone quarries and a stone-built harbour,[96] which like Seaham before it would not only bring prosperity and jobs but would also be 'a harbour of refuge'.[97] This was emphasised at the official opening of Carnlough harbour as it had been at the laying of the foundation stone at Seaham, where Lord Londonderry proclaimed to have, 'no selfish motive'.[98] Mixing altruism with personal gain was ingrained in paternalism. In a speech on Thursday, 20 September 1856, in the new town hall, at a dinner given for 300 tenants, the Third Marchioness, now a dowager, declared 'poverty has disappeared'.[99] In visiting tenants, 'in general', she found 'industrious people and contented spirits'.[100] However, whilst praising social and industrial development she stated, 'I wish I could speak as strongly as to the advance of agriculture ... much, very much is still to be done'.[101] This, despite her giving prizes to those who had adopted better farming practices. In the speech she declared her fondest wish, almost a feudal wish, certainly a paternalistic wish, was 'to live in the hearts of my tenantry'.[102]

Table 3, comparing the population in Frances Anne's townlands between 1841 and 1851, before most of her industrial development, suggests whether she lived in the hearts of her tenantry or not she deserved gratitude. Between 1841 and 1851, the population of the estate showed a drop of 3 per cent, compared to a 20 per cent average for Ireland.[103] Numerically, at 56 people, Ballymacaldrack, visited by the Londonderrys in 1846, and whose unfortunate emigrants were noted by Lanktree, showed the largest decline; but even here, at 17 per cent, it is below the national average. Twelve of the townlands, recorded in Lanktree's reports, showed an increase in population. Whilst his reports recorded misery, emigration and even death by starvation, the Antrim Estate of the Third Marchioness of Londonderry did not suffer as badly as Ireland suffered.

That the Marchioness supported her husband's opposition to the 1832 Reform Act and, especially, the 1842 Mines and Collieries Act, leaves her on the wrong side of history. She could not 'understand how her workers could be so misguided against their paternal rule in such a detestable organisation as a trade union'.[104] Yet, at the same time, her collieries provided 'free medical treatment at the local infirmary and practically free education for their children at the local schools'. She organised the free distribution of warm clothing for children, wives, and old people.[105] A concern for the distressed was also evident during the Famine. It could be argued that Frances

Table 3: Third Marchioness of Londonderry Antrim Estate Population

Townlands	1841			1851				
Barony of Lower Glenarm	M	F	Total	M	F	Total	Pop. Change (Number)	Pop. Change (%)
Aghalum	32	29	61	29	29	58	-3	-4.9
Bellair	62	42	107	47	35	82	-25	-23.4
Ballyvaddy	114	99	213	105	110	215	2	0.9
Carnlough	145	158	303	155	173	328	25	8.3
Druninagh	9	13	22	18	12	30	8	36.4
Doonan	49	45	94	57	51	108	14	14.9
Drumcrow	81	78	159	86	80	166	7	4.4
Drumnacole	19	17	36	17	13	30	-6	-16.7
Galboly U	28	30	58	29	27	56	-2	-3.4
Galboly L	14	11	25	11	15	26	1	4.0
Gartford	11	11	22	8	9	17	-5	-22.7
Gortcarney	16	14	30	19	16	35	5	16.7
Gortin	13	10	23	14	15	29	6	26.1
Mullaghconnelly	12	13	25	10	13	23	-2	-8.0
Stoney Hill	15	14	29	3	3	6	-23	-79.3
Unshinagh n	27	36	63	17	30	47	-16	-25.4
Unshinagh S	12	9	21	13	8	21	0	0.0
Barony of Upper Glenarm	M	F	Total	M	F	Total		
Capanagh U	6	4	10	5	6	11	1	10.0
Barony of Kilconway	M	F	Total	M	F	Total		
Ballymacaldrack	156	173	329	132	141	273	-56	-17.0
Ballyreagh	125	167	292	137	161	298	6	2.1
Carrowcowan	48	47	95	55	60	115	20	21.1
Drumavaddy	22	19	41	25	17	42	1	2.4
Drumnaglea	51	68	119	52	67	119	0	0.0
Legnagrane	53	60	113	37	45	82	-31	-27.4
Torcrum	N/A							
Total			2290			2217	Gross loss 73	Gross % loss 3%

(Source –1851 Census of Ireland)

Anne showed up nine years late, that in Davidson's time, as hinted at by the Ballymacaldrack tenants, she was an absentee landlord with a disinterested agent. Her return, however, coincided with the start of the Famine and she showed the same concern for her tenants in Antrim as she did for her pitmen in Durham.

It has been pointed out that the building of Garron Tower at a cost of over £2,000, and the lavish entertainment that followed, vastly exceeded the few hundred pounds spent on a school.[106] Removing rundale on the site created landless labourers. However, Frances Anne's investment in housing, education, social amenities, and industry, during and immediately after the Famine, brought prosperity, including jobs for the displaced. Rundale would have been removed regardless of building Garron Tower. Anne Casement makes the argument that Lord Londonderry, and by marital extension Lady Londonderry, have been misjudged by popular opinion; that given his moral philosophy and 'in the light of his financial position' at the time—servicing debt, being responsible for relatives, investing in his mines, port and industries, providing employment for hundreds from clergymen to pitmen—his actions deserve 'a more accurate and fair and informed judgement'.[107] Hector MacDonnell, a descendant of Francis Anne, an artist and family historian, suggested that Frances Anne's concern went well beyond that of her husband.[108] Given that the Newtownards Poor Law Union was down 6 per cent in population and Frances Anne's townlands were down 3 per cent, between 1841 and 1851, the census figures offer support to Hector's loyalty.[109]

In widowhood, Frances Anne remained an entrepreneurial paternalist, but not a remote one. Disraeli described her surrounded by her collieries, blast furnaces, railways and 'unceasing telegraph',[110] and in Antrim, where Edith wrote of Frances Anne making, 'a point of visiting the most remote farms on the estate',[111] she liked to be perceived as the head of a great family, caring for her children.[112] On the Antrim Coast Road the Third Marchioness of Londonderry had a limestone famine stone inscribed with a tribute to 'England's generosity in the year 1846–1847'. It was, even then, insensitive. It was defaced in the 1920s.[113] The wording was of her class and of her ethnicity reflecting a narrow, hierarchal, paternalist view of Irish society; but generosity has no class, no religion. Frances Anne, who from childhood was concerned about children's welfare, who moved to relieve destitution in the coalfields of Durham, who moved to meet immediate needs in the cabins of Antrim, who used her business acumen to improve the lives of her tenants on her Antrim Estate is defined by the Census population figure of a three per cent loss between 1841 and 1851 as a famine hero.

NOTES

1. Diane Urquhart, *The Ladies of Londonderry: Women and Political Patronage* (London: Bloomsbury Academic, 2007), p. 2.
2. Ibid., p. 1.
3. Edith, Marchioness of Londonderry, *Frances Anne: The Life and Times of Frances Anne the Marchioness of Londonderry and her husband Charles, Third Marquess of Londonderry* (London: Macmillan & Co. Ltd., 1958), p. vii.
4. Ibid.
5. Angela Day and Patrick McWilliams (eds), *Ordnance Survey Memoirs, vol 13: County Antrim IV, 1830–38* (Belfast: Institute of Irish Studies, 1991), p. 7.
6. John Lanktree, *Antrim Estate Second Report for the Year 1845* (Public Record Office of Northern Ireland—hereafter, PRONI—D2977/6/3/A). As Lady Londonderry's agent, in this report, he enumerates with rents and arrears all the townlands he is responsible for.
7. Irish and Local Studies Library, Armagh. Census of Ireland 1851, Baronies of Lower Glenarm, Upper Glenarm, and Kilconway, pp 383–384.
8. Third Marchioness of Londonderry, the Antrim Estate (PRONI D/2977/6/3), Charlotte, Francis Anne's mother's sister, inherited most of the Antrim estate and the title, Countess of Antrim.
9. Married Women's Property Act 1882. www.legislation.gov.uk/ukpga/1882/75/pdfs/ukpga_18820075_en.pdf
10. Typed copy of Francis Anne's Autobiography, dated 27 December 1848 (PRONI, D 3084/C/A/7), p. 1.
11. Ibid., p. 2.
12. Ibid., p. 3.
13. Ibid.
14. Ibid., p. 4.
15. Ibid.
16. Ibid., p. 5.
17. Ibid., p. 4.
18. Ibid.
19. Ibid., p. 6.
20. Ibid.
21. Londonderry, *Frances Anne*, p. 31.
22. Autobiography, p. 32.
23. Londonderry, *Frances Anne*, p. 32.
24. Ibid.
25. Ibid., p. 33.
26. Autobiography, p. 19.
27. Castlereagh to Lord Londonderry, 11 April 1818 (PRONI D/3030/p/157/1).
28. Urquhart, *Ladies of Londonderry*, p. 16.
29. Autobiography, p. 39.

30. Urquhart, *Ladies of Londonderry*, p. 19.
31. Frances Anne to her mother, 26 December 1822 (D/3084/C/A/7).
32. Ibid.
33. Sir Archibald Alison quoted in Londonderry, *Frances Anne*, p. 207.
34. Ibid., p. vii.
35. Anastasia Crosswhite, 'Women and Land: Aristocratic Ownership of Property in Early Modern England', *New York University Law Review* 77 (2002), p. 1125.
36. Keith Wilson (1987), 'Political radicalism in the North East of England, 1830–1860': Issues in historical sociology, Durham University. Available at Durham E-Theses Online: http://etheses.dur.ac.uk/1680/
37. Ibid.
38. Urquhart, *Ladies of Londonderry*, p. 39.
39. United Kingdom Parliament, Coalmines. www.parliament.uk/about/living-heritage/transformingsociety/livinglearning/19thcentury/overview/coalmines/#:~:text=The%20Mines%20and%20Collieries%20Bill,frequency%20of%20accidents%20in%20mines
40. Ibid.
41. Londonderry, *Frances Anne*, p. 231.
42. Ibid.
43. Ibid., p. 70.
44. Ibid., p. 71.
45. Autobiography, p. 53.
46. Ibid.
47. Londonderry, *Frances Anne*, p. 229.
48. Ibid., p. 228.
49. House of Commons, *Her Majesty's Commissioners of Enquiry into the state of the Law and Practice in respect of the Occupation of the Land Ireland* (Devon Commission), (Dublin: H.M. Stationery Office, 1845), p. 592.
50. Angela Antrim, *The Antrim McDonalds* (Belfast: Ulster Television, 1978), p. 50.
51. Ibid.
52. Devon Commission, p. 594.
53. Ibid.
54. Ibid.
55. Ibid., p. 597.
56. Ibid., p. 593.
57. Ibid., p. 596.
58. Lanktree's 1844 Report was the first one and was addressed to Lord Londonderry.
59. Anne Casement, *The Management of the Londonderry Estates during the Great Famine* (Belfast: Ulster Historical Foundation, 2005), p. 32.
60. Jimmy Irvine, 'Lady Frances Anne Vane's County Antrim Estate', *The Glynns* 3 (1975). https://antrimhistory.net/lady-frances-anne-vanes-county-antrim-estate-by-jimmy-irvine/
61. Lanktree to Lord Londonderry, Report 1844 (PRONI D/2977/6/3).
62. Devon Commission, p. 593.

63. Felix McKillop, *Glencloy; Local History including Carnlough* (Glenarm: Local History, 1996), p. 63.
64. Lanktree to Lady Londonderry (PRONI D/2977/6/3/A), p. 1.
65. Ibid., p. 2.
66. Ibid.
67. Ibid.
68. Ibid., p. 12.
69. Ibid.
70. Lanktree to Lady Londonderry (PRONI D/2977/5/1/8/1–10).
71. Urquhart, *Ladies of Londonderry*, p. 49.
72. Antrim Estate Statistical Report for the Year 1847 (PRONI D/2977/6/4B).
73. Ibid.
74. Casement, *Londonderry Estates,* p. 30.
75. Lanktree to Lady Londonderry (PRONI D/2977/5/1/8/8/10).
76. Notes from Rev. Waddle to Glencloy Relief Committee (PRONI D/2977/5/1/8/4/3).
77. Lanktree to Lady Londonderry (PRONI D/2977/5/1/8/8/21–30).
78. Antrim Estate Statistical Report for the Year 1848 (PRONI D/2977/6/4C).
79. Lanktree to Commissioners of Education, Dublin (PRONI ED3 P71).
80. Antrim Estate, 1848.
81. Ibid.
82. Ibid.
83. Ibid.
84. Ibid.
85. David Roberts, *Paternalism in Early Victorian England* (New Brunswick: Routledge 1979), p. 5.
86. Paul Magill, *Garron Tower, County Antrim* (Belfast: Magill, 1990), p. 2.
87. Edith, Marchioness of Londonderry, *Letters from Benjamin Disraeli to Francis Anne Marchioness of Londonderry* (London: Macmillan & Co., 1938).
88. David Roberts, *Paternalism*, p. 3.
89. Lanktree to Lady Londonderry (PRONI D/2977/5/1/8/11/21).
90. Lanktree to Lady Londonderry (PRONI D/2977/5/1/8/8/41–46). Tenant Right allowed the departing tenant to sell his lease. The price would reflect any improvements the tenant had made and the level of competition for land. Lord Londonderry allowed Tenant Right on all his Irish estates but in his evidence to the Devon Commission Davidson disapproved, because when an incoming tenant paid too much, he had little money to further improve the farm, or pay his rent.
91. Magill, *Garron Tower*, p. 5.
92. Ibid., p. 37.
93. Ibid.
94. Casement, *Londonderry Estates,* p. 40.
95. Richard Wilson to Lady Londonderry (PRONI D/2977/9A–B).
96. Magill, *Garron Tower*, pp 54–59.
97. Londonderry, *Frances Anne*, p. 154; *Belfast News-Letter*, 25 August 1855.

98. Londonderry, *Frances Anne*, p. 156.
99. *Belfast News-Letter*, 20 September 1856.
100. Ibid.
101. Ibid.
102. Ibid.
103. Census of Ireland, 1851.
104. Londonderry, *Frances Anne,* p. 232.
105. Ibid.
106. Casement, *Londonderry Estates,* p. 41.
107. Ibid., p. 56.
108. Hector McDonnell, Personal communication.
109. The Mount Stewart Estate covered most of north County Down including the Newtownards Poor Law Union. North Down consisted of good soils and communications. The Antrim Estate was mainly isolated and mountainous.
110. Londonderry, *Frances Anne,* p. 268.
111. Ibid., p. 266.
112. Ibid., p. 280.
113. Christine Kinealy, *Charity and the Great Hunger. The Kindness of Strangers* (London: Bloomsbury, 2013), pp 281–282; *Belfast News-Letter*, 30 October 1928.

CHAPTER SEVEN

FREDERICK HAMILTON-TEMPLE-BLACKWOOD (1826–1902)

Marquess of Dufferin and Ava

Eamonn McKee

> *In all probability they are as selfish, as interested, and as unscrupulous as any other collection of human beings possessing the same amount of education and intelligence.*
>
> Dufferin on Irish landlords.[1]

It was said of Lord Dufferin that he was caught between his conscience and his circumstance.[2] This duality formed his life's thread: humanitarian and landlord, proud Irishman and self-professed Englishman, advocate for home rule in the Empire but silent on Irish Home Rule, man of the world nostalgic for the past, egalitarian elitist, a chivalrous admirer of women who was dominated by his mother.

For the first half of his adult life, Dufferin focused on reform in Ireland, for the second on the promotion of Empire. Dufferin thereby escaped his inner conflict and came to epitomize the age of Victorian imperialism. Yet his career ultimately anticipated not the dawn of the future, but the twilight of the landed aristocracy, Victorian Britain, the Empire, and the nineteenth century world order he had helped to stabilise and sustain. Dufferin's presentiments about the new age were accurate, yet they could not save him from grievous personal loss and public scandal when he retired to the decorous romanticism of his estate at Clandeboye in County Down.

Dufferin's public life began with his first attempt to reconcile his conscience to his new circumstances. A student at Oxford on the cusp of becoming a leading Irish landlord, he determined to verify reports of famine in Ireland, exaggerated according to the London *Times.* With his friend George Boyle, he dashed to Dublin in February

1847. They were advised to go to Skibbereen, already infamous for its suffering.[3] They reached Athy and were reassured by the sense of organisation and the soup kitchen as they walked around its districts: 'There were misery and hunger it is true, some deaths too had occurred, but still the village seemed brisk and lively, more distressed than famished'.[4] On the road to Cork, they noted public works with gaunt, sickly men 'languidly hammering stones by the way-side'. More unnervingly, 'at every stage, the coach was surrounded by crowds of wretched creatures begging for something to eat, wan little faces thrusting themselves in at the window, praying "the kind gentleman just for one ha'penny to buy a penn'orth of bread"'.[5] With almost a theatrical intervention, they met a priest on the Bantry Mail who affirmed that despite the deprivation, the poor had been law-abiding and the relief efforts of the government appreciated. Still, the conditions deteriorated as they travelled southwards, with fields unattended, wretched horses abounding, and ominously new deal coffins appearing. At Clonakilty, a government ship was docked with provisions.[6] It was the last sign of hope as they approached the bleak mountain pass to Skibbereen: 'After this the scenery became even still more wild and desolate, the road wound through barren bleak mountains, no vestiges of labour or cultivation, while occasionally pools of stagnant bog water stretched out on either side the way'. Entry to the village through a cluster of deal coffins revealed an eerily listless crowd of mainly women and children, 'the most wretched beings one had ever beheld.' Pushing through the crowd to get to their inn and deposit their luggage, 'nothing seemed doing, there was no stir and bustle of business, and the shop-keepers from lack of customers stood idle at their doors'.[7]

The students' Stygian guide to the horrors of Skibbereen was a doleful Rev. Townsend, his wife stitching shrouds from a pile of linen on the floor. Their two maids had died of typhus. Local deaths of over 100 had outpaced available coffins and Christian burials. The workhouse was full, in cottages 'dead bodies had laid putrifying [sic] in the midst of the sick remnant of their families, none strong enough to remove them, until rats and decay made it difficult to recognise that they had been human beings'.[8] In a hovel stripped of furniture, the wife of a respectable tradesman only two months previously crouched over a small peat fire, suffering from diarrhoea, family members lying obscured in the dark recesses. Daily, Dufferin learned, carts circulated with calls of 'bring out your dead' and bodies were unceremoniously buried in shallow pits beneath the ruins of an abbey.[9] In one corner of the graveyard, an acre of uneven and freshly-turned earth barely concealed the coffins and corpses of the newly dead piled up, their ends protruding:

> by these graves, no service had been performed, no friends had stood, no priest had spoken words of hope, and of future consolation in a glorious eternity! The bodies had been daily thrown in, many without a coffin, one over another, the uppermost only hidden from the light of day by a bare three inches of earth, the survivors not even knowing the spot where those most dear to them lay sleeping.[10]

The gravediggers reported that they had buried ten the previous day and six more were expected that evening. At one removal from a cottage where the sick family were unable to assist, the barely-clad remains of one women was unceremoniously removed by the querulous gravediggers, 'the livid lifeless arms as they hung down swinging and knocking against the ground'.[11]

Over dinner at the inn, the conversation with three gentlemen was focused on the spread of typhus. Later that evening, horror piled on horror as the indefatigable Dr Donovan[12] confirmed the Reverend's reports and illustrated the state of Skibbereen thus:

> At some distance from Skibbereen there was a cottage, in which lay a man and his wife both sick of the fever; the woman died, and the husband had just sufficient strength to crawl out and bury the body in his garden. During the night he distinctly heard dogs scratching and howling over what he but too well knew was the lately made grave; he sent out his little girl to drive them away, but they only bit at her, and frightened her back into the cottage. The following day one of the neighbours brought back the head of the unfortunate woman, saying, 'that his dog had brought it home!'[13]

Next morning 'we determined to hurry on by any conveyance which could be procured, as we had seen quite enough to satisfy us, and a further stay would have been both painful and unnecessary'. Word soon spread that the young gentlemen had sent for an immense basket-full of loaves. Flinging bread to 'the screaming, the swaying to and fro of the human mass', they fled on a jaunting cart over sun-hardened ruts. We wondered, Dufferin wrote, 'what legislation and influences could soonest make Ireland happy and cheerful, and its poor people industrious and independent'.[14] After eight days, they were back in Oxford.

Rev. Townsend, impressed by his young visitors, sent a long letter to the *Cork Constitution* outlining the horrors they had witnessed while in Skibbereen. He explained that they had intended to stay for an extra day, and accompany Dr Donovan on his rounds, but they had left early, Dufferin explaining he 'could look on no more'. Before departing, he presented the minister with 'a large sum' of £50, collected in Oxford, together with a personal donation of £10.[15] Back in Oxford, Dufferin not only determined to write an account of his experiences in the south of Ireland, but to continue to raise donations. Only weeks later, Townsend reported receiving further sums of money, including £683 from Dufferin, leading him to state, with unjustified optimism, that if similar amounts continued to be sent to him, 'we shall be able to feed the people and keep them alive'.[16] Sadly, this would not be the case. By the end of 1847 most donations had dried up, while in May 1850, Townsend contracted 'famine fever' when visiting the local workhouse. He died days later.[17]

In Oxford, Dufferin continued fundraising and personally donated £1,000. His relatives were chagrined at such activities that his mother deemed a first act of independence, though 'quixotic'.[18] Dufferin's donation matched Queen Victoria's first donation, and that of the Sultan of Turkey. Victoria's appeal of January 1847 had encouraged charitable donations of £50,000 by mid-March, notes Christine Kinealy in her ground-breaking work, *Charity and the Great Hunger in Ireland. The kindness of strangers*. At the behest of the Prime Minister Lord John Russell, this was followed by the Queen's announcement of a Fast Day on 24 March to appeal for divine assistance, although the Queen herself was sceptical about the rationale and implication ('almost blasphemous'). The effort raised another £172,000.[19] Public Works were shut down at the same time, with dire consequences for those who had relied on this employment, prompting panic and exodus when the potato crop failed again, this time island-wide. As Kinealy points out, interventions by the British Relief Association, the Quakers and the churches, funded by charitable donations, were a vital supplement for a cumbersome and often failing governmental response.[20] International fund-raising ranged from New York to Calcutta, from the elites to prisoners and Indigenous Peoples in the United States and Canada, who themselves were in highly straitened circumstances.[21] In Britain, the compassionate response had to overcome the determined opposition of the *Times* and the *Economist* that argued that it was unnecessary and unwise to offer relief.[22] Dufferin's eye-witness affirmation of the horrors afoot in Ireland was all the more vital at a time when charitable donations directly saved lives. Moreover, in his rapidly published account, Dufferin contradicted the *Times* and admonished the government:

> Surely no sacrifice would be too great by which they could be alleviated. If ever a prudential foresight for future competence is to be sacrificed to the urgent necessities of our fellow-creatures, this is the occasion. Depend upon it, none will hereafter suffer from a present simple and trustful generosity.[23]

How differently an Irish parliament might have responded was indicated at a representative meeting of Irish peers and MPs at the Rotunda in Dublin in 1847. They were 'deeply critical of the policies of the British government', called for food to be sold under cost, and condemned the export of massive amounts of food. As with the demands of corporations in Dublin, Belfast, Cork, and Derry to close the ports, their views were ignored.[24] Even prior to the Famine, as Kinealy points out, the approach to Ireland's poor was substantially different compared to the England's poor: all relief was to be indoor in deliberately appalling conditions in workhouses, there was no legal right to relief, and relief was only available to the 'destitute' poor.[25] Moreover, Britain denied to the Irish poor the legal entitlement to aid prevailing in England, closed public works before soup kitchens were operational and on which some three million people—40 per cent of the population—would come to depend,[26] and declared the Famine over in August 1847, ending most of the vital international fundraising. The Poor Law Extension Act thrust the cost of providing for both the destitute and the sick on the Irish taxpayer, and denied relief to any who occupied more than a quarter acre of land. That this incentivised landlords to evict tenants or be bankrupted, and tenants to choose between starvation and their small holding, was an intended outcome to socially engineer a new middle class of small, landed proprietors.[27]

Neither the Famine, nor Dufferin's role in providing relief, ended in 1847. Dufferin did not complete a degree at Oxford University, but left after two year's study. Increasingly, he turned his attention to being an 'improving landlord' on his County Down estate, and to forging a diplomatic career in London. His on-going concern for victims of the Famine was again evident in 1849, when most charitable bodies had ended their involvement through a lack of funds. In June, he donated £100 to the General Central Relief Committee in Dublin.[28] A few weeks later, he sent a further £400 to the committee to provide relief in the south and west. They responded, 'This princely gift is doubly valuable coming as it does at a time when it is peculiarly needed. We are just now in a lull—in a lull of charity, but not a lull of death'. They added:

> By this act Lord Dufferin has raised himself above the level of rank to the elevated dignity of humanity. We trust he will become the leader of his class, and the leader of Ulster, in this glorious work of saving life on which he has so nobly entered.[29]

The young Lord Dufferin had proved to be a true friend to the Irish poor during the Famine. He was now about to commence a new phase of his life that would place him at the heart of the imperial project and take him far from his beloved Clandeboye Estate.

Awakenings

After his father's untimely death in 1841,[30] Dufferin came into his majority six years later in June 1847, with an estate of 18,000 acres outside Belfast and title of 5th Baron of Dufferin and Clandeboye.[31] Second only to Clandeboye in Dufferin's heart, Oxford University, along with Eton, had been a carefree time with friendships formed that would sustain his career. Now a landlord, Dufferin believed his immense responsibilities were both managerial and moral. To his perplexed mother Helen, he declared 'the improvement of Ireland [is] the one great purpose and interest in my life'. He trudged to visit his 6,819 tenants. Appalled at their conditions with cottages damp green outside and smoked brown inside, Dufferin's grim prognosis was confirmed by a tour of the west of Ireland. Ireland was overpopulated and underdeveloped.[32] Improving Ireland would be daunting as panic-stricken famine refugees flooded out of the country. In this infamous year, records show 106,812 men, women and children, mostly Catholic, departed for Canada on crudely adapted lumber ships. On average 26 passengers died on each voyage, 6116 on the passage, and following quarantine and travel within Canada, there were over 17,000 recorded deaths.[33] The bulk of the Irish exodus switched to the United States the following year and it continued unabated for generations. Combined with the one million dead from starvation and disease, this eventually cut Ireland's population by half.

As Dufferin wondered what best to do, Roscommon landlord, Major Denis Mahon, approved a scheme of sponsored emigration from his newly inherited and heavily indebted estate at Strokestown.[34] His efforts to ensure the safe passage of 1,490 tenants and their dependents to Canada were frustrated: the verified death toll was 387, though it may have been almost double that.[35] The *Toronto Globe* reported the shocking state of the passengers who disembarked from the *Virginius* at the quarantine station at Grosse Île, ravaged by cholera and typhus after 63 days at sea. Of 476 passengers, 267 or 56 per cent died either on the voyage or during 13 days in quarantine.[36] An investigation was ordered and a new description coined, 'coffin ships'.[37] Mahon's murder in November 1847, at the hands of an unknown assassin, rocked Ireland and made international headlines. Yet, unlike the revolutions sparked a year later in Paris, Rome, and Berlin, the short violent farrago of rebellion in County Tipperary demonstrated that Ireland's outrages would remain agrarian not revolutionary, at least for now.

With gallows humour winning his audience of 500 guests at a dinner in Newtownards to honour his agent, John Howe, on 30 December, Dufferin said of Irish landlords, 'Never were a class of men placed in such embarrassing circumstances ...

who does not get rent ... a well-dressed gentleman who may be shot with impunity'. If the landlord was father to their tenants, he said, an agent was their nurse, and it would be a pity to shoot Howe. Ireland needed to be wrested from 'the sputtering of musketry, the dropping fire of the peasant sharp-shooters,' by defying the Molly Maguires. He passionately asserted that 'the great object of all landlords, whether they live in the North or in the South, is to attain the confidence of their tenantry'. His duty was to encourage the fullest advantage of the soil's natural capacities. He did not believe that Ireland should forever be a monument to national idleness, a blot on the face of Europe.[38] Loyal to family and class, and determined to manage his estate effectively, Dufferin's heart 'was tormented with shame and pity at the plight of the Irish tenants'.[39]

Though he retained the utmost contempt for absentee landlords, Dufferin himself had considered flight from Irish landlordism. Before the indelible trip to Skibbereen, Dufferin fantasised about selling up and establishing himself as a laird at Inveraray, and researched deeply into his family's Scottish roots. Yet Clandeboye would not let him go because it was 'home, home, home, *home*,—amid drenched fields, leafless bushes and a misty mockery of a park—which against my better reason, I cannot help loving more than any place in the world'.[40] Dufferin implemented his Newtownards commitments in two ways. The first was palliative, though personally expensive, remitting rents of £2,000 a year to his tenants, generously compensating outgoing tenants, and investing £78,000 without increasing rents. He funded public works to enhance Clandeboye's landscape, including a folly in the Scottish baronial style, intended as a gamekeeper's lodge but later a shrine to his mother.[41] His princely donations to famine relief in contrast to his peers were lauded by *The Freeman's Journal*, raising him 'above the level of rank to the elevated dignity of humanity'. Dufferin's second and longer term approach was to advocate national solutions: emigration and land reform.

These thoughts weighed heavily on Dufferin at Clandeboye but he enjoyed the company and attentions of his mother, Helen Selina, née Sheridan. Helen's grandfather was the renowned playwright Richard Brinsley Sheridan. Her father Thomas and her mother Caroline had enjoyed royal family support, he with a lucrative appointment in South Africa and she, when suddenly widowed, with apartments at Hampton Court in which to raise her children.[42] Her daughters Georgina, Caroline and Helen were beautiful, vivacious, and talented writers: 'the glory, and at times, the scandal of their age'.[43] In this favoured milieu Helen met and married Price Blackwood in 1825, her lack of wealth casting a pall of disapproval that prolonged their Italian honeymoon. Dufferin's birth in Florence in 1826 almost cost Helen her life. Only 18, the birth began an obsessive lifetime bond with her only child. Eventually reconciled with the Blackwoods, Price died in 1841, two years after inheriting the family seat.

Dufferin quickly established himself in London and by 1849 was Lord-in-Waiting, a function at court suited to his good humour and dandyish charm. Helen pushed him to declare himself a Whig, contrary to his Tory inclinations. Prime Minister Lord John Russell elevated him to the House of Lords, though a seat in the Commons would have aided a political career.[44] Dufferin got the measure of his own talents as well as tastes in London which fed a growing ambition. Something else was brewing in him too, a strongly visceral and very Victorian instinct to escape. With the Crimean War underway, Britain and France blockaded Russia in the Baltic. A keen sailor, Dufferin arrived on his yacht, the *Foam*, at the Åland Islands, Finland, in the summer of 1854. Invited on board *HMS Penelope* he had more than a ringside seat of the bombardment of the Russian-held fort of Bomarsund.[45] Later, amidst more shot and shell as the fortress was stormed, Dufferin again displayed insouciant Victorian sangfroid. His physical courage was not in any doubt. Dissuaded from voyaging to Crimea, he joined Lord John Russell's delegation in 1855 at the abortive talks in Vienna. Russell became bored but the experience whetted Dufferin's appetite for diplomacy.

His appetite for adventure unquenched, Dufferin readied the *Foam* for a trip to Iceland and Spitzbergen in 1856. *Letters from High Latitudes*, his account of the trip, was an instant bestseller with five quick editions.[46] The account is thrilling and chilling, Dufferin in death defying attempts of seamanship all the while threatened with fatal entrapment in sea ice. Death denied him its own form of grim escape and *Letters* was an undoubted success in presenting Dufferin indomitable but good company, the manly man, the adventurer that Victorians admired and, more to the point, the Empire needed.[47] An extensive Mediterranean cruise also completed, with a miserable but determined Helen along, Dufferin's rise was marked when in 1860 Lord Palmerston nominated him to the commission investigating a Druze massacre of Christian Maronites in which Turkish soldiers occasionally collaborated. International opinion was outraged, London and Paris disturbed by the Ottomans' imperial failure to maintain order in Lebanon and Syria. Dufferin played his hand superbly, and proved adept at the daring-do of power politics. He had found his vocation. An offer of the governorship of Bombay followed but he declined. Probably seen as a stepping stone to the coveted prize of Viceroy, Dufferin served as Under-Secretary of State for India in 1864–1866. After a stint as Under-Secretary of State for War in 1866, and as Chancellor of the Duchy of Lancaster, he was appointed Paymaster General (1868–1872). It amounted to an official apprenticeship, though Dufferin became anxious for greater preferment as he entered his mid-forties.

After years of courtly flirtations and aristocratic matches never concluded, Dufferin had married the young and inexperienced Hariot Georgina Rowan-Hamilton in 1862.[48] Helen approved the match, for though it did nothing for her son's position in English society, or for his wealth, it freed her to marry a much younger admirer, Lord Gifford, just before her son's nuptials.[49] Later in life, Dufferin cast a veil over his relationships by expunging the topic from his diaries.[50] Distant cousins, Dufferin's marriage to Hariot united Hamiltons and Blackwoods whose intertwined histories dated to local colonial settlement two centuries earlier. Generations previously, a scandalous feud over a will was resolved by the Dublin probate court splitting assets so assiduously it included a mathematical line through Killyleagh Castle.[51] Restoring the Gatehouse in the best mock Gothic fashion, Dufferin could claim that, with the exception of his mother, the greatest influence on his character had been the novels of Sir Walter Scott.[52]

Momentously for Dufferin, Helen died from breast cancer in 1867, she was aged 60. Dufferin was simultaneously liberated from, and reconciled to, her. Ever afterward, mention of her or sight of Helen's Tower glimpsed through the windows at Clandeboye prompted reverent sadness by all in deference to Dufferin's well known loss.[53] Helen's death came as Dufferin's campaign on emigration and land reform was nearing its climax. He had immersed himself in research, displayed in speeches and at hearings of parliamentary committees and government commissions. His expertise and views appeared in letters to the *Times*, eventually published as a book. Induced, he declared, solely by the 'uncontrollable conviction' of the injustice of the allegation concerning 'the exterminating policy of Irish landlords', Dufferin's *Irish Emigration and The Tenure of Land in Ireland* is testament to his extraordinary commitment.[54] The landlords of Ireland had an exemplary advocate in Dufferin who set the available statistics (drawn from the Devon Commission evidence) in both their historical context and current practices.[55] Tenants, Dufferin averred, were renting land as a merchant would a ship. If there was to be land reform, it had to be based on principles of justice and 'present policy', namely private property.[56] He rejected notions of reversing the confiscations of earlier centuries as unworkable and iniquitous. Hence his preference was for state purchase. *Irish Emigration and the Tenure of Land in Ireland* presented a cogent and principled analysis that hints at an alternative narrative had Dufferin's prescription of land purchase been followed in 1870 with the force that it enjoyed only decades later, and after such bitter campaigns of political and agrarian conflict. Hero of the famine he may have been for his visit to Skibbereen, but Dufferin was a hero too for devoting more than 20 years to land reform. The fate of his proposals would turn on whether Britain accepted that Irish landlords were land-owners or remained expropriating colonists.

In an arresting analysis, Dufferin said he had been told that 'this frantic clinging of the Irish to the land was natural to their genius, and not the result of commercial restrictions.' [57] Just as penal laws and religious intolerance had 'vitiated our social atmosphere', he asserted, attachment to the land had resulted from Britain's repression of Ireland's attempts at commercial diversification: 'One by one, each of our nascent industries were either strangled in its birth, or handed over, gagged and bound, to the jealous custody of the rival interest in England, until every fountain of wealth was hermetically sealed'.[58] The land could support three or four million but, without industry, not the current level. He pointed to the one exception, linen. Manchester had tried to deprive Ireland yet again but 'justice and reason for one prevailed and the one surviving industry of Ireland was spared'.[59]

> How has it repaid the clemency of the British Parliament? By dowering the crown of England with as fair a cluster of flourishing towns and loyal centres of industry as are to be found in any portion of the Empire. Would you see what Ireland might have been—go to Derry, to Belfast, to Lisburn, and by the exceptional prosperity, which has been developed, not only within a hundred towns and villages, but for miles and miles around them, you may measure the extent of the injury we have sustained.[60]

Citing the contrasting conditions in Ulster and elsewhere in Ireland, Dufferin wrote that had Ireland been allowed develop her abundant resources, 'the equilibrium between the land and the population dependent upon the land would never have been disturbed, nor would the relations between landlord and tenant have become such a subject of anxiety'.[61] Moreover, the landlord was restricted by lack of capital to improve the land. Rents had been outpaced by the value of Irish agriculture output. Yet evictions, contrary to belief, were low and it was tenants who benefitted from the competition for land, not landlords. The value of the Ulster Custom, payable by the succeeding tenant, required heavy debts, bedevilling the management of tenure by landlords and their agents, an infuriating obstacle that merely underscored the revenue lost to landlords. The opprobrium fixed to Irish but not Scottish landlords, limited the scope for clearances in the switch to more profitable pasturage. If not for his exculpation of landlords, Dufferin's powerful exegesis sounded like the *cri de cœur* of an ardent nationalist. Logically, his argument should have led him to Home Rule, but he halted at the frontier between economics and politics.

As with so much of his life, and that of Ireland *writ large* for that matter, both Dufferin's title and his career path in London were a direct result of the Act of Union 1800. His great-grandfather, Sir John Blackwood, died in 1799, family lore holding as he put on his boots to go vote against the Union. His son James voted in favour and accepted the proffered peerage on behalf of his mother Dorcas Blackwood (née Stevenson) who became the 1st Baroness of Dufferin and Clandeboye. The act ended the Ascendancy's platform for eighteenth-century success and their proudest physical and functioning expression, the Irish parliament.[62] Robbed of the parliament that had done so much to counter London's interests and advance the island's economic and social interests, Ireland's metrics declined. Had the parliament endured, as a leading landlord with a sense of duty, Dufferin would inevitably have served there, as had been the tradition in his family. The history of Ireland from 1800 to the Famine demonstrated that local government, even if exclusively Protestant, trumped government at a remove. Had the Irish parliament endured, in other words, there might have been no need for young Dufferin to visit Skibbereen. Moreover, as the history of poor law relief and land reform legislation both demonstrated, the proposed solutions were always a step short of resolution squeezed by Westminster party politics and the limits of British public opinion. Yet, to condemn the Act of Union would have required Dufferin to censure the decision of his family and his class to support it. On the contrary, Dufferin was a convinced advocate for the Union. Repeal, he believed, had been a dead horse until it was married to the land question, as he put many years later.[63] Dufferin's tours of his estate and of Ireland conveniently convinced him that the Union was better than an Ireland run by what he characterised as the equally feckless landlords and peasantry.

Dufferin was left in no doubt about the case against him, acidly put by historian and essayist James Cotter Morison after a visit to Ireland in 1868. In *Irish Grievances Shortly Stated*, Morison laid the cause of Ireland's ills firmly on Dufferin, his class, and England's 'habitual apathy'. Irish landlords were an 'alien proprietary' who were endowed with the land 'with the express understanding that the original owners and inhabitants should be carefully expelled from it'.[64] He rejected the notion that the Irish were the source of their own problems. Irish landlords maintained their tenantry in uncertainty and ruled them though bye-laws 'which place the tenant for practical purposes in a state of serfdom'[65] that was 'coincidental with their pecuniary self-interest, their privileges and their pride'.[66] This 'fatal want of certainty' undermined investment in agriculture and the consequent lack of savings inhibited urban and industrial growth.[67] Worse, Morison charged, the alien propriety acted as a 'waste pipe' draining off what little capital accumulation there was.[68] Having seen the wrong of the Established Church, it was time to see the wrongs of the Ascendancy.[69] Morison argued that it was the responsibility of the State to regulate the relationship between landlord and tenant, for example by mandating 30-year leases.[70] The Union needed to be reappraised, Morison counselled, 'one of the most nefarious transactions in human history, and now proved calamitous in its effects'.[71] Morison's arguments and Dufferin's campaign for land were fought at Westminster, not Dublin's College Green. Instead of convincing his fellow Irishmen, Dufferin had to convince an assembly of British politicians in which Irish representatives were a distinct minority dependent for their influence on electoral flukes like a hung parliament. More than land reform was at stake. In abolishing their own parliament in 1800, Irish landlords had surrendered political agency, reduced to supplicants of the British Government with all its budgetary concerns, ideology, ignorance, and whims. Ultimately, the British parliament determined their fate and eventual extinction.

Dufferin became William Gladstone's *consiglieri* on the land question as the first election under the 1867 Reform Act hoved into view, or so he liked to think. The moment seemed at hand in 1868 when elected Liberal Prime Minister Gladstone declared it was his mission to 'pacify Ireland'. Dufferin harboured expectations of a cabinet post as Lord Lieutenant of Ireland, highly unlikely for reasons plain to everyone but Dufferin. Sure of his ground and of his principles, notably on the inviolability of private property, Dufferin was combative.[72] He stoutly supported Gladstone on the disestablishment of the Church of Ireland, but Gladstone kept Dufferin from the cabinet's inner discussions. He was rightly wary that Dufferin would resist his preference for fixity of tenure and the Ulster Custom. By the same token, Dufferin suspected that Gladstone was capable of repealing the Union.[73] On sight of the draft legislation, Dufferin threatened resignation, supported by his friend Argyll, the Scottish landlord. Not for the first time would a Gladstonian mission to settle the Irish question founder on hostile British interests. In this context, writes Gailey, Dufferin's counter proposals offered Gladstone a compromise: 'For Dufferin was more sympathetic to reform than his vehement defence of landlordism implied .... ready to consider the legalising of the Ulster Custom where it existed and provisions of compensation for improvements and for eviction other than non-payment of rent ... Dufferin encouraged [the] proposal for state-aided land purchase'.[74]

Inevitably, the 1870 Land Act disappointed tenants and outraged landlords. Astute but insubstantial, in the view of historian Roy Foster, it indeed fixed in law the Ulster Custom but only where it already existed. Cautious provision for compensation, purchase and rent control, as Foster notes, would have applied to few. Provision for fixed leases threatened the continuous traditional tenancy that applied to 77 per cent of holdings. Yet for all its hesitancy, the Act admitted 'the Irish tenants' *moral* property in his holding' as Gladstone accepted 'the Irish historical sense of a certain vested right in the land that had allegedly been expropriated from their ancestors'.[75]

Dufferin could just about suffer the implied tenant right but only if the 1870 Act was a final settlement. Where Dufferin saw land reform as an antidote to Repeal of the Union, however, Gladstone saw it as but one step toward settling the Irish question that might embrace repeal of the Act of Union. Gladstone later endorsed more land reform and eventually Home Rule. Dufferin, who subscribed to the theory that Irish 'revolutionists' would undo the Empire, was horrified.[76]

Twenty-three years after the Newtownards speech, the 1870 Land Act marked a watershed in Dufferin's life. Massive emigration was creating a new class of strong tenant farmers, which validated Dufferin's Malthusian prognosis, but promised more assaults on the landlord class. They faced parliamentary agitation under the leadership of Isaac Butt and the coming man, Charles Stewart Parnell. The threat of agrarian violence added menace to the land war. It was futile, as Morison had noted, to say the farmers were not Fenians. 'The Fenians are the fighting division of Irish disaffection', he wrote, drawing their 'moral strength and capital' from the sympathy of the majority of tenants.[77] Morison's warning had been stark: 'maltreat men by laws and arrangements which only exist because you choose to make them, and then the fiercest passions in the human heart declare against you. Persist in them after remonstrance and fair warning, then prepare for the day of wrath and vengeance which is surely coming'.[78] It was a sentiment that neatly encapsulated why Gladstone was so determined to resolve the 'Irish problem'. Britain responded with a series of further land reforms, each falling short in Westminster of what was required in Ireland.[79] Outside Ireland, industrialisation, urbanisation, instantaneous communication, technological innovation, mass democracy and demotic media, sealed the fate of the landed aristocracy. Dufferin determined a new path, leading not to the future but an idealized past at Clandeboye, not to Ireland, but to the Empire.

Denied senior office, excluded from inner councils, frustrated by the legislative outcome of his campaign, Dufferin declared he was finished with politics, and wanted an earldom along with retirement at Clandeboye to write an instructive history of Ireland. Gladstone opined coolly that both literature and history would benefit.[80] Yet Dufferin got his earldom, applied and failed to get the Viceroyalty to India, but gratefully took second best as Governor General of Canada in 1872. Harold Nicolson sums up the outcome of Dufferin's long struggle since Skibbereen:

> The fact that he was unable for so long to achieve any fitting adjustment between his divided Irish loyalties, dislocated his political career and all but damped his ambition. It was only when he escaped from this dilemma to the wider fields of diplomacy and empire that any real harmony was achieved between his purpose and his opportunity, between his ambitions and his functions, between his conscience

> and his circumstances. But for this escape, Ireland might well have broken *his* heart also; and ruined an imperial career.[81]

After many rocky years of his absences and her postnatal depressions, Dufferin and Hariot embarked to Canada and their happiest years.[82] With a new career paying an impressive salary of £10,000, Dufferin put his home affairs in order.[83] Already heavily mortgaged, Dufferin began doing stealthily from 1872 onwards what he had failed to persuade the state to do; selling off his land, aware how momentous this was for him and his family. In parcelled sales totalling 11,000 acres by 1880, he realised some £370,000. The switch to liquidity, however prescient, was not without risk, but he had cleared his debts. In June, Dufferin and Hariot were welcomed at Quebec by Prime Minister John A. Macdonald.[84] Alexandrina and Frederick would be born there, joining their siblings Helen, Archibald, Terence, Hermione, and Basil.

In Canada, Dufferin simply turned a Nelsonian eye to Irish demands for what Canada had been granted, responsible government since the 1840s and dominion status in 1867 with its own parliament and government. Since Ireland was not looking forward to Home Rule *ab initio* but its restoration, like Banquo's ghost the spectre of the Irish parliament contradicted claims that the Empire was a handmaiden to democracy and progress. Since there was no reconciling this awkwardness, Dufferin simply excised the Irish experience from his advocacy for national autonomy within a munificent Empire avowedly devoted to progress.[85] Dufferin's silence was all the more impressive since the Fenians (the Irish Republican Brotherhood or IRB) had invaded Canada in 1866 and 1870 in the cause of Ireland's freedom, and Green and Orange tensions had been imported to Canadian towns and cities from Halifax to Toronto.[86] Moreover, transatlantic colonialism had brought generations of Irish to Canada since at least the mid-seventeenth century and Irish influence was heavily evident: shaping Canada's politics, law, literature, education, policing, Indigenous relations, science and business.

Dufferin dedicated himself to making the first Dominion a success. In the Victorian view, 'the dependencies of the Empire were at that time in comparative infancy, and far from attaining the expansion, wealth, and importance, which under enlightened statesmanship and active encouragement from home, have since combined to raise them to the dignity of living bulwarks of our Empire beyond the seas'.[87] As Tindley points out, Dufferin pushed hard against the boundaries of his role in Canada, at times acting as more head of government than representative of the head of state. He lost each battle and, on his departure, new Letters Patent circumscribed the Governor General's role.[88] Rather, Dufferin's success rested on his 'imperial assurance, his affirmation of Canadian nationality, his sense of compromise, and his charm and wit. When combined with his wife's quiet ambitions and effective social skills, his abilities allowed them together to create a viceregal court. A Canadian political and bureaucratic elite took form socially under their cultivation'.[89] Travelling extensively, Lord and Lady Dufferin sought to bind the public in its loyalty to the mother country in what was his core message during relentless public appearances.

It is a little remarked fact that Dufferin was the third successive Irish Governor General of Canada. Charles (Viscount) Monck from Tipperary served before and after Confederation, working assiduously on this historic departure with fellow-Irishman Thomas D'Arcy McGee MP. Monck had decided on Rideau Hall as the official residence for the Governor General of the new dominion. John Young (Lord Lisgar) followed.[90] Lord and Lady Dufferin enhanced and popularised the office in a critical transition period. They entertained lavishly and toured extensively. They enthusiastically engaged with all ranks as well as Indigenous Nations and Bands. Dufferin's view of the Indigenous People was romantic and fateful; they were 'savages' doomed by progress.[91] This was a belief widely shared, including by the Irish: Nicholas Flood Davin's report in recommending the establishment of the Indian Residential Schools was posited on such beliefs.[92]

While touring in the summer of 1874, Dufferin expounded on Canada as a destination of choice for 'the over-thronged countries of the older world.' He published speech extracts, with third person commentary most likely written by himself. Dufferin grasped the new influence of the press, funding traveling journalists in his entourage and even correcting their copy. He used his multiplicity of speaking engagements to laud Canada in all its respects of society, economy, governance, underling its happy loyalty to the Mother country. In the necessary ellipsis required of him on the awkward question of Home Rule catalysing Canada, Dufferin made no mention of his views on emigration as a solution to Ireland's ills. He was more candid, however, once his successful six-year term was drawing to a close. As sectarian tensions brewed in Toronto, he passionately appealed to the Irish Protestant Benevolent Society that to import into the stainless paradise of Canada 'the bloodthirsty strife and brutal quarrels of the Old World' was Cain-like and insane, having seen first-hand in Belfast the murderous effects of 'ancient feuds ... hateful quarrels [that] feed on their excess'. His oratory had its limits; the Jubilee riots broke out the next day and continued sporadically into October.[93]

There is a startling declaration about his identity in one of his concluding remarks in Toronto, after a tour involving some 120 speeches: 'Words cannot express what pride I feel as an Englishman in the loyalty of Canada to England'.[94] In September

1878, in one of his last speeches before leaving, Dufferin commended the qualities of his successor, Lord Lorn, save for one congenital defect: 'Lord Lorn is not an Irishman!' As least, he noted, Lorn was a Celtic Highlander. With unconscious irony, he went on, 'There is no doubt the world is best administered by Irishmen'. Citing a host of Irish surnames in imperial administration: from Canada and the West Indies to India and Australia, he told his audience they had been spoiled by having three Irish Governor Generals in succession.[95]

Dufferin's diplomatic career continued with a posting as Ambassador to Russia (1879–1881), as special commissioner to Egypt (1882–1883), and a posting in Constantinople (1881–1884). He was again strikingly successful, notably in Egypt where he earned the moniker the 'pacificator'. While he led the diplomatic intrigues that held Turkey at bay, another leading Irish imperialist commanded the audacious military intervention, General Sir Garnet Wolseley from Dublin. An Irish diplomat and an Irish general firmly secured Egypt and Suez for Britain.[96] Egypt made Dufferin an international figure and added to his growing celebrity. Constantinople confirmed Dufferin as the diplomat *par excellence*. He honed the presence and skills of an ambassador, understanding that his role as an influencer combined tact, information, and performance.[97] Yet Dufferin's performative diplomacy was grounded not just on a cultivated presence and gracious hospitality but on a genuine liking for all, no matter their rank or social position. He put everyone at ease. His egalitarian approach and abiding sense of fairness impressed all those with whom he engaged socially or worked professionally.[98]

In 1884, Dufferin was finally awarded the prize of Viceroyalty of India.[99] In India he could exercise his executive instincts. There was action aplenty, notably the invasion of Burma in which his was the critical role, and overseeing plans for railways, ports, defences, and expeditions, managing the opium trade, responding to the Indian National Congress, reforming the civil service, legislative councils and land tenure—notably, intervening in the Bengal Land Tenure bill to defend landlord rights. Dufferin was in his element. He had plenty of Irish company too with Irish soldiers comprising some 40 per cent of the British Army there, and many Irish in the civil service. By the 1890s, notes Jane Ohlmeyer, 'Irishmen ran seven (out of eight) of the Indian provinces (including Burma)'.[100] Yet, back in London, Irish MPs 'dominated parliamentary debates on India', while Parnell, Davitt, Hyde, and Yeats offered models for Indian modes of passive resistance and indigenous cultural assertion.[101]

Lady Dufferin also made a substantial contribution with the formation of the National Association for Supplying Female Medical Aid to the Women of India. It funded training as well as the establishment of wards and dispensaries, all under female supervision, treating some four million women by 1915.[102] It was a remarkable achievement for one women. Hariot's successful use of her position was a measure too of how much repressed female leadership subsisted beneath the restrictions of the patriarchal order.[103] The pomp associated with the viceroyalty reached a blazing crescendo of military reviews, speeches, awards and fireworks to celebrate Queen Victoria's jubilee in Dufferin's third and penultimate year, 1887.[104] On his recall, Dufferin asked that his reward for service in India of a marquessate be known as 'Dufferin and Quebec.' London demurred for obvious reasons so it was 'Dufferin and Ava' after the former Burmese imperial capital (now known as Inwa or Innwa) not far from Mandalay. The British intervention was, as Gailey has written, 'a catastrophe for the native Burmese', and it was Dufferin who signed the invasion order that sent 10,000 soldiers on the march.[105] Responsibility for the futile and destructive violence rested largely on him. The pillage of India first by the East India Company and then the British Government saw Britain impoverish the subcontinent and switch its textile manufacturing prowess to Manchester and other industrial centres in the United Kingdom, including Belfast.[106] Whether seizing suzerainty over Egypt from Turkey or securing the Northwest frontier, Dufferin was the Empire's indefatigable servant.

To judge Dufferin's imperial career is to judge the British Empire and vice-versa. Tindley's thorough analysis parses the presumptions shared by Dufferin and his fellow imperialists, among them aristocratic privileges paid 'through onerous duty to the Crown and country'.[107] Yet, behind the public affirmations of the Empire's beneficent rule, Dufferin's Irish experiences informed his imperial perspective, privately counselling that mistakes in Ireland should not be repeated in India:

> … the present condition of Ireland is our own fault, and the fault of English statesmen, and of that intolerable and vulgar brutality which the strong English race always manifests toward inferior and more sensitive populations. We are irritating the natives out there in exactly the same manner as for hundreds of year we have been irritating the Irish, and now they are beginning to borrow Irish methods of political agitation.[108]

Dufferin never uttered such insights publicly, but they demonstrated the degree to which he carefully curated the frontier between his private thoughts and public role. As with his views on Britain's suppression of Ireland's commerce, this hints at the very different figure that Dufferin might have cut in Irish history had he not been such a determined performer in the name of family loyalty, class duty, and imperial promotion.

For all his success, governing cabals in London could be dismissive of Dufferin, painting him effete, overly decorous, plodding and intellectually insubstantial.[109] As

Tindley points out: 'The role played by Dufferin as that man on the spot was far from ornamental; it consisted of the exercise of significant power with long-lasting consequences for both parties'.[110] This was true of Dufferin's repeated diplomatic achievements at sensitive interfaces of the great powers that many thought could spark global warfare if mishandled. He well deserved the monikers imperial trouble-shooter and pacificator. Dufferin was rewarded with plumb postings as Ambassador in Rome (1889–1891) and Paris (1891–1896). In France, the shock of a hostile press was new and unnerving to a man so sensitive to criticism,[111] though he carried off his duties with the lavish confidence of experience and fame. Italy afforded him the chance to explore the places of his earliest years. He was thrilled to find Barberino de Mugello, the small castle in the Apennines in which his father and mother had stayed in 1826, even if the housekeeper resolutely refused him entry. Nonetheless, he imagined his mother, 'so proud and happy with her baby in her arms, she herself being almost still a child'.[112] Dufferin's romanticism was fuelled not by ignorance of world affairs but the acute awareness of them that had made him such a successful diplomat. It made him fearful that the global conflict so long anticipated since his time in Egypt and on the Northwest Frontier was at hand. In a speech in June 1889 to the British Chamber of Commerce in Paris, he viewed Europe with alarm:

> little better than a standing camp numbering millions of armed men, while a double row of frowning and opposing fortresses bristles along every frontier ...Thanks to the telegraph, the globe itself has become a mere bundle of nerves, and with the slightest disturbance at any one point of the system sends a portentous tremor through its morbidly sensitive surface ... like in a heaven overcharged with electricity, the existing condition of unstable equilibrium which sustains the European political system would be upset, and war would be waged in circumstances of greater horror than has been hitherto known to the experience of mankind, and might eventually envelop not Europe alone but two, nay all, four continents at once.[113]

With such foreboding, Dufferin retired to Clandeboye where his days were busy, overseeing more improvements to the estate, reading Greek in his library, and honing his Persian. Still a public figure and accomplished public speaker, he was regularly called on for engagements, taking in visits to his clubs in London.

Yet, outside Clandeboye, the world in which he had moved with such skill and grace was fast crumbling. The Boer War looked to threaten Britons' assumptions of martial supremacy. In January, telegrams arrived to say that Archibald, Dufferin and Hariot's dashing if directionless eldest son, had died after a head wound suffered at Waggon Hill. Dufferin's youngest son, Frederick, was also wounded in action but survived.[114] It was a devastating price of Empire.[115] 'From that moment, the lavish gaiety of Clandeboye became a thing of the past'.[116] Struggling to deal with a new form of guerrilla war, Britain's tactics of scorched earth and concentration camps, all to enforce imperial rule over the Boers, threatened assumptions held by many Britons of the moral purpose of their Empire, none more so than by Dufferin himself.

There was at least one last occasion to celebrate the grand old days as Dufferin travelled to Dublin in April to greet Queen Victoria, part of a recruitment campaign for the Boer War. Wheeled ashore at Dun Laoghaire, the Queen cut a very different figure from the spritely young woman who had visited Ireland in 1849. He was, she said, one of the few left to her whom she could consult. Almost deaf, he bowed over her hand.[117] In January 1901, Queen Victoria, that regnal lynchpin of the Empire and of Dufferin's career, died. By now Dufferin was embroiled in a national financial scandal. He had invested in and taken the chair of the London and Globe Finance Corporation, a holding company with a sprawling portfolio of mining interests. In December 1900, the Corporation announced its insolvency. Dufferin as chair shouldered the blame as thousands of small investors lost savings. Investigations followed public outrage. Dufferin was not only publicly humiliated but financially broke.[118] As the outside world closed in on him and visibly ailing, Dufferin took solace in his last literary effort with the compilation of *The Book of Helen's Tower*, poems by and about his mother. Copies were distributed to family and friends for Christmas 1901.[119] By February, Dufferin was on his death bed.[120] He died from stomach cancer on 12 February and was buried at Clandeboye.

That Dufferin was privileged was an accident of birth. That he was conflicted by his conscience was a measure of his humanity. Dufferin's compassion informed his trip to Skibbereen, his fundraising, and his decades-long determination to address Ireland's problems. The appositeness of his prescriptions can be debated. Land purchase schemes were unlikely to staunch the demand for Home Rule as nationalist confidence rose and Canada's model loomed large as Ireland's inchoate future. However, Dufferin's intentions were clear, admirable, and heartfelt. Defeated but not bowed by the 1870 Land Act, he escaped to the international stage. His triumph was to mould from the conflict between his conscience and his circumstance such a polished and internationally admired public persona. To do so, it was his fortune that he was granted much of the second half of the nineteenth century at the peak of Victorian self-confidence. Though Clandeboye endures and his grandiose statute at Belfast City Hall casts him as the confidant imperial guardian, Dufferin himself has largely been lost to public memory, an epitome of an age overwhelmed by the new.[121]

In his lifetime, Ireland changed beyond recognition. Dufferin had assessed his part in this recovery, had done some good, and tried to do more. The population may have dipped to half the pre-Famine level at four million but nationalism was on the move: a Gaelic cultural revival, a rising middle-class educated by a confident Catholic Church, and a new generation of assertive parliamentarians. British obduracy and delays in granting Home Rule primed Ireland for a climatic confrontation. The IRB endured as a determined minority and though denied the grist of an alienated tenantry, awaited an opportunity to strike again. Like many Irish landlords, Dufferin had set himself outside and against these developments. In the years before his death, he had become a hero for Irish unionists. Yet Dufferin was less alone as an Irish imperialist than the backward glance at those times has allowed. The crowds welcoming Queen Victoria on her trips to Ireland in 1849, 1853, 1861 and 1900 reflected the widespread aim of mainstream nationalist Ireland to have what Canada had, or in Daniel O'Connell's phrase, two parliaments and one crown. Like D'Arcy McGee, nationalists insisted that Ireland would be as loyal as Canada if they had their own parliament. This was not to be. The IRB might have been a minority of a minority of a minority, but their rebellion changed everything. If, as Yeats asserted, the IRB's Rising in 1916 had created a terrible beauty, it was too a terrible simplicity about what constituted Irish identity.[122]

Reading history forward not backward, and though distinguished by privilege and the fabulous persona he had created, Dufferin represented a variated but widespread Irish involvement in the Empire. Most were willing, some, like the Famine emigrants, were victim participants in colonialism. Similar to Dufferin, they wrestled with the bonds of circumstance, with what being Irish meant within the island, across the class, political and religious divides, and spanning the Irish Sea.[123] He saw himself as neither Ascendancy nor Anglo-Irish, but Irish, even if his affiliation with Ireland had meant increasingly Clandeboye as a place, and not the Irish as a people. Divided or multiple calls on identity were complex and pervasive in Ireland until 1916, while partition clarified, institutionalised, and reduced these complexities into a rough, at times ferocious binary. 'Many in Ireland have, however, either conveniently forgotten our imperial past or are simply oblivious to it', writes Ohlmeyer.[124] Yet, these multiple, complex, and even contradictory strands of Irish identity have been ever-present. In the spectacular life and times of Lord Dufferin, we find many of those strands illuminated by this hero of the Famine, reforming Irish landlord, and celebrity imperial diplomat.[125]

NOTES

1. *Irish Emigration and Land Tenure in Ireland* (London, 1867), p. 49.
2. The pithy summary belongs to Harold Nicolson in his reminiscence, *Helen's Tower* (London, 1937), p. 85, in which his uncle Dufferin is the central character and the eponymous Helen is Dufferin's mother. Nicolson, well connected with the next generation of Britain's political and literary figure is regarded, admiringly, as a second ranked witness to the great events of his time. His analysis of Dufferin's dilemma, pp 79–86, informs his account that is insightful and evocative.
3. Dufferin, *Narrative of a journey from Oxford to Skibbereen during the year of the Irish famine* (Bangor: Books Ulster, 2023) first published in Oxford by John Henry Parker, 1847. Unusually for an Irish place-name, no reliable etymology of Skibbereen/Sciobairín is recorded in the usual sources.
4. Ibid., p. 6.
5. Ibid., p. 7.
6. Ibid., p. 8.
7. Ibid., pp 9–10.
8. Ibid., p. 11.
9. Ibid., p. 19. The epistolary structure, the daily chronology of conveyances changed here and there, the passage over the mountains into a landscape of the virtually undead, the vivid details and horrified responses of our witnesses, irresistibly evoke a fictional traveller beset with strangeness and horror, Jonathan Harker in *Dracula*, published 50 years later. For a brilliant exegesis of Dracula as a metaphor of colonialism, see Joseph Valente, *Dracula's Crypt, Bram Stoker, Irishness and the Question of Blood* (University of Illinois Press, 2002).
10. Dufferin, *Narrative*, p. 15.
11. Ibid., p. 18.
12. See Marita Conlon Mackenna, 'Dr Daniel Donovan. A Famine Doctor in Skibbereen', in Christine Kinealy, Jason King and Gerard Moran, *Heroes of Ireland's Great Hunger* (Cork University Press, 2021), pp 115–130.
13. Dufferin, *Narrative*, p. 21.
14. Ibid., p. 23.
15. 'Progress of the Pestilence and Famine', *Dublin Evening Packet and Correspondent*, 6 March 1847; 'State of the Country', *Warder and Dublin Weekly Mail*, 6 March 1847.
16. 'Richard Boyle Townsend to *Southern Reporter*', 15 March 1847, *Southern Reporter and Cork Commercial Courier*, 18 March 1847.
17. Abbeystrewry Church, Skibbereen. https://skibbheritage.com/abbeystrewry-church-skibbereen/
18. Andrew Gailey, *The Lost Imperialist* (John Murray, 2015), p. 34. He estimated that it would be £100,000 in 2006.
19. Christine Kinealy, *Charity and the Great Hunger: The kindness of strangers* (Bloomsbury, 2013), pp 108–115.
20. Ibid., pp 278–79.

21. Ibid., p. 277.
22. Ibid., pp 113–14.
23. Dufferin, *Narrative*, pp 11–12.
24. Ibid., pp 27–28.
25. Ibid., pp 19–20.
26. Ibid., p. 29.
27. Ibid., pp 34–35.
28. *Dublin Evening Packet and Correspondent*, 12 June 1849.
29. 'An example for Ulster. Splendid contribution from Lord Dufferin', *Freeman's Journal*, 27 June 1849.
30. From an accidental morphine overdose as he was rushing to catch the steam packet at Liverpool bound for Belfast, following his meeting with Dufferin. Gailey assesses the suspicion of suicide, p. 22.
31. Dictionary of Irish Biography, RIA. See also Charles Edward Drummond Black, *The Marquess of Dufferin and Ava, diplomatist, viceroy, statesman* (London, 1903), pp 15–16. Drummond Black's biography is highly informative and thoroughly partisan, very much a hagiography of a Victorian by a Victorian. It has the benefit of interviews with Dufferin by the star-struck author. The biography authorised by Lady Dufferin was written by Sir Alfred Lyall, *The Life of the Marquis of Dufferin and Ava* (London, 1905).
32. Gailey, *The Lost Imperialist,* pp 36–37. As Gailey records, Dufferin changed the name of the family seat from Ballyleidy to Clandeboye, adding the 'd' as Walter Scott had spelled it in his poem *Rokeby*, p. 42.
33. Mark McGowan, *Death or Canada, The Irish Famine Migration to Toronto, 1847* (Novalis, 2009), Appendix A.
34. Ciaran Reilly, *Strokestown and the Great Irish Famine* (Dublin, 2014), pp 62–63. In one of the estates, there was more than one person per acre: 475 families of 2,444 people on 2,105 acres, according to the census taken by land agency Guinness and Mahon.
35. Ibid. Reilly puts the final death toll at 700, p. 73.
36. McGowan, *Death or Canada*, p. 30.
37. Ibid, pp 69–77.
38. Henry Milton (ed.), *Speeches and addresses of the Right Honourable Frederick Temple Hamilton Earl of Dufferin* (John Murray, 1882), reprints from the collection of the University of Michigan Library.
39. Ibid., p. 78.
40. Quoted by Nicolson, *Helen's Tower,* p 86. Dufferin paid tribute to his fantasy with a trip to Inveraray on the way to Iceland; the depth of his Scottish research is evident in Letter III, *Letters from High Latitudes*.
41. Ibid., p 84. Helen's Tower was constructed between 1848 and 1861 and Dufferin commissioned poems in his mother's honour by leading poets, including Tennyson, Browning, and Kipling.
42. DIB. On the death of Thomas in the Cape, 10-year-old Helen Selina returned with her mother and siblings to London, via St Helena's, where she observed the portly Napoleon in his garden under a large straw hat. Nicolson, pp 59–60.

43. Nicolson, *Helen's Tower,* p 52. Georgina became the Duchess Somerset. Caroline had a storied life as society hostess, a prolific if acerbic writer, and a social reformer in the matter of child custody and women's right to their property and income in the event of divorce. As Nicolson states, following the disaster of her marriage to George Norton, 'Mr Norton was not an easy husband even as Mrs Norton was not an easy wife', p. 53.
44. Drummond Black, pp 23–24.
45. Ibid, pp 27–27; for a vivid account, see Gailey, *The Lost Imperialist,* pp 59–61.
46. Dufferin and Ava, Marquis of Frederick Temple Blackwood, *Letters from High Latitudes* (Alpha Editions, 2022). With eighteen editions by 1915, it remains a popular read: Gailey, *The Lost Imperialist,* p. 69.
47. 'Manly' is used by Drummond Black repeatedly, often in appraising his speeches. As a quality esteemed by Victorians and emulated by nationalist counterparts, it is rightly the focus of academic study. See, for example, Joseph Valente, *The Myth of Manliness in Irish National Culture*, 1880–1922 (University of Illinois Press, 2011); Rebecca Anne Barr, Sean Brady, and Jane McGaughey (eds), *Ireland and Masculinities in History* (Palgrave Macmillan, 2019).
48. Of course it was Nicolson, so seasoned on the affairs of the heart and of the bedroom, that noticed that the age gap between Dufferin, at 37, and Hariot at 19. The 18 years' gap was the same as between Dufferin and his mother, or as he put it, the girl-mother and girl-wife, p. 143.
49. Dufferin understood the point and slyly reordered events putting her marriage *after* his own.
50. Gailey on the marriage, pp 97–100.
51. Nicolson, *Helen's Tower,* p. 39.
52. Ibid., pp 34–40.
53. Ibid., p. 61.
54. Preface (Willis, Southeran, & Co, London).
55. Dufferin, *Irish Emigration and The Tenure of Land in Ireland*, p. vii.
56. Ibid., p. 139.
57. Ibid., p. 135.
58. Ibid., pp 129–30.
59. Ibid., pp 135–36.
60. Ibid., p. 136.
61. Ibid., p. 138.
62. J.C. Beckett makes the point in *The Making of Modern Ireland 1603–1923* (London, 1966), Prime Minister William Pitt's objective was achieved in a narrow window of Anglo-Irish fright in the wake of the rebellion of 1798, agrarian violence, a large British Army presence, and the threat of French invasion: 'Had there been peace abroad and stability at home, no Irish parliament would ever have consented to its own extinction', p. 274, and 'However unrepresentative, ineffective, or venal, it had stood for more than five hundred years as a symbol of Ireland's separate place among the nations of Europe', pp 282–3.
63. Letter to Sir William Gregory, July 1886, quoted in Lyall, pp 140–41.

64. *Irish Grievances Shortly Stated* (Longmans, Green, Reader, & Dyer, 1868), pp 70–72, footnote 1; Morison recounts attempts at extermination under Elizabeth, plantation under James, and expulsion west of the Shannon under Cromwell, all failures because it was not in the interest of the adventurers for lack of English tenants.
65. Ibid., pp 34–35.
66. Ibid., p. 53.
67. Ibid., p. 43.
68. Ibid., p. 59.
69. Ibid., p. 82.
70. Ibid., pp 46–7.
71. Ibid., p. 83.
72. Gailey, *The Lost Imperialist,* p. 113.
73. Lyall, pp 139–140.
74. Ibid., p. 112.
75. R.F. Foster, *Modern Ireland 1600–1972* (Allen Lane, 1988), p. 396.
76. Annie Tindley, *Lord Dufferin, Ireland and the British Empire, c. 1820–1900. Rule by the Best?* (Routledge, 2021), p. 124.
77. *Grievances*, pp 31–32.
78. Ibid., p. 68.
79. Dealing with a variety of issues from purchase to rent arrears, legislation was enacted in 1881, 1882, 1885, 1887, 1896 until the definitive land purchase deal of the Wyndham Land Act, 1903, followed by compulsory purchase in amending legislation 1909. Foster, *Modern Ireland,* p. 435, fn vi.
80. Nicolson, *Helen's Tower,* p. 137.
81. Ibid., p. 85.
82. Ibid., p. 60.
83. Gailey, *The Lost Imperialist,* pp 115–116.
84. Drummond Black, pp 82–83.
85. For the disastrous economic impact of British imperialism on India, see William Dalrymple, *The Anarchy, The Relentless Rise of the East India Company* (Bloomsbury, 2019).
86. On this topic, see Mark G. McGowan, *The Waning of the Green, Catholics, The Irish, and Identity in Toronto 1887–1922* (McGill-Queen's University Press, 1999) and David Wilson *Canadian Spy Story, Irish Revolutionaries and the Secret Police* (McGill-Queen's University Press, 2022).
87. Drummond Black, p 76. This was not a description attributable to Ireland, even 20 years after it was written by this admiring biographer in 1903.
88. Tindley, pp 118–119.
89. DCB.
90. Though born in Bombay, Young's father had laid the town plan for Bailieborough, County Cavan, and the family seat was at Lisgar Hall.
91. Tindley, pp 125–126.
92. Flood Davin was born in County Limerick and in Canada had a varied career as lawyer, journalist, politician, and author of *The Irishman in Canada*, a survey of the Irish impact

there. He was tasked by Prime Minister John A. Macdonald to review the American industrial school system for Indigenous children which informed his report recommending a similar system for Canada.

93. Many years later, Lady Dufferin published her letters home as *My Canadian Journal* (John Murray, Albemarle Street, London, 1891) following her earlier publication, *Our Viceregal Life in India: selections from my journal, 1884–1888* (London, 1889).
94. *Canada, the place for the emigrant, as shown by speeches delivered by his Excellency Lord Dufferin, Governor General etc. et. etc. during a tour made in the summer of 1874* (Toronto, 1874), p. 29.
95. Speech in reply to the joint address of the municipal corporations of the province of Ontario, 5 September 1878, *Speeches* (Reprints from the collection of the University of Michigan Library), pp 272–73. Dufferin cites Lords Palmerston, Mayo and Monck, along with the Robinsons, Kennedys, Laffans, Callaghans, Gores, and the Hennesseys.
96. Wolseley led the military intervention against Riel's first resistance in Canada after a legendary and pioneering march that avoided the easier route through the USA. Gailey misses the Irish connection as so often the Irish role in Britain's imperial aggrandizement is overlooked. In the nineteenth century, some 30 per cent of Britain's army was Irish.
97. Lyall, *Personal Reflections*, Sir Henry Mortimer Durand, p. 317.
98. Ibid. Durand's personal recollection is deeply admiring of Dufferin and rueful that he did not fully appreciate him until his passing.
99. The foundation of the British Raj was laid by Richard Colley Wellesley during his tenure as Governor General between 1798 and 1803, supported in the field by his brother Arthur, a major general. As William Dalrymple points out (pp 385, 387, 382) Richard conquered more territory than Napoleon and added 50 million subjects to the Crown, on his own volition and with little oversight or even knowledge in London. Arthur would reshape Canada, investing in defence infrastructure to deter the USA from further thoughts of invasion and annexation after the War of 1812.
100. Jane Ohlmeyer, *Making Empire, Ireland, Imperialism, & The Early Modern World* (Oxford University Press, 2023), p. 166.
101. Ibid., pp 166–67.
102. Gailey, *The Lost Imperialist,* p. 270. Tindley notes that Hariot's medical facilities are still used today, p. 170.
103. See Appendix, *The Countess of Dufferin's Fund*, in Lyall, op cit., pp 321–323.
104. Held in January to avoid the heat of July: see Drummond Black, pp 317–318.
105. Ibid., p. 240.
106. Dalrymple, p. 14: in 1608, India, with 150 million people, had a fifth of global population and was the leading exporter of textiles, manufacturing a quarter of the world's goods. The Moghul Emperor's income at £100 million a year, he notes, made him 'by far the richest monarch in the world'. By the mid-nineteenth century, the Emperor, Shah Alam, was an impoverished puppet of the EIC that was by then producing almost half of Britain's trade (p. 388). Victorian Britain was the world's wealthiest and most industrialised country. The last Sikh Maharaja Duleep Singh, a child favourite at Victoria's court, died impoverished in a Paris hotel room in 1893.

107. Tindley, pp 103–104.
108. Ibid, p. 104, and Gailey, *The Lost Imperialist,* pp 276–86, citing Dufferin to Sir Henry Verney, 6/1/1888.
109. Durant summarised this view: see *Personal Reflections*, Lyall, pp 312–19.
110. Tindley, p. 143.
111. Lyall, p. 316.
112. Quoted in Nicolson, *Helen's Tower*, p. 63.
113. Cited in Drummond Black, pp 351–52.
114. Frederick won the DSO, fought and was wounded twice in WWI, and succeeded to the peerage after the death of his surviving brother Terence in 1918. He served as Speaker of the Northern Ireland Parliament between 1921 and 1930 when he died in a plane crash.
115. Basil was killed in action near Ypres in June 1917.
116. Nicolson, *Helen's Tower,* p. 264.
117. Ibid, p. 265.
118. Gailey, *The Lost Imperialist,* pp 335–41.
119. Drummond Black, pp 375–77.
120. Ibid, p. 381. The Managing Director who founded the company, Whitaker Wright, had certainly schemed in switching monies between the holding companies, mostly involved in mining. In mitigation, he argued investment in mining was known as a risky gamble. Convicted of fraud in 1904, and facing seven years in prison, he adjourned to an anteroom and committed suicide by cyanide.
121. In Tindley's neat description looking 'almost comically ornate', p. 4.
122. For pioneering research on Irish involvement in the British Empire, see Jane Ohlmeyer, *Making Empire*.
123. On the Irish in Canada, for example, see Mark G. McGowan, *The Imperial Irish, Canada's Irish Catholics Fight the Great War, 1914–1918* (McGill-Queen's University Press, 2017).
124. Ohlmeyer, *Making Empire*, p. 199.
125. I want to thank Patrick and his son Liam of McGahern's Antiquarian Book Shop, Byward Market Ottawa, for supplying me critical texts, including Dufferin's *Emigration and Land Tenure in Ireland*, his pamphlet of speeches on emigration to Canada, and Harold Nicolson's *Helen's Tower*. These were drawn from Patrick's lifetime of collecting books related to Ireland and the Irish in Canada.

CHAPTER EIGHT

THE IRISH ODESSEY OF JAMES REDPATH (1833–1891)

Reporting Famine in Ireland

Catherine B. Shannon

By the early 1870s, timely information about political and economic conditions in Ireland were more available to the American Irish diaspora than during the Great Hunger of 1845 to 1852. Technological advances such as the trans-Atlantic cable laid in 1866, an expanded railway system in Ireland, and a large increase in the number of local Irish newspapers, were important factors in allowing journalists to document the return of famine conditions in the west of Ireland in the late 1870s. Moreover, the expanding Irish American population, anxious for information about their homeland, encouraged major papers in New York, Chicago, Boston and elsewhere to cover Irish developments. The *New York Tribune*, the *New York Herald* and the *Boston Globe* were notable in this regard. The *Pilot* of Boston and the newly founded *Irish World and Industrial Liberator,* whose subscribers were predominantly Irish, were especially effective in documenting the return of famine-like conditions in Ireland, and in rallying their readers and the wider public to contribute money to various Irish relief efforts.[1] Thirty years after the tragedy of the Great Hunger, regardless of a dramatic fall in the Irish population and a revolution in global communications and transport, famine continued to be endemic in the west of Ireland. As had been the case in the 1840s, the role of sympathetic eye-witnesses proved to be crucial in saving lives.

James Redpath, an experienced American journalist with long ties to the *New York Tribune*, played a major role in informing Americans about the extent and depth of the economic and food crisis that gripped the west of Ireland and sparked the Irish Land War between 1879 and 1882.[2] In many respects, Redpath was an unusual advocate for Ireland as he was born in Berwick-on-Tweed in Scotland on 24 August 1833 and raised within a strict Presbyterian tradition.[3] Upon completing his formal education at age 13, in a school run by his father Ninian, James became an apprentice printer. The family emigrated to Allegan County, Michigan in 1849, where his father abandoned teaching for farming. Young James Redpath worked in newspapers in Kalamazoo and Detroit as a printer and occasional reporter. In 1852, at the invitation of Horace Greeley, owner and editor of the *New York Tribune*, he headed to New York City to take up a junior reporter's position at this influential newspaper. Redpath's stenographic skills and strong work ethic were apparent and, within two years, he was working as an exchange editor responsible for gathering articles from other newspapers across the country for reproduction in the *Tribune.* His curiosity about the workings of slavery in the American south was sparked at this time and led to his 'Facts About Slavery' columns.[4] Although Redpath had abandoned formal religion, his opposition to slavery derived partly from his Presbyterian heritage that held that all men were equal in the eyes of God and must be given equal rights no matter what their colour, religion or ethnic background. Equally important in forming his moral compass was the Presbyterian opposition to class hierarchies and a belief in the necessity of individual self-determination and civil rights. These principles were central to Redpath's republican anti-monarchical and anti-aristocratic views both in relation to the American south and later to the Irish situation.

In 1854 Redpath travelled to the southern slave states to see for himself the plantation system and the living and working conditions of enslaved African Americans. This tour took him to Virginia, North Carolina, and Georgia where he gathered detailed information on every aspect of the oppressive system. A second tour followed in autumn to Georgia, Alabama and New Orleans where he witnessed a large slave auction. Henceforth, Redpath would be an ardent and active abolitionist. His strong critiques against slavery were published as letters in the *New York Tribune*, *the Liberator* of William Lloyd Garrison, and the *National Anti-Slavery Standard*, but signed under the pen-name of 'John Ball, Junior' to protect him from potential physical attacks from pro-slavery individuals. These were eventually published in 1859 as *The Roving Editor* or *Talks with slaves in the Southern States*. Although he was a reporter for the *Daily Missouri Democrat,* Redpath soon took a partisan role by giving unqualified support to John Brown, the leader of the Kansas free-soil militia, despite the latter's suspected association with murderous attacks against pro-slavery settlers. At Brown's suggestion, in 1858 Redpath relocated to Boston for the purpose of recruiting northern moral and financial support. Redpath's reputation as an influential journalist who used both statistics and emotional human interest portraits and interviews of the oppressed in support of his chosen cause began at this time, and would be replicated in his coverage of Irish affairs between 1880 and 1882.[5]

In 1879 Redpath experienced financial reversals and personal complications following his divorce from his wife of 20 years. Redpath approached William Whitelaw Reid, the new owner of the *New York Tribune*, with a proposal that he go to Ireland as a special correspondent to investigate the veracity of reports that Ireland was facing another famine crisis. The wide publicity surrounding Charles S. Parnell's arrival in New York on 1 January 1880, and his national fund-raising tour for the recently formed Irish Land League, reinforced to Reid the relevance of Redpath's offer, most especially as a means of attracting more readers from New York's growing Irish population.[6] Although sceptical of Irish claims of distress and of Parnell's charismatic style of leadership, Reid accepted Redpath's proposal, agreeing to finance his expenses and ordering him: 'First find the facts and report them!'[7] During three trips to Ireland between 1880 and late 1881, Redpath followed Reid's instructions with the same energy, curiosity and commitment he had previously displayed in reporting on American slavery.

At the time of the Great Hunger, Redpath was a teenager living in Scotland. Given his intellect and his employment in the press, he would have been aware of the tragedy unfolding in nearby Ireland. His upbringing, however, may have precluded him from sympathizing with the plight of the 'sister isle', especially as British newspaper coverage was largely antipathetic. Three decades later, as a mature and experienced reporter, observing the suffering first-hand proved to be a life-changing experience. Arriving in Dublin in early February 1880, Redpath spent the next month compiling comprehensive data on the extent of Irish distress through his interviews with government officials and civic leaders. He fully examined the books, letters of appeal, and reports of the three major relief agencies, which were the Duchess of Marlborough Fund, the Mansion House Relief Fund, and the Irish National Land League Relief Fund. He concluded that the alarming reports of widespread distress in Ireland were not exaggerations but accurate and dire warnings about the looming potential for famine conditions similar to the 1840s unless significant aid was provided.

In Ireland, Redpath had a three-hour interview on 20 February with Lord Randolph Churchill who was overseeing his mother's fund. Churchill provided county by county information of distress, noting that £26,000 out of the £54,000 collected since December 1879 had been distributed. Churchill was confident that between this fund and the other charities providing relief, along with agricultural employment starting in the spring, famine would be avoided. Churchill's statement that 'We do not intend to support the pauper class but seek to prevent the self-supporting classes from sinking into it' was revealing if not ominous, and Redpath later reported that the local Marlborough Fund officials often rejected appeals of individuals in dire need on the basis of their politics or religion or because they qualified for poor-law relief. Redpath was sceptical of the accuracy of Churchill's figures and gathered sufficient data to show that at least 100,000 more people were in distress than Churchill stated.[8]

Unlike the Marlborough Fund, the Mansion House Committee had a long tradition of providing relief. First formed in response to the food shortages of 1822, they had reconstituted in 1831. The failure of the potato crop in 1845 again brought them into existence, the committee members then including Daniel O'Connell and the Lord Mayor of Dublin.[9] They reconvened during the shortages of 1862 to 1863, and again after 1879. Redpath was critical of their efforts in the latter period. When Dublin Mayor, Edmund Dwyer Gray MP, head of the Mansion House Fund, cabled American and Canadian mayors in early July for more donations to supplement the diminishing Mansion House funds, Redpath launched a ferocious attack, claiming that the mayor and his committee of landlords and gentry were political lackeys who were ignoring their responsibilities to assist their fellow countrymen. He claimed that Gray was using the Atlantic cable 'as a begging bowl as a beggar's dog to catch a few more pennies for the paupers whom these merciless and mercenary miscreants had created'.[10] He questioned why Gray as an Irish MP did not press the new Gladstone administration to provide a grant of a million pounds for Irish relief, and summed up the government policy as 'Landlords, let the Americans feed your tenants until September, and *then* go in and seize the crops that foreign bounty enabled them to raise for your rack rents now due'. Protesting against a single dollar being sent to the Mansion House Committee, Redpath urged his readers to send their donations to Mayor F. O. Prince of Boston who was serving as an almoner of the American Land League.[11] Redpath's attack on Gray and the Mansion House Committee was unfair in not acknowledging the distributions that the committee had made. Its final report indicated that it had spent £187,350 on life-saving aid to 500,000 people, mostly residents of counties Donegal, Mayo and Galway. This was the highest amount distributed by any of the three major relief funds. Although Redpath had earlier documented that fishermen in these areas suffered from the lack of safe piers, seaworthy boats and equipment,[12] he apparently was unaware of the work of the Mansion House Committee in arranging for £9,700 from the Canadian government's donation of $100,000 for pier construction and repairs and the purchase and repair of fishing boats and gear along the northwest coast. This programme employed 490 men on 23 piers, while the £11,037 invested in fishing boats and gear quickly tripled this amount in the value of the fishing catch.[13] Redpath later learned from Land League treasurer, Patrick Egan, that part of the Canadian government donation of $100,000 was used to build piers and assist fishermen in the west when local landlords refused to engage in loan programs for relief schemes that the government had provided for earlier. Upon learning this, he wondered why the British government had become involved in this project only after the Canadian donation was made.[14] His dismissal of the Mansion House effort also ignored the service that some local resident landlords and gentry as well as 1,319 Catholic priests provided on the local Mansion House committees.[15] By this time, Redpath was politically and emotionally committed to the Land League and, like Parnell, he wanted any future American donations to go through the League to enhance its reputation and influence over the Irish populace.[16]

In addition to reading the hundreds of appeals made to the main charities, Redpath reached out to Irish bishops requesting information about the extent of distress in their dioceses and for permission to contact their priests who had the best knowledge of local conditions. In response, nine bishops sent accounts of the dire conditions in their localities while over 80 parish priests sent graphic descriptions of the destitution and suffering of their parishioners.[17] Among those who sent reports to Redpath were Bishops James Donnelly of Clogher, Patrick Dorrian of Down and Conor, John P. Leahy of Dromore, Francis McCormack of Achonry in Sligo, Hugh Conway of Killala, and Daniel McCarthy of Kerry. Redpath sent Bishop McCarthy's full report on his diocese to the *Pilot* which conveyed the urgent need for relief for 31,000 people in County Kerry.[18] Thus Redpath developed a network of valuable informants and, in some cases, guides and hosts when he later toured of the country. To ensure that the unfolding Irish crisis remained in the American news in March while he was traveling to Galway, Mayo and Cork, Redpath sent the *Tribune* extracts from letters of local priests, thereby countering the more positive views that Churchill and the pro-landlord London and Dublin press disseminated. Redpath's Irish American readers were presented with highly emotive reports of destitution in locations where they may have had family connections, increasing the possibility that they would contribute to the American relief funds for Ireland. Moreover, Redpath proved skilful in choosing stories that would arouse the compassion and sympathy of his readers. From Killybegs, Rev. James Stephens reported that English machine competition had destroyed the local hand weaving industry and that 'the looms have been broken for firewood'. Rev. J. Maguire of Clonmoney noted that his parishioners who used to earn £8 as seasonal agricultural workers in England were now earning only £2, and that absentee landlords in his district were collecting £5,000 in rents and making no effort to relieve distress in the area. Rev. J. J. McFadden of Gweedore reported that only 50 families of the 1,000 in his parish were free from distress. Rev. Charles Davis of Skibbereen wrote, 'I have not seen anything like this since the memorable famine year of 1847' and indicated that the two local landlords, Henry Beecher and Lord Carberry, had given no rent reductions or aid to the local relief committee. As had been the case in the 1840s, reports of women and children having no proper clothing were frequent.[19] Canon James McDermott from Buninadden, County Sligo reported that the good land in his parish was in the hands of graziers. His district included 27 absentee landlords and the three resident landlords in the area were too poor themselves to provide any help so that evictions were mounting. Rev. Thomas Donagh of Cumer-Ballylunn wrote that only two landlords in his district had shown any sympathy for the starving multitudes, while the richest man in the parish, with an income of £8,000, who had 58 tenants on the local relief list, refused to provide a donation to the local relief committee, saying 'I prefer selecting my own objects of charity to having them chosen for me'. The request of Rev. Kenny of Corofin to local landlords for help was denied on the grounds that 'political agitators have raised the cry (of hunger) for their purposes'. Conditions in Connemara were especially dire given that 600 of 750 families in Spiddal, and 600 of 700 families in Letterfrack were in absolute destitution.[20]

Redpath called at the Land League headquarters soon after arriving in Dublin and was surprised that Michael Davitt, the founder of the organization, had no hesitation in providing him with full access to the League's financial books and correspondence including over 500 letters of appeal from all areas of the country.[21] The next day, Davitt took Redpath to Knockaroe in Queen's County to witness a Land League protest against the eviction of a substantial tenant farmer named Malachy Kelly. Even though Kelly had been a tenant for 30 years and had made and paid for many improvements on his holding, he was evicted for arrears of one and a half years. No consideration was given to Kelly or many others, that forces beyond their control were responsible for their insolvency. These forces included a potato crop failure as well as a diminished grain crop, three seasons of bad weather, competition from American agricultural products and a general economic depression. Davitt urged the large gathering of Land League supporters to ostracize anyone who dared take up the vacant holding. Redpath was appalled at the cruelty of this eviction and also by the heavy presence of the Royal Irish Constabulary and of government note-takers, which he saw as a violation of free speech.[22] Davitt's commitment to seeking economic justice for Ireland's tenant farmers and poor cottiers won Redpath's immediate admiration, leading him to compare Davitt to his abolitionist heroes.[23] Davitt's knowledge and sympathy was largely derived from what he referred to as 'the English-made famine of 1846–47'.[24] During this time, his family had been evicted from their home in County Mayo and forced to emigrate to England. When Davitt arrived in New York in May 1880 to organize and expand the newly formed American Land League, Redpath assisted Davitt in finding an office and securing a secretary for the organization. Redpath hailed Davitt at a huge welcoming reception on 22 May at Jones's Woods, describing him as a statesman who has 'the gift to see a wrong and the cause of it, and to apply the remedy that will cure it' by working to abolish the Irish landlord system so that every farmer is owner of the land he tills.[25] A year later Redpath dedicated his *Talks About Ireland*, a collection of his *Tribune* letters and speeches in Ireland and America, to Michael Davitt and he allocated some of the book proceeds to the Parnell's Defense Fund after his arrest in October 1881.

In March 1880 Redpath travelled to counties Roscommon, Mayo and Sligo where he witnessed first-hand the extreme poverty and hunger that his clerical correspondents had described. A common theme that emerged from the priests he met at Athlone, Westport, and Claremorris was that greedy absentee landlords who charged exorbitant rents, often double their government evaluation, were the principal cause of the poverty and desolation in the west of Ireland. Redpath saw many examples where improvements made and paid for by tenants frequently resulted in landlords arbitrarily raising their rents, thereby reducing the incentive to make improvements and encouraging widespread emigration of young people to America.[26] One young woman emigrant he met at Cork told him 'We are only wasting our time here'. Yet Redpath was disturbed by the sad emotional scenes of young Irish women at rail stations crying and hugging their mothers for one last time as they began their sojourn to America. He praised them for their courage and their willingness to send remittances home to save their elderly parents from eviction.[27] While admiring their devotion to family, Redpath was disturbed that their hard-earned wages went to the landlords. Redpath described the current emigrants as better educated and skilled than those of the 1840s and eager to seize the opportunities in America. He favoured voluntary emigration schemes that would bring emigrants to places like Minnesota or the mid-Atlantic states where land and opportunities were greater than in the urban areas of the northeast.[28] Redpath was shocked and outraged at conditions in the Westport area after visiting the 39 tenants of Colonel Logan in the townland of Shabeen where the total rent was £179 although the government valuation was only £77:

> The appalling wretchedness, the filthy cabins, the haggard mothers, the blue legged and ragged children, the gaunt and careworn women, the grey headed wrinkled woman, who look more like the witches of MacBeth on a stage than the grandmothers of comely girls in Mayo–I grew sick and faint at these sights everywhere, and I mounted my horse and left them behind me as fast as I could gallop.

Calling on Lord Sligo and Colonel Logan, both absentees, to visit their estates, Redpath proclaimed 'May the scorn of a great nation haunt you in your clubs and castles if you neglect your duty'.[29] These descriptions, and the absence of relief from many landlords, especially absentee ones, were redolent of scenes from the Great Hunger.

Redpath was in Cork when Parnell returned from his successful 62-city American tour. He witnessed the large and enthusiastic receptions that the Irish leader received in both Cobh and Cork City with at least 30,000 in the latter location. Redpath subsequently debunked the false report of the pro-British *New York Herald* that Parnell had a cold reception upon his return.[30] Within days of returning to New York, Redpath had a wide-ranging interview with *Pilot* editor, John Boyle O'Reilly, who hoped to recruit his old friend as the *Pilot*'s Irish correspondent. Redpath acknowledged the crucial work that the three different Irish funds along with the *New York Herald* Fund and the Philadelphia fund did in providing relief. However, he recommended Americans to give directly to the Land League which did not have the bureaucracy and red tape associated with the Marlborough Fund and the Mansion House Fund. While he credited the Duchess of Marlborough with being the first to initiate a relief scheme in December 1879, Redpath thought her individual contribution of £250 should have been substantially more considering that her husband's official salary was equivalent to $100,000.[31] His strongest criticism was aimed at Queen Victoria who gave only £250 despite her annual income of £2 million, comparing her donation unfavourably with what James Gordon Bennett, the owner of the *New York Herald*, had raised for the *USS Constellation* effort. Redpath also contrasted the contributions of the Queen and the Duchess with the donations that Irish servant girls in the United States sent to Ireland. He reported that one young Boston seamstress had given him $50, the equivalent of six months savings. She declined to give her name, saying 'God knows my name'.[32] Redpath estimated that at least 350,000 people would be totally dependent on charity over the summer months so that continued American help was essential. He held some hope, soon to be dashed, that the newly elected Gladstone government would be shamed into providing significant additional direct relief from government resources.

Between May and late July 1880 Redpath addressed enthusiastic Irish American audiences in New York and Boston and other cities describing what he learned on his Irish sojourn. His most popular lecture, 'Famine and the Landlords', received full press attention and was included later as the introductory chapter in his book, *Talks About Ireland.* Redpath's initial lecture in Boston on 9 May was so popular that the local Irish leaders asked him to repeat it the following week with its proceeds assigned to the Land League.[33] His graphic descriptions of suffering women and ragged children living in hovels worse than those in the American south were emotionally powerful and caused some in the audience to weep. Redpath also provided extensive statistical information on differing conditions of distress in each of the provinces, noting that the comparatively better situation of Ulster farmers was the result, not of their Protestant religion, but of the 'Ulster Custom' which gave them some rights to the financial value of improvements they made. Redpath attributed the misery and destitution he witnessed in Ireland to the greed, arrogance and neglect of Irish landlords whose privileged status was protected by existing land laws and a British government dominated by aristocratic landholders. His references to Irish landlords as Shylocks, and his contention that Dante would have consigned them to his *Inferno*, were received with enthusiastic applause. He concluded by proclaiming:

> Irish landlordism is in the dock today charged with high crimes and misdemeanor of a starving and great people. I am one of the jury that has sat and taken evidence... 'Guilty or not guilty?' My verdict is guilty. The Irish people will never be prosperous until Irish landlordism is abolished. (Long applause).[34]

In this lecture and subsequent articles and talks Redpath expressed great admiration for Irish priests and their extensive efforts to help their parishioners to survive the on-going food and economic crisis. His initial appreciation of the crucial role of the priests in seeking assistance derived from the letters he read in Dublin and was fully confirmed when he witnessed their tireless work during his first and second tours of the west and northwest, in March 1880 and the late summer and autumn of 1880. In concluding his talk on the role of the Irish priests in saving their flocks from starvation and resisting excessive demands of landlords, Redpath promised 'Whenever I see the white banner of the Irish priest pass by, I shall dip my own colors in salutation to it, in memory and in honor of the beneficent devotion to the famished Irish peasants during the famine of 1880'.[35] Redpath also praised the efforts of the Sisters of Mercy in Claremorris for their care of 200 to 300 destitute children.[36] Reporting on his July 1880 visit to Kerry, Redpath praised the work of the Nun of Kenmare (Mary Ellen Cusack) in providing food, clothing and shelter for 100 children with funds sent from America. According to Redpath, Lord Lansdowne contributed nothing, even though his estate abutted her school. Lansdowne was portrayed as a cruel and heartless landlord for having recently responded to the begging pleas of a tenant with eight children, 'I am not responsible for your large family'.[37] Redpath stayed in contact with the Nun of Kenmare and published her April 1881 letter to him in which she condemned the government's coercion policy and land bill. Thanking Redpath for his work on Ireland, she urged him: 'In the name of justice go on and make America ring with the truth about Ireland until your great people do themselves the justice to ask justice for us'.[38]

Although Irish Americans had sent relief funds to Ireland as early as December 1879, Redpath's letters and lectures during spring 1880, were important in validating the extent of the crisis among non-Irish, non-Catholic readers.[39] In the *New York Independent*, Redpath made a special appeal to American Protestants to contribute to Irish relief as a humanitarian obligation and dismissed accusations that American relief funds were diverted to the Pope and the Irish hierarchy. A donation of just $1, he wrote, would provide a three weeks' supply of Indian corn to save a large Irish family from starvation. Moreover, these donations would teach Irish Protestants a lesson of religious toleration. He urged his readers to send their donations to the *Pilot* whose editor, John Boyle O'Reilly, was helping to co-ordinate Irish relief.[40] At least 20 *Independent* readers from areas as diverse as Massachusetts, Maine, Pennsylvania, Ohio, New York and Wisconsin quickly responded by sending $90 to the *Pilot* for Irish relief. Meanwhile, in August the *Pilot* reported receiving $145, proceeds from a Redpath lecture for the Land League fund.[41] In his speech at Leenane, County Mayo, on 28 August Redpath claimed that his reports of destitution and constabulary threats to free speech and assembly in Ireland infuriated his readers, motivating them to contribute £20,000 through the *Pilot*. That he was responsible for raising this large sum may have been an oratorical exaggeration since donations in the spring and summer of 1880 to the *Pilo*t and Patrick Ford's *Irish World* followed pleas by other Irish and Irish American leaders. Redpath calculated that by August 1880, the total amount of relief to Ireland from various American funds was five million dollars.[42]

Redpath's reports were praised by other newspapers such as the *Boston Globe*, the *Pilot*, the *Chicago Inter-Oceania*, the *Boston Daily Advertiser*, as well as Michael Davitt and other Land League leaders for providing factual and balanced accounts of the extent of the subsistence crisis and its structural causes.[43] The New York Parnell Club echoed these encomiums stating: 'We owe a lasting debt of gratitude to James

Redpath, the correspondent of the *Tribune* for his pen pictures of the condition of our people'.[44] Redpath's second visit to Ireland lasted from July to November 1880 and once again he reported landlord and government indifference to continuing distress in Mayo, Waterford, Tyrone, Carlow, Clare and Queen's County.[45] He was impressed by the growing strength of the Land League campaign against exorbitant rents and evictions and how its funds were being allocated to help evicted tenants. By this time, the Land League agitation had spread beyond Connacht to south and west Munster, fuelled especially by the August defeat in the House of Lords of a limited government proposal to provide tenants with some compensation for their improvements. These slightly better off tenants were also in debt as a result of falling grain prices stemming from American agricultural competition. Redpath heralded Davitt as the 'tribune of the people' and commended Thomas Brennan, Thomas Kettle, and Patrick Egan for their commitment to the cause. After observing House of Commons debates on Ireland, he praised Parnell and his principal lieutenants for their obstructionist tactics to protest against Gladstone's Irish policy. John Bright and Chief-Secretary W. E. Forster were the targets of Redpath's cutting satire, while Lord Randolph Churchill was dismissed as 'a fop … whose speeches are inferior both in style and argument to the average speech of any New England town meeting'.[46]

On this second tour, Redpath moved beyond his reportorial role to become an outspoken supporter and agitator for the Land League. While he was proud that his first visit had increased American relief donations, his mission now was 'to expose the crimes of the Irish landlords' and to vindicate Irish peasants as '…the most frugal, and thrifty and industrious races on the face of the earth'.[47] For Redpath, temporary measures such as extending outdoor relief, government loans to landlords for relief works on their estates, or relying on more foreign charity did nothing to address the landlord system, or the political powerlessness of the majority of Irish people, which were the fundamental causes of Irish poverty. He thought efforts to enshrine in law the '3 Fs' (fair rents, fixity of tenure and free sale of tenant interest) would not fundamentally improve the conditions of the tenants and cottiers.[48] Like Davitt, Redpath's top priority was the complete abolition of the landlord system, a goal he proclaimed in three public speeches between late August and late September. At Leenane in County Mayo on 28 August he declared: 'There will be no prosperity in Ireland until every tenant is his own landlord, and every landlord is his own tenant'. Two weeks later, Redpath participated with 600 men, women and children in a Land League organized grain harvest gathering at Ballintaffy, also in County Mayo. To the 2,000 people attending the rally, Redpath proclaimed 'Landlordism in Ireland must die, if the Irish were ever to be a happy, contented and prosperous people. Irish landlordism had better tell its heirs and executors what sized coffins it wore; for the bondage of time has given warning that its hour of doom has come'. Always aware of the value of performative acts, when the Land League supporters and their bands passed a landlord's residence enroute back to Claremorris, Redpath suggested that the band play a funeral dirge. The 'Death March of Saul' was loudly applauded while Redpath and the local Land League officials waved sheafs of oats as a symbol of holding the harvest.[49]

Tensions in Mayo and Galway were particularly high and both Davitt and Redpath were nervous that violence might lead to government repression and a renewal of the law restricting free speech and assembly.[50] Redpath insisted that bloodshed and violence would do nothing to abolish landlordism and he invoked Daniel O'Connell's dictum that, 'whoever commits a crime strengths the enemy'. He warned that violence would undermine the growing support of the tenants' cause in America and Europe and delay the day of justice for Ireland.[51] At his 28 August speech at Leenane, Redpath urged the audience to employ the tactics of social ostracism against any individual who supported rack-renting landlords, their agents or their families. If the whole community stood shoulder to shoulder to impose social isolation, there was nothing the landlord or the British government could do since such tactics did not break the law.[52] Redpath quoted Father John O'Doherty's assurance given in 1880 that 'boycotting' was not contrary to Catholic doctrine, citing an instance when Rev. James McFadden had refused sacraments to a tenant who had taken a holding without providing compensation to the out-going tenant.[53] In fact, 'social ostracism' was already being used on the nearby estate of the Earl of Erne whose agent, Captain Charles Boycott, was being ostracized for not meeting the wage demands of local harvesters to bring in Erne's crops. Redpath provided a detailed account of this famous Land League-inspired resistance in his book.[54] The workers went on strike and no one in the area would engage with the Captain, his family or household employees, be it on the street, in the local store or at the chapel. The Protestants that Boycott brought from Ulster to harvest the crops, who required protection by the RIC and the army, ended up costing far more than the total wage demands of the local workers. Boycott was defeated and soon departed County Mayo.

Redpath was pleased that his Leenane advice had been followed so successfully, but he was concerned that the term 'social ostracism' was too vague a term for the average small tenant and he asked Father O'Malley if he could suggest a better rallying cry. The priest came up with the term 'Boycott', as the appropriate term to convey an effective, but peaceable, action plan against landlords and their agents. It was a tactic and rallying cry that would be invoked widely over the next 18 months. Redpath subsequently made the term a household word in Ireland and America through his journalism and speeches, claiming that 'It (boycotting) taught the people of the West of Ireland that, without bloodshed or outrage, they could successfully resist the aggressions of the landlord'.[55] At one point, he urged Americans to boycott British products, including Irish linen, to force the London government to stop acting as a protector of Irish landlords.[56]

Redpath's final public speech was on 26 September at Clonbur where Lord Mountmorres had been murdered the previous day. Redpath condemned the murder, again advocated 'social ostracism' or boycotting, to break the power of the landlords and their alliance with the British government. He absolved the Land League from any involvement in the murders of Lords Mountmorres and Leitrim, attributing their deaths to allegations that they were implicated in the ruin of young Irish girls.[57] Redpath contended that emigration to America caused by landlord oppression was creating 'a hurricane of hate' since 'Every Irish exile becomes a missionary of hate, to quicken, to keep alive, and to fan every spark of animosity against England'.[58] This was a perceptive observation given the broad Irish American moral and financial support for the Land League, and later for Home Rule and the Irish War of Independence. Patrick Ford of the *Irish World* and John Devoy of the *Irish American* made similar claims of growing Irish American opposition to England.[59] At this stage, according to Rev. James Corbett of Claremorris, Redpath's name was a household word in every cabin for exposing the iniquities of Irish landlordism and vindicating the moral character of the Irish clergy and people. Prior to his departure from Ireland in mid-November, a banquet in honour of Redpath was held at Cork with leading Land League figures in attendance.[60]

Upon returning to the United States Redpath embarked on an extensive lecture tour in which he championed the Land League and pilloried various prominent landlords for exploiting their tenants. By early 1882 Redpath had given lectures in 100 cities including Boston, New York, Chicago, Baltimore, and Montreal, as well as smaller cities where Land League chapters had been established.[61] His lecture in the Music Hall in Boston, where the audience of 600 included Parnell's mother Delia and Ellen Ford, sister of Patrick Ford, generated $800 for the Land League, while his appearance in Worcester, Massachusetts raised $400 from 2,500 listeners. Smaller events also generated donations: $57 was raised from the 281 attendees in East Cambridge.[62] Redpath's stump talk was, 'What I know about Boycotting', but prominent Irish landlords who were absentees were also frequent targets. In addition to citing statistics showing that rents were at least double the government valuations, Redpath's incorporation of the names and stories of individuals who had suffered from landlord misdeeds made his attacks even more forceful. In his indictment of Lord Sligo and his agent John T. Browne, Redpath quoted at least eight former tenants who reported instances of cruelty and oppression: they included forcing tenants to pay poor rates and the county cess that were Sligo's legal responsibility; evicting tenants for sub-letting to, or housing, poor relatives; marrying without securing permission from the estate; charging tenants for collecting and drying seaweed on estate beach-fronts; and imposing tolls on farmers bringing their goods into the Westport market.[63] Redpath used a similar approach in his indictment of Lord Lucan whose property encompassed Castlebar and its surroundings. According to local priest, Father John O'Malley of Islandealy, Lucan's evictions over three decades and his exorbitant rents had reduced the parish's population from 1,800 families to 600.[64] Holdings emptied by eviction and emigration had been turned over to cattle and sheep graziers which brought Lucan greater financial returns. Lord Lansdowne's requirement that tenants do 'duty work' ranging from six to 14 days of labour on the estate farm or face a fine of £5 fine, was used as another example of landlord oppression.[65]

Colonel E. H. King-Harmon, a resident landlord who served on the Mansion House committee as agent for the *NY Herald* Fund and was often portrayed by himself and the pro-landlord press as a model landlord, was subject of a lengthy and fierce attack by Redpath. King Harmon held properties in five counties, with those in Longford and Roscommon accounting for 58,000 acres out of a total of almost 80,000 acres. As usual, Redpath provided statistical information showing that King-Harmon's claim that his rents were at or below their government valuation was false. The total government valuation of his properties was £49,105 while the rentals amounted to £200,000. Poverty was extensive on his estates, with some rents being paid solely by remittances from America or England. Redpath provided the names of individual tenants who were evicted for minor offences of 'estate rules', or who were heavily fined for their infringements. In January 1881, when 700 tenants whose rents were 50 per cent over the government valuation requested a reduction of 25 per cent, King Harmon refused, accusing them of 'ingratitude' for all his supposed benevolence. Yet his tenants had not been compensated for their improvements at the end of their lease, and more frequently faced large rent increases if they continued as tenants. For Redpath, King-Harmon was a symbol of the 'moral malaria' that was Irish landlordism.[66] In a published interview in the *Boston Globe,* Redpath challenged the claims of the *Boston Herald* that Cork landlord William Bence Jones was a model landlord who was victimized by the Land League. According to Redpath's local informants, Jones was infamous for his contempt for his tenants, his exorbitant rents, his refusal to donate to the local relief fund or support relief works in the district. Redpath also denied that the Land League was involved in incidents of agrarian outrages and insisted the League leaders were actually working to prevent them. Reports to the contrary, he claimed, were the result of misinformation emanating from the hostile anti-Irish London press.[67] As shown by several historians, the League leaders were not able to fully banish 'Captain Moonlight' from the Irish countryside.[68]

Prior to returning to Ireland in July 1881 for his third tour, Redpath was honoured for documenting the suffering of the Irish people by the New York Land League, with a testimonial dinner at Delmonico's restaurant. From July through October 1881 Redpath continued to investigate the misdeeds of Irish landlords. However, owing to an injury he suffered in Donegal, his reports were not published in America until late 1881 and early 1882. Meanwhile, the Gladstone government launched a two-pronged effort to fight Irish land agitation through a carrot and stick approach. The carrot consisted of giving statutory status to the '3 Fs' and establishing a land court to implement the new policy. The stick was renewed coercion measures allowing the Irish government to suspended habeas corpus in proclaimed districts, incarcerate League agitators, seize fire-arms, and ultimately outlaw both the Land League and the Ladies' Land League, which had kept the agitation going when the male leaguers were imprisoned. In February 1881 Davitt was the first victim of this new coercion policy and by spring 1882 over 1,000 Land League agitators had been imprisoned, including Parnell. Redpath opposed the land legislation on principle as well as its details. It did not deliver the goal of peasant proprietorship and its provisions did little to address the grievances of the most impoverished tenants in areas like Mayo and Donegal, whose high rent arrears prevented them from applying to the land court for reduced rents.[69] Parnell used this issue of the rent arrears of small holders as one of the reasons for withholding his full assent to the legislation. On the eve of his October departure for America, in a speech to the Queenstown and Cork Land Leagues, Redpath roundly condemned the coercion policy and urged 'No Compromise' on the land bill, telling his audience:

> Let your war cry be the total and immediate abolition of Irish landlordism; drag the crimes of the landlords into the light of day, make their names a hissing and a by-word in every nation, and before long they will fall on their knees and call for the rocks to cover them.[70]

Despite the acceptance of the 1881 Land Act by most tenant farmers, Redpath remained critical of the legislation and quoted his friend, Rev. James McFadden, that the legislation did nothing for the poor of Gweedore.[71] Redpath attacked the United States Ambassador to Britain, James Russell Lowell, for his failure to protest the imprisonment without trial of three American citizens who were involved in the land agitation.[72] When Gladstone boasted in the House of Commons in February 1882 that the land court had delivered average rent reductions of 23 per cent, Redpath labelled them as insufficient and insisted the Irish peasant would still be unable to eat anything but potatoes or provide decent clothing or housing for his family. He provided statistical data for each county showing that current rentals were well above Griffith's valuation.[73]

Toward the end of his third tour, Redpath gained an influential convert to his analysis of the Irish situation. He took David H. Locke, editor of the *Toledo Blade*, to the Galtee area of County Cork where the destitution that Locke witnessed on the Kingston and Buckley estates shocked him into abandoning his negative views about Parnell, the Land League campaign, and the Irish people. Using his pen name 'Nasby', Locke joined Redpath in condemning Irish landlordism in newspaper articles, lectures, and his book *Nasby in Exile*.[74] Redpath embarked on an extensive lecture tour after returning from Ireland in November 1881 and published *Talks About Ireland*, which was a selection of his Irish speeches and news articles. His appearances continued to benefit the Land League: his talk at Charlestown, Massachusetts generated a donation of $100 for the Parnell Defense Fund.[75]

The political climate in Ireland changed greatly in late spring of 1882 with the Kilmainham Treaty between Gladstone and Parnell whereby the Irish leader was released from prison in exchange for backing of the Land Act and the dismantling of the Land League. Redpath realized the necessity of accepting the 1881 Land Act as a significant step forward and he opposed Davitt's brief campaign for 'land nationalization'. He criticized Jeremiah O'Donovan Rossa and his physical force policy as counter-productive and condemned the May 1882 Phoenix Park assassination of Irish Chief Secretary, Lord Edward Cavendish, and his assistant, T. H. Burke. Redpath supported Parnell in making Home Rule the top priority.[76] In fact, from his earliest days in Ireland Redpath had contended that 'Land for the people is not enough; you ought never cease to insist that Ireland must be ruled by the Irish ... If I were an Irishman I should never cease to work for the independence of Ireland'.[77] Redpath was a delegate at the Philadelphia meeting in April 1883 when the American Land League was transformed into the Irish National League of America. In July 1882, Redpath established his own weekly magazine and continued to advocate for Irish self-government for the two-year duration of the magazine.[78]

Redpath's strong ideological commitment to peasant proprietorship and his genuine horror at the living conditions of the most impoverished small holders account for his blanket demonization of Ireland's landlord class. Nonetheless, he insisted that the Land League and its members always operated within the law as Ireland was once again highlighting the ravages of famine and Redpath wanted to expose the reasons behind the perennial crises that Ireland faced, as many had done during the Great Hunger. His descriptions of the Irish poor during a time of food shortages mirrored the images of the suffering that had occurred in the late 1840s. What was palpably obvious was that, despite the dramatic fall in population and generous remittances from overseas, the poor in the south and west of Ireland remained vulnerable to harvest failures. Similar to earlier famines, many of the landlord class, rather than coming to the assistance of their tenants, saw each subsistence crisis as an opportunity to evict their tenantry. As had been the case during the Great Hunger, it was left to philanthropy to help fill the gap left by inadequate government relief policies and landlord indifference. In raising funds and increasing awareness of the suffering in Ireland, Redpath proved to be an excellent spokesperson for, and friend to, Ireland's most vulnerable population. Moreover, his voice was heard on both sides of the Atlantic.

Redpath's analysis provided little space for reporting examples of sympathetic landlords or for explaining the extent to which the inherited indebtedness of many landlords, especially middling resident ones, prevented them from showing more compassion.[79] Likewise, any admission that many petty and personal disputes were violently settled under the cover of the Land League would have damaged the reputation of the movement in America where crucial financial support was sought. Redpath's descriptions of the Land League movement as a socially unified one ignored both the class and political tensions that existed within the movement, tensions that became evident in the aftermath of the Land Act of 1881 and the Kilmainham Treaty when thousands of tenants applied to the land court to obtain rent reductions.

Despite biases in his reporting, James Redpath deserves much credit for his journalistic and public speaking on the Irish crisis from 1879 to 1882. Like external benefactors such as Asenath Nicholson, James Hack Tuke and many others during the Great Hunger, Redpath provided valuable eye-witness testimony of the suffering of the poor, from a sympathetic vantage point. His writing and oratorial style were informative, powerful, and often entertaining. His early 1880 articles and later his public lectures helped to sustain the flow of American donations to save the cottier population in the rural west when the crisis was at its worst. His well-researched articles served as an anti-dote to the British and the Anglophile American press which downplayed the extent of the crisis. He showed that Davitt and Parnell were championing the interests of the Irish people in language that resonated with his American readers. Redpath's pen portraits of Irish people showed them as hard working, industrious and honest people whose current destitution was not the result of character flaws, but of an oppressive landlord system and perennial crop failures that were beyond their control. Redpath's advocacy of peaceful protests and 'social ostracism', as opposed to violence tactics, was a positive contribution in helping to prevent a more serious disruption of the social order in rural Ireland during very tense times. His damning reports helped to generate sympathy for the Irish people and their struggles among the wider American population. Redpath had great faith in the power of the press to inform people of social and political realities and to shape public opinion to bring positive change as was evident when he wrote in November 1881:

> That modern banshee—the steam printing press—has made its dreaded appearance, and it is now the hour for British misrule to prepare its shroud and order its coffin in that fair and gentle land that it has desolated and decimated so cruelly and so long.[80]

It would take another three decades before the landlordism that Redpath decried was dead and buried, but he played an important role in shaping the political opinion that eventually killed it, replaced it with peasant proprietorship and, consequently, fewer famines. Redpath's immense contributions in raising relief funds for Ireland and promoting the cause of Irish self-government was recognized when the *Pilot* reported his death in February 1891: 'The world at large has lost a noble, broad-minded, great-hearted friend in the death of James Redpath'. [81]

NOTES

1. See Catherine B. Shannon, 'Patrick Donahoe (1811–1901): The *Pilot* and Irish Famine Relief, 1845 to 1882', in Christine Kinealy, Jason King, Gerard Moran (eds), *More Heroes of Ireland's Great Hunger* (Hamden, CT: Quinnipiac Press, 2022) for the role of another journalist in raising humanitarian aid for Ireland.
2. For a comprehensive account of Redpath's life see John R. McKivigan, *The Forgotten Firebrand: James Redpath and the Making of Nineteenth Century America* (Ithaca: Cornell University Press, 2008).
3. James Redpath, *Talks About Ireland* (New York: P. J. Kennedy, 1881), p. 32.
4. Ibid., p. 6, *New York Tribune,* 16 February 1854.
5. For details of Redpath's abolitionist activities, see McKivigan, *Forgotten Firebrand*, pp 1–83, 98–113.
6. Ibid., pp 153–155.
7. *Pilot,* 24 April 1880.
8. *New York Tribune,* 5 March 1880.
9. *Report of the Mansion House Committee on the Potato Disease* (Dublin: J. Browne, 1846).
10. *New York Tribune*, 24 July 1880.
11. Ibid.
12. Ibid., 3 July 1880; Redpath, *Talks About Ireland,* p. 22.

13. *Report of the Joint Committee of the Duchess of Marlborough Relief Fund and the Mansion House Fund for the Relief of Irish Distress,* Appendix No. 3.
14. *Pilot,* 23 July 1881.
15. Gerard Moran, 'Near Famine: The Roman Catholic Church and the subsistence crisis of 1879–82', *Studia Hibernica,* no. 32 (2002/2003) p. 164.
16. Donnacha Sean Lucy, 'Power, politics and poor relief during the Irish Land War, 1879–82', *Irish Historical Studies,* xxxvii (November 2011) pp 584–598.
17. Redpath, *Talks About Ireland,* p. 10; *Milwaukee Daily Sentinel,* 8 May 1880.
18. Redpath, *Talks About Ireland,* pp 19–20; see *Pilot,* 27 April 1880 and *New York Tribune,* 12 April 1880 for the full report of Bishop Daniel McCarthy.
19. See chapter by Christine Kinealy on the involvement of women in providing relief during the Great Famine.
20. *New York Tribune,* 17 March 1880.
21. Redpath, *Talks About Ireland,* p. 10.
22. Ibid., pp 14–15; Michael Davitt, *The Fall of Feudalism in Ireland* (Dublin: Irish Academic Press, 1970) pp 223–225; Redpath, *Talks About Ireland*, pp 14–15; L. P. Curtis, Jr., *The Depiction of Eviction in Ireland, 1845–1910* (Dublin: University College Press, 2011) p. 92.
23. *Pilot,* 29 May 1880, McKivigan, *Forgotten Firebrand*, p. 158.
24. Davitt, *Fall of Feudalism*, p. 159.
25. Redpath, *Talks About Ireland,* p. 36.
26. Ibid., 1 May 1880.
27. Redpath, *Talks About Ireland,* pp 63–64.
28. *Boston Globe,* 18 April 1880; *New York Tribune,* 1 May 1880.
29. Ibid., 19 April 1880.
30. *Pilot,* 24 April 1880.
31. For details on the *New York Herald* fund, see Harvey Strum, 'America's Errand of Mercy to Ireland', in Christine Kinealy, Gerard Moran (eds), *Irish Famines Before and After the Great Hunger* (Hampden, CT: Quinnipiac University Press, 2020).
32. *Pilot,* 24 April 1880.
33. *New York Tribune,* 6 May 1880; *Pilot*, 15, 22 May 1880.
34. Redpath, *Talks About Ireland,* p. 30.
35. Ibid.; Moran, 'Near famine', pp 155–177.
36. *New York Tribune,* 1 May 1880.
37. *Pilot,* 21 August 1880.
38. *Boston Globe,* 2 April 1880. Redpath's admiration for Mary Ellen Cusack led him to include her photograph in his book, *Talks About Ireland.*
39. For efforts to raise relief for Ireland prior to Redpath's involvement see Catherine B. Shannon, 'Boston and the Forgotten Famine of 1879–82', Kinealy and Moran, *Irish Famines*, pp 195–212; Ely M. Janis, *A Greater Ireland: The Land League and Transatlantic Nationalism in Gilded Age America* (Madison: University of Wisconsin Press, 2015). In addition to the *New York Tribune*, most of Redpath's articles were published in the *Pilot*, the *Boston Globe*, and the *Irish World* which had a combined circulation of 120,000. Shannon, p. 199.

40. *Milwaukee Daily Sentinel,* 8 May 1880.
41. *Pilot,* 15 May, 7 August 1880.
42. In his *New York Times* obituary of 11 February 1891, $100,000 is given as the total that Redpath had raised for Ireland, which would be roughly equivalent to £20,000. See also Shannon 'Boston and the Forgotten Famine of 1879–82' and Ely Janis for further data on fund-raising during these years. *New York Tribune,* 15 August 1880.
43. *New York Tribune,* 8, 10, 16, 19, 23 May, 12 June 1880; *Boston Globe,* 9 May 1880; *Boston Daily Advertis*er, 12 May 1880; *Daily Inter Ocean,* 25 May 1880.
44. *New York Tribune,* 28 May 1880.
45. *Pilot,* 7 August 1880.
46. Ibid., 18 September 1880.
47. Redpath, *Talks About Ireland,* p. 45; *Pilot,* 9 October 1880. In the *Dictionary of Irish Biography* entry on Redpath, Patrick Maume contends that Redpath was elected as a Land League member in October 1880. https://doi.org/10.3318/dib.009582,v2.
48. *Pilot,* 2 October 1880.
49. Ibid.; Redpath, pp 42, 51. For details on the performative aspects of Land League protest meetings, see L. P. Curtis, Jr. *Depictions*, pp 96–98. Fanny Parnell's poetic advice to Irish farmers to 'Hold the Harvest' was first published in the *Pilot* on 21 August 1880, and soon gained status as the anthem of the Land League.
50. Redpath, *Talks About Ireland,* p. 39; Curtis, *Depictions,* p. 96.
51. Redpath, *Talks About Ireland*, p. 54.
52. Ibid., pp 39–49.
53. *Pilot,* 4 March 1882.
54. Redpath, *Talks About Ireland,* pp 78–85.
55. Ibid., p. 83.
56. Ibid., p. 85; *Pilot,* 25 February 1882.
57. Redpath, *Talks About Ireland,* p. 54; *Boston Globe*, 3 January 1881, 23 December 1882.
58. Redpath, *Talks About Ireland,* p. 59.
59. Janis, *A Greater Ireland,* p. 6.
60. Redpath, *Talks About Ireland,* p. 44; *Boston Globe,* 15 November 1880.
61. *Pilot,* 14 January 1882.
62. *Boston Globe,* 11, 23 January, 15 February 1881.
63. *Pilot,* 25 February, 18 March 1882.
64. Redpath, *Talks About Ireland,* p. 9.
65. *Pilot,* 4 March 1880.
66. Ibid., 18 February 1882.
67. *Boston Globe,* 25 January 1881; Redpath, *Talks About Ireland*, pp 67–71.
68. R. V. Comerford, 'The Land War and the Politics of Distress', in W. E. Vaughan (ed.), *A New History of Ireland,* vol. vi, *Ireland Under the Union, 1870–1921*, p. 45; Curtis, *Depictions,* p. 92; Laurence Geary, *The Land War in Ireland: Famine, Philanthropy and Moonlighting* (Cork University Press, 2023).
69. *Boston Globe,* 20 July, 5 November 1881.

70. *Derby Daily Telegraph,* 6 October 1880.
71. *Pilot,* 24 December 1881.
72. *Boston Globe,* 16, 20 November 1881, 15 January, 19 April 1882.
73. *Pilot,* 4 March 1882.
74. Ibid., 3 November, 31 December 1881, 4 February 1882.
75. Ibid., 3 December 1881.
76. McKivigan, *Forgotten Firebrand*, p. 164.
77. Redpath, *Talks About Ireland,* p. 47.
78. Ibid., pp 163–164; *Redpath's Illustrated Weekly,* 7 December 1882.
79. For instance, Lord Dillon gave abatements of 20 to 30 per cent to his Mayo and Roscommon tenants in 1879. Lord Kenmare spent £33,645 on abatements and estate improvement that brought employment to his tenants, see Curtis, *Depictions,* p. 88, p. 94. For a nuanced and comprehensive analysis of the economic plight of Irish landlords during this era, see Curtis, 'Landlord responses to the Irish Land War, 1879–87', *Eire-Ireland,* xxxviii, Fall/Winter, 2003. The Countess of Kingston in Cork was an example of one landlord whose inherited indebtedness helps explain her refusal of rent abatements. At the time of Redpath's visit, she was paying annual interest of £10,000 on a loan of £236,000 from the Church of Ireland. Curtis, *Depictions,* p. 169.
80. *Boston Globe,* 27 November 1881.
81. *Pilot,* 14 February 1891.

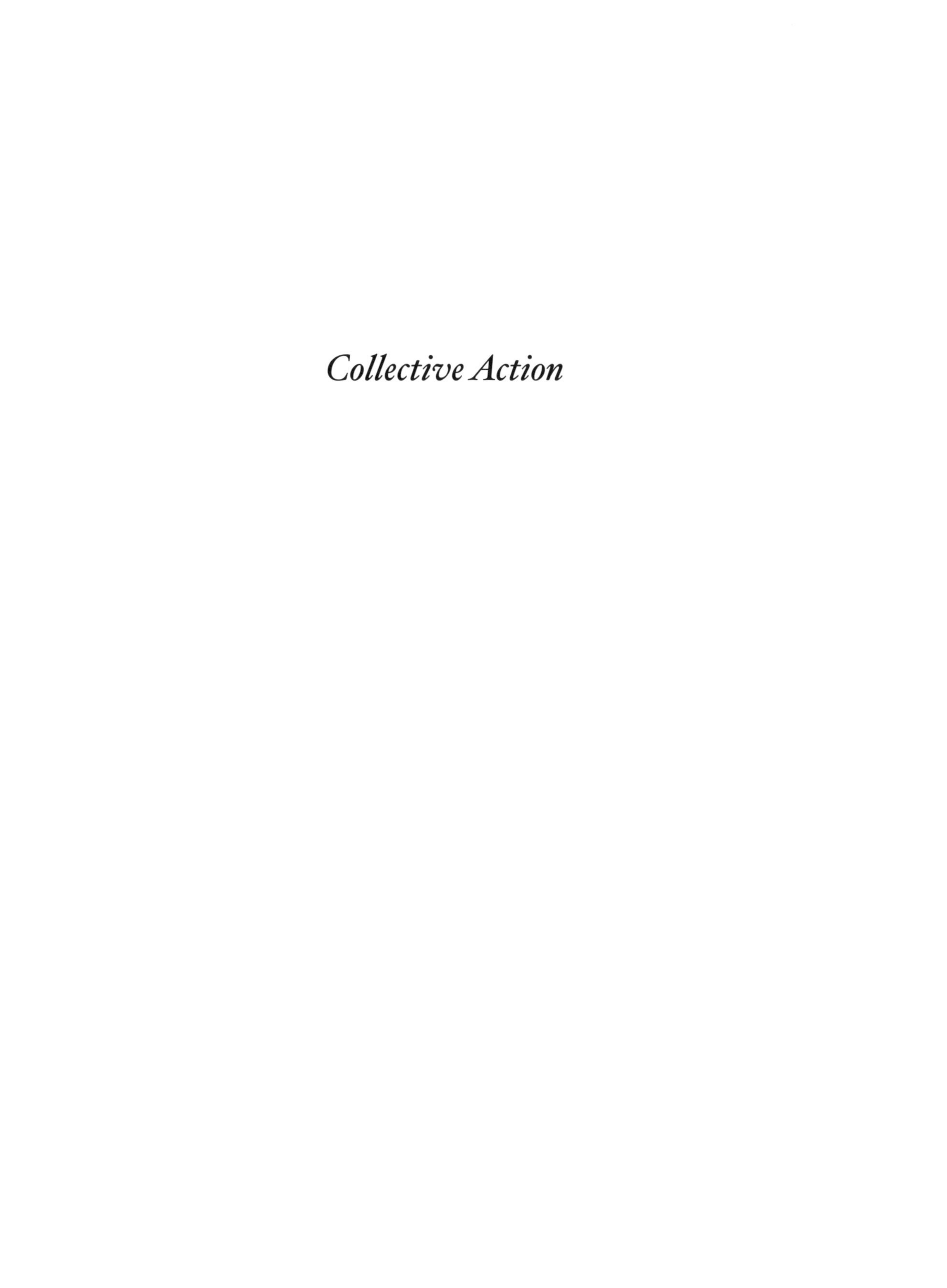

Collective Action

CHAPTER NINE

QUAKER HEROES OF THE FAMINE

Rob Goodbody

> *It is not for man to command success; but it is his Christian duty, under circumstances of doubt and difficulty such as those presented by the recent famine, to labour from day to day, acting for the best according to Him who sees the end from the beginning, and who alone can bless the work.*
>
> Preface to *Transactions*[1]

There is a dichotomy in recording Quaker heroes of the Great Famine in Ireland, as those who form the subject matter would not have regarded themselves as heroes, nor would they have wanted their works during the Famine to be broadcast as heroic acts. An essential tenet of Quaker belief and practice was humility, and this is seen in the lack of portraits of Quakers of this period and earlier and the absence of headstones over their graves. Changes to Quaker practice began not long after the Famine; in Ireland the ban on headstones in burial grounds was lifted in 1856, subject to strict regulation, while easing of restrictions on other practices began shortly afterward.[2] As a result, we have portraits of some of those involved in the Famine relief work who survived the Great Hunger, while those who died left no portraits.

Members of the Religious Society of Friends, or Society of Friends, are often just called Friends, though they are more commonly known as Quakers. The Quaker Famine relief operations began in the autumn of 1846, after the second appearance of the blight. The severity of the blight in 1846 was much greater than in the previous year, the government had changed and much of people's reserves had been used up. It was inevitable that the ensuing year would bring great hardship. Individual Quakers, and local Quaker communities undertook relief efforts during the Great Hunger, but their works were largely undocumented and hence it is not possible to quantify the work or to single out individuals who were most involved in these efforts. It is known, for instance, that Quakers in Monkstown, County Dublin, ran a soup kitchen during the Famine, though the minutes of Monkstown Quaker Meeting do not refer to this. Similar efforts were carried out by many of the Quaker meetings around the country, also unrecorded in their minutes.

A critical factor in Quaker relief efforts was the almost entire lack of overlap between the distribution of Quaker communities in Ireland and the location of the worst hit areas. The Quakers in Ireland in the 1840s, numbering approximately 3,000, were overwhelmingly concentrated in the area lying roughly eastwards of a line connecting Coleraine with Bandon via Limerick. In 1846 there was only one Quaker meeting in Connaught, at Ballymurry, between Roscommon and Athlone. Only one family remained there, however, and the meeting was closed in 1848 following the death of the father of the family.[3] While the Famine affected all parts of Ireland and Quaker relief would be of benefit wherever there was a Quaker community, any significant relief effort would have to be based on a more formalised basis that would include substantial fundraising and an efficient system for the distribution of assistance.

Quaker relief efforts on the larger scale began simultaneously in Dublin and London. Irish Quakers met in Dublin on 13 November 1846 'to combine their efforts towards mitigating the widespread distress now prevailing in Ireland' and the result was the establishment of the Central Relief Committee of the Society of Friends in Ireland. Four days earlier, British Quakers had met in London and decided to raise funds to send to Ireland and had established the Committee of the Society of Friends in London. The two committees worked closely together throughout the Great Hunger with the London committee concentrating on collecting funds, food and clothing and lobbying parliament, while the Dublin committee was responsible for distribution of relief. Soon after this, contacts were made with Quakers in the United States and this provided a third centre of operations, concentrating on raising donations of food and money. Within Ireland subcommittees were established to spread the load, including subcommittees for food, clothing and a Dublin soup kitchen and auxiliary subcommittees in Waterford, Clonmel, Limerick and Cork to reduce the workload of the central committee in Dublin. Another important element of the relief efforts was fact finding and, to this end, many Quakers travelled through the worst-hit areas to determine the extent of the problem and to identify places where efforts could be concentrated or where new approaches were appropriate.

Many Quakers were involved in these efforts in the three countries, and it is only possible here to acknowledge the contribution of some of the principal actors. While it will never be known how many of Ireland's 3,000 Quakers were in any way involved in Famine relief, either centrally or in their own home areas, some idea of the numbers may be seen in the 45 members and corresponding members of the Central Relief Committee, 36 members of the auxiliary committees in Munster and 46 working at the soup kitchen in Dublin. Many more served on the various subcommittees in Dublin and elsewhere or ran soup kitchens in other locations. In addition, there were 20 members of the committee in London and substantial numbers of other Friends in Britain working on fundraising, purchase of commodities or gathering donations of clothing, while still more worked in the United States. Some of these lost their lives during the relief efforts, through contracting famine fever or through overwork. Those who survived were generally deeply affected and some followed on through the rest of their lives to try to improve living conditions in Ireland.

Joseph Bewley

With the arrival of the potato blight in 1845, Joseph Bewley was one of the first Quakers to establish a soup kitchen. He was a merchant, in partnership in his father's business, which was originally involved in the silk trade and expanded to include trade in a range of products from around the world. However, Joseph Bewley's principal concern was the Society of Friends rather than commerce and having earned a sum sufficient to live on he retired from business to devote his time to spiritual and charitable matters.[4]

When the blight returned in 1846 and resulted in a total failure of the potato crop it was clear that the coming year was going to be one of crisis throughout Ireland. While a number of relief efforts were established both locally and on a wider scale, Joseph Bewley believed that Quakers could have a role to play by providing some kind of assistance to the populace. He called a meeting of Quakers in Ireland on 13 November 1846 and at that meeting, a decision was taken to establish a committee, to be known as the Central Relief Committee of the Society of Friends in Ireland, to raise funds for distribution and to gather information as to the exact nature of the problem so that the best means of relief could be organised. At the meeting, 21 Quakers were appointed to the committee, a significant number of whom were merchants and other businessmen who possessed the skills to acquire goods and to transport them across distances, and who also had a network of contacts throughout the country. All of the committee members were based in the Dublin area to allow for the holding of frequent meetings. A further 21 Quakers from around the other parts of the country acted as corresponding members, feeding information back to the central committee.[5]

Joseph Bewley was an obvious choice to be a member of the Central Relief Committee, having been, in effect, the instigator and having the necessary skills as a merchant. He was also retired, which ensured that he would be free to attend frequent meetings. The committee needed a secretary to coordinate the workload and two people were appointed to this role as joint secretaries, to share the load. Again, Joseph Bewley was an obvious choice, and his fellow joint secretary was Jonathan Pim. In view of the amounts of money and goods that were likely to be handled, the decision was made to have three joint treasurers and, again, Joseph Bewley was appointed to this role, along with James Perry and Thomas Pim junior.

Once the Central Relief Committee met it decided that to operate most efficiently and effectively most of the work would be done by a subcommittee that would meet three times a week, with a quorum of three. The committee was to consist of the two secretaries, the two treasurers and three others, so Joseph Bewley was committed to a busy workload. In practice, the subcommittee met five days a week for a considerable period, often for long hours, though the workload was somewhat reduced by ignoring the requirement for a quorum. In addition, the two joint secretaries coordinated the work of a significant number of subcommittees, maintained contacts with corresponding members and overseas colleagues, raised funds, negotiated with the authorities in Dublin Castle, considered projects other than the distribution of food and clothing, wrote minutes and produced reports for distribution.

One of the fundamental beliefs of Quakers during the Famine was that while it was necessary to feed and clothe the destitute in order to save lives, the longer-term need was to establish the means of ensuring that the populace could be freed from the unreliability of the potato and be provided with sufficient means to earn a living and grow or purchase foodstuffs that could be depended upon. In the later stages of the relief operations, early in 1849, the Central Relief Committee acquired land in County Galway on which to establish a model farm and Bewley served on the committee of this project.[6] The Central Relief Committee had been established to run a relief operation until the new harvest of 1848 and, in common with other operations, it kept going as the Famine stretched out over a longer period. It was not until 1851 that the committee finally considered it time to wind down its operations and to write its final report to donors. As with the relief operation itself, the initiative for writing the final report came from Bewley and it was published in 1852 as *Transactions of the Central Relief Committee of the Society of Friends during the Famine in Ireland in 1846 and 1847*. Joseph Bewley did not live to write Transactions. In the introduction to the volume the delay in its publication was explained:

> A main cause of the delay ... was the delicate state of health of Joseph Bewley, one of our honorary secretaries; and by his decease ... we were deprived of his important and highly valued assistance. He was the first promotor of this Committee, and as he had throughout taken a much larger share than any other of its members, of the labour and responsibility attendant on its proceedings, we hoped that he would have been able to prepare the report of its transactions.[7]

Worn out by five years of hard work on the relief operations, Joseph Bewley went with his family to Castlewellan, County Down, for a rest, but collapsed and died after going for a walk. He was 56 years old.[8]

Jonathan Pim

The Pim family had arrived in Dublin from Mountmellick in the eighteenth century and had made their mark on the city's commercial community. The partnership of Pim Brothers was established by Jonathan Pim's father and his three uncles, working in imports and exports to England, North America and the West Indies. Jonathan Pim was born in Dublin in 1806 and became a partner in the family firm and managing director when the firm became a limited company. By that stage, Pim Brothers also had extensive manufacturing premises at Greenmount, Harold's Cross.[9]

Jonathan Pim was appointed joint secretary of the Central Relief Committee, along with Joseph Bewley, and his functions on that committee were as described above in the section on Joseph Bewley, including the position on the subcommittee handling the day-to-day running of the relief efforts. In January 1847, Jonathan Pim and William Todhunter travelled to County Mayo to join William Forster on his fact-finding tour of the west, accompanying him to investigate conditions at Ballina, Crossmolina and Killala and to make contacts with local people who could help in their localities. In March and early April, Jonathan Pim travelled westward again, this time with James Perry, visiting Galway, Roundstone, Clifden, Westport and Newport. Along the route they had a meeting with Count Strzelecki, agent for the British Relief Association, which was also running a relief operation.[10]

In late March 1847, Pim confided in Joseph Bewley that the stress and strain of running the relief operation were seriously affecting his mental and physical health and that his business was totally neglected. As a result, the system of working was revised, including the establishment of subcommittees to take on part of the workload.[11] This solved his immediate problem, though he still served on several committees and subcommittees. In addition to his work with Famine relief, Pim found time to write and publish a volume entitled 'The Condition and Prospects of Ireland and the Evils Arising from the Present Distribution of Landed Property with Suggestions for a Remedy', published in 1848. This was a significant work, amounting to some 300 pages, with a further 50 pages of appendices.[12] Famine relief work was not the only cause taken up by Jonathan Pim as he was also a founder member of the Dublin Statistical Society, founded in 1847, and served on its council and as its president and presented a number of papers to the society.[13]

In 1865, Pim was elected MP for Dublin University and took up a number of causes in parliament, the principal one being the land question over the next nine years. During this time, he published *The Land Question in Ireland* in which he proposed a detailed bill as a replacement for the Landlord and Tenant Act of 1860. While this bill was not adopted, the British politician, William Gladstone, availed of his knowledge of the Irish landholding system in the drafting of the 1870 Land Act. Further publications included *Ireland and the Imperial Parliament,* (1870) and *A Review of the Economic and Social Progress of Ireland since the Famine* (1876).[14]

Jonathan Pim died in 1885 at the age of 79.

Henry Perry

Henry Perry was born in County Laois in 1796 and moved to Dublin in 1817 with his brother, James Perry, when they took a lease on a shop in Pill Lane, now Chancery Street. From these premises they ran an ironmongery business, dealing in Sheffield cutlery, locks, hinges and articles of brass and iron. The business expanded into the adjacent premises, which they operated as haberdashery. They also became the proprietors of the Ringsend Iron Works, just outside Dublin.[15]

In November 1846, Henry Perry was one of the four Quakers to write to members of the Society of Friends in Ireland to call the meeting that was to establish the Central Relief Committee and he was appointed to sit on that committee. As the workload of the Friends' relief operation broadened and increased, numerous committees were established to look after specific aspects of the operations. Amongst these was a clothing committee, set up in recognition of the inability of those most affected by the Great Hunger to acquire clothes to replace those that were wearing out, particularly in the light of the harsh winter. Donations of clothing were collected by Friends in Britain and sent to the clothing committee in Dublin for distribution wherever they were needed. This became one of the most important committees, with a substantial workload that necessitated the employment of a paid secretary, while the volumes of clothing collected was sufficient to warrant the use of a warehouse. Henry Perry was treasurer of this committee and attended its meetings regularly.[16] In addition, he attended a number of other meetings on which he was not formally a member, such as the committee set up to establish a soup kitchen in Dublin.

Henry Perry's death is not noted anywhere in the Quaker records. His name just ceased to appear among those in attendance at committee meetings at a time coinciding with his date of death as recorded on his grave marker in 1848.[17] His death was noted in the Dublin press, however, they simply noting that Henry Perry, who was a member of the Society of Friends, had died at his home, Obelisk Park, on 1 February.[18] Perry was aged just 52 years, and it is tempting to conclude that his death was caused either by contracting famine fever or that was due to the excessive workload through running a thriving business while also attending to the many duties arising from his work on Famine relief.

William Forster

William Forster was born in London in 1784, where his father was a land agent and a surveyor. A devout Quaker from an early age, he was recognised as a minister by the Society of Friends by the time he was 20—signifying that he was approved to preach the Quaker message. He was also a passionate abolitionist and spent three years touring in the United States. His marriage to Anne Buxton brought him financial independence, facilitating his travels to preach and to campaign against slavery. Living in Dorset after their marriage, William and Anne Forster moved to Norwich in 1844.[19]

At the same time as Irish Quakers were considering what they could do to alleviate suffering during the Famine, Quakers in Britain had similar thoughts and a meeting was held in London on 9 November 1846. The outcome was a decision to contact Friends in Ireland, as a result of which a second meeting was held on 25 November, at which a committee was established to assist relief operations in Ireland, to raise funds and to lobby parliament when necessary. One of the most immediate needs identified by both the London and Dublin committees was to find out more detail as to the situation around Ireland so as to formulate the most effective means of providing relief. This need was particularly important given that the distribution of Quakers in Ireland was skewed towards the east of the country, while the worst effects of the Great Hunger were likely to be in the west. Even before he knew of the decisions of Friends in Ireland, Forster was considering the need to determine the extent of the distress and had discussed it with London Quakers. Just five days after the second meeting in London, Forster set out for Dublin to meet with the Central Relief Committee prior to commencing his fact-finding tour.[20]

William Forster did not travel alone, but was accompanied by others along the way, though his companions varied, and he was the only one to undertake the full journey. His travels extended over four and a half months, lasting until 14 April 1847. During this time, he travelled through counties Roscommon, Leitrim, Fermanagh, Donegal, Sligo, Mayo, Galway, Longford and Cavan. He inspected each of these counties carefully, particularly those areas that were more remote or particularly poor. Throughout the journey he was in constant contact with the Central Relief Committee, sending back information as to the state of the populace and providing advice as to how relief might be managed.[21] The findings of his journey were invaluable. The extent of the destitution that he discovered was much worse than had been anticipated, a finding that was of particular importance given that some of the English newspapers were claiming that the distress was being exaggerated. His contacts with the local gentry and professionals allowed him to encourage them to become involved in relief measures locally, helped by promises of assistance from the Central Relief Committee. Through Forster, many of these people were put in contact with the relief efforts in Dublin, providing efficient and trustworthy agents for the distribution of aid in areas far from the locations where there Quaker communities.

The winter of 1846–1847 was a harsh one and William Forster travelled in primitive conditions through areas with little in the way of home comforts. As the *Transactions* put it, he went 'in the depth of a very inclement winter, deprived of many of the comforts to which he was accustomed, and his feelings often painfully excited by witnessing so much misery beyond his power to relieve'.[22] He was not in the first flush of youth at the time, being 62 years old. William Forster subsequently continued his campaign against slavery, travelling throughout Europe for four years, visiting about a dozen countries and meeting with kings, emperors, statesmen and officials. He returned to the United States in an attempt to reconcile slave owners and slaves and died in Tennessee in 1854 at the age of 70.

Abraham Beale

Abraham Beale was the proprietor of the Monard Ironworks and the Kilcully Iron Works, near Cork, and had a warehouse for iron goods in St Patrick's Quay in that city.[23] In 1820, when he was 27 years old, he ran into difficulties with his business interests and was bankrupted, leading to his being disowned by the Quaker community, which demanded that the business and private lives of its adherents be conducted with care and without unwarranted risk.[24] Through diligence he was able to pay his creditors and discharge his bankruptcy and was readmitted to the Society of Friends.

Beale was an active supporter of various charitable institutions in Cork and when the potato crop failed, he was one of the Cork Quakers who established a committee to organise relief works in the city.[25] This committee soon realised that while there was a great deal of suffering in Cork city, it was even more intense in west Cork, and so they began to distribute relief in that area in December 1846.[26] In January 1847, the Munster Quarterly Meeting of the Society of Friends established four auxiliary committees based on its meeting houses in Cork, Clonmel, Waterford and Limerick to act as agents for the Central Relief Committee in Munster. Beale served as clerk of the Cork Auxiliary Committee and devoted a great deal of his time and energy to organising the relief measures in counties Cork and Kerry.

During the first eight months in which the Cork Auxiliary Committee was operating Abraham Beale's work was unrelenting to the detriment of his health. He was aware of this, and that the nature of the relief work brought those involved into close contact with the diseases that accompanied famine. He was determined that this would not affect his input to the relief operations. In August 1847, he contracted typhus fever and died a few days later.[27] He was aged 54 years.

William Bennett

William Bennett was an English Quaker in his mid–40s when the potato blight arrived in Europe. He was a businessman and for more than 20 years had been running the family tea dealership in London.[28] He believed that a significant element of the relief efforts should include the distribution of seeds of green crops in the remote districts of Ireland to provide the people with an alternative to the now failed potato. The London committee was too deeply involved with its own measures to take on this project and so William Bennett decided to do it himself. He collected funds from English Quakers and was also given three large bales of clothing by the Ladies' Irish Clothing Committee.[29]

Early in March 1847 Bennett set off for Ireland, accompanied by his eldest son. He spent three days in Belfast, gathering information and meeting with local Quakers. From Belfast he travelled by the recently opened railway line to Dublin, where he attended a meeting of the Central Relief Committee. He was impressed at the committee's organisation and business methods and noted:

> it was said that they had as extensive a correspondence to conduct as any mercantile counting-house in Dublin. Some Friends devote almost their whole time, giving up day and night to its concerns and management, and to the work of the subcommittees.[30]

The Central Relief Committee was not convinced of the value of distributing seeds at this stage. William Bennett was not discouraged by the lack of support and arranged with the firm of W. Drummond and Sons, Dawson Street, Dublin, for the purchase of suitable seeds. Drummonds provided advice on types of seed that would be suitable and arranged for distribution to remote areas, along with simple printed directions for sowing and cultivating. The seeds selected included several varieties of turnip, principally swedes, the white Belgian carrot and mangel-wurzel. Some cabbage, flax and parsnip were latter added.[31]

On 12 March, Bennett set off by coach, with two hundred weight of seeds, en route for Boyle, County Roscommon. Over the next two weeks he travelled far, through Boyle, Ballina, Tobercurry, Crossmolina, Belmullet, The Mullet, Ballycastle, Killala, Ballina and Sligo. From there, he moved on to Ballyshannon, Glenties, Dungloe and Templecrone. Not confining his journey to the mainland, he crossed from Burtonport to Arranmore Island, following which he went on to Dunfanaghy. Leaving Donegal on 26 March, Bennett returned to Dublin, travelling via Letterkenny, Armagh and Portadown to Moira. While there, he visited Brookfield Agricultural School before setting out on his journey back to Dublin. Bennett spent a few days in Dublin, attending a meeting of the Central Relief Committee. He then set out on his travels again, once more with supplies of seeds, taking the train to Carlow and onward by coach to Clonmel, Cahir and Mitchelstown, before moving on to Cahirciveen. He took a boat out to Valentia Island, and on his return visited Maurice O'Connell at Derrynane and from thence to Kenmare via a 26-mile walk. Leaving Kenmare, he travelled from Cork to Clonmel and from there to Waterford, taking the packet boat from Dunmore East to Milford Haven on 16 April.

On his return, Bennett wrote an account of his journey, which he published as a book, with the proceeds going to famine relief.[32] While in Ireland he had not only undertaken an exhausting journey, but met with many people involved in famine relief, including Quakers, members of the clergy of other denominations, landed gentry, members of the aristocracy, professionals and others. His published account, written as a series of letters, provides a great deal of information about the conditions he encountered along the route and the aid he was able to provide.

James and Mary Ellis

James Ellis was the son of a farmer, although he was apprenticed to a corn miller and later established a milling and malting business with his brother-in-law in Bradford in the north of England. He married his second wife, Mary Wheeler, in 1837. Upon becoming an advocate for temperance, he left the malting business and entered the worsted trade, becoming very successful, which enabled him to retire at the age of 55 in 1848.[33] Shortly after his retirement, in July 1848, James Ellis travelled with his wife to Ireland to investigate the state of the country, influenced by the reports circulated by the London committee and by James Hack Tuke, who was the son of Mary's cousin.[34] As a result, they began to consider becoming landlords in an impoverished area, so that they could provide employment to relieve the suffering. In April 1849, James Ellis leased about 1,000 acres at Letterfrack, near Clifden, County Galway and he and Mary moved from England to live on the estate.[35]

The land that they had acquired was mainly mountain and bog and they set out to improve it and make it more productive. This involved land drainage, tree planting and the construction of walls and roads. A village was founded where there had been no buildings and included a school, a dispensary, a shop, a temperance hall and slated, stone-built workers' cottages. Mary managed a distress fund, provided assistance to the poor, distributed clothing donations, established employment in craft work and was involved with the school and the shop.[36] The Ellises remained in Letterfrack for eight years until 1857, when James's health began to decline, and they returned to England. They left behind them land that had been improved and a population that had been given the opportunity to learn new skills and grow new crops. Their actions had long-term effects in the area and are remembered and celebrated in Letterfrack today.[37]

Jacob Harvey

Jacob Harvey was born near Limerick in 1797 and left Ireland at the age of 12 when his family emigrated to the United States. He entered into business with fellow Quaker, Abraham Bell, in New York.[38]

In December 1846, Jonathan Pim wrote to Jacob Harvey, sending a copy of an address to Quakers on the matter of the Great Hunger and the proposed relief works. As a result, Harvey began to tap into every contact that he had in the United States, including the Quaker community, a Roman Catholic bishop, and wealthy bankers. The result was that a substantial amount of donations flowed from the United States to the Central Relief Committee and, what is less recognised, the approach to the Irish Catholic community led to a significant amount of funds being sent from this group to their relatives back in Ireland.[39] Through 1847 and into 1848 Harvey served as secretary of the General Relief Committee of New York.[40]

Harvey was of the opinion that the population of Ireland could not be supported if the potato was absent and, given that the potato had now proved unreliable, the only option was to encourage emigration. New York State passed an act appointing commissioners to take charge of all immigrants arriving in New York and Jacob Harvey was appointed to this commission.[41] In October 1847, Harvey's correspondence with the Dublin committee was from Hyde Park, on the Hudson River, north of New York City, where he had gone for a fortnight 'to recruit my health, which has not been very strong; and after a fortnight's quiet sojourn there, I feel much better'.[42] Nevertheless, he continued his work to raise contributions to be sent to Ireland and to assist emigrants arriving from that country to New York. His letters, while full of succinct accounts of work in progress or proposed, give brief notes of his own position, which, in November 1847 included 'I have been so much an invalid this summer ... but nothing has been neglected I believe', and in January 1848, 'I shall try to collect the returns for the whole of 1847, when I get stronger'.[43] He continued his work for Famine relief and emigrants over the next three months. His last letter to Dublin, dated 1 April 1848, expressed hope that the situation in Ireland was improving, while continuing to encourage emigration, as the United States needed the workers. However, two weeks later he died, aged 51.[44]

William Todhunter

William Todhunter was born in Dublin in 1802.[45] It is not clear what he did for a living, but he may have worked with his brother, Thomas, in his late father's timber, slate and corn merchant's business on Sir John Rogerson's Quay.[46] It is also possible that he worked with his brother-in-law, Jonathan Pim, in the Greenmount Spinning Factory, as he lived at Parnell Place Upper, adjacent to the factory, in a house owned by Pim.[47]

At the meeting in Dublin in November 1846, William Todhunter was appointed to the Central Relief Committee. In January 1847, he travelled with Pim to Ballina, County Mayo, to join William Forster, spending three days there, including visits to Crossmolina and Killala and their environs. Shortly after the establishment of the auxiliary subcommittees in Munster, the workload of the Central Relief Committee in relation to food distribution was delegated to subcommittees for the provinces of Leinster, Connaught and Ulster, and William Todhunter served as an active member of the Connaught subcommittee.[48] In March 1847, the government offered to donate a substantial quantity of green-crop seeds to the Central Relief Committee for distribution. The task was taken on by Todhunter. It was late in the season for planting and to expedite the distribution, he decided to use the postal system as the most efficient and speedy method of dispersal.[49] In total, he distributed 36,196 lb of seeds, equivalent to 16,418 kg, to 40,903 recipients, resulting in the sowing of 9,652 acres, or 3,906 hectares, and this was estimated to have produced 193,040 tons of food.[50] In the following February a seed committee was established, with Todhunter as a member. This committee distributed almost 11,000 lb of seeds donated by the government and more than 120,000 lb purchased by the committee, with similar results.[51]

During the summer of 1847 the Central Relief Committee decided to improve the future prospects for fisheries off the west coast. The problem was considered to be the lack of larger sea-going fishing boats and lack of training amongst the fishermen, along with the inadequacy of coastal charts. There was a belief that the waters off the west coast were teeming with fish and that trawling would be the most effective method for harvesting the seas. William Todhunter spent three months on a trawler examining the seas off Galway, Mayo, Kerry and west Cork, finding that the rich fishing grounds did not exist and that with a few exceptions the sea bed off the coast was too rocky to allow for trawling.[52] When not at sea on the trawler, William Todhunter was also managing the distribution of loans to fishermen to allow them to fit out their boats and return to being self-supporting following a season when the herring had failed to appear off the coast.[53] In 1848, the Central

Relief Committee entered into agreements with certain landowners to take on land and cultivate it, training people in agricultural methods and cultivation, while also producing food. William Todhunter drew up the agreements with the landowners and established the systems on which these ventures would operate, and a number of projects were undertaken from 1848 into 1850.[54] As these short-term agricultural projects wound down a decision was taken, on the suggestion of Dr Edward Bewley, to acquire a significant tract of farmland and to establish a model farm to provide training in agricultural methods in the longer term. Todhunter was appointed one of the directors of the venture.

Having devoted a substantial amount of time and energy into a variety of relief measures from the autumn of 1846, William Todhunter's health broke down and he died in January 1850, aged 46.[55]

James Hack Tuke

The Tuke family were tea merchants in York from 1753, when William Tuke inherited the business from his aunt. James Hack Tuke was the fourth generation to enter the business, though when his father retired in 1852, James also left the tea trade and went into banking.[56] His family had a tradition of concern for the disadvantaged, notably when his great-grandfather, William Tuke, established The Retreat, a psychiatric hospital in York that pioneered humane, patient-centred care, an establishment that inspired the founding of Bloomfield Hospital in Dublin, which still provides care after more than two centuries.[57]

In December 1846, when aged 27, James Hack Tuke travelled to the west of Ireland to join William Forster in his tour of Donegal and Sligo, following which he issued a report to the Central Relief Committee.[58] Deeply affected by what he had seen on this tour, Tuke returned to Ireland later in 1847 and spent time in Connemara. On his return he wrote an account of his findings for the benefit of the Central Relief Committee, and this was published in book form. Arising from responses to this publication he revisited the west, travelling through Mayo to the Mullet, as a result of which he published a revised edition that included a postscript on the topic of evictions in Erris, which included the Mullet.[59] After the Famine, James Hack Tuke continued to be involved with projects to assist the disadvantaged, serving as a member of the National Freedmen's Aid Association to help former slaves following their emancipation in the United States. He was also heavily involved in education in

England, including the establishment of a college for the higher education of women that was a forerunner of Girton College, Cambridge. In 1870, he was a commissioner of the Friends' War Victims' Relief Committee, which provided relief to non-combatants after the Franco-Prussian War.[60]

Tuke's experiences during the Great Hunger in Ireland left a lasting impression, leading him to consider the potential for actions to improve living conditions, particularly in the west. In the wake of the hardship that had returned to Ireland in 1879–1881, Tuke travelled to Ireland to represent Friends in the distribution of relief. From his previous visits he had formed the opinion that the poverty in the west was largely due to the inability of the land to support the population, concluding that the population needed to be reduced and that this would occur either through starvation, as had happened before, or through emigration. In 1881 he published an article in which he advocated that assistance should be given to provide those who wished to emigrate with financial and other assistance. This led to the establishment of the Tuke Fund which provided funds that helped many to make the journey to the United States and Canada. Between 1882 and 1884 almost 9,500 people emigrated from Clifden, Newport, Belmullet and Oughterard, assisted by this scheme.[61]

When Famine returned in 1885–1886, the government sought Tuke's aid and he raised funds for the purchase of seed potatoes, supervising their distribution in the west of Ireland, following which he published his observations and recommendations. When the Congested Districts Board was established in 1891 James Hack Tuke was appointed to the board and travelled to Ireland for its meetings each month until 1894. He died in 1896.[62]

The Central Relief Committee's account of its work during the Famine referred more to its failures and mistakes than to its achievements, stating that:

> Although public opinion has, on several occasions, been favourably expressed as regards our proceedings, we feel that we can only claim the merit of an honest intention, to dispose of the funds under our care to the best of our ability.[63]

However, the best of their ability brought succour to many, often to the detriment of their own health. The few heroes noted here represent only some of those from a small religious group who gave so much without thought for the personal cost, while the names and works of many of their co-religionists during the Famine remain undocumented.

NOTES

1. William E Hearn (ed.), *Transactions of the Central Relief Committee of the Society of Friends during the Famine in Ireland in 1846 and 1847* (1852; facsimile edition, Dublin: Edmund Burke Publisher, 1996).
2. Yearly Meeting of Friends in Ireland, *Rules of Discipline,* 2nd ed. With corrections and additions to 1858 inclusive (Dublin: Webb and Chapman, 1841).
3. David M Butler, *The Quaker Meeting Houses of Ireland* (Dublin: Irish Friends Historical Committee, 2004), p. 17.
4. Helen Andrews, 'Samuel Bewley and Joseph Bewley', *DIB,* www.dib.ie/biography/bewley-samuel-a0644, accessed 22 December 2023; Richard S Harrison, *A Biographical Dictionary of Irish Quakers* (Dublin: Four Courts Press, 2008), p. 53.
5. William E. Hearn (ed.), *Transactions of the Central Relief Committee of the Society of Friends during the Famine in Ireland in 1846 and 1847* (1852; facsimile edition, Dublin: Edmund Burke Publisher, 1996), pp 2, 129–131; National Archives of Ireland, Society of Friends Relief of Distress Papers, *Committee Book No. 1*, 2 506 2, 1A 42 139.
6. National Archives of Ireland, Society of Friends Relief of Distress Papers, *Origins and Objects of Model Farm and Agricultural School,* April 1849, 2 507 7.
7. Hearn, *Transactions*, pp 1–2.
8. *The Annual Monitor for 1851* (London, 1850), pp 6–8.
9. Richard S Harrison, 'Pim Brothers – merchants, manufacturers and entrepreneurs of nineteenth-century Dublin', *Journal of the Friends Historical Society,* vol. 59, no. 2, 2002, pp 236–250.
10. For more on his role see Christine Kinealy, 'Paul de Strzelecki: A Polish Count in County Mayo' in Kinealy, Moran and King (eds), *Heroes of Ireland's Great Hunger* (Cork University Press, 2021), pp 21- 38.
11. Helen Hatton, *The Largest Amount of Good: Quaker Relief in Ireland, 1654–1921* (Kingston & Montréal: McGill-Queen's University Press, 1993), pp 163–164.
12. Jonathan Pim, *The Condition and Prospects of Ireland and the Evils arising from the Present Distribution of Landed Property with Suggestions for a Remedy* (Dublin: Hodges and Smith, 1848).
13. Kieran Rankin, Paul Sweeney and Bill Keating, *Biographical Portraits of the Past Presidents of the Statistical and Social Inquiry Society of Ireland*. www.tara.tcd.ie/bitstream/handle/2262/73814/biographical%20portraits%20of%20the%20past%20presidents%20of%20the%20Statistical%20and%20Social%20Inquiry%20society%20of%20ireland%20final%20-%20last%20updated%20april%202004.pdf?sequence=8&isAllowed=y
14. James Quinn and Bridget Hourican, 'Jonathan Pim', *Dictionary of Irish Biography* (Dublin: Royal Irish Academy, 2009).
15. Rob Goodbody, *Obelisk Park* (Bray: private circulation, 1995), pp 20–21.
16. Hatton, *The Largest Amount of Good*, p. 105.
17. Henry Perry's grave, Mount Jerome Cemetery, Dublin.
18. 'Deaths', *Dublin Evening Mail*, 2 February 1848; *Limerick Reporter*, 4 February 1848.

19. Edward H. Milligan, 'William Forster', *Oxford Dictionary of National Biography* (Oxford University Press, 2004).
20. Hearn, *Transactions,* pp 38–40.
21. Ibid., pp 145–160.
22. *Transactions*, p. 39.
23. Billy Wigham and Colin Rynne, *A Life of Usefulness: Abraham Beale and the Monard Ironworks* (Blarney: Sitka Press, 2000), p. 33.
24. Ibid, p. 2; Database of Disownments, Friends Historical Library, Dublin.
25. *The Annual Monitor for 1848* (York: William Alexander, 1847), pp 164–165.
26. Ibid, pp. *165–166*; Rob Goodbody, *A Suitable Channel* (Bray: Pale Publishing, 1995), p. 6.
27. *The Annual Monitor for 1848*, pp 167–170.
28. Edward H. Milligan, *Biographical Dictionary of British Quakers in Commerce and Industry, 1775–1920* (York: Sessions Book Trust, 2007), p. 45.
29. Except where otherwise noted, the entry for William Bennett is based on William Bennett, *Narrative of a Recent Journey of Six Weeks in Ireland in Connexion with the Subject of Supplying Small Seed to some of the Remoter Districts* (London and Dublin: Charles Gilpin, 1847).
30. Hearn, *Transactions*, p. 160.
31. For more on Bennett's time in Ireland, including an annotated reprint of his published account, see 'William Bennett. *Six Weeks in Ireland'* in Christine Kinealy (ed.), *The History of the Irish Famine* (London: Routledge, 2019), pp 221–300.
32. Bennett, *Narrative of a Recent Journey.*
33. Milligan, *Biographical Dictionary of British Quakers*, p. 165.
34. For more on Tuke see Gerard Moran, 'James Hack Tuke. An English Quaker Philanthropist' in Kinealy, Moran, King, *Heroes*, pp 3–20.
35. Joan Johnson, *James & Mary Ellis: Background and Quaker Famine Relief in Letterfrack* (Dublin: Historical Committee of the Religious Society of Friends in Ireland, 2000), pp 18–19, 28–33.
36. Ibid., p. 36.
37. Ibid., pp 65–69.
38. Richard S. Harrison, *A Biographical Dictionary of Irish Quakers* (Dublin: Four Courts Press, 2008), p. 116.
39. Hearn, *Transactions*, pp 216–220, 285–292.
40. Christine Kinealy, *Charity and the Great Hunger in Ireland. The kindness of strangers* (London: Bloomsbury Press, 2013), p. 59.
41. Hearn, *Transactions*, p. 289.
42. Ibid., pp 314, 322, 325.
43. Ibid.
44. Ibid., p. 327.
45. Irish Quaker Database, Friends' Historical Library, Dublin.
46. Alexander Thom, *Thom's Irish Almanac and Official Directory for the year 1847* (Dublin: Alexander Thom & Co, 1847), p. 396.
47. Ibid., County Dublin Directory, p. 28; Valuation Office Dublin, Cancelled books, Harold's Cross, vol. 1.

48. Hearn, *Transactions*, p. 37; National Archives of Ireland, *Society of Friends Relief of Distress Papers, Connaught Subcommittee*, 2 505 25, 1A 42 120.
49. Kinealy, *Charity and the Great Hunger*, p. 74.
50. Hearn, *Transactions*, p. 385.
51. Ibid., pp 387–389.
52. Ibid., pp 410–415.
53. Hatton, *The Largest Amount of Good*, p. 206.
54. Ibid., pp 189, 192.
55. *The Annual Monitor for 1851* (London, 1850), p. 65.
56. Milligan, *Biographical Dictionary of British Quakers*, pp 445–446.
57. Glynn Douglas, Rob Goodbody, Alice Mauger and John Davey, *Bloomfield: A History, 1812–2012* (Dublin: Ashfield Press, 2012), pp 5–10.
58. Hearn, Transactions, pp 147–153.
59. James H. Tuke, *A Visit to Connaught in the Autumn of 1847 ... with Notes of a Subsequent Visit to Erris* (London, 1848).
60. Milligan, *Biographical Dictionary of British Quakers*, pp 445–446.
61. Gerard Moran, 'James Hack Tuke and his schemes for assisted emigration from the west of Ireland', *History Ireland*, vol. 21, 3, May-June 2013, pp 30–33; Clifden & Connemara Heritage Society, *Mr Tuke's Fund: Connemara Emigration in the 1880s* (Clifden, 2014), pp 20–23.
62. David Murphy, 'Tuke, James Hack', *Dictionary of Irish Biography* (Dublin: Royal Irish Academy, 2009).
63. Hearn, *Transactions*, p. 5.

CHAPTER TEN

'OUR MOST EFFICIENT ALMONERS'
Women and Relief

Christine Kinealy

The multiple contributions of women during the Great Hunger, both individually and collectively, have received relatively little attention in Famine historiography.[1] Following the second harvest failure in 1846, however, women, both within Ireland and further afield, were galvanized into taking actions that took them beyond the domestic sphere and into the lives, and sometimes homes, of the poorest members of society. Moreover, they proved to be effective as fund-raisers, as conduits for collecting clothes and blankets, as book-keepers, at running industrial schools, establishing soup kitchens, and as effective providers of direct relief. The Quakers, who distributed money and relief in some of the remotest and poorest parts of Ireland, admitted that they preferred to work with women as they had proved to be 'our most efficient almoners'.[2] Nonetheless, many of these women simply appear as a name in a list of donors or as a member of a relief committee. An even greater number of women remain nameless and invisible in the historical record and the historiography. For the most part, they are hidden in history and overshadowed by their male counterparts. This chapter explores the involvement of a small number of Irish women who engaged in famine philanthropy in a variety of capacities, while providing some context to their lives and the work that they undertook.

By the 1840s, women were no strangers to charity work—along with abolition, it was one of the few areas where it was acceptable for middle-class and upper-class females to be visible. Their involvement in both no doubt helped to hone their skills and their sense of agency. Within Ireland, philanthropy tended to follow accepted religious and sectarian divisions.[3] During the Famine, it mostly cut across these traditional divides. It reflected the pattern of most charity work, commencing at the end of 1846 following the second harvest failure, and being most intense in the early months of 1847 when the transition between the public works and the government-run soup kitchens resulted in widespread suffering. By the end of the year, most charitable donations had dried up.

Women were overwhelmingly excluded from sitting alongside men on the main relief bodies. Two of the largest committees, the British Relief Association, and the Central Relief Committee of the Society of Friends, both founded by religious minorities, namely Jews and Quakers, had male-only committees. Women, however, were both contributors to, and beneficiaries of, their work. At the end of 1846, women were applying to the newly established private relief committees for financial assistance. Moreover, Quaker women, who were involved in every aspect of famine relief, formed their own auxiliary relief committees. They developed their own areas of speciality regarding the collection and distribution of clothing. As Daphne Wolfe has demonstrated, the lack of clothing hampered people from being able to go into public spaces and receive relief. Moreover, the winter of 1846 to 1847 was the coldest on record for 100 years.[4] Most of the garments were collected in England. The logistics of transporting large amounts of bulky clothing and bedding was a task that soon overwhelmed the men on the Quaker's Central Committee in Dublin. In January 1847, a special committee was established, run by women, who co-ordinated the 'receiving, sorting and delivering' of these goods. They were assisted by being given free transport from the railway companies in England, and free passage on the steam ships to Ireland. A warehouse for storage was also made available to them.[5] In Dublin, the distribution of clothing largely fell to the capable hands of Susanna Pim.[6] Born in 1806, Susanna Jane Todhunter had married Jonathan Pim in June 1828.[7] Her father was John Todhunter, who, like Jonathan, was a successful Dublin merchant.[8] In 1846, Jonathan became one of the secretaries of the Central Relief Committee.[9] The effectiveness of the women's clothing committees was evident to Asenath Nicholson who, when visiting a convent in Tuam, was informed by a nun that all 400 children were wearing clothes provided by the Society of Friends. The nun added, 'The good Quakers have kept them alive'.[10] Despite playing a pivotal role, Susanna's name rarely appeared in public records or in the Quakers' own record of the Famine, which they published in 1852. This was part of the self-effacing nature of Quaker philosophy. As the *Transactions* recorded, 'it is not our province to record the noble self-denial shown in individual cases'.[11] Elsewhere though, it was noted:

> Clothing was distributed by Susanna Pim, while Isabelle Pim was involved with the Kingstown Industrial Society which supplied new nets to fishermen. Food was also distributed by Mary Greenwood Pim and by Ruth Pim of the Liberty Infant School. In rural areas, the Moss family was distributing aid in Kilteman, and the Barringtons near Bray.

Clearly, there is a far larger story to be told about Quaker women during the Great Hunger. Susanna's public involvement did not end with the Famine. In 1862, she donated £1 to a relief fund established in Lancashire in the north of England to support unemployed families who had refused to work with cotton imported from the Southern slave states in America.[12] Susanna died in 1868, her passing being noted in the Quaker records. Her age was given as 61.[13] Jonathan survived until 1885.

Women throughout Ireland proved to be adept at forming relief committees. The Belfast Ladies' Association for the Relief of Irish Destitution was formed on 1 January 1847. It brought together females from all religious denominations and political persuasions, including the indomitable Mary Ann McCraken, then aged 77.[14] A number of the women, including McCracken, Maria Webb and Mary Ireland, were actively involved in the abolition movement and so were familiar with operating in the public sphere.[15] From the outset, the 115 all-women committee showed its determination to operate as a professional body with several sub-committees being established including the Corresponding, Clothing, Industrial, Collecting, and Bazaar Committees.[16] For fund-raising purposes, Belfast was divided into a number of districts, each with its own subscription list. Donations were also sought from Britain. Relief was to be provided throughout all of Ireland with no distinction based on 'doctrinal differences'.[17] Nicholson, who witnessed the committee's work at first-hand, was impressed with the efficiency and harmony with which the women worked together.[18] The majority of requests for assistance came from counties Antrim, Donegal, and Mayo. As conditions deteriorated in Belfast, exacerbated by a down-swing in industrial production, a separate organization was established to look after the needs of the poor in the town.[19]

The meticulous records kept by the Belfast Ladies' Association testified to the remarkable efforts being made by women to assist in their communities. One such woman was Mrs Hewetson from Rossgarrow near Milford in County Donegal. In February 1847, she appealed to the Belfast committee for clothing to be sent to her.

She explained that she and her daughters, together with several local women, had formed an Industrial Committee for which she acted as both Treasurer and Secretary. She had already received small grants from the First and Second Unitarian churches in Belfast, and from the Society of Friends, which had been quickly used up. The Belfast Committee had sent her a consignment of clothing, but its arrival coincided with 'a bitter snow storm', consequently, demand had exceeded supply. She explained:

> The children, in particular, are never half covered, and their few things seldom made to fit ... Some men are now working on the roads in thin linen jackets; and many starving beings, male and female, some of tender age, are now expecting employment on them, and anxiously imploring a covering from the exposure they are subject to, at such work.[20]

Hewetson received £5 worth of clothing from the Ladies' Association.[21] A few days later, she received a grant of £5 from their Industrial Committee.[22]

The Hewetson family came to the notice of Nicholson, as she toured the country, providing valuable, forthright, eye-witness accounts of the suffering and of those who sought to alleviate it. She first became acquainted with a 'Miss Hewitson' [sic] when she was staying in Belfast, who informed her that her family resided in Donegal where the suffering was very great.[23] Nicholson took the coach to Derry where she was met by Mrs Hewetson and her son and they 'took tea at a delightful little mansion on the sloping side of one of Ireland's green lawns'. They then travelled to the family home, a thatched cottage overlooking a lake, which Nicholson described as 'one of the most pleasant retreats I had met'.[24] Hewetson's husband had served in the military, and spent time in America, but he was now retired. In the previous months, he had been employed as an overseer for the Boards of Works, but 'his heart had sickened at the scenes which came under his eye'.[25] As was the case in many places, the public works had proved to be an ineffective tool for providing large-scale relief. In December 1846, the local Catholic and Protestant clergy had sent a joint memorial to the Lord Lieutenant pointing out that while 700 families were existing in a state of misery, only 118 individuals had been employed on the works.[26] Nicholson recorded that her host woke up every day when it was still dark to make breakfast for her family and to weigh out cornmeal, the latter having been supplied by the Society of Friends. The local poor gathered early outside the Hewetson's home, and the glass window in the kitchen had been replaced with a board, 'this having been broken by the pressure of faces continually there'.[27] For Nicholson, such suffering affected nature itself:

> Who could eat, who could work, who could read, or who could play in such circumstances as these? Certainly, it sometimes seemed that the sunshine was changed,

> that the rain gave a stranger pattering, and truly, that the wind did moan most dolefully. The dogs ceased their barking, there were scarcely any cocks to be heard crowing in the morning, and the gladsome mirth of children everywhere ceased … The young laughing faces, and brilliant eyes, and buoyant limbs, had become walking skeletons of death![28]

When Nicholson left Donegal and returned to Belfast, Mrs Hewetson accompanied her. Before departing, the usual relief had been distributed. Nonetheless, 'the starving were crowding about and pressing her for food, following the carriage—begging and thanking—blessing and weeping'. Hewetson's comment on leaving was, 'Many of these poor creatures will be dead on my return'.[29] In Belfast, there was a donation waiting for Nicholson, which she gave to Hewetson. The latter said she eked the money out for months as it was the only gift she received during the remainder of the year.[30] What became of the kindly Hewetson family? While it is hard to know definitively, a family of this name from Rossgarrow emigrated to America in 1850. The woman of the house, Hannah Hewetson, died in Charleston, South Carolina, in 1856. Her husband, Barry Drew Hewetson, died in the same location in 1869.[31]

At the southern end of County Donegal, another woman was demonstrating similar resourcefulness and benevolence. Susan Hume lived in Glen Lodge, close to the small sea-port and fishing village of Killybegs. Her husband was a Justice of the Peace who had signed an Ulster-wide petition in 1841 in support of the union with Britain.[32] Nonetheless, they were both critical of the government's response to the hunger in Ireland. On 3 February 1847, Susan wrote to the Belfast Ladies' Association requesting financial support to establish a knitting group. She explained:

> The aid which has been obtained, by Government employing some on the public roads, is very inadequate to the extent of want. The limitation of one only being employed out of large family, at 9*d* per day, affords to a labouring man, with six or eight children, scanty pittance for their support. The females are totally unemployed, in a state of wretchedness and want, and would require some active efforts to relieve them, by giving work. [33]

On 22 February, Susan again wrote to the committee, thanking them for sending the first half of a grant of £10. She promised that she would 'expend it judiciously', and explained that the local women had only been employed in manual labour previously, working in a field.[34] Both of her letters were published in the press by the Ladies' Association, alongside many other heart-felt appeals. In May, she received a further grant of £10 from the Association.[35]

Susan's frustrations with the government's relief measures were shared by her husband. In April, William wrote to William Stanley, secretary to the Relief

Commissioners in Dublin, and painted a dismal picture of the local situation. The letter concluded:

> I must confess, as a Landlord (not receiving any rent) my inability to assist the poor tenants in their need. But the plan of the Commissary General, I suppose, accords with the views of Government, to procrastinate relief, until starvation and death ensues. This is, I assure you, the general impression.[36]

William died on 3 November 1849. His death notice stated that his passing occurred 'after a long illness borne with Christian firmness and resignation'.[37] William was buried in St Columba's Anglican church in Columcille.[38] How did Susan fare following the passing of her husband? In 1853, she was recorded as appearing in the Encumbered Estates Court.[39] At the end of 1856, over 10,000 acres of land from the estate was put up for sale.[40] In 1857, Glen Lodge and other family possessions were sold in the Court. The property was described as:

> Glen Lodge, heretofore the residence of the proprietors, is situated on the Townland of Drimroe, and consists of two storeys, with Out-offices and walled-in Garden and a Farm of about 30a[cres]. 0r. 7p. attached. There is a daily post to the Glen, the office being convenient to Glen Lodge. The Lands lies 5 miles from the rising town of Carrick, and 11 from the seaport town Killybegs. From the nature of this Estate, and its varied and valuable resources and attractions, it offers great advantages for safe and remunerative investment of capital; and it is specially recommended to the consideration of English and Scotch capitalists.[41]

The final sentence was a telling insight into how post-Famine Ireland was regarded. After selling Glen Lodge, Susan disappeared from sight. In 1847, however, both she and William had not only highlighted how government policies were failing the people, but Susan had also intervened in a practical way to help the local poor.

Philanthropic relief to Ireland in 1847 came from all parts of the world and from all levels of society, from convicts to heads of state. Inevitably, a large portion came from North America where, even before the Famine exodus, there had been large-scale emigration. Two sisters from the small town of Dunmanway in County Cork, which contained approximately 3,000 inhabitants, fearlessly made an appeal to women, in both Britain and America.[42] A small group of women, drawn from the gentry classes, responded to the potato failure in 1846 by forming the Dunmanway Indian Meal Ladies' Committee. The committee consisted of the sisters Martha Deane Cox and Katherine Anne Cox, Harriet Maria Shuldham, Ellen Jagoe, Isabella Sullivan, and Anna Maria Galbraith. Its patrons were Lady Carbery and Mrs Major General Shuldham.[43]

The Anglo-Irish Cox family had been in Dunmanway since 1688 and were credited with being the founders of the town. In the 1840s, much of the local land was owned by two unmarried sisters, Martha and Katherine Cox. They were known to be benevolent landlords who had donated part of their property for the building of a new Catholic Church.[44] In 1845, even before the potato blight had fully appeared in Ireland, they had promised that there would be no rent increases for tenants who held leases. They were held up in the local press as an example that 'may be generally adopted by those who are placed on this earth as the Stewards of God's bounty to His children, the poor'.[45] As the impact of the blight started to be felt, they immediately lowered rents. In January 1846, following Mass, a meeting of over 1,000 people was held in the yard of the chapel to thank the sisters for granting a renewal of their leases, with no conditions and below its real value. The local parish priest, Father James Doheny, praised them for their 'humane conduct', while several other speakers held them up as an example to other Irish landlords. That evening, Father Doheny held a large banquet in honour of the sisters but, due to the delicate health of one, the Coxes could not attend. They were toasted frequently in their absence.[46] Accounts of the celebrations were reprinted in multiple Irish newspapers.[47]

Poor health did not deter the sisters from playing an active role in the Dunmanway Indian Meal Committee. Following the second crop failure, the Dunmanway women had opened a soup kitchen on 61 and 62 Main Street, which was rented in the name of Anna Galbraith and Miss Cox.[48] As demand expanded, they required financial assistance to purchase further kitchen apparatus. On 11 January, they sent a request to the Irish Relief Association, which had been established in Dublin in September 1846,[49] for a grant to enable the purchase of two large boilers.[50] The request was signed by the women who formed the committee. In the covering letter, they explained the limitations of relief provided under the public works, most especially that wages were too low for a man to support his wife and children during a time of inflated famine prices. Moreover, many local merchants were deliberately overcharging, consequently, 'many have been saved by the exertions of a few in underselling the extortionate millers and merchants of this place—and the soup shop saves many more'. While the request was granted, the Dunmanway Committee was told that any future requests for assistance should be directed to the Ladies' Association in Dublin.[51]

Demonstrating an initiative and a mettle that was rare even amongst male fundraisers, the enterprising ladies of Dunmanway extended their appeals to England and to the United States—both directed to women. The emotional appeal to women in England simultaneously paid tribute to the forbearance of the Irish poor. It was dated 1 January 1847:

> The Christian Ladies of England are earnestly called up by their Irish sisters to help them in 'saving alive in Famine the perishing people of Ireland'. The Irish are not regardless of their country's misery and have done what they could to relieve it; but so total and so widespread is the destitution, that it is beyond their power to remove it. In former times, the Irish cottier was ready to divide his last meal with the hungry, and the best potatoes in the bowl was preserved for the widow and the fatherless; but now there is not one to divide—the daily morsel is consumed at once, and he has nothing left to save the perishing neighbour from dying at his door. Fever and other deadly diseases have set in on famine, and unless we can procure foreign aid, Ireland must soon be one wide field of the dying and the dead.
>
> If you, dear lady, into whose hands these papers may be placed, would make a collection of sums, however small, among friends and neighbours, and send it by Post-Office Order, on to the Cork Post-Office, to any of the undersigned committee, who will gratefully acknowledge them, such aid will save many lives. When were the Ladies of England appealed to in vain?[52]

The appeal to the United States was widely circulated.[53] On 9 February 1847, a mass meeting was convened in Washington by the Vice President, George Dallas, to raise relief for Ireland. During the proceedings, Dallas read a letter from the Cox sisters:

> Oh! That our American sisters could see the labourers on our roads, able-bodied men, scarcely clad, famishing with hunger, with despair in their once cheerful faces, staggering at their work ... oh! That they could see the dead father, mother, or child, lying coffinless, and hear the screams of the survivors around them, caused not by sorrow, but the agony of hunger. They, whose hands and hearts are ever open to compassion, would unite in one mighty effort to save Ireland from such misery.[54]

The 'Address to the Ladies of America' was reprinted in full in the anti-slavery *Liberator*, which was published out of Boston. The paper's editor, William Lloyd Garrison, appealed to abolitionists to assist if they could.[55] The response was immediate and generous. John W. Sullivan of Boston consigned to the Mayor of Cork, to be forwarded to Isabella Sullivan of Dunmanway, 'two cases of goods, two barrels of clothing, one barrel of barley, one barrel of potatoes, one box of soda biscuit'. Additionally, the same gentleman sent 'two barrels of clothing, one barrel of barley, one barrel of potatoes' for 'Miss J. Bruce', who was part of a ladies' relief committee in Kilbolane, also in County Cork.[56] Misses White and Griffin, acting on behalf of the women of Binghampton in New York, raised almost $500 which was to be shared amongst the committee in Dunmanway and the poor in Skibbereen.[57] A merchant in New York, Mr Connolly, moved by the letters of the Cox sisters, purchased $400 cornmeal to be sent to Dunmanway on board the *Macedonian*.[58] His wife raised the same amount, 'without noise or pretext', which she used to purchase clothing, totalling 600 items of dress. A further $450 was raised in New York state to be sent to Dunmanway.[59] The thanks of the Cox sisters to the people of New York appeared in a number of Irish newspapers.[60]

In 1848, in recognition of the multiple kindnesses of the Cox sisters, Father Doheny presented them with a silver tea service. It was comprised of a tea pot, a water jug, a sugar bowl, and a milk jug, and was made by a renowned silversmith in London. Its embellishments included the Cox crest and the inscription read:

> Presented to the Misses Cox of the Manor House, by the Rev. James Mahony, P. P., on the part of the tenants as a small token of their gratitude for the unsolicited renewal of their leases. February 1848.[61]

By that stage, most private philanthropy had dried up, with some evidence of 'donor fatigue'. Despite this, the Dunmanway soup kitchen continued to operate throughout 1848 and was providing limited assistance as late as 1851.[62]

In April 1847, Martha had privately expressed her concern to a relative in America of the long-term impact of the exodus that was taking place in all parts of Ireland. She wrote, 'all the best of our people are flying to America, leaving behind them an inconceivable legion of idleness, filthiness and beggary to drag the whole nation into the gulph of Pauperism'.[63] At that stage, she could not have foreseen that famine would continue for a further four years and that the population of the Dunmanway area would drop from 31,000 in 1841 to 21,000 in 1851, and would continue to fall.[64] Overwhelmingly, those who died were from the poorest class. A few years later, the Cox family faced their own financial difficulties. In 1858, the sisters offered 7,000 acres of their estate, which included the town of Dunmanway, for sale through the Encumbered Estates' Court.[65] The sale marked the ending of almost 200 years close association with the town and the local people.[66] Martha died in 1860, but Katherine continued to live in the Manor House until 1863, when it was announced that the house was to be sold as 'Miss Cox' was moving to Queenstown. In addition to the farm equipment and animals, the furniture was also offered for sale, including carpets, lamps, telescopes, bookcases, feather beds and horse towels.[67] Katherine died in 1889. Neither sister had ever married. As was the case with many Irish landlords, the Famine and the Encumbered Estates Acts ultimately brought to an end the privileged position that the Cox sisters held in society. The actions of these two women were an example not only of female agency, but of the benevolent intentions of a small number of Irish landlords and landladies, who themselves became the scapegoat for the inadequacies of the response of the British government to the crisis of the late 1840s.

The fate of another member of the Dunmanway Meal Committee, Harriet Maria Catherine Shuldham, was very different. Harriet had been born in Bombay in 1821 when her father was serving in the British Army.[68] The family was involved in providing famine relief in a variety of ways. Major General Edmund William Shuldham, Harriet's father, was a Poor Law Guardian of the local workhouse. In November 1845, he had been appointed a magistrate for County Cork.[69] Harriet Shuldham, his wife, and a patron of the Meal Committee, died in July 1847 after contracting 'famine fever'.[70] The major died in November 1852, aged 73.[71] Only a few months earlier, he had 'given away' his only daughter upon her marriage to Lord Carbery in the Cathedral Church in Cork. The lavish wedding of 'the beautiful bride' was reported in the Irish and British press:

> The bride ... wore a dress of moire antique, with guipure flowers, looped up with orange blossoms, a veil of the same costly material tastefully falling from a wreath of orange blossom, and white satin shoes. The bridesmaids, twelve in number ... wore dresses en suite of pink glacé silk, under white tarlatan, trimmed with the richest lace, and lace bonnets trimmed with wreaths of shamrocks. After the ceremony, the brilliant assembly ... and a large number of the invited gentry, returned to the Imperial Hotel, when, after partaking of a superb dejeuner, prepared in the best style, and toasting the bride and bridegroom's health, the happy pair departed for Castle Freke, the princely residence of the bridegroom, there to spend the honeymoon ... the bride wore Limerick lace bonnet, and shawl of the same, over a peach-coloured satinet dress.[72]

Lady Hariet Carbery, died at her home, Phale Court in Dunmanway in 1884. She was aged 63.[73] As a young woman, she had been part of a group of women who had fearlessly brought the plight of the Dunmanway poor to the attention of people thousands of miles away, including the Vice-President of the United States. Fittingly, she died in the place she had done so much to help during the Great Hunger.

Soup Kitchens

Soup kitchens, run privately, were a popular way of providing large scale relief economically. News of the visit of celebrity chef, Alexis Soyer, to Dublin in March 1847, prompted a public debate about the nutritional value of such a diet.[74] For upper class women, from Lady Londonderry in County Antrim to Lady Carbery in west Cork, opening a soup kitchen on their estates was an efficient way of feeding their tenants. In the case of the former, she was feeding 480 people daily, although it is unlikely that she, or other women of her class, had direct contact with the recipients.[75] Nonetheless, the importance of having a landlord, or a landlady, who was resident proved to be significant in determining who had access to relief—a fact noted by the Quakers, who were highly critical of absentee landowners. This situation was evident in the small townland of Kilbolane, also in County Cork, but close to the Limerick border.

For women of the upper classes in Ireland, patronage of charitable causes was an expectation, part of an unspoken 'moral economy' of what the women of the 'Big House' regarded as their duty. Many of them were of Anglo-Irish origin and belonged to the Church of Ireland. Rather than have direct involvement with tenants, therefore, they frequently worked through the local Anglican ministers. This included Lady Mary Dillon Massy of Doonass House in County Clare. Like Lady Carbery, Lady Massy was a patroness of 'The Limerick Protestant Orphan Committee', which hosted fund-raising bazaars on behalf of the children.[76] Together with many other titled female gentry, she was also a patroness of 'The Ladies' Association for the Encouragement of Industry among the Female Peasantry of Ireland'.[77] The people of Doonass had suffered greatly following the first appearance of blight in 1845. A special correspondent of the *Freeman's Journal* who visited the area in May 1846 reported that 250 families had no food, nor any means of procuring it, and 'were it not for the exertions of the Catholic clergy these unhappy people would at the present moment be without the scanty allowance which is afforded to them'. The report added, 'I cannot omit mentioning a gratifying fact namely, the Rev. Mr. Allen, a Protestant clergyman, has been most active in this parish in assisting the Rev. Mr. McMahon and his curates'.[78] Lord Massy had given £100 for the purchase of Indian corn but then left for Dublin, an act that was bitterly criticized.[79] In early January 1846, Sir Hugh and Lady Massy took up residence in Dublin.[80] In April, they relocated to Cheltenham,[81] and, in late May, it was reported under 'fashionable entertainments' that Sir Hugh and Lady Massy had arrived in London.[82] In June, they commenced a tour of the Scottish lakes.[83] In contrast to their leisurely perambulations, as late as June 1846, the public works had not commenced in Doonass, despite appeals by the local relief committee.[84] The situation in Doonass, although not unique, revealed the task that faced private relief efforts, which were attempting to fill a vacuum resulting from inadequate government relief provision.

Lady Massy's involvement in famine relief followed the second appearance of blight. In December 1846, she sent £10 to Rev. Somers H. Payne for the Castle-Connell Relief Committee.[85] Payne, an Anglican minister, had established a soup kitchen locally. At the beginning of 1847, Lady Massy also gave a number of donations to the Rev. James Hastings Allen.[86] Rev. Allen, who had been born in County Clare in 1805 and educated in Trinity College, was the local rector in Clonlara village, land owned by the Masseys.[87] Lady Massy was not the only Massy female involved in these activities, as her mother-in-law, the Dowager Lady Massy, also made a number of donations to the local relief committees.[88] These donations were intended for a variety of ends–the local soup kitchen, the sick poor, the local ladies' relief committee, and employment of poor females in spinning.[89] By March 1847, the Massys were back in Dublin where they were frequent attendees at events in Dublin Castle.[90] At this stage, Doonass was a stronghold of Whiteboy activity,[91] with frequent attacks on cattle, magistrates and land agents.[92] The Massys were not immune as, in April, their home was attacked by nine armed men and two guns taken from it.[93] A few weeks later, an attack was made on a lumber boat on the canal, but the perpetrators were disappointed as it was not carrying food.[94] The backdrop to this unrest was extreme poverty, exacerbated by the closing of the public works, with the local poor being described as 'starving and wretched creatures'.[95]

Following the harvest of 1847, charitable donations to Ireland largely dried up. Clearly, the Famine was not over but for wealthy landowners like the Massys, life continued to be a series of pleasurable activities. In August 1847, as the government soup kitchens were closing and the New Poor Law was coming into operation, they attended an event at Dromoland Castle, to celebrate the election of Sir Lucius O'Brien to the British parliament. The guests were described as 'the most elite of the county'. At the farewell luncheon, 'the sideboards groaned beneath the weight' of the food and elaborate tableware.[96] In early 1848, the Massys were living in their residence in the fashionable Fitzwilliam Square in Dublin.[97] They were frequent guests of the Viceroy.[98] It was not until May 1848 that the Massys returned to Doonass House.[99] In early October of that year, they holidayed in the pretty seaside village of Kilkee in County Clare.[100] Two weeks later, they travelled to the fashionable spa town of Leamington in England, a favourite with the British and Irish upper classes.[101] By the end of the month, they were back home and dining in the Swinburne Rooms in Limerick City. The room was decorated with Union flags and portraits of Queen Victoria and Prince Albert, while 'the confectionery and other refreshments were supplied by Mr Goggin in his usual profuse and exquisite style'.[102] As the Famine showed no signs of abating in the west of Ireland, most notably in County Clare, Lord and Lady Massy continued to socialize with people of their own class, always on a lavish scale.[103] A highlight was the visit of Queen Victoria to Ireland in August 1849. Lady Massy was present at the ball in Dublin Castle and wore, 'a corsage and train of sky glace silk, trimmed with Limerick lace; petticoat of sky glace with rich

Limerick lace flounces. Head dress—plume of Ostrich feathers and wreathes of flowers, Honniton lappets; ornaments, diamonds'.[104] For the royal visitor, it must have appeared that the Famine was truly over.

How did Lady Massy fare after the Famine? In November 1858, approximately 6,000 acres of the Doonass Estate were advertised for sale in the Encumbered Estates' Court. In the 1870s, she still owned 4,625 acres of land in County Clare.[105] Sir Massy died in 1870 and a monument was erected to him in Clonlara village, allegedly by grateful tenants to thank him for having waived their rents during the Famine. A few decades later, it was described as an eyesore, and was covered with ivy and brambles.[106] Lady Massy died in January 1890, aged 80. She left an estate worth £6,000 a year, together with a considerable private income.[107] Her role in famine relief had been short-lived and, in the context of her wealth, miniscule. An examination of her activities during those years reveals that she continued to enjoy a life of privilege, mostly spent hundreds of miles away from her estate. Lady Massy represented one end of a wide spectrum of women who donated to famine relief. While it is hard to characterize her role as heroic, contributions such as hers helped to keep soup kitchens open, and to offer a lifeline to the poor, when no other relief was available. Her involvement, and that of other upper-class women, add a more nuanced understanding of this tragedy and its impact across the social classes.

In contrast to the hands-off attitude of Irish upper-class women, middle class females were more directly involved in providing relief. In early 1847, Anne Bruce, the Secretary of the Kilbolane Ladies' Soup Committee, wrote to the press saying that 'in this remote part of Cork' over 3,000 people were in the 'greatest destitution'. There were only three resident gentry 'and Mrs Barry and myself, the only ladies in the neighbourhood, are united and unceasing in our endeavours to alleviate the misery around us and, if possible, save the lives of our suffering fellow creatures'.[108] There was a lot of disease, brought on by a lack of clothes and food. When their own resources had become exhausted, the two women continued their work because of the benevolence of individuals in Ireland and England and opened two soup kitchens, feeding 120 families daily for free, with a small charge for those employed, namely, a half-penny per quart of soup. They were also providing medicine to the sick. Because everything had to be purchased in Cork City, which was 37 miles away, they were faced with additional expenses. Anne had written to the press because their resources were fast diminishing, and with no other relief being available, they were appealing for assistance.[109] Her letter was included in a general appeal for famine relief made by *Bell's Life in London and Sporting Chronicle*. It clearly had yielded some results, with Anne also thanking the donors through the columns of this paper.[110]

The Kilbolane Soup Kitchen operated separately from Kilbolane Relief Fund, which undertook its own fund-raising activities. By mid-April, it had raised almost £200. This fund was run by two men: Jonathan Bruce, was the Treasurer, and William Barry, the Secretary—they being the spouses of the women who ran the soup kitchen.[111] Jonathan was the son of a Church of Ireland minister.[112] Anne, née Maxwell, and Jonathan had married in 1829.[113] The involvement of the Bruces and Barrys offers insights into the complexities of providing relief, and how gender continued to create separate spheres of influence. It is also a reminder of the multiple ways in which Irish women and men were seeking to find solutions to the crisis in their country.

The involvement of a husband and wife in famine relief was not unusual. In late April, the Dublin Ladies' Committee sent £15 to Mrs Ellen Scott of the Pallasgrean Rectory, which she used to purchase clothing.[114] Pallasgrean, or Pallasgreen, was a small village in east Limerick, on the border with Tipperary. Ellen's husband, the Rev. William Scott, received two donations of £20, which he forwarded to the New Pallas Relief Committee.[115] William, originally of Carrick-on Suir, and Eleanor Elmina Chadwick, daughter of a rector, had married in County Tipperary in 1812.[116] When Ellen died in January 1851, aged approximately 61, her death was noted in the Limerick press and also in an American newspaper.[117] She was survived by her husband William and at least two sons.

Working at close quarters with the poor during the Famine was not without risks for women. Brendan Hoban's chapter describing the role of Anglican clergy in the small town of Ballina in County Mayo briefly mentions the wives and daughters of minsters who caught 'famine fever', some fatally. Sadly, many more women lost their own lives coming to the assistance of the poor. One such casualty was Alicia Moylan Kenefick of Ballindeasig, who died of fever while giving out charity.[118] The Kenefick were a wealthy family of Catholic merchants in County Cork.[119] Despite being the mother of six children, during the Great Hunger Alicia not only raised money, but she also personally distributed relief. Her donors included Lady Shannon.[120] Alicia died on 3 April 1847.[121] Notice of her death was reported in the British press including in the *Stirling Express* in Scotland [122] It was also included in the London *Morning Post*, which reported that 'A vast number of persons of the upper ranks of society have already fallen victim to the fever among the distressed poor'.[123] Alicia's was the only female death to be mentioned. Newspapers in Ireland also covered her death. One Dublin newspaper explained that she had caught fever 'while in attendance of the poor in her neighbourhood'.[124] A notice in the *Southern Reporter and Cork Commercial Courier* provided a fuller account of Alicia and her involvement:

> The late Mrs. Kenefick, of Ballindeasig, who died of fever caught in the exercise of charity, ordered the following acknowledgements of Poor Relief to be gratefully made. Through the Countess of Shannon, £106–10*s*, including £20 for Poor Females, during their confinement, from the Queen Dowager. It is but due to Lady Shannon to say that her heart is, more than her Coronet, a type of her nobility. From the Rev. Mr. Salt, Leamington, £5; Constable Maxwell, Esq., Yorkshire, £7; Mrs. Hardy, Mount-street Crescent, Dublin, £2; through Miss A. M. Moylan and Mrs. H. McDonnell, Dublin, £6–5*s*; from the Ladies' Association, Dublin, through Miss Digges LaTouche, £15; from the Society of Friends, Cork, through A. Beale. Esq. £5 and a Sack of Rice; from the Rev. C. Corkran, P. P. to provide breakfasts for the girls in the Work School, £2–10*s*. This school, opened for the distribution of clothing and bedding for destitute lying-in cases, will be kept in active operation, and the other monies expended according to the intention of the Donors.[125]

The article offered an insight into the scope of the relief work carried out by one woman, now largely forgotten, who lived in a small townland in Ireland. In this case, she paid for her actions by sacrificing her life. The family's involvement did not end with Alicia's death as her daughters took over her charitable work.[126]

In conclusion, this small sample of women's activities during the Great Hunger provides a microcosm of what was being replicated in many townlands, villages, and towns throughout Ireland. For the most part, the work of women remained unnoticed and unrecorded. While women were at forefront in dispensing food, usually soup, they understood that the needs of the poor extended beyond this, and so it was not uncommon for them to provide clothing, blankets, and medicine. For the Quakers, who selflessly traversed Ireland after 1846, it was clear that women were the backbone of a massive network of relief givers. When William Harvey and Joseph Harvey visited Kinsale in west Cork in February 1847, they had several meetings with the local women who had formed themselves into a committee and opened a well-run soup kitchen. Before departing, they left a sum of money with the women, noting, 'but for the activity and benevolent care of the Ladies' Committees ... it is possible that many might have perished altogether'.[127] This praise could be extended to hundreds of women elsewhere in Ireland who, for the most part, were invisible heroes, but whose actions, however small, helped to save some of the poor of Ireland from perishing in 1847 and beyond.

NOTES

1. Exceptions include work by Margaret Kelleher, Christine Kinealy, and Maureen Murphy
2. *Transactions of Central Relief Committee of the Society of Friends in 1846 and 1847* (Dublin: Hodges and Smith, 1852), p. 56.
3. Maria Luddy, *Women and Philanthropy in Nineteenth-Century Ireland* (Cambridge University Press, 1995), p. 1.
4. Daphne Wolfe, '"Nearly Naked". Clothing and the Great Hunger', in Christine Kinealy, Jason King and Ciarán Reilly (eds) *Women and The Great Hunger* (Hamden, CT: Quinnipiac University Press and Cork University Press, 2016), pp 83–93.
5. *Transactions*, p. 70.
6. 'The Quakers in Ireland'. www.quakers-in-ireland.ie/history/charity
7. They were married at Sir John Rogerson's Quay in Dublin, 'Marriages', *Limerick Chronicle*, 25 June 1828.
8. 'Pim, Jonathan', *Dictionary of Irish Biography*. www.dib.ie/biography/pim-jonathan-a7349
9. See chapter by Rob Goodbody on Quaker involvement.
10. Mrs A. Nicholson, *Annals of the Famine in Ireland in 1847, 1848 and 1849* (New York: E. French, 1851), pp 235–236.
11. *Transactions*, p. 32.
12. 'Lancashire Distress Fund', *Dublin Evening Post*, 8 November 1862.
13. Quaker death records are available on Find My Past. www.findmypast.com/transcript?id=IRE%2FQUAKER%2FBURS%2F55345
14. See Peter Murphy, 'Mary Ann McCracken of Belfast: "Better to wear out than to rust out"' in Christine Kinealy, Gerard Moran and Jason King (eds), *Heroes of Ireland's Great Hunger* (Cork University Press, 2021), pp 71–86.
15. Maria Webb was born in Lisburn but moved to Belfast following her marriage to William Webb in 1828. Mary Ireland corresponded with Maria Weston Chapman, who was prominent in the abolition movement in Boston. All three Belfast women had met Frederick Douglass during his visit to the town in 1845 to 1846. See Christine Kinealy, *Frederick Douglass and Ireland* (London: Routledge, 2018).
16. *First Report of Belfast Ladies' Committee* (hereafter BLC), 6 March 1847 (Belfast: s.n., 1847), p. 1.
17. Ibid., pp 4–5.
18. Asenath Nicholson, *Annals of the Famine in Ireland* (New York: E. French, 1851), pp 76–77
19. Ibid., pp 7–8; Christine Kinealy and Gerard MacAtasney, *The Famine in Belfast* (London: Pluto Press, 2000).
20. Mrs Hewitson, Rossgarron [sic]. 18 February 1847, *Report of BLC*, pp 17–19. The name is more commonly spelled Hewetson.
21. 'Grants of Clothing', *Northern Whig*, 9 March 1847.
22. Ibid., 'Belfast Ladies Association', 16 March 1847.
23. Nicholson, *Annals*, p. 79.
24. Ibid., p. 80.
25. Ibid., p. 81.

26. 'Ireland. Destitution', *Oxford University and City Herald*, 2 January 1847.
27. Nicholson, *Annals*, p. 82.
28. Ibid., pp 82–83.
29. Ibid., pp 110–111.
30. Ibid., pp 117–118.
31. Addendum, John Hewetson, *Memoirs of the House of Hewetson or Hewson of Ireland* (London: Mitchell & Hughes, 1901).
32. 'Great meeting in Belfast', *Northern Standard*, 16 January 1841.
33. Mrs Hume, Glen Lodge Killybegs, 3 February 1847, *Report of BLC,* p. 33.
34. 'Ladies Relief Association', *Northern Whig*, 9 March 1847.
35. Ibid., 25 May 1847.
36. William Hume to William Stanley, 2 April 1847, Relief Commission Papers, National Archives, Dublin, RLFC 3/2/7/0. Quoted in Christine Kinealy, *Charity and the Great Hunger. The Kindness of Strangers* (London: Bloomsbury, 2013), p. 149.
37. 'Died', *Derry Journal*, 28 November 1849.
38. Headstone Inscriptions', St Columba's Church of Ireland. http://donegalgenealogy.com/stccofi.htm
39. 'Incumbered Estates' Court', *Cork Constitution*, 21 June 1853.
40. 'Encumbered Estates' Court', *Belfast Mercury*, 15 December 1856.
41. The advertisement appeared several times: 'In the court of the commissioners for the sale of incumbered estates', *Dublin Evening Post*, 6 January 1857; Ibid., *Londonderry Standard*, 14 May 1857.
42. 'Dunmanway', *Lewis's Topographical* (1837). www.libraryireland.com/topog/D/Dunmanway-East-Carbery-Cork.php www.libraryireland.com/topog/D/Dunmanway-East-Carbery-Cork.php
43. Hugh James Rose and Samuel Roffey Maitland, *The British Magazine,* vol. 31, p. 240.
44. Pat Crowley, '1848 Landlord Listing, Dunmanway Union, West Cork (2023). www.academia.edu/110131523/Landlord_Listing_Dunmanway_Union_West_Cork
45. *Cork Examiner*, 10 September 1845.
46. 'Important meeting in Dunmanway', *Cork Examiner*, 4 February 1846.
47. 'An example for Landlords', *Southern Reporter and Cork Commercial Courier*, 19 March 1846; *Cork Examiner*, 20 March 1846.
48. 'The Dunmanway Indian Meal Ladies' Committee and the famine soup kitchen as referenced in the valuation office house books for the town of Dunmanway, 1848 and 1851'. https://mccarthythesquare.com/2018/12/28/the-dunmanway-indian-meal-ladies-committees-and-the-famine-soup-kitchen-as-referenced-in-the-valuation-office-house-books-for-the-town-of-dunmanway-1848-and-1851/
49. This committee had initially been founded to assist with food shortages in 1831. See Kinealy, *Charity*, pp 261–265.
50. 'Schedule of Grants', Irish Relief Organization, *Distress in Ireland* (Dublin: P.D. Hardy, 1847), p. 23.
51. Dunmanway Ladies' Committee to Irish Relief Association, Application No. 271, 11 January 1847, Royal Irish Academy, Dublin, 27. Q. 24.

52. Ibid. Unlike the American appeal, Isabella Sullivan's name did not appear on this appeal.
53. It was dated 28 December 1846.
54. *National Intelligencer*, 11 February 1847.
55. 'Address to the Ladies of America', *Liberator,* 12 February 1847.
56. 'American Sympathy', *Morning Advertiser*, 21 May 1847.
57. 'Relief for Ireland', *Southern Reporter and Cork Commercial Courier*, 27 March 1847.
58. 'Active Benevolence', *Dublin Evening Mail*, 9 April 1847.
59. 'Important from America', *Kerry Evening Post,* 14 April 1847.
60. *Southern Reporter and Cork Commercial Courier*, 1 May 1847.
61. In 2011, descendants of the Cox family returned the tea service to Dunmanway, 'Historic Silver Service returned by Cox Descendants to Dunmanway', *The Southern Star,* 21 May 2011.
62. 'The Dunmanway Indian Meal Ladies' Committee and the Famine Soup'. https://mccarthythesquare.com/2018/12/28/the-dunmanway-indian-meal-ladies-committees-and-the-famine-soup-kitchen-as-referenced-in-the-valuation-office-house-books-for-the-town-of-dunmanway–1848-and–1851/
63. Martha Cox to Sophia H. Cox, 28 April 1847. Cormac Ó Gráda was shown this private letter in Washington. Quoted in Ó Gráda, *Ireland. A New Economic History, 1780–1939* (Oxford: Clarendon Press, 1994), p. 488.
64. James S. Donnelly Jr, *The Land and People of Nineteenth-Century* Cork (London: Routledge and Kegan Paul, 1975), pp. 95–96.
65. Landed Estates Database, NUI Galway. www.landedestates.ie
66. 'Court of the Commissioners ...', 25 September 1858.
67. 'Auction', *Cork Examiner*, 3 April 1863.
68. 'General registry of births, deaths and marriages', *Bombay Gazette*, 21 March 1821.
69. 'The Magistracy', *Kerry Evening Post*, 5 November 1845.
70. Her death was reported widely, although the cause of death was rarely mentioned: *Dublin Evening Post*, 7 August 1847; 'The Late Doctor Lynch', *Daily News* (London), 11 October 1847.
71. 'Deaths', *Saint James's Chronicle*, 30 November 1852.
72. From *Morning Post, Stamford Mercury,* 13 August 1852; 'Marriage in High Life', *Northern Whig,* 14 August 1852 *John Bull*, 14 August 1852.
73. *Morning Post*, 20 August 1884.
74. See chapter by Christine Kinealy on Alexis Soyer.
75. Henry Stewart, Rathbarry Vicarage, 1 April 1847, Ireland, *Bath Chronicle and Weekly Gazette,* 15 April 1847.
76. 'Ladies' Bazaar', *Limerick Chronicle*, 7 October 1846.
77. *Dublin Evening Post*, 30 March 1847.
78. 'The Famine in the South', *Weekly Freeman's Journal*, 9 May 1846.
79. 'Famine in Ireland', *Limerick and Clare Examiner*, 9 May 1846.
80. *Limerick Chronicle*, 10 January 1846.
81. Ibid., 18 April 1846.
82. 'Fashionable Entertainments', *Dublin Evening Mail*, 22 May 1846. It was also reported in *Saunders's News-Letter*, 22 May 1846.

83. *Limerick Chronicle*, 24 June 1846; 'Miscellaneous', *Statesman and Dublin Christian Record*, 26 June 1846.
84. *Limerick Chronicle*, 27 June 1846.
85. Ibid., 30 December 1846.
86. Allen became Dean of Killaloe in 1862, a position he held until his death in 1880.
87. Donations to Rev. Allen in February 1847 included ones from Lady Massy, the Dowager Massy, Mrs Clarke from Plymouth, and the Lord Lieutenant, *Limerick Chronicle*, 10 February 1847.
88. *Limerick Chronicle*, 13 March 1847.
89. Ibid., 21 April 1847.
90. 'Fashionable Intelligence', *Freeman's Journal*, 5 March 1847.
91. The Whiteboys were a secret Irish agrarian organization who took vigilante action to defend tenants' rights. Their name was derived from their tradition of wearing white smocks during their nightly raids
92. 'Attempt to Assassinate a Land Agent', *Belfast Protestant Journal*, 17 April 1847.
93. 'State of the Country', *Dublin Evening Herald*, 6 May 1847.
94. 'State of the Country', *Pilot,* 4 June 1847.
95. 'New Phase of Relief Measures', *Tipperary Free Press*, 21 April 1847.
96. 'Fete at Dromoland', *Limerick Chronicle*, 21 August 1847.
97. *Limerick Chronicle*, 19 February 1848.
98. 'Viceroy Court', *Dublin Evening Post*, 4 March 1848.
99. *Limerick Chronicle*, 10 May 1848.
100. Ibid., 30 September 1848.
101. 'Arrivals', *Leamington Spa Courier,* 14 October 1848.
102. 'The Assembly Room Swinburne's Rooms', *Limerick and Clare Examiner*, 28 October 1848.
103. *Limerick and Clare Examiner*, 28 October 1848.
104. 'Ladies' dresses', *Dublin Weekly Register*, 11 August 1849.
105. 'Massy', *Landed Estates Records.* https://landedestates.ie/family/2004
106. 'Clonlara', I.T.A. Topographical and General Survey 1942/3. https://www.clarelibrary.ie/eolas/coclare/history/ita_survey_1942/clonlara.htm
107. *Portsmouth Evening News*, 28 January 1890.
108. Anne Bruce, Secretary, Prohurst, Charleville, *Bath Chronicle and Weekly Gazette*, 15 April 1847.
109. Ibid.
110. 'Famine in Ireland. Our Appeal', *Bell's Life in London and Sporting Chronicle*, 4 April 1847.
111. 'List of Subscribers. Kilbolane Relief Fund', *Cork Examiner*, 14 April 1847.
112. *Journal of the Institute of Bankers in Ireland* (Dublin: Hely's, 1904), p. 169.
113. 'Married', *Cork Constitution*, 16 July 1829.
114. *Limerick Chronicle*, 21 April 1847.
115. Obituary: Scott, Ellen January 11, 1851. www.igp-web.com/IGPArchives/ire/limerick/obits/s/scott4309ob.html
116. 'Married', *Limerick Gazette*, 8 September 1812.
117. 'Deaths', *Limerick Chronicle*, 11 January 1851; *Irish American Weekly*, 15 February 1851. https://www.igp-web.com/IGPArchives/ire/limerick/obits/s/scott4309ob.html

118. 'Thanks', *Southern Reporter and Cork Commercial Courier*, 10 April 1847.
119. Alicia Moylan had married Richard in 1815. See Anthony McCan, *The rise and fall of the Kenifecks of Ballindeasig house* www.kenefick.com/Kenifecks_of_Ballindeasig_House.pdf
120. 'Thanks', *Southern Reporter and Cork Commercial Courier*, 10 April 1847.
121. McCan, *Rise and Fall.*
122. 'Increase of Fever', *Stirling Observer*, 15 April 1847.
123. Ireland', *Morning Post*, 7 April 1847. The same article noted that Rev. Traill's condition was precarious. Reprinted in *Bell's New Weekly Messenger*, 11 April 1847, and *Stirling Observer*, 15 April 1847.
124. 'Died', *Dublin Evening Post,* 6 April 1847.
125. 'Thanks', *Southern Reporter and Cork Commercial Courier*, 10 April 1847.
126. Ibid., 29 May 1847.
127. *Transactions*, p. 176.

CHAPTER ELEVEN

'OUR FELLOW BEINGS'
Famine Relief and Indigenous Resistance

Anelise Hanson Shrout

On a freezing and cloudy Saturday morning in March 1847, a crowd gathered at Fort Gibson in the Cherokee Nation to raise funds for Ireland.[1] Fort Gibson, a United States army outpost in what is now Arkansas, was established in 1824 so that the American army could intervene in the politics of Indigenous Nations who had been pushed west by Anglo-Americans.[2] By the 1840s, Fort Gibson had become an administrative centre for what representatives of the United States called 'Indian Territory'.[3]

The famine fundraisers met in the fort's chapel, which was separated from Cherokee land by a large gulch and an imposing gate.[4] Perhaps speaking from the pulpit, or perhaps standing among the assembly, United States Lieutenant Colonel Gustavus Loomis 'made a few pertinent remarks relative to the extraordinary distress in Ireland, and the object of the meeting, and requested a gentleman present to read some newspaper accounts of the famine'. According to a local newspaper, following this reading, 'the persons present contributed $103.30, which sum was increased by a collection after the service on Sunday the 14 March to $130'.[5] Fort Gibson, and the chapel within it, were explicitly White spaces, but Cherokees were present as participants and donors. A few months after the meeting, the *Cherokee Advocate*—the first Indigenous newspaper published in Indian Territory—would celebrate the Fort Gibson meeting as 'evidence of the liberality of our red brethren in the far west'.[6]

Cherokee donors at Fort Gibson, along with the Choctaw donors in Schullyville and Doakesville, were part of a global community of famine philanthropists who sent money to Ireland between 1845 and 1852.[7] The scale of participation in Irish famine relief was unprecedented. In the decades before the Famine, most charity was local, which meant that the people giving aid could immediately see the results of their benevolence.[8] The Irish famine and resulting transnational relief revolutionized the charitable ecosystem. Famine donations were prompted by accounts of Irish suffering in newspapers from places as far flung as Mexico, France, and India.[9] People with no previous personal interest in Ireland learned of, and then began to comment on, the best way to relieve Irish starvation. As if by common agreement, thousands of people from hundreds of locales collectively sent millions of dollars to help the Irish.

This widespread interest in famine relief can be explained by the fact the Irish Famine could be put to many and varied political uses.[10] This was a dramatic story of suffering that was taking place close to the heart of the British Empire, in the midst of contests over land, nationalism, trade, and imperial rule. These contexts allowed the Famine to become a global media event that could be made to take on multiple, conflicting meanings simultaneously. Around the world, different groups tied these meanings to local interests, and famine relief became a way to bring local interests to the fore of public consciousness.

This chapter explores the ways in which Indigenous donors used famine philanthropy as a political tool, focusing on the donations made by Cherokees at Fort Gibson. First, it describes how Cherokee donations, and others like them, undermined White Americans' claims of Native 'incivility,' at a time when the United States' Federal policy relied on those same negative stereotypes. Second, it details the ways in which famine philanthropy allowed commentators to juxtapose widely-condemned British imperialism with the United States' government's policies of Indigenous marginalization and expropriation. The fact that their donations had political uses does not undermine the degree to which Cherokee, and other Indigenous donors, were moved by compassion and empathy for suffering strangers. Rather, it points to the ways in which these donors folded their sympathy towards Ireland into existing projects of philanthropy and resistance.

Undermining Stereotypes

The United States' policies towards Indigenous Nations broadly, and towards the Cherokees in particular, were built on racist stereotypes about Indigenous 'backwardness' and incompatibility with 'settled' White society. These stereotypes were inherited from a long tradition of British colonial projects, which paired the conversion of Indigenous inhabitants with justifications for the establishment of permanent colonies and the seizure of land.

For example, the *Laudabiliter*, a possibly apocryphal, but nevertheless much-referenced document purportedly written by Pope Adrian in the twelfth century, ostensibly granted the English King Henry II full authority to extend papal control over Ireland. The document was the foundation of policies used to justify centuries of English conquests of Ireland.[11] This logic was also used by prospective colonists in North America. One 1641 pamphlet pointed to the duty of Britons to 'Propagate the Gospel in America' and save 'the immortall souls of innumerable men, who still sit in darknesse'.[12] By the early nineteenth century, missionaries in the United States had become preoccupied with transforming Indigenous communities into mirrors of White American society. These missionaries did not necessarily aim to seize land, but did seek to control it by 'planting' churches which would perpetuate the Gospel.[13] This is a gloss of centuries of rhetoric linking conversion missions and control, but each of these examples required a convertible, but not yet converted, people in order for religious leaders to claim authority in new spaces. In the decades before the Great Hunger, missionaries seeking to maintain a foothold among Cherokees were incentivized to rhetorically construct Indigenous people as ignorant, pitiable heathens who could benefit from American and Christian knowledge.[14]

Governments, too, adopted this rhetoric of Indigenous 'backwardness' as a way to justify control and colonization. British settlers in the seventeenth century asserted that the constructions of houses and fenced-in gardens were the markers of settled land, and that Indigenous People had no claim on land they did not develop.[15] This rhetoric persisted after the American Revolution, and was serially adopted by politicians in the United States. In the half-century before the Famine, Indigenous People living in the southeastern United States were cast as insufficiently 'civilized' to appropriately steward the land, and too volatile to live in proximity to White settlers.[16] When those settlers—many of them of Irish descent—began to encroach on Cherokee land in Georgia, the Carolinas, Alabama and Tennessee, the United States federal government abrogated earlier treaties that had recognized Cherokee sovereignty.[17] For missionaries and federal officials alike, the idea of Indigenous 'incivility' was an essential part of justifying control over Cherokee land and people in the early nineteenth century.

In 1830, President Andrew Jackson proposed a national plan of 'Indian removal' from the American southeast. Federal officials coerced Cherokee leaders with threats and actual violence to exchange over two million acres of their ancestral homelands for land west of the Mississippi, which the federal government renamed 'Indian Territory'.[18] This land was already occupied by Caddos, Wichitas, Comanches, Kiowas, Apaches, Arapahos, Cheyennes and Osages.[19] Factions within the Cherokee Nation strategized various, and often divergent, ways to resist their dispossession.[20] Some, including the Principal Cherokee Chief, John Ross, sought to claim the inherent right to remain on their ancestral homelands, and worked to consolidate tribal governments and enact laws that would protect communal landholdings.[21] Others leveraged alliances with missionaries who feared that removal would undermine their proselytization efforts.[22] While the majority of the Cherokee Nation publicly and adamantly rejected removal, some opposed removal in principle, but believed that moving west was the best way to protect the integrity of the Cherokee Nation as a political entity.[23] This latter group included a minority of Cherokee elites, who believed that neither federal nor state authorities could be trusted to treat the Cherokee Nation justly. For these leaders, giving up their ancestral homelands was preferable to continuing to be assaulted by violent White settlers.[24] In 1835 this smaller group signed a removal treaty on behalf of the entire Cherokee Nation. The federal government used this treaty to claim authority to violently expel men and women who refused to leave their lands. Cherokees, along with other Indigenous People, were forced to march hundreds of miles along what would come to be known as the 'Trail of Tears'.[25] Records of the dispossession and forced march west are scant, but scholars estimate that one in four Cherokees died, and that every family lost at least one relative.[26]

Tensions in the Cherokee Nation between those who had supported the removal treaty and those who had opposed it travelled west with them. Hostilities escalated throughout the 1840s.[27] Legal and political structures, disrupted by removal, were not sufficient to prevent a series of coordinated assassinations of treaty signers.[28] Government representatives used this unrest to further their political ends and marginalize Cherokees. In late 1846, the United States Agent to the Cherokees, Colonel James McKissick, sent a letter to the Office of Indian Affairs in Washington, D.C., reporting 'cases of outrage' in the Cherokee Nation. The federal official who responded to McKissick's letter lamented that it was troubling to hear that 'every member of the Cherokee Community' was not 'obviously impressed with the many advantages secured to them by the late treaty'.[29] It was against this backdrop of dislocation and political disruption that Cherokees contributed to famine relief.

Cherokee donors learned of the Famine in Ireland through both Indigenous and White newspapers. The primary non-Native newspaper serving the region around Fort Gibson, and the paper which first reported the Cherokee donation, was The *Arkansas Intelligencer*, published six miles from the border of Indian Territory, and distributed by Native agents within the Cherokee Nation.[30] Cherokees also had access to Native newspapers, in the tradition of Elias Boudinot's *Cherokee Phoenix*, which had been established in Georgia in 1828. Boudinot used the paper to foster a Cherokee reading public and to interject Cherokee experiences into a public sphere that was largely dominated by White culture and writing.[31] The *Cherokee Phoenix* was key to Cherokee efforts to resist United States encroachment, developing what Hillary Wyss called a community of 'Writerly Indians', who used both English and Indigenous writing technologies to articulate sovereignty, political autonomy, and personal identity.[32]

In 1844, as one of its first official acts after removal, the Cherokee Nation government established the *Cherokee Advocate* with similar aims to the *Phoenix*. The slogan of the new paper was 'Our Rights, Our Country, Our Race'. Like the *Phoenix*, the *Advocate* was published in English as well as in the Cherokee syllabary and sought to reach as wide a range of readers as possible, both within and beyond Indian Territory. In fact, the prospectus of the *Cherokee Advocate* claimed that 'our location, and station we occupy relative to the Creeks, Chickasaws, Choctaws, Osages, Senecas, Delawares and other Indians, are such as will enable us at all times to furnish the readers of the paper with the latest and most correct border news'.[33]

The *Arkansas Intelligencer* was quick to cast Indigenous donations as evidence of White superiority. An article on the Choctaw donation from Schullyville celebrated it as a 'voice of benevolence from the western wilderness' and championed '[t]he "poor Indian" sending his mite to the poor Irish!' The writer continued to develop this theme, enjoining readers to note:

> [w]hat an agreeable reflection it must give to the Christian and the philanthropist, to witness this evidence of civilisation and Christian spirit existing among our red neighbors. They are repaying the Christian world a consideration for bringing them out from benighted ignorance and heathen barbarism. Not only by contributing a few dollars but by affording evidence that the labors of the Christian missionary have not been in vain.[34]

This article claimed that Indigenous donations were a credit to missionaries' efforts, but also argued that those efforts were incomplete. Despite this act of startling generosity, the article went on to remind (presumably White) readers that their 'red neighbors' were still only a few steps away from 'benighted ignorance and heathen barbarism.' For missionaries, the fragile success of Christianizing projects was evidence that they should be allowed to continue to operate in Indian Territory. A letter to the editor of the *Intelligencer* expressed similar sentiments, marvelling that 'is this not a sublime spectacle? The Red man of the New, bestowing alms upon the people of the Old World? With them, it be literally complying with that golden rule of Christianity, of returning good for evil'.[35] This language echoed longstanding attempts by missionaries to claim any Indigenous success as their own.[36] However, the *Cherokee Advocate* explicitly challenged the view that the Cherokee and Choctaw donations were evidence of Indigenous Peoples' need to be redeemed by White Christians. In July 1847, the *Advocate* reprinted an article from the Philadelphia-based *United States Gazette* which proclaimed:

> Among the many noble deeds of disinterested benevolence which the present famine in Europe has called forth, none can be more gratifying to enlightened men than the liberality of our red brethren [...] displayed at a late meeting in the Cherokee nation.[37]

The writer went on to note that Indigenous philanthropy was 'the more acceptable that it comes from those upon whom the white man has but little claim. It teaches us that the Indian, made like as we are, has a humanity common among us'.[38] This article implicitly referenced traditional Indigenous charitable practices, wherein giving did not signal the giver's superiority over the recipient, but was rather a reciprocal necessity born of the need to constantly redistribute goods to the benefit of the community, however broadly construed.[39] In the Cherokee Nation in the first half of the nineteenth century, charity included local infrastructure projects, as well as gift-giving that constructed broad Indigenous communities. Cherokees and Choctaws were familiar with aiding others, and considered giving a necessary part of community and political life.[40] The editors of the *Cherokee Advocate* chose not to reprint claims that Indigenous donations were evidence of the superiority of White, Christian morality. When they reproduced White writing on the donations, they drew on an article that explicitly argued for Indigenous humanity and for the significance of Indigenous giving practices. In doing so, the editors of the *Cherokee Advocate* challenged prevailing White interpretations of Indigenous philanthropy.

The *Cherokee Advocate* also explicitly called for readers to give to Ireland. In May 1847, it celebrated the fact that 'in all the large cities, in the towns and villages, and throughout the country public meetings have been held and speedy and energetic measures adopted'. It particularly lauded that 'our neighbors, the Choctaws, have lent a helping hand, and so have the Cherokees'. Like the article reprinted from the *United States Gazette*, this article did not cast Indigenous donations as evidence of missionaries' success. It did make an explicit link between the shared experiences of Irish sufferers and of Native donors. It called on readers 'not to hesitate' to give even though 'the sufferers are separated from us by hundreds of miles. It should be enough for us to know that those who are dying for bread are our fellow beings'.[41] For the *Cherokee Advocate,* Indigenous donations to famine relief were not merely the expression of generosity, but the natural and appropriate behaviour of one group of 'fellow beings' to another.

In sum, while the White press was content to claim Cherokee and Choctaw donations as evidence of the success and the ongoing need for projects to 'civilize' Indigenous People, the Cherokee press argued that famine relief was in fact evidence of Indigenous morality, undermining claims made by both missionaries and United States' officials that Native Nations were inferior to White Americans.

Challenging Settler Colonialism

Public expressions of charity helped the Cherokees to craft an alternative to the dehumanizing rhetoric which underpinned the United States' Indian Removal policies. Choosing to give to Ireland, however, had particular potential, reflected in the *Advocate*'s claim that Cherokees and the Irish were 'fellow beings'. This claim of fellowship connected Ireland's colonial history to Cherokee experiences of settler colonialism, and facilitated parallels between Irish experiences of the Great Hunger and Indigenous experiences of the Trail of Tears. In fact, the tactics that the United States used to implement Indigenous dispossession were inherited from Britain. While the United States frequently repudiated its imperial predecessor, scholars have noted that the American Revolution was in many ways an attempt to enact settler colonialism without oversight from London.[42] The antecedents to Andrew Jackson's Indian Removal policies could be found both in pre-Revolutionary British treaties with Native Peoples and in the actions of British settlers in pre-Revolutionary North America.[43] This meant that the treatment of the Irish by Britain, and Indigenous People by the United States, came from the same body of laws and practices. Indigenous expropriation was a central strategy of both British and American settler colonialism, a strategy that the British sought to perfect in Ireland.[44] This made comparisons between Irish and Cherokee People fertile political ground.

There is ample evidence that the Indigenous press paid particular attention to Ireland. This focus is surprising because many Cherokees were descended from Scottish Highlanders who had traded and lived among Cherokees in the southeast.[45] In fact, John Ross, the Principal Chief of the Cherokee Nation, argued that it was 'particularly incumbent on the Cherokee People' to send relief to Scotland, because many Cherokees, including Ross himself, were 'themselves descended from Scottish ancestors'. Despite these kinship connections, Ross noted that the 'the attention of the benevolent community has seemed to be directed more to Ireland'.[46] Ross's speech suggests that he did not think that Irish famine donations reflected some special kinship between Cherokees and the Irish, and opens up other possible interpretations of this extraordinary act of famine relief.

In her history of Cherokee diplomatic correspondence, Claudia Haake argues that people subject to colonial violence often have to choose between radical and covert acts of resistance. Radical acts of resistance have the potential to result in 'political annihilation'. Covert acts, which often involve seeking legitimacy through the logic of the dominant order, have the potential to effect more immediate change.[47] This is similar to James Scott's framework of 'hidden transcripts': actions which carry one meaning for a dominant culture and still another 'unstated' meaning for subordinate groups. Donations like those collected from Cherokees at Fort Gibson should be read as a covert act of resistance which created a fictive bridge between two groups subject to the violence of colonialism. In the years prior to removal, Indigenous leaders and thinkers accused the United States' government of coercion, neglect and bad faith, using language that presaged more trenchant critiques of American imperialism later in the century, and which often drew on Britain as the exemplar of abusive imperialism.[48] For example, a letter from the Cherokee Nation addressed to Congress in 1829, and published in the *Cherokee Phoenix*, argued that the United States government took advantage of its comparative strength to seize lands long inhabited by Cherokees, and codified by treaty. The petitioners wrote:

> the land on which we stand we received as an inheritance from our fathers, who possessed it from time immemorial, as a gift from our common father in heaven ... this right of inheritance we have *never ceded*, nor ever *forfeited*. Permit us to ask, what better right can a people have to a country than the right of *inheritance* and *immemorial peaceable possession*?[49]

Despite 'the faith and pledge of the United States, repeated over and over again, in treaties made at various times,' the petition warned that the Cherokee Nation would soon be 'forever divested of our country and rights'. It closed by noting that 'your memorialists humbly conceive, that such an act would be in the highest degree oppressive'.[50]

A pamphlet recounting a meeting in support of Indigenous rights held in Philadelphia in 1830 made a similar claim. One speaker asked, 'shall a government founded on that celebrated exposition of the rights of man, which accompanied our declaration of independence, grossly violate those rights in others?' Referencing the American Revolution, the speaker went on to ask, 'if *dependent nations* have a right *to declare themselves independent*, ought not *independent nations* be permitted to *remain independent*?' Furthermore, given that Indigenous Nations had long been treated as independent and sovereign, 'can a people be viewed as the friends of liberty at home, who are ready to avail themselves of superior strength to exercise tyranny abroad?'[51] Speaking against removal in Boston in 1832, the Cherokee Chief, John Ridge, compared 'his people,' with Bostonians' revolutionary ancestors, whose 'first resistance was made against the designs of Great Britain to enslave this people' of Britain's American colonies.[52] Ridge cast the Cherokees as allied with the United States against imperial tyranny—and a tyranny that most White Americans would condemn.[53] As these examples illustrate, in the decade before removal, Indigenous People couched their experiences vis-à-vis the United States in the context of settler colonialism, often using Britain as an example of dangerous imperial power.

Participating in famine relief enabled the extension of this comparison. Like Cherokees, the Irish had experienced violent settler colonization. The Indigenous press made Britain's imperial failure clear in its famine reporting. In March 1847, the *Cherokee Advocate* reprinted an account by a Catholic clergyman, who blamed Ireland's crisis on 'the unfortunate misgovernment of this country,' on 'the want of parental sympathy for the people,' and on 'not timely interfering and rescuing a generous, noble, and a devoted people'.[54] In May, an article in the *Advocate* wrote that it was the 'oppressed condition' forced on the Irish by Britain, rather than any intrinsic failures of Irish people or soil, 'that is to be deplored'. The author continued, 'The Irish nation is tithed and taxed and rented until the energies of the people are subdued, until there is no wonder that they suffer and die—these facts even thus succinctly stated, we believe will be of interest to our readers'.[55] In articles like these, the Irish Famine served as an opportunity to critique British governance, and particularly Britain's arbitrary power over colonial spaces, in language that echoed Cherokee critiques of the United States' government in the years before removal.

The Indigenous press also highlighted specific Irish experiences that might have resonated with their readers. In April 1846, the *Cherokee Advocate* reported:

> In Roscrea, an important and populous district, the poor are living on the refuse of diseased potatoes and crowds may be seen from morning till night in the fields, grubbing the stray potatoes that may have remained on the ground after digging ... wherever one looks, the misery of the poor is really heart rending.[56]

The article closed by editorializing that these conditions constituted 'a new and an awful phase in the type of Irish misery and woe'.[57] When, one year later, the paper wrote of the 'famine lands' of Ireland in which 'old and the young, the feeble and the stout hearted, have been stricken down and hurried to another world', the descriptions were so terrible that the unnamed author posited that readers might 'hardly credit the reports of the sufferings, disease and death which have reached us'.[58] In writing this, the Indigenous authors were perhaps hoping that their own experience might be as heart-rending to readers as that of the Irish.

Like Cherokees, Irish people had experienced firsthand what it meant to be a disposable population within an expanding polity. In the wake of the 1840s' crop failures, thousands of Irish were forcibly evicted from their lands, either to be virtually imprisoned in poorhouses or forced to emigrate overseas on insalubrious ships.[59] Experiences of dispossession and forced removal suffered by Cherokees tribes were equally, if not more horrific. James Mooney, an amateur ethnographer, recounted the process of removal as told to him 'from the lips of the actors in the tragedy':

> Stockade forts were erected for gathering and holding the Indians preparatory to removal. From these, squads of troops were sent out to search with rifle and bayonet every small cabin hidden away in the coves or by the sides of mountain streams, to seize and bring in as prisoners all of the occupants, however or wherever they might be found. Families at dinner were startled by the sudden gleam of bayonets in the doorway and rose up to be driven with blows and oaths along the weary miles of trail that lead to the stockades ... in many cases, on turning for one last look as they crossed the ridge, they saw their homes in flames.[60]

The men and women who suffered the Trail of Tears might well have seen parallels to their experiences in an article in the *Cherokee Advocate* from June of 1846 reporting that:

> The quays at Cork, as we read, are crowded to inconvenience with passengers and their luggage. Already one vessel has sailed with a full complement of passengers, and twenty-three others with nearly four thousand emigrants are preparing at that port for sea.[61]

A few months later, the *Advocate* reprinted an article from the *Liverpool Times* arguing that 'the number of persons in the most utter destitution, arriving from Ireland' in British cities 'still continues'. The article closed by observing 'it is clear, however, that this evil cannot be allowed to proceed without the most ruinous consequences'.[62] For both Irish and Indigenous Peoples, the experience of dislocation was fresh in memory.

Just as evictions meant starvation and disease for Irish people, so too did American government policies mean starvation and disease for dispossessed Indigenous people. For example, the Choctaw district chief, Greenwood Leflore, reported in 1830 that 'a considerable portion' of the people he represented were 'poor and leaving with means hardly sufficient to sustain them on their journey,' and that they would 'reach the place of their future residence in a very destitute condition'.[63] Similarly, the missionary Alexander Talley disclosed that those forced west on the Trail of Tears had 'perished with cold and hunger' and had been left to sleep in 'a deep and extensive forest ... in a linen tent covered with ice and snow for a week, with but two blankets to cover a bed of grass'.[64] Eviction led, unequivocally to death.

For Indigenous People and for the Irish, the traumas of removal, eviction, and expropriation were bound up not only in the physical experience of being uprooted, but in exile from ancestral lands. The 1829 testimony of one Cherokee Elder illustrated this attachment to the Nation's spiritual home. In a speech resisting removal, he declared:

> My aged bones will soon be laid under ground, and I wish them laid in the bosom of this earth we have received from our fathers who had it from the Great Being above. When I shall sleep in forgetfulness, I hope my bones will not be deserted by you.[65]

Colonel George S. Gaines, who was tasked with overseeing Choctaw removal, recounted the same ties to the land: 'The feeling which many of them evince in separating, never to return again, from their own long cherished hills, poor as they are in this section of the country, is truly painful to witness'.[66] A traveller who passed groups of Cherokees en route to Indian Territory remarked, 'We learn from the inhabitants on the road where the Indians passed that they buried fourteen or fifteen at every stopping place, and they made a journey of ten miles per day only on an average'.[67]

In the spring of 1847, just before the famine relief meeting, the *Cherokee Advocate* printed a litany of accounts of Irish death. Many of these featured people who died far from home, or who could not be buried with appropriate rites or ceremony. One described men being forced to labour on public roads who had 'not energy enough to keep their blood in circulation, and they drop down from the united effects of cold and hunger, never to rise again'.[68] Another recounted that, 'a whole family ... ill with fever, having lost two of its number within two days', were evicted from their home by an 'unfeeling landlord [who] had unhinged the door, took off their blankets, and left them to die without shelter, clothing or food'. The same article described a scene in which 'four corpse lay in that town as they had died, without preparation of any kind'.[69] These descriptions of dislocation and death at the hands of Britain mirrored the Cherokee and Choctaw experiences at the hands of the government of the United States.

Interspersed with these accounts, the *Cherokee Advocate* published articles pointing to the United States government's failures to attend to the needs of Cherokees and Choctaws. One, from 4 March 1847, opined that government representatives 'must know what we have been subjected to, during and prior to, our forcible removal west'. This included being deprived of 'the comforts and enjoyments of domestic life' and left in 'absolute poverty'.[70] Two weeks later, in an article following numerous accounts of horrific Irish deaths, an anonymous author asked, 'Why has there not been a disposition of Cherokee affairs? It can be answered in but one way—because there was not a will *just now*'.[71] Lack of political will to attend to the needs of marginalized people had real consequences. For the Irish it meant degrading deaths, often far from home; for Cherokees, it meant starvation and roadside burials in the 1830s and continued poverty in the 1840s. For Indigenous People, who buried their relatives by the roadside on the Trail of Tears, or who wished they could have buried their children among their ancestral kin on tribal lands in the American Southeast, stories of Irish distress would have evoked both memories and profound sympathy. Giving to the Irish cemented parallel experiences, linking these 'fellow beings' with material aid in addition to rhetorical support.

For Cherokee donors, and other contributors to Famine relief who had been expropriated by the United States' federal government, aiding Ireland had two potential political uses. The first was to challenge the logic of Indigenous incivility, which underlay both the United States' Indian Removal policies and White missionaries' claims of the need for their presence in Indian Territory. In claiming that donations from 'our red brethren' were evidence of Indigenous morality, separate from missionizing efforts, commentators undercut claims that White intervention was required to improve Indigenous lives. The second was to continue to highlight parallels between the United States' behaviour towards Indigenous Nations and Britain's behaviour towards the Irish. These parallels continued a tradition of rhetorical resistance that had begun before the Indian Removal Act, whereby Indigenous leaders accused the United States of British imperial caprices. These two political uses, however, do not devalue the incredible generosity evinced by Cherokee and Choctaw donors. Rather, their generosity was paired with thoughtful and strategic manipulation of a distant crisis for local ends.

NOTES

1. United States. Dept. of the Army. Office of the Surgeon General and Lawson, *Army Meteorological Register, for Twelve Years, from 1843 to 1854, Inclusive*, pp 198–199.
2. The reference to 'Indian uprisings' can be found in Brad Agnew, *Fort Gibson, Terminal on the Trail of Tears* (Norman, OK: University of Oklahoma Press, 1980), p. 30. http://archive.org/details/fortgibsonterminooagne. For a discussion of the politics that led to the Osage-Cherokee conflict in Arkansas, see Kathleen DuVal, *The Native Ground: Indians and Colonists in the Heart of the Continent* (Philadelphia: University of Pennsylvania Press, 2007), pp 197–200, http://ebookcentral.proquest.com/lib/nyulibrary-ebooks/detail.action?docID=3441510.
3. For an overview of the role of agents from the perspective of the United States, see R. S. Cotterill, 'Federal Indian Management in the South 1789–1825', *The Mississippi Valley Historical Review* 20, no. 3 (1933): pp 333–52, https://doi.org/10.2307/1886843.
4. Grant Foreman, *Fort Gibson : A Brief History*, 1930, p. 12; John S. (John Shaw) Billings and Royal College of Physicians of London, *A Report on the Hygiene of the United States Army: With Descriptions of Military Posts* (Washington, D.C.: Government Printing Office, 1875), p. 263.
5. *Arkansas Intelligencer* (Van Buren), 20 March 1847.
6. *Cherokee Advocate*, 15 July 1847.
7. Christine Kinealy, *Charity and the Great Hunger. The Kindness of Strangers* (London: Bloomsbury Press, 2013).
8. Robert A. Gross, 'Giving in America: from charity to philanthropy,' in Lawrence Jacob Friedman and Mark D. McGarvie (eds), *Charity, Philanthropy, and Civility in American History* (Cambridge, UK; Cambridge University Press, 2003), p. 31; Merle Curti, *American Philanthropy Abroad* (New Brunswick, NJ: Rutgers University Press, 1963), pp 4–5.
9. The *American Flag*, published in Matamoros, Mexico, along with the *Daily American Star* and *El Monitor Republicano*, both published in Mexico City, routinely carried news of the Famine. Peter Gray, 'Famine and land in Ireland and India, 1845–1880: James Caird and the political economy of hunger,' *Historical Journal* 49, no. 1 (2006), pp 193–215; Norbert Götz, Georgina Brewis, and Steffen Werther, *Humanitarianism in the Modern World: The Moral Economy of Famine Relief* (Cambridge University Press, 2020), pp 36–42.
10. Anelise Hanson Shrout, *Aiding Ireland: The Great Famine and the Rise of Transnational Philanthropy* (New York University Press, 2024).
11. Anne J. Duggan, 'The power of documents: The curious case of Laudabiliter,' in Brenda M. Bolton, Christine E. Meek (eds), *Aspects of Power and Authority in the Middle Ages* (Turnhout, Belgium: Brepols, 2008), http://ebookcentral.proquest.com/lib/nyulibrary-ebooks/detail.action?docID=5205968.
12. William Castell, *A Petition of W.C. Exhibited to the High Court of Parliament Now Assembled, for the Propagating of the Gospel in America, and the West Indies; and for the Setling of Our Plantations There; Which Petition Is Approved by 70 Able English Divines. Also by Master Alexander Henderson, and Some Other Worthy Ministers of Scotland*, 2008, p. 7. http://name.umdl.umich.edu/A78294.0001.001.

13. Emily Conroy-Krutz, *Christian Imperialism: Converting the World in the Early American Republic*, The United States in the World (Ithaca, NY: Cornell University Press, 2015), pp 104–105.
14. Laura M. Stevens, *The Poor Indians : British Missionaries, Native Americans, and Colonial Sensibility* (Philadelphia: University of Pennsylvania Press, 2004), p. 18.
15. Patricia Seed, *Ceremonies of Possession in Europe's Conquest of the New World, 1492–1640* (Cambridge University Press, 1995), p. 28, https://hdl.handle.net/2027/heb01808.0001.001.
16. Pekka Hämäläinen, *Indigenous Continent: The Epic Contest for North America* (New York: Liveright Books, 2022), p. 349.
17. Cotterill, 'Federal Indian Management in the South 1789–1825,' p. 339. Grant Foreman, *Indian Removal: The Emigration of the Five Civilized Tribes of Indians* (University of Oklahoma Press, 1972); Anthony F. C. Wallace, *Jefferson and the Indians: The Tragic Fate of the First Americans* (Cambridge, Massachusetts; London, England: Belknap Press of Harvard University Press, 1999).
18. Julie L. Reed, *Serving the Nation: Cherokee Sovereignty and Social Welfare, 1800–1907* (University of Oklahoma Press, 2016), p. 62.
19. Donna L. Akers, *Living in the Land of Death: The Choctaw Nation, 1830–1860* (Michigan State University Press, 2004), p. 73, http://ebookcentral.proquest.com/lib/bates/detail.action?docID=3338325.
20. Akers, *Living in the Land of Death*, p. 87.
21. Reed, *Serving the Nation*, p. 62; Theda Perdue, 'Race and culture: writing the ethnohistory of the early South,' *Ethnohistory* 51, no. 4 (2004): p. 710.
22. Clara Sue Kidwell, *The Choctaws in Oklahoma: From Tribe to Nation, 1855–1970* (University of Oklahoma Press, 2008), p. 4
23. Ibid., p. 4.
24. Andrew Denson, *Demanding the Cherokee Nation: Indian Autonomy and American Culture, 1830–1900* (University of Nebraska Press, 2004), pp 42–49.
25. Foreman, *Indian Removal*; William G. McLoughlin, *Cherokee Renascence in the New Republic* (Princeton University Press, 1986), p. 411; Theda Perdue, 'The conflict within: The Cherokee power structure and removal', *The Georgia Historical Quarterly* 73, no. 3 (1989); Akers, *Living in the Land of Death*, p. 112.
26. Reed, *Serving the Nation*, p. 76.
27. Denson, *Demanding the Cherokee Nation*, pp 42–49.
28. Reed, *Serving the Nation*, p. 78.
29. 14 January1847. Letters sent by the Office of Indian Affairs, National Archives Microfilm Publication M21, Roll 39, Records of the Bureau of Indian Affairs.
30. These agents were listed in the 15 February 1845 issue of the *Arkansas Intelligencer*. They included Peter Pitchlynn, a notable Choctaw political leader and Daniel Folsom, the editor of the *Choctaw Telegraph*.
31. Meta G. Carstarphen, 'To sway public opinion: Early persuasive appeals in the Cherokee Phoenix and Cherokee Advocate,' in *American Indians and the Mass Media*, Meta G. Carstarphen and John P. Sanchez (eds), (Norman, OK: University of Oklahoma Press, 2012), p. 66, https://papers.ssrn.com/abstract=2142508.

32. Hilary E. Wyss, *English Letters and Indian Literacies: Reading, Writing, and New England Missionary Schools, 175–183* (Philadelphia: University of Pennsylvania Press, 2012), pp 6–7, http://ebookcentral.proquest.com/lib/nyulibrary-ebooks/detail.action?docID=3441995.
33. Quoted in Carstarphen, 'To Sway Public Opinion,' p. 66.
34. *Arkansas Intelligencer*, 3 April 1847.
35. Ibid.
36. Lee Irwin, 'Freedom, law, and prophecy: A brief history of Native American religious resistance', *American Indian Quarterly* 21, no. 1 (January 1, 1997), pp 35–55; Circe Sturm, *Blood Politics: Race, Culture, and Identity in the Cherokee Nation of Oklahoma* (Berkeley: University of California Press, 2002), p. 17, http://site.ebrary.com/id/10051192.
37. *Cherokee Advocate*, 15 July 1847.
38. Ibid.
39. Ronald Austin Wells, *The Honor of Giving. Philanthropy in Native America* (Indiana University Center on Philanthropy, 1998), p. 75; Laura W. Wittstock, 'American Indian giving and philanthropy: The Overlaid Relationship', *Hubert H. Humphrey Institute of Public Affairs: University of Minnesota-Home Page. Retrieved May* 30 (2010).
40. Reed, *Serving the Nation;* Akers, *Living in the Land of Death*, p. 44; LeAnne Howe, 'Ima, Give,' in Padraig Kirwan and LeAnne Howe (eds), *Famine Pots: The Choctaw–Irish Gift Exchange, 1847–Present* (East Lansing: Michigan State University Press, 2020), pp 135–38, http://muse.jhu.edu/book/76002.
41. *Cherokee Advocate*, 13 May 1847.
42. E. H. Gould, *Among the Powers of the Earth: The American Revolution and the Making of a New World Empire* (Cambridge, MA: Harvard University Press, 2012), p. 3.
43. Fred Anderson and Andrew Cayton, *The Dominion of War: Empire and Liberty in North America, 1500–2000* (Penguin, 2005), p. 66.
44. Patrick Wolfe, 'After the Frontier: separation and absorption in US Indian policy,' *Settler Colonial Studies* 1, no. 1 (2011): pp 13–51.
45. Colin G. Calloway, *White People, Indians, and Highlanders: Tribal People and Colonial Encounters in Scotland and America* (Oxford University Press, 2008), pp 150–56.
46. *Cherokee Advocate*, 6 May 1847.
47. Claudia B. Haake, *Modernity through Letter Writing: Cherokee and Seneca Political Representations in Response to Removal, 1830–1857* (Lincoln: Nebraska, 2020), p. 6.
48. Denson, *Demanding the Cherokee Nation*, p. 25.
49. *Cherokee Phoenix*, 20 January 1830.
50. Ibid.
51. Robert Hare, *A Vindication of the Cherokee Claims: Addressed to the Town Meeting in Philadelphia, on the 11th of January, 1830*, 1830, p. 4.
52. *The Liberator*, 17 March 1832.
53. John M. Coward, *The Newspaper Indian: Native American Identity in the Press, 1820–90* (University of Illinois Press, 1999), pp 79–80.
54. *Cherokee Advocate*, 18 March 1847.
55. Ibid., 6 May 1847.

56. Ibid., 23 April 1846.
57. Ibid.
58. Ibid., 13 May 1847.
59. Cian T. McMahon, *The Coffin Ship: Life and Death at Sea during the Great Irish Famine*, The Glucksman Irish Diaspora Series (New York: New York University Press, 2021).
60. James Mooney, *Myths of the Cherokee* (Washington, D.C.: Courier Dover Publications, 1996), p. 128.
61. *Cherokee Advocate*, 4 June 1846.
62. Ibid., 18 March 1847.
63. Quoted in Foreman, *Indian Removal*, p. 39.
64. Ibid., p. 41.
65. *Cherokee Phoenix*, 24 October 1829.
66. Mobile *Commercial Register*, 12 November 1831.
67. New York *Observer*, 26 January 1839.
68. *Cherokee Advocate*, 18 March 1847.
69. Ibid.
70. Ibid., 4 March 1847.
71. Ibid., 18 March 1847.

CHAPTER TWELVE

IN 'RELIEF OF OUR DESTITUTE WHITE BRETHREN'

Upper Canada's Indigenous Peoples and the Irish Famine, 1847

Mark G. McGowan

The Irish Famine of 1846 to 1852 was one of the most traumatic events in modern Irish history. With the repeated failure of the potato crop, upon which two-thirds of Ireland's eight million people depended, the social and economic fabric of Irish life was torn to pieces. By the early 1850s, one million people had perished from hunger or disease and another 1.5 million simply left Ireland. During the tragedy relief money flowed into Ireland from all over the world. Queen Victoria gave £2,000 for relief, the Sultan Abdul Medjid Khan of the Ottoman Empire offered £1000, Pope Pius IX roused Catholics all over the globe to donate to Irish relief, and Archbishop Daniel Murray of Dublin became the principal collector of these funds and distributed them to parishes throughout Ireland.[1] In Canada, Archbishop Joseph Signay, who was to become a pivotal figure in the reception of Irish refugees to Quebec, initiated a fund-raising drive within his vast diocese. Relief committees were founded in the United Kingdom, the United States, and British North America, to raise money within the Irish diaspora to assist the starving Irish and the Highland Scots, who had also been severely affected by the potato blight. The British Relief Association, alone, raised £400,000 for distribution in Ireland and Scotland.[2]

One of the unsung episodes of the Famine was the donation of $170 (the figure is disputed) or about $6,300 USD in today's currency, from the Choctaw Nation in the

United States to Irish relief.[3] There is much irony in this act of generosity from the Choctaw. They themselves were destitute having been forced to relocate from their traditional lands in the southeastern United States, to the designated 'Indian Territory' in present-day Oklahoma. From 1831 to 1833, this 'Trail of Tears', initiated by President Andrew Jackson, himself of Irish descent, caused the deaths of thousands of Choctaws, Creeks, Cherokees, Chickasaws, and Seminoles.[4] Yet only 15 years later, the Choctaw and Cherokee, in their own poverty, recognized the plight of the Irish, identified with it, and scraped up what meagre resources they had to share with their fellow human beings living an ocean away. According to Choctaw historian and writer LeAnne Howe: 'buried deeply within the Choctaw body politic is a sense of giving shelter, food, and/or aid to our relatives, friends, and allies. Ima, giving, is a cultural lifeway'.[5] Historian Anneliese Shrout has written that 'It is difficult to imagine a people less-well positioned to act philanthropically'.[6] The Irish in Ireland have not forgotten the gift and have erected a large monument, highlighted by a massive circle of eagle feathers, to the Choctaw gift, named 'Kindred Spirits', at Midleton, near Cork City.

What has gone virtually unheralded in Canadian history is similar gifts made by Indigenous Peoples to Irish migrants who arrived in Canada, fleeing the Famine. In 1847, the traditional Haudenosaunee territory of Hochelaga, then Montreal, was the scene of tremendous suffering and death. Afflicted with typhus and other serious infections, thousands of Irish migrants were herded into hastily built sheds at Point St. Charles, just west of the downtown area. Tens of thousands of Famine emigrants continued their journeys into Canada West (now Ontario). When asked by Director of the Indian Department in Upper Canada (Canada West), the Haudenosaunee and Anishnaabe Peoples of the province gave generously out of their government annuities to the Irish and Scottish Famine Relief Committee. At the time, the Governor General, Lord Elgin, wrote to the Colonial Office indicating that 'several Indian tribes expressed a desire to share in relieving the wants of their suffering white brethren'.[7] This chapter focuses on the gifts of the Haudenosaunee and Anishinaabe peoples of Upper Canada and the significance of these gifts to the starving Irish. When seen through the understanding of these Indigenous Peoples, the gifts were expressions of these peoples as treaty peoples, who regarded their generosity as integral to keeping the spirit of their treaty with the Crown, regarding such assistance as a responsibility to the 'relief of our destitute white brethren'.[8]

Indigenous Peoples in Upper Canada

The Indigenous Peoples of what became Upper Canada had a long history in this region of Turtle Island.[9] At the time of first contact with Europeans the area was home to a variety of nations with varied traditions, ways of life, and languages. The Huron-Wendat and other Haudenosaunee peoples such as the Neutrals and Petuns were the largest groups and were noted for their permanent fortified settlements and their focus on agriculture, particularly the growing of corn (maize), beans and squash. The Huron-Wendat were decimated by diseases brought by the European traders in the seventeenth century and their principal villages were destroyed in warfare forcing many Wendat to leave and resettle in other territories. The Anishinaabe, mostly Algonquins, inhabited the eastern sections of the region and were nomadic hunter-gatherers, who summered near the many lakes and rivers, where they fished and hunted. By 1701, other Anishinaabeg peoples, through conquest and treaty, occupied much of what became Upper Canada, having defeated the Haudenosaunee peoples, and expanded their hunting territories from the lower Great Lakes to the Ottawa River. Subdivided into Ojibwa, Mississauga, Potawatomi, and Algonquin bands, these groups allied with the French until 1760.[10]

The First Nations of Upper Canada first encountered European traders, explorers, and soldiers in the early seventeenth century. The initial contact was made by the French and its adventurer and explorer Samuel De Champlain. The territory which became Upper Canada and is now Ontario (Haudenosaunee for 'Shining Water'), was under the jurisdiction of New France until the British conquest, whose sovereignty over the region was formalized in 1763, through the Treaty of Paris. Unlike the English settler colonists to the south, in what is now the United States, the French never aspired to establishing a settlement frontier. While the French Crown laid claim to the territories, particularly for trade, they permitted usufructuary rights to the Indigenous Peoples to use the land, an ideology that was not completely understood in indigenous cultures.[11] The French Regime established military and trade centres at Fort Detroit, Fort Rouille (Toronto), and Fort Frontenac (Kingston), but essentially the French settlement frontier was restricted, by government policy, to the St Lawrence Valley and adjacent land in what became Lower Canada and is now Quebec.

With the British conquest of this portion of Turtle Island in 1763, it appeared at first that indigenous title to their own territories would be preserved in the region. The Royal Proclamation Act of the same year confirmed the rights of First Nations over the newly 'conquered' lands east of the Ottawa River, essentially confirming this as Indian Territory.[12] The proclamation also underscored the fact that First

Nations would have to be compensated if outsiders wished to settle on their lands. Should the British Crown intend to extend its settlement frontier it would have to negotiate with First Nations and negotiate treaties.[13] The Anishinaabeg Peoples and the Haudenosaunee Peoples had long traditions of treaty making, most notably The Dish With One Spoon agreement, that brought both indigenous groups into a sharing arrangement with the lands which became Upper Canada;[14] and, before that, the Great Law-inspired Confederacy of the Haudenosaunee brought five peoples (Mohawk, Oneida, Onondaga, Cayuga, and Seneca) into alliance with each other. In 1722, the Tuscarora joined the Confederacy, forming a new Six Nations.[15]

The British had been historically allied to the Haudenosaunee Peoples throughout the colonial period. When the American War for Independence began in 1775, the Mohawk and some Oneidas allied themselves with the British Crown against the settler-colonial Americans. When General George Washington's Continental Army invaded their territory in 1779, the Onondagas, Senecas, and Cayugas allied themselves with the British Crown.[16] With the defeat of the British, in 1784, the Crown, through Lieutenant Governor Frederick Haldimand, granted the New York-based Haudenosaunee resettlement in their traditional lands north of Lake Ontario. The Haldimand Deed prompted the Haudenosaunee to settle on 694, 910 acres purchased by the Crown from the Mississauga, along the Grand River.[17] The Crown also arranged for Mohawks under John Deseronto to settle 69,000 acres in the Bay of Quinte area, in 1784, which became known as Tyendinaga Township nine years later.[18] A second group of Oneida arrived in Canada in 1840 and purchased near Munsey, south of London, at a site which became known as Ona Yo Te Aka.[19]

The allied members of the Haudenosaunee and Anishinaabe had been helpful in the British forces defending against American invasions of the province in 1812 to 1814. By the 1830s, however, Indigenous Peoples were no longer needed as military allies and colonial officials now considered their former partners as obstacles and impediments to the settlement of what had become the Province of Upper Canada in 1791.[20] In the 1830s, with the military threats not as pressing, and the Indigenous Peoples appearing more 'in the way' of new settlers, the Crown transferred responsibility for the First Nations from the military to civilian authorities. Now, relations between the Crown and Indigenous Peoples would be handled by the Department of Indian Affairs, which in the United Province of Canada after 1841, would have a superintendent in each of the Canada East (formerly Lower Canada) and Canada West (formerly Upper Canada) sections. The superintendents in Canada East and Canada West, respectively, reported to the Civil Secretary to the United Province of Canada. In 1847, the Governor General, Lord Elgin, would remain ultimately responsible for Indian Affairs and he reported directly to the Colonial Office in London, and its head, Earl Grey.

In 1845, Thomas G. Anderson replaced Samuel Peter Jarvis as the Superintendent of Indian Affairs in Canada West.[21] Jarvis had a less than stellar reputation with many First Nations, including the Haudenosaunee of Grand River, whose money he invested, without their permission, in a dubious, and ultimately failed, scheme called the Grand River Navigation Company.[22] Jarvis worsened his relations with the Haudenosaunee because of the questionable, if not immoral, extraction of several chief's signatures, without Confederacy Council consent, that ended in the loss of all but 55,000 acres of Governor Haldimand's original grant to the Haudenosaunee. The '1841 Surrender' still resonates as an example in which the 'Crown again failed to fulfill its promises in regard to protecting the significantly reduced Six Nations' land from white squatters'.[23] Anderson, as the new superintendent, had plenty of fences to mend.

Thomas Gummersal Anderson was born in Sorel, near Montreal, in 1779, to Captain Samuel Anderson and Deliverance Butts, a family of Loyalists who had recently escaped from the American War of Independence. He spent nearly 13 years as superintendent and moved the S.I.A. office from Toronto to Cobourg in 1847. He had inherited poor relations with the Haudenosaunee, thanks to Jarvis, and ongoing negotiations with the Anishinaabe Peoples who for several decades had been engaged in treaty-making with the Crown. By the time Anderson ascended to the superintendency, the Ojibwa, Mississauga, and Pottawatomi, had ceded much of what is now southwestern Ontario to the Crown, in exchange for gifts, an annuity, and hunting and fishing rights on their former lands. Also, in this mix, were surviving members of the Huron-Wendat, who had moved into the territories of some of their Anishinaabe neighbours. Anderson's mandate was to manage the treaty obligations, engage with the nations on their reserve lands (See Table 1), and effect new treaties with Indigenous Peoples occupying their unceded traditional lands, notably the Saugeen on the Bruce Peninsula and the Odawa and Ojibwa of Manitoulin Island and the northern shores of Lake Huron and Lake Superior.[24] According to historian Peter Schmalz: 'Many agreements made by the British with the Ojibwa were unconscionable. The few that were agreed upon in good faith were later broken through government manipulation of band funds'.[25] The negative relationships that developed between Indigenous Peoples and the Superintendency, after the 1830s, made the solicitation of funds by the Crown for Famine relief even more remarkable.

Irish and Scottish Famine Relief

In Montreal, in February 1847, local Irish and Scottish citizens met at Daly's Hotel and established the Fund for the Relief of the Destitute Poor in Ireland and Scotland.[26] Initial donors to the fund included Governor General, Lord Elgin (£70), Montreal Mayor John Mills (£100), and the Catholic Seminarians of Montreal (£100).[27] The clamour to support the fund spread from the greater Montreal area to west of the Ottawa River. In February, a special meeting in Toronto saw the subscription of £800 to Irish and Scottish Famine Relief.[28] This mass meeting was followed by several other similar, but smaller, gatherings across Canada West. By the end of March, the province had raised £2,797 for Irish and Scottish Famine relief.[29] In Nova Scotia, a separate colony at that time, the Provincial Legislature added £1,000 to relief funds, despite the fact that farmers in eastern Nova Scotia were also experiencing the destruction of their potato crop by the same blight attacking the fields in Ireland.[30] Similarly, Quebec's Archbishop Joseph Signay initiated a collection and raised £1,602 by the end of March.[31] In many of the fundraising areas, the relief committee was clear—to divide the proceeds for each country based on the decision of individual donors. Irish relief was the overwhelming recipient.[32]

On St Patrick's Day, 1847, Thomas Anderson issued an invitation to the Indigenous Nations within his jurisdiction to donate to the fund. The following petition was sent to all the Haudenosaunee, Anishinaabe, and Wendat reserve settlements in the western portion of the province:

> My Dear Brethren,
>
> There are a few of you who have not at some period of your lives felt the cravings of hunger, but a merciful God has thus far preserved you from the miseries of famine and none of you have seen their children, their fathers and mothers, their husbands or wives dying around them from want of food!
>
> Brethren, this is now the lamentable case with some of your white friends—hundreds in Ireland and Scotland are daily passing into the land of Spirits because they have not food to keep them alive.
>
> Brethren, Your Great Mother the Queen and all your white brethren throughout the world are collecting money & other necessities to save their lives. You also have the means of contributing to the relief of your suffering and dying fellow subjects inform me by letter of the amount you wish to give and I will forward your Great Father at Montreal who is pleased when we show acts of kindness to our fellow creatures.[33]

Within the next six weeks, at least 16 bands answered the call for donations. Representing a population of about 6,103 persons, Indigenous Bands raised £172 10*s* or the equivalent of about $19,130.85 in Canadian dollars (2023).[34] (See Table 1) Most of the responses to Anderson's requests were formulaic and written by either the band's missionary or school master. The one exception was the Mississaugas of the Credit River, whose letter was written in the hand of Peter Jones, Kahkewaquonaby (Sacred Feathers), who was both a leader of the Credit band and a Methodist missionary.[35] The letters usually expressed that Anderson's petition had been received by the band and that the question was taken to the Council, who, in turn, deliberated on the matter. In almost all cases the result of the deliberation included the expression that the council expressed its sympathy for 'our suffering fellow subjects and Christian brethren in Ireland and Scotland', and that a donation would be made despite the band's poverty. In several cases, the band expressed that if it had not been for that poverty, more funds out of their government annuity would be allocated to relief. Such was the case with Chief Brant of the Mohawks of Quinte who explained to Anderson that: 'We feel we have too many poor among ourselves to give much but we beg you will accept our sum of twelve pounds ten shillings as a small proof of our sympathy with them'.[36] By the middle of May, the Mohawks, Haudenosaunee of the Six Nations of Grand River, Chippewa (Ojibwa), Delaware, Wyandotte, and Mississauga Peoples had donated £115. By early June, with further donations from the Saugeen, Ojibwa of Lake Huron, the Ojibwa of Rama, and Moravian Delaware, the total indigenous gift to the relief fund was £172 10*s* (See Table 1).

Two letters, however, stand out from the letters received by Anderson. The first was the letter signed by Chief Nang of the Mississaugas of Mud Lake, now Chemong and Curve Lake. At Chemong Lake, which had a tiny population of only about 94 persons, Chief Nang conceded, as had Chief Brant at Quinte, that his community was poor and would have liked to have given more. He added this urge to help, however, arose from 'the friendships we have received from them [British settlers] in former times'.[37] No doubt Chief Nang was referring to the settlers, many of whom were Irish from the Peter Robinson migration scheme, who had populated several areas of Peterborough County, within Mississauga lands, since 1825. Significantly, it was the only mention among the letters that the Indigenous Bands had positive relations with the settlers who had occupied their lands. Generally speaking, many of the bands in Anderson's agency had been set upon by squatters and European emigrants who had successfully lobbied colonial officials for further concessions from Indigenous Peoples. Somehow, the Mississaugas of Chemong Lake were able to overcome these past wrongs, and able to identify the starving people of Ireland with their Tipperary and Cork neighbours who had made their homes only 20 years before in the region.

Table 1: Indigenous Peoples of Canada West, 1845

Location	Old Name	Nation	Population	Donation/ annuity
Six Nations	Grand River	Haudenosaunee*	2,223	£25 -- --
Thames	Fairfield	Delaware	153	£ 5 -- --
Chippewas of the Thames	Munsey	Ojibwa	620	£7 10s --
OnaYoTeAka	Delaware Twp	Oneida	430	
Wyandotte-Huron		Wendat, Ojibwa, Shawnee	308	£ 5 -- --
St. Clair-Sarnia		Ojibwa, Pottawatomi	741	£20 -- --
Walpole Island		Ojibwa, Odawa, Pottawatomi	1,140	unknown
Manitoulin		Odawa, Ojibwa	1,098	unknown
Tyendinaga	Quinte	Mohawk	383	£ 12 10s --
New Credit	Credit River	Mississauga	239	£ 12 10s --
Alderville	Alnwick	Mississauga	220	£ 10 -- --
Hiawatha	Rice Lake	Mississauga	114	£ 10 -- --
Chemong-Curve Lake		Mississauga	94	£ 12 10s --
Scugog Island	Balsam Lake	Mississauga	90	£ 5 -- --
Rama		Ojibwa	184	£ 10 -- --
Beausoliel		Ojibwa	232	£ 10 -- --
Georgina	Snake Island	Ojibwa	109	£ 5 -- --
Saugeen Lake Huron		Ojibwa	197	£ 10 -- --
Nawash	Georgian Bay, Owen Sound	Ojibwa	130	£ 12 10s --
Bedford/Kingston		Algonquin	91	unknown
			8,862	£172 10s

*Mohawk, Seneca, Oneida, Onondaga, Cayuga, Tuscarore; Source: Bagot Report, 1845, p.25, col.2; LAC, RG10, vol. 162-163, Indian Affairs, Civil Secretary's Office, Correspondence (2301-2400) 1844-1847. £172 10s =$690 USD = £142 sterling

Similarly, Chief Brant at Quinte would have had frequent contact with the large Irish settlement in Tyendinaga Township in Hastings County, which bordered Mohawk reserve lands. Brant, like many other respondents, commented that 'we have too many poor among us to give much'.[38] Nevertheless, as was the case of the Mississaugas of Chemong Lake, the Mohawks donated £12 10*s* each, reflecting perhaps both a concern for the starving in Ireland and Scotland, but also familiarity with the Irish settler/colonists who had been their neighbours for over two decades. By the 1820s, the Mohawks had been selling portions of their original grant of 92,700 acres to incoming settlers, many of whom formed a strong Irish enclave in the township.[39] Brant added the further condition that they were 'fellow subjects and Christian Brethren', which points to recognition of the Irish and Scots as both fellow subjects under the Crown, and fellow Christians to the Mohawks, of whom many belonged to the Church of England. How much the local missionary and the interpreter, Isaac Hill, who co-witnessed to the latter, were influential in the language used, remains unknown.[40]

The letter from Peter Jones and Joseph Sawyer from the Credit River, however, also stands out for different reasons. First, it was written by Jones himself, who was one of the few Mississauga leaders who was fluent in English and had frequent engagements with settler colonists and Methodist clergy. Jones wrote the letter 22 March 1847, only five days after the plea from Anderson, making it one of the first responses, possibly due to the proximity of the Mississaugas of the Credit to Toronto, Anderson's early headquarters for the Indian Office. The cruel irony of the letter was made clear on 23 March, when the Mississauga lands were put up for sale by the government.[41] Because the encroachment of white squatters and aggressive settlers, the Mississauga remitted their 3,189 acres at the Credit,[42] and were moving to the Grand River Valley, to settle on 6,000 acres provided for them by the Six Nations Haudenosaunee.[43] The second irony was that these lands were previously sold by the Mississauga to the British Crown, so that the Haudenosaunee could be deeded them as compensation for their alliance with the Crown during the American Revolution. The added tragedy of the Mississaugas was that Jones and Sawyer explained to Anderson that, although they were willing to offer £12 10*s* out of 'our land payments', it would have been more pleasing to them 'to have given a larger amount but we regret to inform you that our people here are in a very destitute state arising from their not having raised any quantity of produce during last summer'. The cause of this, they asserted, was the news of their surprise removal from their lands, and the failure of their own potato crop.[44]

The collection of letters from the Anishinaabeg and Haudenosaunee peoples are remarkable in several ways. First, given the self-confessed poverty of these bands, the nature and amount of the gifts represent acts of self-giving generosity, not from a surplus but from their very means of survival. It helps to place the amounts donated in perspective. In 1847, at Chemong Lake, a yoke of oxen cost £16 5*s*, or just over the £10 12*s* offered by the Mississaugas to the relief fund.[45] When one realizes how essential oxen were to clear and plow the land, one appreciates how this Anishinaabeg Band had sacrificed from their own potential livelihood. Similarly, the Ojibwa at Munsey on the Thames made a request to Anderson for £56 5*s* for six month's pay for the schoolteacher and a blacksmith, or a rate of just over £9 per month. Their donation to the relief fund was £7 10*s*, or just under what it cost to pay the teacher and a blacksmith for one month.[46] Finally, numbering 90 members, the tiny band of Mississaugas of Scugog, was the smallest group in Anderson's agency. Their bequest of a modest £5 to the relief fund, represented just under one-third of the cost to hire a translator for the band.[47] Moreover, this group gave amidst rather unfortunate circumstances. With fellow Mississaugas at Rice Lake and Chemong Lake, in 1818 the Scugog band had sold 1,951 million acres in exchange for an annuity of £760. They moved to Balsam Lake, but found it infertile, so they relocated their band to 600 acres on Lake Scugog, which they had to purchase back from the British Crown out of their annuity.[48] Despite all these indignities, their donation was forthcoming, and was substantial according to their small population and their own needs, in this case a translator. Thus, while the Indigenous donators apologized for their poverty, their actual gifts were substantial considering their needs of the day.

Understanding the Donation

In the United States, contemporary commentators on the Choctaw and Cherokee donations to Famine relief framed the generosity as coming from the 'fact' that they were more civilized or Christianized 'Indians'. According to the *US Gazette*: 'The unexpected contribution is the more acceptable that it comes from those upon whom the white man has but little claim ... Christianity has taught them that 'God hath made of one blood all nations of men to dwell upon the face of the earth'.[49] In a similar light, the *Cherokee Nation* reported a conversation originating among the white elites of Philadelphia, one of whom wrote to Chief John Ross thanking the Cherokee for the donation, seeing it as 'evidence it affords your people having already attained to a higher and purer species of civilization derived from the influence of our holy religion, by which we are taught to view the sufferings of our fellow beings wherever they exist as our own'.[50] Historian Shrout confirms that for the bourgeois settler society of the time charity was considered one of the 'marks of morality, civility, and social status'.[51] Shrout even suggests that both the Choctaw and Cherokee, with developed print media and access to international news, were sympathetic to the Irish and their predicament of oppressive British rule.[52] In the end, both Shrout and Choctaw scholar/poet, LeAnne Howe dismiss such settler/colonist notions of native 'civility' and consider the gift as part of a long tradition of charity within First Nations.[53] For Howe, the donation was the result of a generosity embodied in the Choctaw concept of *Ima,* or giving.[54]

The idea that religion and growing assimilation of Indigenous Peoples to Upper Canadian settler norms does not explain convincingly the motivation of the First Peoples of British North America to contribute to Irish Famine relief. While some Mississauga, particularly Peter Jones' band at the Credit River, would have been nominally Methodist, some Haudenosaunee were Anglican, and the Delaware were Moravian Brethren, most of the Indigenous Bands who donated to Famine relief still retained their traditional spirituality. Only the Mohawks of Quinte mentioned a possible link of their donation to the fact that the starving Irish and Scots were 'Christian Brethren'.[55] The *Bagot Report* of 1845 was clear that in Upper Canada, the First Nations were an 'untaught, unwary race'.[56] The settler authors of the report described the contrasting situations regarding indigenous Christianity in the two sections of the United Province of Canada: 'In Canada West, in the contrary, to which the influences of the Jesuits and Roman Catholic clergy did not extend, the Indians remained until a very recent period, in a state of heathen barbarism'.[57] The ethnocentric and racist language of the report notwithstanding, it is evident that Canadian observers, unlike American witnesses to the Famine donations by Indigenous Peoples, could not credit Christianity or western-style aspirations to civility and social status as the primary reasons for the donations.

Perhaps the motivation for the donations rests in the way in which the First Nations understood and honoured their treaties and alliances with the British Crown. Given the history of unrequited promises and unfulfilled treaty obligations from the British Crown, land hungry settlers and white squatters on indigenous lands, and the failure of settler colonists to allow the hunting and fishing rights of these First Nations, the fact that Indigenous Peoples, with near unanimity, rallied to the Famine crisis in Ireland is astounding. As allies, the Anishinaabe, Wendat, and Haudenosaunee peoples had rallied to the aid of the British Crown in numerous colonial wars, and they continued to support imperial endeavours, including the coming war in Crimea in the 1850s.[58] This sense of alliance and treaty obligation lay at the heart of the indigenous response to Anderson's petition.

The Haudenosaunee had longstanding military alliances with the British Crown which may have made the Mohawks of Quinte and the Six Nations of Grand River receptive to Anderson's petition. From the time of the Kaswentha Wampum, which established a trading alliance with the Dutch in 1613, and the extension of these treaty relations to the British in 1664 and 1677, when they assumed the Dutch territory, the 'Silver Covenant Chain' was a living agreement between the Haudenosaunee and the British Crown.[59] Despite the British turning a blind eye to squatters and settler land hunger, the Haudenosaunee held to their treaty commitments. While the British regarded treaties as a means of securing ownership of indigenous lands, Joseph Brant of the Mohawks reminded his treaty partners that treaties were undertaken with 'the belief that family members have an obligation to provide for each other'.[60] It is possible to see the donation of 1847 to Famine relief as a Haudenosaunee extension of what they regarded as the obligations of a treaty people, helping their treaty partners who were in distress.

Similarly, the donations made by the Anishinaabeg peoples also suggest that their generosity was a product of how they viewed their treaty relations with the British Crown. Most of the letters from the Anishinaabeg bands were signed with the doodem of the signatory band chief. This was not a personal signature, as was assumed by the settler administrators who received them. They were the marks of the clans who had met in Council to make a collective decision on treaties, or in this case, Anderson's petition. Many bands used these same doodemag on these letters as they had on treaties with the British Crown. According to scholar Heidi Bohaker, the doodem informed:

> respective understanding of time, space, history, law, philosophy, ethics, and most significantly, the foundational relationship between human beings and the world in which human beings live. Anishinaabeg leaders wrote these images on documents pertaining to their lands, at councils held on those lands, reflecting the discussions of those councils. These images were expressions of Anishinaabe law.[61]

When a doodem was assigned to a document or treaty it was an expression of communal consent, arrived at in council, and then expressed by a symbol that was integral to Anishinaabeg notions of personhood. Thus, the appearance of doodemag on these letters was far more than assent to a 'one off' donation; instead, it was an expression of how the Anishinaabe understood themselves as treaty people in their relationship with the British.

The importance of the use of doodemag on these letters should not be underestimated. The doodem was both a sign of kinship or clan, but also a representation of the Anishinaabe's symbiotic relationship with the non-human and natural world:

> Anishinaabe use of the doodem as a category of kinship is also an articulation of Anishinaabe philosophy and law—one that places humans in an interdependent relationship with other-than human beings who are persons with a soul and also relatives to whom one owes a duty of care.[62]

In this relationship with the animal and natural world it is not surprising that the doodemag were representations of animal kin: the eagle, cariboo, deer, crane, serpent, crayfish, pike, or bear, to name a few. Each doodem embodied a characteristic for the Anishinaabeg people to emulate. The crane, for example, featured in several of the letters, was the embodiment of 'eloquence for leadership'.[63] Thus in making treaties with the British Crown, the Anishinaabe, as well as the Haudenosaunee, had far different notions about land ownership, and their responsibility to treaty partners both socially and materially.[64] Treaties made by Council and inscribed with doodemag represented more 'responsibility to' the treaty partner as opposed to the Crown's and settlers' notions of 'authority over'.[65]

While in the United States, after 1817, Indigenous Bands rarely used doodemag on legal documents, instead adopting the use of the 'x',[66] Canadian Anishinaabe continued their use, both on treaties and in regular correspondence with the Provincial Government. At least nine Anishinaabeg bands signed their responses to Anderson with doodemag: Peter Nagy (Serpent) of Chemong Lake; James Mushannog (Pike) and John Mundwa (Caribou) of Munsey Town; Chief Wawanosh (Caribou) and Chief Mishebeshee (Caribou) of St. Clair; Chief John Sunday ('puckwith' or Wind swirl) of Alnwick; George Paudash (Crane) and John Copway (Crane) of Rice Lake; John Aissance (Crane) of Beausoliel Island; Jacob Crane (Crane) of Scugog; Joseph Snake (Fish) and James Snake (Fish) of Snake Island; and Joseph Sawyer (Eagle) of the Mississaugas of the Credit River. Peter Jones, the co-author of the response from the Mississauga of the Credit often used his Eagle doodem,[67] although not on this particular letter, of which he was the principal writer in English.

The Anishinaabeg Bands' treaties with the British Crown, signed with doodemag, bound them in a reciprocal relationship with their treaty partners. These donations were manifestations of the responsibilities that treaty partners had to one another. Although they had never seen those who were in need, thousands of kilometers away, they acknowledged their responsibilities to assist 'our destitute white brethren' who were fellow children of the Crown. George Paudash and fellow leaders among the Mississaugas of Rice Lake, near Peterborough, were clearly motivated by compassion for the Irish. Indeed, they were crestfallen that their donation was only £10, due to their own poverty, lamenting 'we are sorry it is not in our power to do more as our hearts swell with grief at the thought of any of our fellow creatures dying of want of food'.[68] Paudash's letter, written just ten days after Anderson's request, prefaced the donation by contextualizing their concern within an Imperial context, thus underscoring their awareness that their people, though their alliances, were linked with others under the British Crown:

> [we] are happy to find that our great Mother the Queen, and other great people, are considering their situation, though we are poor indeed and our own wants many, still we feel that we are called upon to do something towards relieving their present distress.[69]

It should be noted that although Haudenosaunee peoples at Quinte and Grand River no longer used their Otara[70] to sign the donation letters, their alliances with the British Crown were no less a significant motivation in this act of giving.

Thus, when viewed through an Indigenous lens, the offerings of relief to the starving Irish were expressions of how First Nations Peoples viewed their treaty responsibilities when called upon. Their gift was an obligation to their ally. This generosity was well expressed by Chief John Aissane of Beausoleil, when he informed Anderson:

> Your brother has read your letter to his brother chiefs, who express great pity for their White Brethren and have unanimously agreed to place at the disposal of their Great Father in Montreal [Lord Elgin] for the relief of our White Friends who are suffering of hunger the sum of ten pounds currency ... The sum is small compared with the large sums that we are told has been sent to our white friends by their brethren but we are poor and give the best of our ability with willingness.[71]

Despite their own hardships, dealing with white settlers and squatters (some of Irish birth and descent), and being marginalized in reserve lands which constituted a sliver of their historic territory, the Anishinaabe, Haudenosaunee, and Wendat Peoples honoured their treaties, despite the often unrequited promises of the British Crown and its emissaries.

I would like to acknowledge the help offered me in conversations with Heather George and Mika Patterson of Six Nations, Grand River, Darin Wybenga of the Mississaugas of the New Credit, Jonathan Hamilton-Diabo of Kahnawake; Tracy Taylor and Donovan Taylor of the Mississaugas of Curve Lake, and especially Elder Duke Redbird, Anishinaabe-Saugeen of Chippewa Hill. My thanks also to Kelly McCann (retired archivist, Library & Archives Canada) who shared his findings with me just as we went to press.

NOTES

1. Christine Kinealy, *Charity and the Great Hunger in Ireland: The Kindness of Strangers* (London: Bloomsbury, 2013), pp 108, 115–119, 131–42.
2. Ibid., p. 195.
3. Ibid., pp 103–104 and Anelise Hanson Shrout, 'A voice of benevolence from the Western Wilderness: the politics of native philanthropy in the Trans-Mississippi West', *Journal of the Early Republic* 35, no. 4 (Winter 2015), p. 553.
4. Padraig Kirwan, 'Recognition, resilience, and relief: the meaning of the gift', in LeAnne Howe and Padraig Kirwan, eds. *Famine Pots: The Choctaw-Irish Gift Exchange, 1847-Present* (Cork: Cork University Press, 2020), p. 9; Alfred Cave, Abuse of power: Andrew Jackson and the Indian Removal Act of 1830', *The Historian*, vol. 65, no. 6 (Winter 2003), pp 1330–1335; Gregory D. Smithers, *The Cherokee Diaspora: An Indigenous History of Migration, Resettlement, and Identity* (New Haven: Yale University Press, 2015), pp 93–114.
5. LeAnne Howe, 'Ima, give: A Choctaw tribalography', in Howe and Kirwan, p. 135.
6. Shrout, 'A voice of benevolence', p. 558.
7. British Parliamentary Papers, House of Commons, vol. 53, 1847, p. 7.
8. Library and Archives Canada [LAC], RG 10, Indian Affairs Department, vol.163, no. 2401–2500, Henry Brandt to Thomas Anderson, 5 May 1847, p. 94952.
9. Indigenous identification of what settler-colonists term North America.
10. Pater S. Schmaltz, *The Ojibwa of Southern Ontario* (Toronto: University of Toronto Press, 1991), p. 35.
11. Cornelius J. Jaenen, 'French sovereignty and native nationhood during the French Regime', *Native Studies Review* 2, no. 1 (1986), pp 83–113.
12. *Report of the Royal Commission on Aboriginal Peoples*, vol. 1; *Looking Forward, Looking Back* (Ottawa: Minister of Supply and Services, 1996), p. 116; p. 8 Victoriae, Appendix EE (1844–45), *Report on the Affairs of Indians in Canada (Laid Before the Legislative Assembly, 20 March 1845*, [hereafter *Bagot Report*], p. 4, col. 1.
13. Olive Patricia Dickason, *Canada's First Nations: A History of Founding Peoples from Earliest Times* (Toronto: McClelland and Stewart, 1992), p. 249.
14. Susan M. Hill, *The Clay We are Made Of: Haudenosaunee Land Tenure on the Grand River* (Winnipeg: The University of Manitoba Press, 2017), p. 34. Hill describes the Dish With One Spoon as 'an agreement for nations to treat each other with care and caution, as instituted by the Great Law, and has implications for contemporary land claims'.
15. Hill, *The Clay We Are Made Of*, p. 111.
16. Ibid., p. 128.
17. *Bagot Report*, p. 26, col. 2. Hill, *The Clay*, pp 150–3. Governor Frederick Haldimand had granted one third more than the 677,000 that eventually was purchased from the Mississauga peoples. His successor, Governor John Graves Simcoe, reneged on Haldimand's original grant by excluding the headwaters of the Grand in his deed of 1793.
18. *Bagot Report*, p. 37, col. 2; Hill, *The Clay*, p. 135.
19. *Akwesasne to Wunnumin Lake: Profiles of Aboriginal Communities in Ontario* (Toronto: Ontario Native Affairs Secretariat and Ministry of Citizenship, 1992), p. 176.

20. Schmalz, *The Ojibwa*, p. 122; Dickason, *Canada's First Nations*, p. 248; *Royal Commission*, p. 138.
21. Dickason, *Canada's First Nations*, p. 252.
22. Hill, *The Clay We are Made Of*, p. 178.
23. Ibid., p. 182.
24. The Odawa of Wikwemikong, on Manitoulin Island, have never ceded their lands.
25. Schmalz, p. xii.
26. Jason King, 'Stephen de Vere (1812–1904) and Kahkewaquonaby's "extended sympathies"' in Christine Kinealy, Jason King and Gerard Moran (eds), *More Heroes of Ireland's Great Hunger* (Hamden, CT & Cork, Ireland: Cork University Press and Quinnipiac University Press, 2022), p. 153.
27. Ibid.
28. *British Colonist*, 23 February 1847.
29. Ibid., 23 March 1847.
30. Ibid., 23 February 1847; see Mark G. McGowan, 'A tale of two famines: famine memory in Nova Scotia, Canada', in Patrick Fitzgerald, Christine Kinealy and Gerard Moran (eds), *Irish Hunger and Immigration: Myth, Memory and Memorialization* (Hamden, CT: Quinnipiac University Press, 2015), pp 57–68.
31. *Journal de Québec*, 30 March 1847.
32. Note the example of Brockville, where £630 was collected with £400 designated to Ireland. In York Township, residents collected £122 of which £80 was designated to Ireland. *British Colonist*, 9 March 1847 and 5 March 1847.
33. LAC, RG 10, vol.162, Anderson Petition, 17 March 1847, p. 94332.
34. In 1841 the Pound Sterling was equivalent to £1 4*s* 4*d* Canadian. Likewise, the Canadian pound was equivalent to $4 United States currency. Population figures were derived from Bagot Report, 1845, p. 25, col. 2; The actual letters are at LAC, RG 10, vol. 162–163, Indian Affairs, Civil Secretary's Office, Correspondence (2301–2400) 1844–1847.
35. An excellent study of Jones is Donald B. Smith, *Sacred Feathers: The Reverend Peter Jones (Kahkewaquonaby) and the Mississauga Indians* (Toronto: University of Toronto Press, 1987).
36. LAC, RG 10, vol. 163, no. 2401–2500, Chief Brant to Anderson, 17 April 1847, p. 94786.
37. LAC, RG 10, vol. 163, no. 2401–2500, Chief Peter Noogie to Anderson, 5 April 1847, p. 94787.
38. LAC, RG 10, vol. 163, no. 2401–2500, Chief Brant to Anderson, 17 April 1847, p. 94786.
39. *Akwesasne to Wunnumin Lake*, p.140; *Bagot Report*, p. 37, col. 2; For Irish settlement see: Cecil J Houston and William J. Smyth, *Irish Emigration and Canadian Settlement: Patterns, Links and Letters* (Toronto: University of Toronto Press, 1990), p. 232.
40. LAC, RG 10, vol. 163, no. 2401–2500, Chief Brant to Anderson, 17 April 1847, p. 94786.
41. Donald B Smith, *Mississauga Portraits: Ojibwe Voices from Nineteenth Century Canada* (Toronto: University of Toronto Press, 2013), p. 65.
42. *Bagot Report*, p. 38, col. 2.
43. *Akwesasne to Wunnumin Lake*, p. 134.
44. LAC, RG 10, vol. 162, part 2, Peter Jones and Joseph Sawyer to Thomas Anderson, 22 March 1847, pp 94354–94345.

45. LAC, RG 10, vol. 164, Jacob Crane, Mud Lake [Chemong Lake] Band Request to Anderson, 18 May 1847, p. 95294.
46. LAC, RG 10, vol. 163, John Riley to Joseph B Clench, 30 April 1847, p. 94967.
47. LAC, RG 10, vol. 163, Jacob Crane to Thomas Anderson, 30 March 1847, p. 94918.
48. *Akwesasne to Wunnumin Lake*, p. 136; *Bagot Report*, p. 40, col. 2.
49. Cited in Kinealy, *Charity and the Great Hunger*, p. 105.
50. Ibid., p. 105. From *Cherokee Nation*, 15 July 1847.
51. Shrout, 'A Voice of Benevolence', p. 561.
52. Ibid., pp 566–567.
53. Ibid., p. 564.
54. Howe, 'Ima', p. 135.
55. LAC, RG 10, vol. 163, no. 2401–2500, Chief Brant to Anderson, 17 April 1847, p. 94786.
56. *Bagot Report*, p. 6, col. 1
57. Ibid., p. 15, col. 2.
58. Peter Jones (Kahkewaquonaby), *History of the Ojibway Indians with Especial Reference to their Conversion to Christianity* (London: A.W. Bennett, 1861), p. 214.
59. Hill, *The Clay We are Made Of*, pp 85–100.
60. Ibid., p. 127.
61. Heidi Bohaker, *Doodem and Council Fire: Anishinaabe Governance thru Alliance* (Toronto: University of Toronto Press, 2020), p. xiii.
62. Ibid., p. xiv.
63. Basil Johnston, *Ojibway Heritage* (Toronto: McClelland & Stewart, 1976), p. 53.
64. Bohaker, *Doodem and Council Fire*, p. 123.
65. Ibid., p. 28.
66. Ibid., p. 36.
67. Ibid., p. 86.
68. LAC, RG 10, vol. 162, part 2, George Paudash, John Crow, and John Copway of Rice Lake to Anderson, 27 March 1847, p. 94346.
69. Ibid.
70. Hill, *The Clay We are Made Of*, p. 5.
71. LAC, RG 10, vol. 162, part 1, John Aissance, Beausoliel Island, to Anderson, 29 March 1847, p. 94341.

CHAPTER THIRTEEN

'TO KEEP THEM FROM STARVATION'

Honouring Anishinaabe and Haudenosaunee Irish Famine Aid in Canada West in 1847

Jason King

On 22 March 1847, the Mississaugas of the Credit *ogimaa* (chief) Newechekeshequeby (Joseph Sawyer, also known as Sloping Sky), and *aanikeogimaa* (second chief, deputy) Kahkewaquonaby (Peter Jones, also known as Sacred Feathers), wrote to the superintendent of Indian Affairs, Thomas Gummersall Anderson, to contribute £12–10 'for the relief of the perishing' Irish and Scots.[1] 'We are exceedingly sorry to learn that our fellow subjects in those parts of the world are visited with such an awful calamity', they added. Their donation was but one of many offered by Anishinaabe, Haudenosaunee, and Wyandotte-Huron First Nations in Canada West (now Ontario) in response to a circular issued by Anderson five days earlier, on St Patrick's Day, to support the Montreal based Fund for the Relief of the Destitute Poor in Ireland and Scotland.[2] Their contribution was especially remarkable because it was offered at the very moment that the Credit Mississauga themselves were facing imminent removal from their model village (west of Toronto) without knowing where they would resettle. 'It would have afforded us great pleasure to have given a larger amount', they insisted, 'but we regret to inform you that our people here are in a very destitute state arising from their not having raised any quantity of produce during the last summer, owing to the suspense concerning their removal, and the few potatoes they planted having also proved a failure ... We fear their sufferings from want of food will be very great'. The Credit Mississauga sought to alleviate the hunger of the 'perishing' Irish even while they themselves were at risk 'from starvation'.[3]

This chapter examines their contribution to Irish famine relief and their struggle against removal as a case study of contested land negotiations and increasingly frayed treaty relations that framed their extraordinarily generous act. Recently discovered Anishinaabe, Haudenosaunee, and Wyandotte-Huron First Nations archival records provide much more detailed evidence of Indigenous Peoples speaking for themselves in their decision making and Band council deliberations about rendering aid than can be found in the better known, and rightly celebrated, Choctaw and Cherokee accounts.[4] Analise Hanson Shrout has argued persuasively that 'writers in the Indian Territory used reports of famine and of famine philanthropy to highlight Native morality and capacity for fellow-feeling in contrast to prevailing American ideas that Indians required white guidance in order to act in a humanitarian way'.[5] Yet, it is important to emphasize that the only Indigenous person named in the few contemporary Choctaw and Cherokee archival records and press accounts that exist is Cherokee Chief John Ross (Coowescoowe or Tsan-Usi), who convened 'a public meeting on May 5, 1847, in Tahlequah, Cherokee Nation (Oklahoma)' to enlist support from 'the very considerable number of the descendants of Scotsmen among the Cherokee [that] is calculated particularly to awaken our sympathy towards that people'.[6] More typical are accolades for the Choctaw Indian Agent, William Armstrong, and Lieutenant Colonel Gustavus Loomis who, as Shrout notes, arranged 'a meeting for the relief of the famishing poor of Ireland ... held in the Chapel at Fort Gibson, Cherokee Nation': 'our military friends have taken the lead in this good work—the bravest hearts melt at the human distress', enthused the *Arkansas Intelligencer* on 20 March 1847. By contrast, the much richer First Nations archival records in Canada West meticulously record correspondence and council deliberations that name each of the individual Indigenous decision-makers who contributed to Irish famine relief on behalf of their peoples. Mark McGowan notes in his chapter's sweeping overview and survey of these archival records that they should be interpreted not in the context of famine philanthropy and 'Native morality' but rather as donations in fulfilment of treaty obligations with the Crown, which were increasingly not reciprocated.

This chapter complements and expands on McGowan's research by closely examining the Credit Mississauga contribution to Irish famine relief at the very moment of their removal as a case study of native generosity, treaty violations, and escalating tension with the Crown. Since the Methodist converts Peter Jones and Joseph Sawyer had established the Credit Mission in 1826, they had sought and failed to secure title to their land.[7] As Donald B. Smith notes, 'it was the central political issue that the Credit Mississauga faced. Throughout Peter Jones's correspondence runs the theme of land tenure'.[8] Jones himself contended in his *History of the Ojebway Indians* that 'as the white man advanced in his encroachments, the Indian retired farther back to make room for him. In this way the red men have gradually been stripped of their hunting grounds and corn fields, and been driven far from the land of comfort and plenty'.[9] On 14 September 1838, he had submitted a petition on behalf of the Credit Mississauga to Queen Victoria in Windsor Castle, who 'approved her colonial secretary's recommendation to grant title deeds',[10] yet, despite her assurance, they were never forthcoming. By the spring of 1847, they had exhausted all appeals to remain on their land yet had nowhere else to go. Indeed, the day after the Credit Mississauga contributed to Irish famine relief on 22 March 1847, their lands were advertised for public auction.[11]

Shortly thereafter, they received an unexpected invitation from the Haudenosaunee Six Nations of the Grand River—the largest contributor to Irish famine relief with a donation of £25[12]—to resettle on their reserve in accordance with what Jones described as 'the ancient treaties that were made by our forefathers'.[13] In fact, the Six Nations of the Grand River Haldimand tract had been granted to the Haudenosaunee on traditional Anishinaabe territory by the Crown in 1784 in recompense for their alliance during the American Revolution and loss of their homeland in New York State. Hence, the legendary Mohawk Chief, John Smoke Johnson, welcomed Jones and Sawyer to the Six Nations with his 'recollection of the friendship and kindnesses that existed amongst each of their forefathers [that] was not forgotten'.[14] However, 1847 was a tumultuous year not only for the Credit Mississauga but also for the Six Nations of the Grand River who were confronted with 'territorial reductions' and forced to consolidate and surrender much of their land.[15] As Susan M. Hill argues, 'British Indian policy began to shift from relationships based on treaty obligations to one of paternalistic oversight, heralding "civilization" to "children" who had once been "brethren"'.[16] Ultimately, the Credit Mississauga and the Six Nations of the Grand River displayed extraordinary generosity to the Irish and fidelity with one another in honouring 'ancient treaty' obligations that the Crown failed to uphold.

'Your White Brethren'

On 2 April 1847, superintendent of Indian Affairs, Thomas Gummersall Anderson, wrote from the Indian Office in Toronto to apprise his superior, George Vardon, Assistant Superintendent General, Indian Affairs, and the Governor General, Lord Elgin, in Montreal, of his endeavours to raise funds for famine relief from First Nations in Canada West: 'I have the honor to enclose herewith the circular', he explained, 'which I took upon myself to address to the Indian tribes within my superintendence, with a view of giving them an opportunity of subscribing to the relief funds for Ireland and Scotland ... which I trust his lordship the Governor General will be pleased to approve'.[17] Anderson was a veteran Indian Agent 'who spoke Ojibwa [and] had worked with the Anishinabeg for nearly half a century',[18] although he was also resented for his 'dictatorial philosophy'.[19] His letter makes it clear that he issued his circular of his own volition, which explains why there is a multitude of contributions from Indigenous Peoples in Canada West, with almost no corresponding documented evidence of similar donations from First Nations in Canada East (now Quebec).[20]

The circular that Anderson issued on St Patrick's Day in 1847 was carefully worded to instil a sense of obligation amongst it recipients. It is worth quoting at length:

> My Dear Brethren,
>
> There are a few of you who have not at some period of your lives felt the cravings of hunger, but a merciful God has thus far preserved you from the miseries of famine and none of you have seen their children, their fathers and mothers, their husbands or wives dying around them from want of food!
>
> Brethren, this is now the lamentable case with some of your white friends—hundreds in Ireland and Scotland are daily passing into the land of Spirits because they have not food to keep them alive.
>
> Brethren, Your Great Mother the Queen and all your white brethren throughout the world are collecting money & other necessities to save their lives. You also have the means of contributing to the relief of your suffering and dying fellow subjects—inform me by letter of the amount you wish to give and I will forward it to your Great Father at Montreal who is pleased when we show acts of kindness to our fellow creatures.[21]

Anderson's salutation of 'My Dear Brethen', in seeking to alleviate 'the cravings of hunger' of the Irish and Scots 'daily passing into the land of Spirits', would seem to address Indigenous Peoples in a conciliatory fashion as fraternal rather than paternal relations of the Crown. As Alan Ojiig Corbiere notes, this 'fictive kin relationship' signified a longstanding 'Nation to Nation relationship' between the Anishinaabe, Haudenosaunee and the Crown following the Treaty of Niagara in 1764 and the defeat of the French in North America during the Seven Years' War.[22]

The Anishinaabe and Haudenosaunee also used the term 'brethren' in their treaty relations with one another. As Corbiere observes, Peter Jones employed 'this idea of brother, instead of enemy' in his description of their treaty alliance after prolonged hostilities in the seventeenth century in his *History of the Ojebway Indians*:

> A treaty of peace and friendship was then made with the Nahdoways [Haudenosaunee] residing on the south side of Lake Ontario, and both nations solemnly covenanted, by going through the usual forms of burying the tomahawk, smoking the pipe of peace, and locking their hands and arms together, agreeing in future to call each other BROTHERS. Thus ended their wars.[23]

Jones also noted that in spite of their treaty 'there has been, and still is, a smothered feeling of hatred and enmity between the two nations, so that when either of them comes within the haunts of the other they are in constant fear'.[24] More to the point, Anderson was not simply employing diplomatic convention when soliciting aid for 'suffering and dying fellow subjects' from his Indigenous 'brethren'. In addressing them as 'my dear brethren', he also sought to ween them from their ostensible sense of dependence on the Crown. Indeed, when first appointed to his position in 1845, Anderson declared: 'My Friends and Brethren, I no longer call you children, as was formerly done when you were a loving unhappy set of people', because 'the further you proceed in the arts of civilized life the more happy of independence you will become'.[25]

'Suspense Concerning Their Removal'

Anderson's insistence on the need for more Indigenous self-reliance was especially disingenuous in relation to the Credit Mississauga. As superintendent, he exerted pressure on Indigenous Peoples in Canada West to abandon hunting for farming, cede and 'surrender' land, reduce the Crown's expenditure in the form of diminished annuities and present distribution from previous land cessions, and relocate to the remote Saugeen (Bruce) Peninsula in the name of 'civilization' and 'independence'. In reality, he was couching the Crown's abrogation of longstanding treaty obligations in these blandishments of improvement. As Corbiere notes, 'the Treaty of Niagara [in 1764] and Covenant Chain did not contain an explicit clause referring to annuities, but the British did promise that the Western Nations and their posterity would never 'sink into poverty'. Moreover, 'the annual delivery of presents was not to be supplanted by an annuity from a treaty. The presents themselves represented something more than clothing—the giving and receiving of presents was the embodying act of the continued alliance between nations'.[26] In the case of the Credit Mississauga, they had already come to embody all of the civilizing ideals that Anderson sought to inculcate after their conversion to Methodism in the early nineteenth century, yet, they too, were deprived of title to their land. By the early nineteenth century, the Credit River Band 'seemed destined for extinction. At that decisive time', claims Schmalz, 'Peter Jones returned to his people in an attempt to bring material as well as spiritual aid. His success became legendary'.[27] In fact, he helped create an exemplary village in 1826 with Chief Joseph Sawyer at Credit Mission: 'This settlement established a precedent and provided the government with a model for all future reserves established for the Ojibwa in southern Ontario and beyond'.[28] Yet, from the Crown's perspective, these achievements were suspect, occurring under the auspices of the Methodist rather than the Anglican Church. 'Suspicious of the American ties to Methodism, the government refused the band's application for a deed', notes Dickason.[29] Indeed, its failures to secure land tenure and pressure from the Crown to relocate to Owen Sound came to a head in the early months of 1847.

The Credit Mississauga were the first recipients of Anderson's St Patrick's Day circular to respond five days later, on 22 March. As noted, Peter Jones and Joseph Sawyer wrote a letter in which they both offered famine relief and revealed that their fellow band members were themselves at risk 'from starvation':

> Feeling the necessity of rendering aid to such as are in real distress, we gladly subscribe the sum of twelve pounds ten shillings ... out of our land payments, and beg you will have the goodness to pay that amount into the hands of our Great Father, the Governor General, that he may forward the same over the Great Water. It would have afforded us great pleasure to have given a larger amount, but we regret to inform you that our people here are in a very destitute state arising from ... the suspense concerning their removal.[30]

As with most of their correspondence, the letter was signed by Peter Jones and marked by Joseph Sawyer with his Eagle doodem.[31] It was profoundly ironic that they were forced to cease farming because of 'the suspense concerning their removal' while 'rendering aid' from 'land payments' for the surrender of their home.[32]

The Mississaugas of the Credit offered their donation in a moment of considerable vulnerability and escalating tension both with colonial officials and between band members themselves. Under persistent pressure, they had reluctantly agreed to relocate to the hinterland of Owen Sound, only to discover that its soil was rocky and much less arable than the Credit Mission that they were leaving behind. On 21 January 1847, Peter Jones wrote to George Vardon to inform him:

> There is quite a dissension amongst our people with regard to their removal to Owen Sound. Our young men who assisted in surveying the boundary line of our intended tract there have brought an evil report as to the quality of the soil... In consequence of these tidings a large majority of our tribe are reluctant to remove to that tract of land... If the land really is as poor as they represent it, I should be the last man to induce any of our people to remove to it, as I am fully persuaded that when Indians emigrate to another part of the country, they ought to settle on a better tract of land than that which they leave.[33]

Jones's point would seem self-evident and, perhaps lined with sarcasm, held little sway. Shortly thereafter, on 6 February, Joseph Sawyer and Peter Jones invited Anderson to Credit Mission for a council they had convened 'on the subject of their removal from this place'.[34] In Anderson's presence, on 9 February, the council became a flashpoint for simmering tensions with the Indian Office and within the tribe itself.

The Credit Mississauga council minutes make clear the pressures that Jones and Sawyer faced both from Anderson as well as from their fellow band members. The former expressed little sympathy for their plight. Anderson chided them with a reminder:

> the Credit Indians agreed to go ... and much expense was incurred ... That after all that has been done it will appear very strange to the Government that they should now refuse to go to that tract of land.[35]

He 'advised them to pause before they made up their minds not to go to Owen Sound'. Peter Jones tried to placate him, which was construed as a provocation by James Young, one of the Tribe's young men who had surveyed the Owen Sound tract. Young 'rose up and said, my Chiefs, you are very great cowards indeed, in being afraid to speak to the Government[;] you know our minds on the subject, and will not speak and tell the same'.[36] After that, 'the council broke up' but before it dispersed 'Peter Jones addressed them and... gave notice of his intention to resign his chieftainship'. 'It would not do to have a coward for a chief', he admonished.[37] Ultimately, he did not resign, but the Tribe had reached breaking point.[38]

Tensions remained in the weeks that followed. On 12 February 1847, the Credit Mississauga council reconvened and passed a unanimous resolution 'that our chiefs Jos. Sawyer and Peter Jones be appointed to wait upon our Great Father, Lord Elgin [the Governor General] with our petition praying that we may be able to select a good tract of land somewhere in the west'.[39] On 15 February, Sawyer and Jones wrote to Anderson requesting 'permission to visit upon their Great Father Lord Elgin at Montreal with their memorial and to explain all the matters on the subject'.[40] They were rebuffed.[41] On 19 February 1847, George Vardon notified Anderson that the

Governor General was 'unwilling ... to comply with their request', though he would accept their petition.[42] 'The Governor General regrets to learn', he added, 'that the Mississaugas of the River Credit who heretofore have taken the lead in the proposed scheme of emigration ... should now vacillate, and abandon a plan which has been already attended with much labor and expense'. Peter Jones was mortified. On 4 March, he complained to Anderson that, 'I am at a loss to conceive what could have induced him to make such a severe attach on us poor chiefs'. He also expressed disappointment in George Vardon, 'whom I have always considered one of my best friends in Canada, but self-defence is the first law of nature'.[43] 'If anything should recur to prevent my going to Montreal', he avowed, 'I shall write to my friends for an explanation on the charges made against the chiefs'.[44]

The Credit Mississauga crafted their petition the following day. Sawyer and Jones also drafted a letter to Vardon in which they reiterated that they 'were grieved and mortified' but insisted that they 'had been misled as to the good quality of the soil' awaiting them, which elicited 'the almost unanimous voice of our people... raised against removing to Owen Sound'.[45] Their petition emphasized that it was their prerogative to choose a better tract of land. In it, they beseeched:

> Father, we humbly beg your Lordship will be pleased to pardon what may appear a reckless and vacillating spirit, in this changing our plans, but being fully convinced that our beloved Great Mother the Queen loves her red children and desires to see them happy and prosperous, and knowing that all of Her Majesty's Great Officers are ever ready to carry their Sovereign's wishes into effect, we feel persuaded that when Your Lordship has heard our reasons, Your Lordship will approve of the course we have taken.
>
> Father, we now humbly pray your Lordship to allow us to select a good farming tract of land.[46]

Their petition concluded with an invocation of 'the blessing of the Great Spirit' followed by the band members' signatures and corresponding 24 doodemag or doodem images described as 'their totems' which extend over two pages at the end of the document.[47] As such, it represented a form of collective 'deliberation in council'.[48] Their petition made it clear that the Credit Mississauga did not simply accept, but actively sought to choose their destination for resettlement.

The Credit Mississauga's contribution to Irish famine relief was also a collective decision inextricably linked with their ongoing land negotiations. McGowan notes in his chapter the underlying expectation that Indigenous Peoples would respond to Anderson's circular as part of their sense of obligation to the Crown. 'These donations were manifestations of the responsibilities that treaty partners had to one another', he asserts. The treaty relationship with the Credit Mississauga was especially frayed as they rendered aid from land payments without knowing where they would resettle. Yet, more broadly, each of the First Nations that provided famine relief did so from its annuities or annual government payments received in exchange for previous land cessions. In short, their destitute 'white brethren' were the beneficiaries of their past and present territorial dispossessions.

'There were no white people'

The Mississaugas of the Credit remained in suspense about their removal until the end of March in 1847. On 29 March, Thomas Anderson delivered the Governor General's reply to their petition in person on a visit to Credit River. 'I am directed to inform you that his Lordship will not oppose the wishes of the tribe, which it is stated is nearly unanimous', wrote Vardon on Lord Elgin's behalf.[49] 'In reply to the petition the Governor General sanctions their removal to the west', records band council minutes that day.[50] The council then proceeded to hold a vote about where to resettle, with 51 families opting for the west, two to remain at Credit River, and only one for Owen Sound. The Credit Mississauga had thus prevented their relocation to the latter destination yet remained uncertain about where they would resettle.

The suspense concerning their removal came to an end the following day. According to the band council minutes on 30 March 1847:

> Chief Sawyer stated that having heard that it was the intention of the Six Nations on the Grand River [also located to the west] to invite our tribe to come and settle on their tract of land which they would give without any charge[,] the Council took the subject into consideration, and when the vote was taken, there appeared 14 men for the Grand River and—16 against it. So that their [sic] was a majority of one against it[.] The Nays were for Muncey Town.[51]

Joseph Sawyer and Peter Jones opted to travel to the Six Nations of the Grand River to learn more about their invitation in hope of preventing a split. A council was convened there on 9 April 1847 to receive them. At its commencement:

> The fire keeper opened the council by the usual ceremony of condolence, after which [Mohawk] Chief John Smoke Johnson addressed the Chiefs from the River Credit, expressing their high gratification in seeing them present on this occasion, and [he] referred to the old treaties and friendships made and which had ever existed between their fathers and those of the Chippewas [Mississaugas].[52]

Joseph Sawyer also referred to these 'old treaties and friendships' when he had returned to Credit River on 12 April. He reported that the Six Nations chiefs remembered that their ancestors had found refuge on Anishinaabe territory and 'they felt a great pleasure in returning the compliment to their descendants'.[53]

This invitation from the Six Nations of the Grand River was especially generous given their own territorial constrictions in 1847. The Grand River reserve had been established in 1784 for the Haudenosaunee Five Nations—Mohawk, Oneida, Onondaga, Cayuga, and Seneca (and later the Tuscarora)—allied with the Crown after its defeat when they were expelled from the United States and fled to Fort Niagara. 'Between 1784—the removal to and settlement on the Grand River—and 1847, the date of the last formal reduction of Haudenosaunee lands along the Grand River tract, the Six Nations... endured great hardships', Hill contends.[54] Each of the Six Nations had originally been allocated their own sections of the vast Haldimand Tract along the Grand River, but white settler encroachment resulted in 'a series of Six Nations territorial reductions. On most occasions, illegal land transactions—violating both Haudenosaunee and British laws—were eventually sanctioned by the imperial government'.[55] 'Through this loss of land', Hill adds, 'the Haudenosaunee found themselves in a very similar position [in 1847] to that faced by their families at the close of the Revolutionary War—forced to abandon their homes and villages and the bones of their ancestors to relocate and build their lives in a new place'. Like the Credit Mississauga, the Six Nations suffered land cessions because of treaty violations by the Crown.

In spite of their disillusionment, the Six Nations subscribed the largest donation for Irish Famine relief—£25—and honoured their 'old treaties and friendships' with the Credit Mississauga. Their adherence to these obligations appears all the more remarkable given what Jones had described as the 'smothered feeling of hatred and enmity between the two nations'. Even so, Mohawk Chief Henry Brant welcomed Joseph Sawyer and Peter Jones to their Six Nations council on 8 April 'giving their right hand of fellowship' after 'rumours had recently reached' them that the Mississaugas 'were now as it were roving about without a home'.[56] Peter Jones translated for Joseph Sawyer who addressed the council in turn expressing both the plight of his Tribe and gratitude that the Six Nations would abide by their treaty obligations: 'I am glad to hear that you remember the ancient treaties', he declared, 'that were made by our forefathers and your people and our people, and they the enemy took from the Six Nations their houses'.[57] In reminding his hosts of his ancestors providing refuge for their forefathers, Jones recollected that 'it was at the head of Lake Ontario where the treaty was held. There were no white people or houses except at Niagara, and there the final treaty was made in General Council'. 'That treaty was made very strong', he added, 'that its effects were not forgotten but renewed again. That the light it gave is still shining'. He then offered a poignant account of his Tribe's current predicament:

> Brother, I have just told you the extent of our lands and I have now to tell you that it is owned by another race of people ... I am now reduced to so little that I have scarcely enough to stand upon.
>
> My brother, I now tell [of] the poverty our people are in. The small tract we have, the white man keeps hemming us in, and is taking away our wood ... I am afraid that my children... will not have wood to make fires to keep them warm ... that we must seek a place where they will not die from cold.[58]

Ultimately, the Mississaugas of the Credit accepted the Six Nations' invitation to resettle at Grand River. They found common ground in the renewal of their ancient alliance.[59]

The suspense concerning the Credit Mississauga's removal had finally been resolved. In sanctioning their relocation, the Governor General also made clear his approval of their contribution for famine relief. Band council minutes on 26 April 1847 register that these land negotiations and philanthropic contribution were closely related. According to the minutes:

> The Governor General's reply to the address of the Credit Indians was read, and the words of his Lordship gave great satisfaction to the council.
>
> His Excellency's reply to the contribution of the Credit Indians in aid of the suffering Scotch and Irish was read.
>
> Major Campbell's [superintendent-general of Indian affairs] letter to Capt. Anderson conveying the Governor General's sanction to the removal of the Credit Indians to the Grand River reservation was read and recd. [received] with deep feelings of thankfulness.[60]

After months of uncertainty and trepidation, the Mississaugas expressed 'great satisfaction' and 'deep feelings of thankfulness' for the resolution of their plight. They had succeeded in selecting their own destination at Six Nations of the Grand River; while 'no white people' brokered their renewal of 'ancient treaties' subsequently approved by the Crown. The Governor General's sanction helped alleviate escalating tension, as did their contribution 'in aid of the suffering Scotch and Irish'. They offered their donation during their struggle against removal in furtherance of their sense of alliance.

In conclusion, the contribution of the Mississaugas of the Credit to Irish famine relief was unique insofar as they faced the imminent prospect of 'roving about without a home' in the spring of 1847. While the Choctaw and Cherokee donations are rightly celebrated for having been offered in the decade after their traumatic journeys to

Indian Territory (now Oklahoma) on the infamous Trail of Tears, the Mississaugas were in the very midst of their removal when they subscribed to Anderson's circular. The archival records, evidence of Indigenous decision-making, and council deliberations in authorizing these donations, are much more detailed and richer for the Anishinaabe, Haudenosaunee, and Wyandotte-Huron First Nations in Canada West than the Choctaw and Cherokee, especially in the case of the Credit Mississauga. Their myriad voices resonate in the Band council minutes, correspondence, and petitions that conveyed their generosity in rendering aid to the Irish and Scots. Their gifts represented a considerable sacrifice. Indeed, Peter Jones makes clear that their contribution to famine relief took place in a moment of 'important crisis'.[61] That crisis of their removal was resolved in accordance with 'ancient treaties', not with the Crown, but between the Anishinaabe Credit Mississauga and Haudenosaunee Six Nations that brought them together near Grand River even while both suffered considerable territorial reductions in 1847. As recounted by Peter Jones: 'their Fathers had fled to Canada, and, when they were without a home, our Fathers readily granted them the land on which they now resided on the Grand River; and now it gave them great pleasure to return a similar kindness by giving us back a small portion from the land reserve they had received'.[62]

Even so, their removal from Credit River elicited great sorrow. 'Not a family but left behind them the sacred dust of some loved relative', lamented Jones. Like the Six Nations, the Credit Mississauga were forced to leave the bones of their ancestors behind. 'The Indians have usually a strong veneration and affection for their old haunts, and consider it a disgrace to abandon the bones of their ancestors', noted a government *Report on Indian Affairs in Canada* (June 1847), 'while the faith of the Crown, and every principle of justice, are opposed to their compulsory removal'.[63] Yet, in depriving them of title to their land, the Crown did not keep faith with the Credit Mississauga—it violated 'every principle of justice' in necessitating their forced migration and compulsory removal. By contrast, the Indigenous Peoples of Canada West honoured their treaty obligations and contributed generously to Irish famine relief for which they deserve lasting recognition. Their acts of kindness in aid of the suffering Scots and Irish should be honoured and not forgotten.

I would like to acknowledge the help offered me in conversations with Heather George and Mika Patterson of Six Nations, Grand River, Darin Wybenga of the Mississaugas of the New Credit, Jonathan Hamilton-Diabo of Kahnawake; Tracy Taylor and Donovan Taylor of the Mississaugas of Curve Lake, and especially Elder Duke Redbird, Anishinaabe-Saugeen of Chippewa Hill.

NOTES

1. Library and Archives Canada (hereafter LAC), RG 10, vol. 162, part 2, Peter Jones and Joseph Sawyer to Thomas Anderson, 22 March 1847, pp 94354–94345. Also see Heidi Bohaker, *Doodem and Council Fire: Anishinaabe Governance through Alliance* (Toronto: University of Toronto Press, 2020), p. 22.
2. LAC RG 10, Indian Affairs Department, vol. 162, Anderson Petition, 17 March 1847, p. 94332. See Mark McGowan's chapter and Jason King, 'Stephen de Vere (1812–1904) and Kahkewaquonaby's "extended sympathies": A Case Study of Famine Irish Emigration and Canadian First Nations' in Christine Kinealy, Jason King and Gerard Moran (eds), *More Heroes of Ireland's Great Hunger* (Hamden, CT & Cork, Ireland: Cork University Pres and Quinnipiac University Press, 2022), p. 153.
3. Ibid.
4. See Christine Kinealy, 'An Ocean of Benevolence' in LeAnne Howe and Padraig Kirwan (eds), *Famine Pots: The Choctaw Irish Gift Exchange, 1847-Present* (East Lansing, MI: Michigan State University Press, 2020), pp 70–105; Analise Hanson Shrout, *Aiding Ireland: The Rise of Transnational Philanthropy* (New York: New York University Press, 2024), pp 103–115; and Analise Hanson Shrout, '"A Voice of Benevolence in the Wilderness": The Politics of Native Philanthropy in the Trans-Mississippi West', *Journal of the Early Republic* (vol. 35, no. 4, 2015), pp 553–557, for detailed studies of Choctaw and Cherokee archival records and especially press accounts of their contributions for Irish Famine relief in 1847.
5. Shrout, 'A Voice of Benevolence in the Wilderness', p. 578.
6. *Cherokee Advocate*, 6 May 1847; Kinealy, 'An Ocean of Benevolence', p. 94.
7. See Donald B. Smith, *Sacred Feathers: The Reverend Peter Jones (Kahkewaquonaby) and the Mississauga Indians*, 2nd ed. (Toronto: University of Toronto Press, 2013), and *Mississauga Portraits: Ojibwe Voices from Nineteenth-Century Canada* (Toronto: University of Toronto Press, 2013), pp 3–32, for compelling biographies of Peter Jones. Smith also profiles Joseph Sawyer in *Mississauga Portraits*, pp 33–67.
8. Smith, *Mississauga Portraits*, p. 22.
9. Peter Jones, *History of the Ojebway Indians: With Especial Reference to their Conversion to Christianity* (London: A.W. Bennett, 1861), p. 27; cited in Smith, *Mississauga Portraits*, p. 22.
10. Smith, *Sacred Feathers*, p. 167.
11. Smith, *Mississauga Portraits*, p. 65.
12. LAC RG 10, vol. 163, Henry Brant et al to Thomas Anderson, 5 May 1847, pp 94951–94952.
13. LAC RG 10, vol. 1011, 'Extracts of the Minutes of a General Council of the Six Nations of Indians Residing on the Grand River... Onondaga Council House ... 23 April 1847', p. 180. Unpublished archival records in this volume include the Credit Mississauga Band Council Minutes (1834–1848), Peter Jones Entry Book, 1831–1848 (Band Council Minutes, Correspondence, Addresses, Petitions), and Band Council Minutes and Correspondence, 1842–1867, which will be examined in detail for the period of the spring of 1847 in this chapter.
14. Ibid., p. 179.

15. Susan M. Hill, *The Clay We Are Made Of: Haudenosaunee Land Tenure on the Grand River* (Winnipeg: University of Manitoba Press, 2017), p. 241.
16. Ibid., p. 240.
17. LAC RG 10, vol. 162, Thomas Anderson to George Vardon, 2 April 1847, p. 94331
18. Smith, *Sacred Feathers*, p. 207. Smith notes that Peter Jones 'viewed Anderson as a vast improvement' over his predecessor Samuel Peters Jarvis who was removed from his position as Chief Superintendent of Indian Affairs for Upper Canada for embezzling funds from the Indian Office but never prosecuted.
19. Peter S. Schmalz, *The Ojibwa of Southern Ontario* (Toronto: University of Toronto Press, 1991), p. 142.
20. It is worth noting that there is an oral tradition of a donation for Irish famine relief in 1847 from the Kahnawá:ke Mohawk Territory near Montreal. As former Chief Christine Zachary-Deom has recollected: 'Our international outlook was also significantly recognized when in the nineteenth century the Irish were experiencing their Potato Famine. Our community was not affluent, but according to a strong oral tradition, it collectively made a small contribution to Irish famine relief. It is said that our community felt distressed over the privations of Irish families during the famine and sent money through the Catholic Church', *Quebec Heritage News* (vol. 9, no. 1, 2015), p. 28. The earliest contemporary documented evidence found to date to corroborate this claim is John Mercier McMullen's contention that 'from the Iroquois Indians of Caughnawaga [Kahnawá:ke], and the Huron and Delaware of western Canada, and from her colored citizens, came contributions in money or in food'. See John Mercier McMullen, *The History of Canada: From its First Discovery to the Present Time* (Brockville, Canada] West: J. M'Mullen, Publisher, 1855), p. 485.
21. LAC, RG 10, vol.162, Anderson Petition, 17 March 1847, p. 94332.
22. Alan Ojiig Corbiere, 'Anishinaabe Treaty-Making in the 18th- and 19th-Century Northern Great Lakes: From Shared Meanings to Epistemological Chasms', unpublished Ph.D. dissertation (Toronto: York University, 2019), pp 258, 255.
23. Jones, *History of the Ojebway Indians,* p. 113; also see Corbiere, p. 260. It is also important to emphasize that in the 'General Council minutes' for their treaty's renewal on 21 January 1840 that the Haudenosaunee 'called the Governor "Brother" and not "Father" as the Ojibways do: the reason why they called the Governor "Brother" was that they might feel themselves equal with the Governor, and so speak more freely to him, which they could not do if he was their father', LAC, RG 10, vol. 1011, 'Minutes of General Council met Tuesday 21 January, 1840', p. 84. See Bohaker for detailed analysis of this renewal of the Anishinaabe and Haudenosaunee alliance (pp 158–167), and Schmalz, who explores the historic enmity and seventeenth-century conflicts between the Anishinaabe and Haudenosaunee in southern Ontario (pp 13–34).
24. Ibid., p. 114.
25. LAC, RG 10, vol. 1011, 'The Speech of Mr Supt Thomas Anderson on his first visit to the Indians under his superintendence, conveying to them by command of His Excellency the Governor General, the views and determinations of the British Government with regard to their future conduct and prosperity', 16 September 1845, p. 122.

26. Cobiere, 'Anishinaabe Treaty-Making', p. 285.
27. Schmalz, *The Ojibwa of Southern Ontario*, p. 159.
28. Ibid.
29. Olive Patricia Dickason, *A Concise History of Canada's First Nations* (Oxford University Press, 2006), p. 138.
30. LAC RG 10, vol. 162, part 2, Peter Jones and Joseph Sawyer to Thomas Anderson, 22 March 1847, pp 94354–94345.
31. Bohaker discusses the significance of the eagle doodem as a 'visual metaphor' on pp 203–205, and p. 256.
32. LAC RG 10, vol. 162, part 2, Peter Jones and Joseph Sawyer to Thomas Anderson, 22 March 1847, pp 94354–94345.
33. LAC, RG 10, vol. 1011, Peter Jones to George Vardon, 21 January 1847, p. 144.
34. Ibid., Joseph Sawyer and Peter Jones to Thomas Anderson, 6 February 1847, p. 148.
35. Ibid., 'Minutes of a Council held at the Credit Village', 9 February 1847, p. 311.
36. Ibid., p. 312.
37. Ibid., pp 312, 313.
38. See Smith, *Sacred Feathers*, pp 210–212.
39. LAC, RG 10, vol. 1011, 'Minutes of Council held at the Credit', 12 February 1847, p. 313.
40. Ibid., Joseph Sawyer and Peter Jones to Thomas Anderson, 15 February 1847, p. 152.
41. Three days earlier (12 February), Joseph Sawyer and Peter Jones had welcomed the newly appointed Governor General on behalf of 'the Chiefs and people of the River Credit Tribe': 'Father, we your red children most respectfully do welcome your safe arrival', they stated, 'to this our native land, and we most humbly beg leave to tell you what is in our hearts'. The Governor General, Lord Elgin, responded graciously 'that your words sink into mine, and [my heart] warms with kindly feelings towards you', LAC, RG 10, vol. 1011, Joseph Sawyer and Peter Jones, 'To our Great Father Lord Elgin, Governor General of Canada', 12 February 1847, pp 145–146, and 'The Governor General's Reply', n.d., p. 146.
42. Ibid., George Vardon to Thomas Anderson, 19 February 1847, p. 153.
43. Ibid., Peter Jones to Thomas Anderson, 4 March 1847, p. 155.
44. Ibid.
45. Ibid., Joseph Sawyer and Peter Jones to Thomas Anderson, 6 March 1847, p. 160.
46. Ibid., Credit Mississauga Petition 'To Our Great Father, The Right Honourable Lord Elgin, Governor General of British North America', 5 March 1847, p. 158.
47. LAC RG 10, vol. 162, part 1, Credit Mississauga Petition 'To Our Great Father, The Right Honourable Lord Elgin, Governor General of British North America', 5 March 1847, pp 93935–93936. The petition is also copied in the Peter Jones Entry Book with band members' signatures but not their accompanying doodemag, LAC RG10, vol. 1011, p. 159.
48. Bohaker, p. 223. 'Regardless of what officials thought at the time', she contends, 'the Ainishiabek knew what their doodem images meant and consistently wrote them on documents that pertained to the work of governance. In turn, Anishinaabe leaders also wrote their doodem images on petitions sent to colonial governments', p. 222.
49. LAC, RG 10, vol. 1011, George Vardon to Peter Jones, 13 March 1847, p. 163.

50. Ibid., 'Minutes of Council held at the Credit, March 29th 1847', p. 314.
51. Ibid., 'Minutes of a Council held at the Credit Village March 30th 1847', pp 314–315.
52. Ibid., 'Memorandum of Proceedings of a General Council of the Six Nations of Indians assembled at the Onondaga Longhouse', 9 April 1847, p. 315. Susan Hill notes that such ceremonies of condolence were 'essential in the Haudenosaunee mind for respectful relations and decision making, (pp 23–24) and featured 'in events ranging from treaty negotiations to the exchange or prisoners', (p. 61). Also, see Hill, pp 61–64.
53. LAC, RG 10, vol. 1011, 'Minutes of a Council held at the Credit Village', 12 April 1847, p. 316.
54. Hill, p. 176.
55. Ibid., p. 241.
56. LAC, RG 10, vol. 1011, 'Extracts of the Minutes of a General Council of the Six Nations of Indians Residing on the Grand River', 8 April 1847, p. 180.
57. Ibid., pp 181–182.
58. Alan Corbiere notes that the 'provision of warmth' served as a metaphor for the Anishinaabeg for honouring treaty relations (pp 274–285). 'After 1815, treaty relationships became reduced to an annual delivery of "Indian Presents" and "warmth" at the council fire, consisting of smoking, giving, receiving, and talking', which were further diminished in the decades that followed, p. 325.
59. 'In effect, this sharing of territory with the Mississaugas meant another reduction in Six Nations land', notes Hill, p. 239.
60. LAC, RG 10, vol. 1011, 'Minutes of a Council held at the Credit Village', 26 April 1847, p. 317.
61. Peter Jones, 'Removal of the Credit River Indians', 22 December 1847, published in *Christian Guardian*, 12 January 1848, p. 9.
62. Ibid. Peter Jones himself relocated not to Grand River but to Muncey Town in the expectation that he would be appointed headmaster of its future, and now notorious, Mount Elgin Residential School. He later declined the position because of failing health and his realization that it would not be under native control. In his letter to the editor of the *Christian Guardian*, he emphasized that Indigenous Peoples flourish not under White tutelage but only when 'highly favoured with the example and influence of *well-informed persons of their Tribe*' (italics in source). Also, see King, pp 154–157.
63. Canada, Legislative Assembly, *Report on the Affairs of the Indians in Canada*, section iii, 24 June 1847, appendix T.

ABOUT THE CONTRIBUTORS

ROB GOODBODY is a building historian and a member of the historical committee of the Religious Society of Friends in Ireland. He has written extensively on the role of the Quakers in the Great Famine, including *A Suitable Channel: Quaker Relief in the Great Famine* (Pale Publications, 1995).

BRENDAN HOBAN is a priest of Killala Roman Catholic diocese, Diocesan Historian and the author of *Ocras, The Great Famine in Killala diocese, 1845–1852* (2021) and *On Our Knees, Famine in the Parishes of Killala Diocese, 1845–1852* (2021), both published by Banley House.

CHRISTINE KINEALY is Director of Ireland's Great Hunger Institute at Quinnipiac University. She has published extensively on the Famine and, more recently, on Ireland's role in the transatlantic abolition movement. Her award-winning publications include *Daniel O'Connell and the Anti-Slavery Movement. The Saddest People the Sun Sees* (2011) and *Becoming Ira Aldridge. A Black Shakespearean Actor in Nineteenth Century Ireland* (2024).

JASON KING is Academic Coordinator of the Irish Heritage Trust and National Famine Museum, Strokestown Park, and a member of the Government of Ireland National Famine Commemoration Committee. He has published extensively on Ireland's Great Hunger and the Irish Famine Migration. His recent publications include *The Famine Diaspora and Irish American Women's Writing* (with Marguérite Corporaal and Peter D. O'Neill, Palgrave, 2024), *The Irish Famine Migration from Strokestown, Roscommon in 1847* (with Christine Kinealy & Mark G. McGowan, Cork & Quinnipiac University Press, 2023), *More Heroes of Ireland's Great Hunger* & *Heroes of Ireland's Great Hunger* (with Christine Kinealy & Gerard Moran, Cork & Quinnipiac University Press, 2022, 2021) and *Irish Famine Migration Narratives: Eyewitness Testimonies,* vol II, *The History of the Irish Famine* (4 vols. Routledge, 2019).

MARK G. McGOWAN is a full professor of history at the University of Toronto and Principal Emeritus at the University of St. Michael's College. He has published widely on the Catholic Church in Canada, Irish migration and settlement, and the Irish Famine migration to Canada. His forthcoming book is *Finding Molly Johnson: Irish Famine Orphans in Canada* (McGill-Queen›s University Press).

A graduate of UCD, **EAMONN McKEE** joined the Department of Foreign Affairs in 1986. On return from a posting at the Embassy Washington, he joined the Good Friday Agreement talks team. He has served as Ambassador to North and South Korea, Israel, Canada, The Bahamas, Antigua and Barbuda, and Jamaica.

GERARD MORAN has lectured in the History Department at the University of Galway and at Maynooth University. He has written extensively on nineteenth-century Ireland and among his most recent publications is *Fleeing from Famine in Connemara: James Hack Tuke and his Assisted Emigration Scheme in the 1880s* (2018).

PETER MURPHY has a lifelong passion for history, obtaining an undergraduate degree in European history from the University of California, San Diego and a Master's degree in American history from Trinity College in Connecticut (2016). He is especially interested in Ireland's history, due in part to his extensive Irish ancestry.

Retired from Anglia Ruskin University, where he worked on higher education projects from Denmark to Myanmar, **ANTHONY RUSSELL** is the author of *Between Two Flags: John Mitchel and Jenny Verner* (2015). He is joint editor (with Patrick Fitzgerald) of *John Mitchel, Ulster and the Great Famine* (2017).

CATHERINE B. SHANNON is Professor Emerita of History at Westfield State University. Her publications include studies of the role of Arthur J. Balfour and Lord Randolph Churchill in Irish affairs. She has published on the role of women in the Northern Irish conflict and peace process. Her recent research focuses on the response of Boston's Irish American community to nineteenth-century Irish Famines.

ANELISE HANSON SHROUT is an associate professor of History and Digital and Computational Studies at Bates College. Her work explores the ways that the Irish diaspora—broadly construed—has shaped the world beyond Ireland. Her first book, *Aiding Ireland: The Great Famine and the Rise of International Philanthropy*, explores the many and varied political uses to which famine philanthropy was put.

FIONA WHITE is programme director and a lecturer in History and Geography at ATU Mayo, where she teaches history, literature and archeology modules. Her main research interests are the Big House and landed estates, and Irish women's history. She has written a number of book chapters and journal articles on these topics.

INDEX